ALL AMERICAN WOMEN

For my father, friend &
comrade on the occasion of
your 64th birthday as we
continue to struggle to be
better, more sensitive men,
and thus more productive
and capable human beings.

With all my love,

ALL AMERICAN WOMEN

Lines That Divide, Ties That Bind

Johnnetta B. Cole
Editor

THE FREE PRESS
A Division of Macmillan, Inc.
NEW YORK

Collier Macmillan Publishers
LONDON

The Free Press
A Division of Macmillan, Inc.
866 Third Avenue, New York, N.Y. 10022

Collier Macmillan Canada, Inc.

Printed in the United States of America

printing number

1 2 3 4 5 6 7 8 9 10

Library of Congress Cataloging-in-Publication Data
Main entry under title:

All American women.

  Bibliography: p.
  Includes index.
    1. Women—United States—Social conditions—
Addresses, essays, lectures.   2. Women—United
States—Economic conditions—Addresses, essays,
lectures.   3. Feminism—United States—Addresses,
essays, lectures.   4. Women—United States—Attitudes—
Addresses, essays, lectures.   5. Minority women—United
States—Addresses, essays, lectures.   I. Cole,
Johnnetta B.
HQ1426.A45   1986   305.4′2′0973   85-24718
ISBN 0–02–906460–0

To the memory of my mother, Mary Frances Lewis Betsch, who would have differed with much that is said in this book, but who, through her example, taught me to respect differences among us.

Contents

Preface

Studies about women, studies by women, studies for women have an unprecedented presence today in scholarly circles. This did not occur by accident, nor as the result of publishers' largesse, sudden enlightenment of scholarly journal "referees," or unbiased generosity by funding agencies. The new presence of feminist studies in the United States results from the concerted efforts of those who see such scholarship as necessary for an accurate view not only of women, but of the world. It is a scholarship which involves analyses from across the disciplines of the academy and comes together as the literature of women's studies.

Contemporary women's studies is a direct outgrowth of the women's movement of the late 1960s and 1970s, just as the black power movement of the 1960s spawned an intellectual wing called black studies. The women's movement itself was much influenced by the earlier civil rights and black power actions, and all in turn were influenced by the nineteenth-century women's rights movement in the United States and the abolitionist movement within which the women's rights movement took root. From this interlocking set of influences and conflicts, the twentieth-century women's movement took inspiration, style, slogans, and even tactics.

Many women's studies programs and departments were founded in the mid-1970s, and with varying degrees of success they remain in place. The objectives of these academic and activist efforts were commonly held. Women's studies would be a corrective scholarship—exposing gender biases in existing academic work. It would also be a pioneering scholarship, cutting through uncharted academic areas. Importantly, it would critique male dominance in the academy itself. Ultimately, the advocates of women's studies sought to place their corrective and innovative scholarship in the service of changing the oppressive conditions of women. (For a summary of the history and objectives of women's studies, see Hunter College Women's Studies Collective 1983: 3–15.)

However, in the act of challenging, and in many instances successfully altering, the male-centered scholarship of the academy, women's studies itself reflected and institutionalized a number of biases. Courses were offered on women's history, women's literature, the sociology of women, women's music—but in reality, these courses addressed, almost exclusively, the particular circumstances of only one group of women. The faculty of women's studies, the overwhelming majority of the students in women's studies, the readings assigned in courses in women's studies, and the speakers and artists brought to campuses under the sponsorship of women's studies tended to voice the experiences of white, middle-class women. (For an excellent critique of racial and other biases in women's studies, see Avakian 1981.)

In women's studies, characteristics assumed to be shared by all women were juxtaposed to what was said to be shared by men. In other words, it was taken for granted that there was something called women's language, women's spirituality, women's history, and women's culture—without modifiers to reflect the influence of race, class, religion, sexuality, language, age, physical ability, ethnicity, geography, and other factors. In academic and popular women's studies literature, we read of female (in contrast to male) modes of thought (Friedan 1984); a female mode of human experience (Gilligan 1982); all women as a class (Daly 1973); a female and a male culture that managers have and practice (Hennig and Jardim 1978); and women's "natural" interest in peace as opposed to men's involvement with war (Tobias 1984).

There were always other voices. Even in those very early days of women's studies, there were voices that spoke of different histories and cultures, of realities that were not addressed in the new feminist scholarship. These were the voices of women of color: Afro-American women, Asian and Pacific Island women, Chicanas, Native American women, Puertorriqueñas, and other women who are often labeled "nonwhite." These were the voices of poor women, lesbian women, older women. These were the voices of working-class women, Jewish women, women with disabilities, and rural women of midwestern and southern Appalachian cultures. Similarly, the women's movement itself was criticized by women of diverse backgrounds and ways of life. That criticism was summarized, for example, by references to the movement as the *white* women's movement, a phrase perhaps too neat in its simplicity yet all too accurate in describing so much of the movement.

How can we explain this narrowness in women's studies and the women's movement as they have developed into the 1980s? Much of it is a reflection of deeply entrenched chauvinism, that is to say, an arrogantly held view that one's own way is the only way. Chauvinism in women's studies takes the form of attitudes and behaviors which ignore or dismiss as insignificant differences of class, race, age, sexuality, religion, ethnicity, and physical ability.

Chauvinism among white women surely influenced much of the direction in which they steered women's studies programs and the women's organizations they have run. Too often even those white feminists who did address "racism" did so almost as a politically correct afterthought, while the substance of their words and actions revolved around the oppression they experienced as white women and ignored the oppression they participated in as white people.

Yet, among white feminists there were and still are important voices raised to challenge white racism. Adrienne Rich has been a powerful white feminist voice struggling "with the meanings of white identity in a racist society, and how an unexamined white perspective leads to dangerous ignorance, heart-numbing indifference and complacency" (1983: 3). Anne Braden, a white Southern woman whose work in antiracist struggles spans four decades, exemplifies her belief that:

> No white woman reared in the South—or perhaps anywhere in this racist country—can find freedom as a woman until she deals in her own consciousness with the question of race. We grow up little girls—absorbing a hundred stereotypes about ourselves and our role in life, our secondary position, our destiny to be a helpmate to a man or men. But we also grow up white—absorbing the stereotypes of race, the picture of ourselves as somehow privileged because of the color of our skin. The two mythologies become intertwined, and there is no way to free ourselves from one without dealing with the other. (1972)

Another white feminist, Bettina Aptheker, observes after exploring the history of the nineteenth-century women's rights movement, from its origins among black and white women in the antislavery movement to its near demise once white women won the vote, that "in the context of American politics, the neglect of or acquiescence in racism would inevitably force the women into a more and more conservative and politically ineffectual world" (1982: 50). Aptheker's study of women's legacy from the past century leads her to state, of the present

women's movement, that the "experiences of women of color must assume a cocentral focus in the shaping of feminist thought and action.
Without this the liberation of women cannot be either envisioned or realized" (1982: 5). And Minnie Bruce Pratt, another white Southern feminist active in antiracist work, offers a concrete application of Aptheker's warning:

> Today the economic foundation of this country is resting on the backs of
> women of color here, and in Third World countries: they are harvesting
> the eggplants and lettuce for Safeway, they are typing secretarial work
> sent by New York firms to the West Indies by satellite. The real gain in
> our material security as white women would come most surely if we did
> not limit our economic struggle to salaries of equal or comparable worth
> to white men in the U.S., but if we expanded this struggle to a restruc-
> turing of this country's economy so that we do not live off the lives and
> work of Third World women. (1984: 54–55)

My own experiences as an Afro-American woman and my knowledge as an anthropologist lead me to question the homogenizing of
women's diverse cultures, languages, sexualities, classes, and ethnici-
ties in the interest of paying homage to a mythical uniformity called
sisterhood.

In the spring of 1984, I took these issues into an anthropology
and women's studies course entitled—pun intended—"All American
Women." A very engaged group of students of diverse backgrounds
joined me in seeking ways to describe and analyze cultural and individual differences among women without denying similarities of circumstances and interests. Readings for the course were chosen to reflect
the many ways of life of women in the United States, and each student
carried out a semester-long series of interviews with an "American"
woman. This anthology is an outgrowth of that rich experience in
teaching and learning. It rests on the conviction that acknowledging
and respecting our differences substantially strengthens feminist theory and action.

The volume is about US women—the great diversity among
women who live in the United States (U.S.) and the commonalities that
exist among us. This duality is explored in the introductory essay,
"Commonalities and Differences." The succeeding five sections are
more detailed explorations of similarities and differences within various spheres of women's lives: work, family, sexuality and reproduction, religion, and politics. These are not the only spheres of activity
within which US women, indeed all women, live our lives, but they are
certainly major ones. The volume would be a more complete and richer
one if it included chapters on expressive culture (music, art, dance,
folklore) and language as shared and used by different women. But

here, as in all such anthologies, certain concessions were made in the interest of space.

Each of the five sections is introduced by a brief essay in which the central issues associated with a particular sphere of activity are explored and related to the major points addressed in each of the articles.

In selecting articles for this volume, the primary consideration was to reflect the range of attitudes, realities, and hopes of women in the United States. In fact, this anthology encompasses more of the diversity of US women than any existing published volume. Several of the articles capture the experiences of women whose lives, like the lives of each of us, fall within more than one "category." There are articles on Afro-American, Asian American, Chicana, Native American, and Puerto Rican women, as well as women of several Euro-American ethnic groups. There are discussions of the conditions of upper-class, middle-class, working-class, and poor women. The volume also includes the experiences and perspectives of lesbian women, women living in rural areas, women living in cities, women with disabilities, and older women.

In selecting articles, priority was given to those in which women "speak for themselves." Thus, in most of the articles, women describe their own realities. Honoring the criteria of diversity and an experiential focus, the articles as a whole portray oppression and resistance, subservience and independence, resignation and creativity. The selection of articles is not perfect, but the weaknesses signal the kinds of work that must be done in women's studies.

The articles included here are about women in the United States today. This focus on our current realities means, of course, that some of the dynamics of change will not be addressed. Yet, in the course of analyzing the current conditions of US women, many of the articles highlight patterns which have developed over time or contrast what appear to be new phenomena with earlier ones. Each of the section introductions also offers some considerations of the histories of the diverse groups represented among US women.

A word about the title of this volume. *All American Women* was originally chosen to capture two meanings. The first is a sense of the inclusiveness which is appropriate when referring to the variety of women in the United States. The second meaning is the suggestion of strength associated with the expression "all-American." For at the same time that women in the United States are subjected to varying degrees of oppression, each group of us also has a tradition and an everyday pool of strength on which to draw.

Yet "American," used to refer exclusively to citizens of the United States, is itself a chauvinistic term. Some of the indigenous peoples of this continent know it as "Big Turtle Island," whereas the white men of Europe named it "America" after one of their kind who arrived here at the beginning of the centuries of conquest. The name was then applied to the entire hemisphere by the white men who expanded their colonial settlement and control across the lands of Indian, Mexican, Innuit, and Hawaiian peoples to carve the United States of North America into its present configuration.

Those of us who live in the United States are Americans, but so, too, are the women who live in Canada, Mexico, Central and South America, and the Caribbean. In recognition of this reality of many American women, the term used most often in this volume is "US women." Here again there is an intentional double meaning. "US women" refers to those of us who live in the United States (U.S.), but it is also used to connote a sense of the commonalities of experience among "us."

The anthology is designed for courses in which instructors and students are prepared to join the struggle to make women's studies truly the study of *all* women. It is also hoped that the different voices that speak out in this volume will be heard by women and men outside of the classrooms of our colleges and universities. To the extent that a minimal condition for the ultimate liberation of US women is an understanding of the lines that divide as well as the ties that bind us, it is time that we all listen.

References Cited

Aptheker, B.
1982   *Woman's Legacy: Essays on Race, Sex, and Class in American History.* Amherst, Mass.: University of Massachusetts Press.

Avakian, A.
1981   "Women's Studies and Racism." *The New England Journal of Black Studies*, pp. 31–36.

Braden, A.
1972   *Free Thomas Wanley: A Letter to White Southern Women.* Louisville: Southern Conference Education Fund.

Daly, M.
1973   *Beyond God the Father: Toward a Philosophy of Women's Liberation.* Boston: Beacon Press.

Friedan, B.
1984   *The Second Stage.* New York: Summit.

Gilligan, C.
1982   *In a Different Voice.* Cambridge, Mass.: Harvard University Press.

Hennig, M., and A. Jardim.
1978   *The Managerial Woman*. New York: Pocket Books.

Hunter College Women's Studies Collective.
1983   *Women's Realities, Women's Choices: An Introduction to Women's Studies*. New York: Oxford University Press.

Pratt, M.
1984   "Identity: Skin, Blood, Heart." In *Yours in Struggle*, with Barbara Smith and Elly Bulkin. Brooklyn, N.Y.: Long Haul Press.

Rich, A.
1983   "Women in Struggle." Unpublished talk at an evening sponsored by *I-Kon* magazine.

Tobias, S.
1984   "Toward a Feminist Position on the Arms Race." *Women Studies Quarterly* xii (2): 20.

Acknowledgments

On this page I express my gratitude to the colleagues, students, friends, and kin folks who helped to make this anthology a reality. But my indebtedness to each of them continues.

Dr. Marion Starling has helped me in so many ways, the most enduring of which is her own example of scholarship and humanity.

Editing a book is a process, Marea Wexler reminded me, and she willingly helped throughout the many stages of that very process. Pamela Wright figured out how to get me to sit in front of a computer, taught me the basics of the machine, and cheerfully helped me to salvage from it parts of this book that I thought were lost forever.

Bob Moore gave me invaluable editorial assistance and shared ideas he has struggled with over years of active involvement in antiracist and antisexist education. I also greatly appreciate the work which Annick Piant did on this anthology.

Each of my sons, David, Aaron, and Che, found different ways of asking in encouraging tones: "How's the book, Mom?"; and they found lots of ways to help me move it along. In the wee hours of the night when jazz musicians are awake and writers like myself wish we weren't, my brother would stop by and introduce me to a cut of music that would soothe the soul. Thanks, John.

Laura Wolff, my editor at The Free Press, "one more time," offered wise suggestions, raised unsettling questions, and through it all, gave me her support and encouragement.

My deepest thanks go to Louise te Boekhorst for the kind of friendship that grows out of shared work. Some of the readings in this anthology are her discoveries; many of the points in the introductory essays were developed in our ongoing dialogues about commonalities and differences among women. And so many of the pieces to the puzzle of this particular book are in place because she believes in and does quality work.

I cannot conclude these acknowledgments without saying thank you to my colleagues who generously shared their ideas, those whose work is reprinted here, and the students who were the inspiration for this book.

Contributors

Paula Gunn Allen is a writer and a professor of women's studies at Berkeley. She is the editor of *Studies in American Indian Literature* (1983), and her novel, *The Woman Who Owned the Shadows*, was published in 1983. Her poetry appears in numerous anthologies.

A. Lynn Bolles is director of the Afro-American Studies Program and a member of the anthropology faculty at Bowdoin College. Dr. Bolles's areas of interest are the Caribbean and black American studies, women's studies, and political economy.

Anne Braden is a journalist who has been active in Southern social justice movements for over three decades. Currently she cochairs the Southern Organizing Committee for Social Justice.

Rosette Capotorto is a freelance writer with a special interest in elder women.

Carol P. Christ teaches women's studies at San Jose State University. Active in the women's movement since the late 1960s, she was among the founders of the nationwide Women's Caucus–Religious Studies. She has published widely on women and religion.

Shellee Colen is completing a Ph.D. in anthropology at the New School for Social Research and teaches in the Metropolitan Studies Program at New York University. Her work centers on issues of race, class, and gender. She is active in the movement for reproductive freedom.

Kathleen Walsh D'Arcy is a freelance writer with a special interest in elder women.

Angela Y. Davis teaches black philosophy and aesthetics as well as courses in women's studies at San Francisco State University. Her published scholarly work and her activism center on issues of race, gender, and class.

Barbara Sinclair Deckard is professor of political science at the University of California, Riverside. Among her published works are the books *Congressional Realignment, 1925–1978* (1982) and *Majority Leadership in the U.S. House* (1983).

Yvonne Duffy is an author, journalist, and speaker. She conducted research among differently abled women in connection with her work . . . *All Things Are Possible* (1981).

Nan Elsasser has taught bilingual education courses at the University of New Mexico and the University of Albuquerque and has held a Fulbright teaching fellowship at the College of the Bahamas, Nassau. She has published on language and ethnicity.

Oliva M. Espín is a practicing psychotherapist and consultant and a member of the faculty of the graduate program in counseling psychology at Boston University. She is currently editing a book on psychotherapy among women of different cultural backgrounds.

Geraldine Ferraro is the first woman to run as a vice presidential candidate of one of the two major U.S. political parties. She taught elementary school and was an assistant district attorney in Queens, New York, before her election to the U.S. House of Representatives, where she has served three successive terms. Congresswoman Ferraro has spearheaded efforts to pass the Women's Equity Act and the Equal Rights Amendment.

Anne Bowen Follis is a founding member and president emerita of Homemakers' Equal Rights Association. She travels frequently, speaking about the women's movement from a Christian perspective.

Betty Friedan was the founder and first president of the National Organization for Women and the original convenor of the National Women's Political Caucus. She has held visiting professorships at Yale, Temple University, the New School for Social Research, and Queens College. In recent years she has been a leader in the fight for the Equal Rights Amendment.

Shirley Glubka holds an M.A. in psychology from the Fielding Institute and spent six years working as a feminist counselor. Her works appear in *Conditions* and the *American Poetry Anthology*. Currently she makes her living as a housecleaner and devotes time to writing.

Jacquelyn Grant has a Ph.D. in systematic theology from the Union Theological Seminary. An ordained minister in the African Methodist Episcopal Church, Dr. Grant is now on the faculty at the Interdenominational Theological Center in Atlanta, Georgia.

Susannah Heschel holds an M.A. from the Harvard School of Divinity and is currently completing a doctorate in modern Jewish thought at the University of Pennsylvania. She has published in the fields of Jewish thought and feminism.

Sasha Hohri is a contributing editor to the journal *East Wind* and a member of the organization The Concerned Japanese Americans in New York City. Ms. Hohri works with the Ms. Foundation.

Amber Hollibaugh is an activist and an author. She was cofounder of the San Francisco Lesbian and Gay History Project. Ms. Hollibaugh is currently an editor of *Socialist Review*.

Gloria I. Joseph is a professor in the School of Social Science at Hampshire College. She has published extensively on black American, Caribbean, and women's issues. Dr. Joseph conceptualized and leads SISA, Sisterhood in Support of Sisters in South Africa.

Rosabeth Moss Kanter is professor of sociology and organization and management at Yale University. Dr. Kanter is also a partner in the organizational consulting firm Goodmeasure in Cambridge, Massachusetts.

Karen Kenyon is a freelance writer who has contributed to *Redbook, Ladies' Home Journal, Newsweek*, and *Life and Health*. In 1975 she received a certificate of merit for poetry from *Atlantic Monthly*. From 1963 to 1966, Ms. Kenyon worked as a secretary.

Elaine H. Kim teaches Asian-American studies at the University of California at Berkeley and is the author of *Asian-American Literature* (1982). Dr. Kim is the executive director of Asian Women United of California and president of the Board of Directors of the Korean Community Center in Oakland, California.

Audre Lorde is professor of creative writing at Hunter College. Her works appear in numerous collections, and among her recent books is *Zami: A New Spelling of My Name* (1983). She is a member of the founding collective of Kitchen Table: Women of Color Press and a founding mother of SISA, Sisterhood in Support of Sisters in South Africa.

Kyle MacKenzie received a Danforth graduate fellowship in connection with her doctoral work in American studies. She has taught English in private schools, and with Nan Elsasser and Yvonne Tixier y Vigil she has published on New Mexican Hispanic women.

Harriette P. McAdoo is a professor in the School of Social Work at Howard University and a research associate at Columbia Research Systems. Professor McAdoo has written extensively on Afro-American families.

Barbara Mikulski served on the Baltimore City Council prior to her election as a representative of the Third Congressional District of Maryland in the U.S. House of Representatives. The Energy and Commerce Committee is among the committees she has served on since her election to the U.S. Congress. Congresswoman Mikulski is an advocate of women's rights.

Elizabeth Oakes is a cultural anthropologist with research interests in the Caribbean, women, and political economy. She has taught at Brown and the University of Massachusetts at Boston. As a postdoctoral Fulbright grantee, she is now doing fieldwork in Grenada.

Lillian Breslow Rubin is research associate at the Institute for Scientific Analysis in San Francisco. A marriage, family, and child counselor, she is the author of a number of scholarly publications.

Melba Sánchez-Ayéndez is a cultural anthropologist in the Department of Social Sciences at the University of Puerto Rico, Medical Sciences Campus. Her areas of specialization are Puerto Rican culture and gerontology, especially aging minority women.

Susan Weidman Schneider is the editor and a founding mother of *Lilith*, the Jewish feminist magazine. Headquartered in New York City, she lectures widely on diversity within Jewish and women's communities.

Barbara Smith has been active in the black feminist movement since 1973. She is the editor of *Home Girls: A Black Feminist Anthology* (1983) and a coeditor of

All the Women Are White, All the Blacks Are Men, But Some of Us Are Brave: Black Women's Studies. Ms. Smith cofounded Kitchen Table: Women of Color Press.

Louise te Boekhorst draws on the Netherlands and the United States as the sources of her biculturalism. She is an undergraduate student and an activist at Hunter College. In 1984–1985, Ms. te Boekhorst worked with Johnnetta Cole as a research assistant.

Yvonne Tixier y Vigil is on the faculty at the University of Nebraska, Omaha. A reading specialist with particular interest in multicultural and bilingual reading materials, she has published articles in education and sociology journals.

Studs Terkel was born Louis Terkel in New York City. A graduate of the University of Chicago Law School, he worked for the depression-era Federal Writers Project and has worked at many different kinds of jobs. He is the author of a number of highly acclaimed books.

1

Commonalities and Differences

Johnnetta B. Cole

If you see one woman, have you seen them all? Does the heavy weight of patriarchy level all differences among US women? Is it the case, as one woman put it, that "there isn't much difference between having to say 'Yes suh Mr. Charlie' and 'Yes dear'?" Does "grandmother" convey the same meaning as "abuela," as "buba," as "gran'ma"? Is difference a part of what we share, or is it, in fact, *all* that we share? As early as 1970, Toni Cade Bambara asked: "How relevent are the truths, the experiences, the findings of white women to black women? Are women after all simply women?" (Bambara 1970: 9)

Are US women bound by our similarities or divided by our differences? The only viable response is *both*. To address our commonalities without dealing with our differences is to misunderstand and distort that which separates as well as that which binds us as women. Patriarchal oppression is not limited to women of one race or of one particular ethnic group, women in one class, women of one age group or sexual preference, women who live in one part of the country, women of any one religion, or women with certain physical abilities or disabilities. Yet, while oppression of women knows no such limitations, we cannot, therefore, conclude that the oppression of all women is identical.

Among the things which bind women together are the assumptions about the way that women think and behave, the myths—indeed the stereotypes—about what is common to all women. For example, women will be asked nicely in job interviews if they type, while men will not be asked such a question. In response to certain actions, the expression is used: "Ain't that just like a woman?" Or during a heated argument between a man and a woman, as the voice of each rises and emotions run high, the woman makes a particularly good point. In a voice at the pitch of the ongoing argument, the man screams at her: "You don't have to get hysterical!"

In an interesting form of "what goes around comes around," as Malcolm X put it, there is the possibility that US women are bound together by our assumptions, attitudes toward, even stereotypes of the other gender. Folklorist Rayna Green, referring to women of the Southern setting in which she grew up, says this:

> Southern or not, women everywhere talk about sex. . . . In general men are more often the victims of women's jokes than not. Tit for tat, we say. Usually the subject for laughter is men's boasts, failures, or inadequacies ("comeuppance for lack of upcommance," as one of my aunts would say). Poking fun at a man's sexual ego, for example, might never be possible in real social situations with the men who have power over their lives, but it is possible in a joke. (Green 1984: 23–24)

That which US women have in common must always be viewed in relation to the particularities of a group, for even when we narrow our focus to one particular group of women it is possible for differences within that group to challenge the primacy of what is shared in common. For example, what have we said and what have we failed to say when we speak of "Asian American women"? As Shirley Hune notes (1982), Asian American women as a group share a number of characteristics. Their participation in the work force is higher than that of women in any other ethnic group. Many Asian American women live life supporting others, often allowing their lives to be subsumed by the needs of the extended family. And they are subjected to stereotypes by the dominant society: the sexy but "evil dragon lady," the "neuter gender," the "passive/demure" type, and the "exotic/erotic" type.

However, there are many circumstances when these shared experiences are not sufficient to accurately describe the condition of particular Asian American women. Among Asian American women there are those who were born in the United States, fourth and fifth generation Asian American women with firsthand experience of no other land, and there are those who recently arrived in the United States. Asian American women are diverse in their heritage or country of origin: China, Japan, the Philippines, Korea, India, Vietnam, Cambodia, Thailand, or another country in Asia. If we restrict ourselves to Asian American women of Chinese descent, are we referring to those women who are from the People's Republic of China or those from Taiwan, those from Hong Kong or those from Vietnam, those from San Francisco's Chinatown or those from Mississippi? Are we subsuming under "Asian American" those Pacific Island women from Hawaii, Samoa, Guam, and other islands under U.S. control? Although the majority of Asian American women are working-class—contrary to the stereotype of the "ever successful" Asians—there are poor, "middle-class," and even affluent Asian American women (Hune 1982: 1–2, 13–14).

It has become very common in the United States today to speak of "Hispanics," putting Puerto Ricans, Chicanos, Dominicans, Cubans, and those from every Spanish-speaking country in the Americas into one category of people, with the women referred to as Latinas or Hispanic women. Certainly there is a language, or the heritage of a language, a general historical experience, and certain cultural traditions and practices which are shared by these women. But a great deal of harm can be done by sweeping away differences in the interest of an imposed homogeneity.

Within one group of Latinas there is, in fact, considerable variation in terms of self-defined ethnic identity, such that some women refer to themselves as Mexican Americans, others as *Chicanas*, others as Hispanics, and still others as Americans. Among this group of women are those who express a commitment to the traditional roles of women and others who identify with feminist ideals. Some Chicanas are monolingual—in Spanish or English—and others are bilingual. And there are a host of variations among Chicanas in terms of educational achievements, economic differences, rural or urban living conditions, and whether they trace their ancestry from women who lived in this land well before the United States forcibly took the northern half of Mexico, or more recently arrived across the border that now divides the nations called Mexico and the United States.

Women of the Midwest clearly share a number of experiences which flow from living in the U.S. heartland, but they have come from different places, and they were and are today part of various cultures.

> Midwestern women are the Native American women whose ancestors were brought to the plains in the mid-nineteenth century to be settled on reservations, the black women whose fore-bears emigrated by the thousands from the South after Reconstruction. They are the descendants of the waves of Spanish, French, Norwegian, Danish, Swedish, Bohemian, Scottish, Welsh, British, Irish, German, and Russian immigrants who settled the plains, and the few Dutch, Italians, Poles, and Yugoslavs who came with them. (Boucher 1982: 3)

There is another complexity: when we have identified a commonality among women, cutting across class, racial, ethnic, and other major lines of difference, the particular ways that commonality is acted out and its consequences in the larger society may be quite diverse. Ostrander makes this point in terms of class:

> When women stroke and soothe men, listen to them and accommodate their needs, men of every class return to the workplace with renewed energies. When women arrange men's social lives and relationships, men of every class are spared investing the time and energy required to meet their social needs. When women run the households and keep family concerns in check, men of every class are freer than women to pursue other activities, including work, outside the home. But upper-class women perform these tasks for men at the very top of the class structure. . . . Supporting their husbands as individuals, they support and uphold the very top of the class structure. In this way they distinguish themselves from women of other social classes. (Ostrander 1984: 146)

Suppose that we can accurately and exclusively identify the characteristics shared by one particular group of women. For each of the women within that group, into how many other groups does she want to, or is she forced to, fit? Or can we speak of similarities *only* with respect to a group such as Puerto Rican women who are forty-three years old, were born in San Juan, Puerto Rico, migrated to New York City when they were five years old, work as eighth-grade school teachers, attend a Catholic church, are heterosexual, married, with two male and two female children, and have no physical disabilities?

Then there is that unpredictable but often present quality of individuality, the idiosyncracies of a particular person. Shirley Abbott, describing experiences of growing up in the South, contrasts her mother's attitude and behavior toward the black woman who was her maid with what was the usual stance of "Southern white ladies."

> I don't claim that my mother's way of managing her black maid was typical. Most white women did not help their laundresses hang the washing on the line. . . . Compulsive housewifery had some part in it. So did her upbringing. . . . There was another motive too. . . . Had she used Emma in just the right way, Mother could have become a lady. But Mother didn't want to be a lady. Something in her was against it, and she couldn't explain what frightened her, which was why she cried when my father ridiculed her. (Abbott 1983: 78–79)

Once we have narrowed our focus to one specific group of women (Armenian American women, or women over sixty-five, or Arab American women, or black women from the Caribbean, or Ashkenazi Jewish women), the oppression that group of women experiences may take different forms at different times. Today, there is no black woman in the

United States who is the legal slave of a white master: "chosen" for that slave status because of her race, forced to give her labor power without compensation because of the class arrangements of the society, and subjected to the sexual whims of her male master because of her gender. But that does not mean that black women today are no longer oppressed on the basis of race, class, and gender.

There are also groups of women who experience intense gender discrimination today, but in the past had a radically different status in their society. Contrary to the popular image of female oppression as being both universal and as old as human societies, there is incontestable evidence of egalitarian societies in which men and women related in ways that did not involve male dominance and female subjugation. Eleanor Leacock is the best known of the anthropologists who have carried out the kind of detailed historical analysis which provides evidence on gender relations in precolonial North American societies. In discussing the debate on the origins and spread of women's oppression, Leacock points out that women's oppression is a reality today in virtually every society, and while socialist societies have reduced it, they have not eliminated gender inequality. However, it does not follow that women's oppression has always existed and will always exist. What such arguments about universal female subordination do is to project onto the totality of human history the conditions of today's world. Such an argument also "affords an important ideological buttress for those in power" (Leacock 1979: 10–11).

Studies of precolonial societies indicate considerable variety in terms of gender relations.

> Women retained great autonomy in much of the pre-colonial world, and related to each other and to men through public as well as private procedures as they carried out their economic and social responsibilities and protected their rights. Female and male sodalities of various kinds operated reciprocally within larger kin and community contexts before the principle of male dominance within individual families was taught by missionaries, defined by legal status, and solidified by the economic relations of colonialism. (Leacock 1979: 10–11)

Even when there is evidence of female oppression among women of diverse backgrounds, it is important to listen to the individual assessment which each woman makes of her own condition, rather than assume that a synonymous experience of female oppression exists among all women. As a case in point, Sharon Burmeister Lord, in describing what it was like to grow up "Appalachian style," speaks of the influence of female role models in shaping the conditions of her development. In Williamson, West Virginia, she grew up knowing women whose occupations were Methodist preacher, elementary school principal, county sheriff, and university professor. Within her own family, her mother works as a secretary, writes poetry and songs, and "swims faster than any boy"; her aunt started her own seed and hardware store; one grandmother is a farmer and the other runs her own boarding house. Summarizing the effect of growing up among such women, Lord says:

> When a little girl has had a chance to learn strength, survival tactics, a
> firm grasp of reality, and an understanding of class oppression from the
> women around her, it doesn't remove oppression from her life, but it does
> give her a fighting chance. And that's an advantage! (Lord 1979: 25)

Finally, if it is agreed that today, to some extent, all women are oppressed, to what extent can a woman, or a group of women, also act as oppressor? Small as the numbers may be, there are some affluent black women. (In 1979, less than 500 black women had an income of over $75,000 a year. Four thousand black men had such an income, as compared to 548,000 white men who were in that income bracket. [Marable 1983: 101–102].) Is it not possible that among this very small group of black women there are those who, while they experience oppression because of their race, act in oppressive ways toward other women because of their class? Does the experience of this society's heterosexism make a Euro-American lesbian incapable of engaging in racist acts toward women of color? The point is very simply that privilege can and does coexist with oppression (Bulkin et al. 1984: 99) and being a victim of one form of discrimination does not make one immune to victimizing someone else on a different basis.

We turn now to an overview of each sphere of women's lives on which succeeding sections will focus: work, families, sexuality and reproduction, religion, and politics. These spheres are examined first in terms of commonalities and shared experiences among US women. Then the coin is turned, exposing differences among US women due to our respective class, race, ethnicity, religion, age, sexual preference, geographical location, and physical ability.

Work

Women work. All over the world women work. A comprehensive view of women's work in the United States must include slave labor, wage labor, unpaid household labor, and voluntary work. In that sense, all women in the United States work whether in prisons (a form of slave labor), out in the "marketplace," in their own households, or for a charitable cause.

The organization of women's labor in the United States has changed over time and in response to the particular economic system in effect. Native American women labored under precapitalistic conditions in their nations and societies prior to European conquest. With colonialism and the advent of capitalism, especially after the rise of industrialization, labor became a commodity and a new sexual division of labor began for most women and men in the United States. Men worked outside of their homes for wages and women continued to work within their homes, without wages. But it is important to note that this new sexual division in the location and valuing of labor did not fundamentally change the type of work women did in precapitalist society: nurturing and socializing of children, care and maintenance of the home, and domestic manufacturing.

Within the sphere of work, major commonalities among women can be stated in terms of two propositions. First, when women work outside of their households, they tend to work in sex-segregated jobs and receive less pay, for comparable work, than men. Second, when women live in households with men or with men and children, the women are "in charge" of the housework. Thus, if women also work outside of the household, they do a "double shift."

Doing "women's work" and getting "women's pay" are phrases which capture the plight of the largest segment of female workers. About 60 percent of the women in the U.S. labor force today (38 million women) work in sex-segregated jobs. Over 99.5 percent of secretaries, 96 percent of registered nurses, and 94 percent of telephone operators are female. Of all jobs, an estimated 96 percent are segregated by sex, with paychecks reflecting the difference between women's pay and men's.

Now, two decades after the 1963 Equal Pay Act and Title VII of the Civil Rights Act, women as an aggregate group in the labor force earn 60 percent of what men earn (Shalala 1983: 3). A study by the National Academy of Sciences sums up the situation in these terms: Not only do women do different work than men, but they are also paid less for what they do. The more an occupation is dominated by women, the less it pays. Yet here too, one cannot avoid reference to differences: the discrepancy between what white women and men earn is less than that between what women of color earn and what is earned by men (Shalala 1983).

Housework is not included in calculations of the U.S. Gross National Product, but it is certainly very much a part of the day-to-day lives of the overwhelming majority of US women. Women doing housework carry out all those tasks which, if done at the dry cleaners, in restaurants, or by maids, would require men's wages to shoot up. Thus, women in traditional marriages who do housework and care for children not only work for free, but work for free for their husband's employer. Although "full-time housewifery" is a declining occupation for women as two wages become a necessity for increasing numbers of

U.S. families, housework continues to be, primarily, women's responsibility. To the extent that increasing numbers of US women work outside of our households, increasing numbers do a double or second shift. Following eight hours of work for less pay than a man would receive, most women in the labor force return home to husband, or children, or both, and begin their "second shift." Women who work outside of their households put in almost as many hours sweeping, cleaning, dishwashing, laundering, and shopping as women who are "housewives." A wife who does not work for wages spends a minimum of forty hours a week maintaining house and husband, and a minimum of thirty hours per week if she does work for wages. Thus, while "outside" employment may mean a degree of economic independence, it does not mean emancipation.

Time-budget studies have found that women still do most of the housework, an average of 70 percent, while husband and children each do about 15 percent. Many women note that even when they manage to get their husbands or grown children involved, the cleaning and cooking and shopping remain "their tasks." Before picking up the broom or turning on the vacuum cleaner, most men will likely ask: "What do you want me to do?" or "How can I help you?"

Perhaps the most telling case of the intimate assocation of women with housework is what happens in the homes of affluent women who are relieved of the drudgery of doing housework themselves. They become, instead, the managers of the drudgery of domestic work done by other women.

It was not until World War II that large numbers of women in the United States began to work outside of their homes. Until then, Euro-American women who lived with their husbands worked outside their home only if they were professional women or extremely poor. Afro-American women, on the other hand, have a long history of working outside of their own households. This particular experience was grounded in the peculiar and barbaric institution of slavery; and after "emancipation", there was often domestic work available for them but not for black men.

In 1963 Betty Friedan described the "problem without a name" as the feeling of boredom and unfulfillment of white suburban middle-class housewives. Yet even in 1963 when she wrote *The Feminine Mystique*, more than one-third of all U.S. women were in the work force; and recent economic circumstances have led unprecedented numbers of women of all racial and ethnic groups and of middle- as well as working-class origin into the paid labor force.

Among women in the paid U.S. work force, a major difference revolves around the kinds of jobs we hold. When viewed as "aggregate groups"—women of color versus Euro-American women—women of color are far more likely to work in less skilled and lower-paying jobs. About 25 percent of Chinese American women still work under harsh conditions in garment shops. In California's "Silicon Valley" women make up 75 percent of the assembly line work force, as they do along Route 128 outside of Boston and in the antiunion, "right to work" state of North Carolina. Forty percent of the workers in these electronics factories are immigrant women. On the West Coast, the majority of the women are Filipinas, Thais, Samoans, Mexicans, and Vietnamese (Fuentes and Ehrenreich 1983).

The situation among Native American women is, in a quantitative sense, the worst of any group of women in the United States. They have the lowest income of any group in the country: while the median yearly income for all Native American women was $1,697 in the 1970s, for those in rural areas it was even less—$1,356. More than a third of all Native American women are employed in service occupations, nearly twice the national average. The plight of American Indian women is reflected in the startling reality that their average life expectancy is in the mid-forties.

Another difference among women in the sphere of work has to do with the amount and intensity of discrimination they face on the job. Women are paid less than men; that is the general rule. And the reason is quite simply that employers find it profitable to do so. "Not only [can] women be forced to absorb unemployment and seasonal work, and to perform the most tedious jobs, but their availability to do so [is] used as a threat against men to keep men's wages and resistance down" (Baxandall et al. 1976: xv). But within this general context of wage discrimination, different women experience other forms of discrimination. For example, in a study of discrimination against lesbians in work places (the first such study of its kind), the researchers conclude that many lesbians both anticipate and experience discrimination in the labor force (Levine and Leonard 1984: 710).

Women's ability to find work also varies. This is well documented in the difference between unemployment for white women and women of color. Bureau of Labor Statistics' figures for July 1985 show the jobless rate as 13.2 percent for black women and 5.7 percent for white women. For comparative purposes, it is interesting to note that for the same period, the jobless rate was 5.6 percent for white men and 12.6 percent for black men, reflecting the decades-long trend of black unemployment at least twice the rate for whites. Unemployment figures of stark proportions which receive very little attention are those of women with disabilities. Estimates are that between 65 percent and 76 percent of disabled women are unemployed. More stark and not so well known is the situation of disabled women of racial and ethnic minorities (Fine and Asch 1981: 233).

And finally, there is diversity among women in terms of whether or not they even need to work. One of the characteristics of upper-class women is their involvement in voluntary or charitable work. The sharp contradictions between the experiences of poor and working-class women, and those of upper-class women, are evident in the response of one of the latter when asked to talk about her voluntary work: "Every summer I get about eighty kids from the [city's black ghetto] and bring them out for a day at my place in the country" (Ostrander, 1984: 126).

What can we conclude about the world of work experienced by women in the United States? Very importantly, work has a centrality in our lives. What kind of work we do, whether or not we work outside of our households, for whom we work, the pay we receive, and the conditions under which we work are key questions not only in shaping the material conditions of our lives, but also in helping to define who we are, as we view ourselves and as we are viewed by others.

Among US women there are radical differences in the answers to these questions. Some women own or are among the owners of the very plants where others work for exploitive wages and under oppressive conditions. Some women clip stock coupons from investments in companies whose profits come, at least in part, from the labor power of other women. Some poor women are the recipients of the charity work of upper-class women. These class divisions cannot be swept away by rhetorical references to a united sisterhood among all US women.

There are also, in the world of work, sharp divisions along racial and ethnic lines. What the overwhelming majority of women of color experience in the work world—whether that is a world of unskilled labor or corporate management—involves "adding insult to injury." In addition to being victims of sex discrimination in employment, Afro-American, Latino, Asian American, and Native American women also experience racial discrimination. And it is this double jeopardy which places women of color at the very bottom of all those comparative statistics between "white" and "nonwhite" women in the labor force.

Not in spite of but in addition to these class and racial differences among US women, there are common, although not identical, experiences among US. As a rule, housework is "women's work." As a rule, the kind of work women do in the labor force is different from that which men do, and as a rule it is labor for which there is less pay.

Families

Among women of different backgrounds, there is no sphere of life, no institution which stirs controversy as does *the family*. It is not only a question of debating similarities and differences among families; it is a matter of widely divergent positions as to what ought to be the very future of *the family*. At stake is a normative issue—what should happen to *the family*—and a political agenda—what is in the best interest of women.

In U.S. society, the term *family* is often used to include and sometimes to stand for "household"; sometimes it means the "nuclear family," i.e., husband, wife, and children; and sometimes the term refers to all of those to whom one has a kinship relationship. Often the term "relatives" is used to distinguish extended family from immediate or nuclear family. "Household," which is actually a spatial term referring to residence, is often a more appropriate term than *family* because it describes a domestic economy which may or may not be limited to biological kin.

Despite the considerable variation in the people *families* are composed of today, the dominant ideology in the United States still presents a family consisting of one man who goes off to earn the bacon, one woman who waits at home to fry it, and roughly 2.5 children poised to eat it. The reality is that no more than 7 percent of all families in the United States are of this type.

While women are the sole bearers of babies and the primary nurturers of children, not all women have children. What sets up a commonality among women is the widespread presumption that those without children are unfortunate individuals who indeed wanted children, but were unable to have them.

While responsibility for young children is shared by most women, how they discharge that responsibility can and indeed does differ. For example, in the homes of the upper class, women can and often do delegate child care responsibilities to other *women*, "nannies" paid to serve as surrogate mothers. Women at the other end of the class continuum also "have help" with the tasks of mothering, but the circumstances involve networks of kin, neighbors, and friends who are not paid monetary sums but are bound together by mutual support and reciprocity. Thus, the children of the rich and the children of the poor are often cared for by individuals other than their biological mothers—but the details of those two situations are in fact quite different. In both cases, the biological mother is "freed" from the day-to-day constraints of child care. In one case, it permits her to engage in voluntary work, to visit with friends, to shop, or to engage in other activities which are not those of necessity. In the other case, the poor woman who is "relieved" of child care responsibilities spends her day working for wages which are not sufficient to monetarily compensate the relative or friend caring for her offspring.

Carol Stack describes the intricate web of relationships in which young black children grow up in the poor urban ghetto where she carried out her research.

> The individual can draw upon a broad domestic web of kin and friends—
> some who reside together, others who do not. Residents in The Flats char-
> acterize household composition according to where people sleep, eat, and
> spend their time. Those who eat together may be considered part of a do-
> mestic unit. But an individual may eat in one household, sleep in another,
> contribute resources and service to yet another, and consider herself or
> himself a member of all three households. (Stack 1981: 352)

Among working-class white families, there is often a sizeable discrepancy between the ideal of an autonomous nuclear family and the
necessity of pooling, borrowing, and sharing resources.

> It is women who bridge the gap between what a household's resources re-
> ally are, and what a family's position is supposed to be. Women exchange
> babysitting, share meals, lend small amounts of money. . . . The working
> class family literature is filled with examples of such pooling. (Rapp 1978:
> 288)

Thus in the variety and importance of friendship and kinship networks for coping with the demands of daily living, working-class white
families share a great deal with poor black, as well as poor white, families. What distinguishes the conditions of these families, however, is
not only that more material resources are available to the white,
working-class family. Families of the black poor are constantly bat-
tling against racist ideology and institutions. Middle-class status and
the even less common status of the black upper class can offer some
protection against racist attitudes and practices; however, no black
family can be totally shielded from white racism. This reality was
starkly captured by Malcolm X when he asked an audience at Harvard:
"What do you call a black person, man or woman, with a Ph.D.? The answer," Malcolm said, "is 'nigger'."

What of the white middle-class family, the suburban family described by Betty Friedan in *The Feminine Mystique*? Until recently
women in these families tended to have full-time responsibility for
child care and housework because necessity did not drive them to
work outside of their homes. Bell Hooks, recalling those days of *The
Feminine Mystique*, writes:

> During the early stages of the contemporary women's liberation move-
> ment, feminist analyses of motherhood reflected the race and class biases
> of the participants. Some white middle class, college-educated women ar-
> gued that motherhood was a serious obstacle to women's liberation, a
> trap confining women to the home, keeping them tied to cleaning, cooking
> and child care. Others simply identified motherhood and childrearing as
> the locus of women's oppression. Had black women voiced their views on
> motherhood, it would not have been named a serious obstacle to our free-
> dom as women. Racism, availability of jobs, lack of skills or education

and a number of other issues would have been at the top of the list—but not motherhood. Black women would not have said motherhood prevented us from entering the world of paid work because we have always worked. (Hooks 1984: 133)

What is clear from this discussion so far is that the opinions of various women about their families address different realities.

The extent to which women are defined in terms of their familial roles and responsibilities is captured in these words of an Asian woman:

> But Asian women are not only oppressed by this American government and society which is based only on what is profitable, Asian women are also oppressed inside our communities by the force of Asian feudal tradition. This tradition continues to define us as so-and-so's daughter, mother, or wife. Such feudal ideas serve to keep us quiet and think "family first." Endless layers and rituals of obligation try to smother us, make us lose ourselves, or we must be "bad" mothers, "bad" daughters and "bad" wives. Is there a balance? (Hohri 1983: 44)

A similar point is made by Ann Wolfe in her discussion of role models for Jewish women, and the extent to which these models come into conflict with feminist perspectives.

> Has tradition enabled these women (fairly affluent and well educated) to feel secure both as women and as Jews? Who are the Jewish heroes that we hope will instill our children with pride in their Jewishness? If we are to believe the texts used in Jewish schools, women, I regret to say, are not much in evidence. One series of widely used Sunday school books about heroes in Jewish history describes thirty-two heroes. Only *one* of these is a woman who is seen as a hero in her own right: Henrietta Szold. Yet her biographical sketch ends with this curious statement: "God made her childless so that she might be mother of thousands." Need I say more? Seven other women are mentioned in these texts—but only in relation to their men: a selfless mother, a devoted daughter, a loyal wife. (Wolfe 1976: 47)

Implicit in the critique of the family voiced by many in the women's movement is that women do all of the work in their households and families but are not given commensurate decision-making powers. Yet, while black women do in fact participate in family decision making more frequently than whites, they are charged with being "black matriarchs"! It seems clear that there is a relationship between decision making in a family/household and contributing monies received from outside the unit. Ostrander makes this point concerning upper-class women:

> One source of subordinance among upper-class women—as a general mode of accommodation and in family decision-making—is the class tra-

dition of women turning over their inheritances to their husbands to manage. When the women give up the control of their money, they give up the freedom to order their own lives and the ability to speak with an equal voice in family decisions. This is not surprising. Low economic power has long been shown to be related to low decision-making power in families in other social classes. (Ostrander 1984: 65)

Here then, in a very striking way, we see a commonality among women in families: the denial of decision making based on economic dependence on men; and conversely, decision-making powers which come with economic independence.

What can we conclude from hearing these various voices on *the family*? It's clear that for women, *families* (in the sense of the kin and fictive kin with whom they live and share a domestic economy) are a source of support in some cases and an obstacle to a woman's development and growth in others. Thus when we talk about women and their *families*, we need to be clear about whom we speak: is it the elderly woman living alone, spending her days wishing that her *family* would spend time with her or ask her to do things for them? Is it the super rich widow who also lives alone and makes a great effort to keep all of the money-hungry *family* from coming around? Is it the poor "bag lady" on the city streets, moving in the winter from one nowhere to another—a woman "freed" of the responsibilities of caring for children and housework, who finds her only *family* are those who drop something in her outstretched palm? Or when we speak of *family* do we mean all of the individuals who provide the support which poor and working women must have if they are simply to make it from day to day? Or is *family* those who live with an upper middle-class woman, helping to create, as Betty Friedan put it, "the problem that has no name"? Is *family* that group of similarly disabled women who stick very close to each other, forming a ring of protection from the gaping stares or disregard of the abled? Or is *family* those who live within a particular household made up of two lesbian women and the boys and girls whom they brought there from previous relationships? *Family* for US women is "all of the above" and more.

Deep emotional and ideological meanings are wrapped up in the concepts and realities of women in families. Nowhere is this emotion more evident than in certain debates between middle-class white women and women of color.

Rayna Rapp, an anthropologist who has written on families in contemporary U.S. society, describes the emotional nature of the issue when she notes that within the women's movement

many of us have been to an archetypical meeting in which someone stands up and asserts that the nuclear family ought to be abolished because it is degrading and constraining to women. Usually, someone else (often representing a Third World position) follows on her heels, pointing out that the attack on the family represents a white, middle-class position, and that other women need their families for support and survival. Evidently both speakers are, in some senses, right. And just as evidently they aren't talking about the same families. We need to explore those differing notions of family if we are to heal an important split in our movement. To do so, we must take seriously the things women say about their experiences in their families, especially as they vary by class. (Rapp 1978: 278–279)

We need also to listen to what women say about experiences in families as they vary by race, ethnicity, and by all other characteristics of family members. If we listen to what different women say about their experiences in their diverse family arrangements, we will acknowledge and come to understand that for women as a group, as well as for individual women, life in families is contradictory—involving restrictions, constraints, and oppressive acts on the one hand and support, protection, comfort, and indeed joy on the other.

Sexuality and Reproduction

Sexuality and reproduction, while closely tied by much of the ideology which surrounds women, are not the same. In order to focus more clearly on the diverse and similar ways in which they are viewed, practiced, and denied, each is discussed here in relative isolation. Actions which violate women's sexuality and personhood (rape, battering, pornography, and so forth) are discussed in the section on politics, for fundamentally they are abusive acts of power.

Sexuality

What is it about sexuality which all US women can be said to share? Certainly the biological characteristics of the female body are a "common denominator" among women. However, the possession of those characteristics is not as important as how they are viewed within a culture and how that cultural view is affected by individual sexual orientation, race, ethnicity, class, age, and other considerations.

One thing shared by US women is the fact that we are the subjects of attitudes, values, practices, a folklore, and "humor" which categorize *all* women as sexual objects who either live up to or fall short of the ideal female sexual being.

US women are being measured against an objectified notion of female sexuality which is eternally young, never fat but "well developed," heterosexual, submissive to "her man," *and* capable of satisfying him sexually. It is striking how this ideal image cuts across racial, ethnic, and class lines. Yet the responses of women to this objectified notion of femaleness are different, as are notions of how close certain groups of women come to the ideal. Indeed, issues of race, ethnicity, and class are very evident in stereotypes of black women as "loose and sexually hyperactive," Asian American women as "exotic/erotic," and affluent women as more prudish than working-class women.

Ideal images of men are also in effect. Indeed, objectification of one gender requires objectification of the other. The difference is that in the case of women, the ideal physical being, carriage, and general personhood are grounded in notions of submissiveness and powerlessness as opposed to strength and power.

The white middle-class women at the forefront of the early women's liberation movement leveled sharp criticisms against this view of women's sexuality and what they considered the oppressive aspects of women's sex lives. Some of these women advocated the destruction of the "double standard" and others called for female sexual permissiveness (a possibility made all the easier because of more ready access to birth control). Lesbian separatists claimed that women should reject all heterosexual relations in favor of nonrepressive homosexual bonds.

Many women, Afro-American women, for example, reacted strongly to these views. In some, perhaps many cases, heterosexist attitudes or "prudishness" were at the base of the reaction. Other Afro-American women, however, were reacting to white middle-class women's indulging themselves in discussing and experimenting with sexuality while black and poor women were struggling to make it through another day in a white racist, capitalist society. The response of many working-class white women was also less than positive as they drew on traditional working-class attitudes about sex and sexuality (Rubin 1976). For many women in Native American, Asian American, and Latino communities, these public discussions of sex and sexuality raised difficulties particular to varying cultural norms. For some Christian fundamentalist women, such open discussion of sexual questions was blasphemous.

There was no all-embracing sisterhood on these questions or on other issues related to women and sexuality. As the women's liberation movement developed through the 1970s, so, too, did a far-ranging discussion of lesbianism as a sexual preference *and* as an empowering choice. However, the discussion was most often centered among middle-class, white women. Yet then, and even more so today, strong voices of lesbian women of various racial and ethnic groups argued for recognition of the particularities of their experiences.

While affirming what is shared with other lesbians, Anita Valerio speaks of her Blackfoot heritage and some of the feelings she experienced in returning to her people:

> Perhaps in the old days, in some way or other I could have fit in there. But today, my lesbianism has become a barrier between myself and my people. What to say when my grandmother or aunt asks if I've met a boyfriend? The perennial lesbian problem—how to tell the folks and what to tell them. . . . Five years ago I dreamt myself walking out of my home in Littleton and out to a flat, long desert. There, beneath a shelter of poles and sticks, an old Kainah woman sat. . . . The old lady looked at me a long time, then she said, "You will return to the Indian way." (Valerio 1981: 44–45)

Audre Lorde, in an open letter to Mary Daly, puts succinctly the important difference color can make for two women who otherwise share a great deal:

> Within the community of women, racism is a real force in my life as it is not in yours. The white women with hoods on in Ohio handing out KKK literature on the street may not like what you have to say, but they will shoot me on sight. (If you and I were to walk into a classroom of women in Dismal Gulch, Alabama, where the only thing they knew about each of us was that we were both Lesbian/Radical/Feminists, you would see exactly what I mean.) (Lorde 1984: 70)

Lesbians of poor and working-class backgrounds have spoken of their alienation from "a brand of lesbianism" associated with the women's movement of the late sixties and seventies:

> The history of my brand of lesbianism is the story of women who ran from towns like the one I fled, who joined the army, navy, or air force or who were busted when discovered with another girl and thrown into juvie hall. Or it is a quieter story of women who form a culture different from the feminist one—a life led in gay bars on Friday and Saturday nights, if you have a lover; every night, if you don't. It is about drinking too much and playing pool with style. It is an underground that runs through the phone company, the Teamsters Union, the Bank of America, and the grocery counters of this country. (Hollibaugh 1984: 2)

An issue which has most clearly divided many women of color from those white women advocating separatist politics is that of relating to men. For many Afro-American, Asian American, Hispanic, and Native American women, who share a range of oppressions with men of their group, a radical feminist position of total separation from all men, who are perceived as the enemy, does not match their day-to-day experiences or aspirations. Lesbian women of color witness the oppression they share with men of color, and they often see their own ultimate liberation as no less a racial than a gender/sexual question.

Some of these dynamics are exposed in this passage from a letter written by a Chinese American woman to her mother.

> I understand all too clearly how dehumanized Dad was in this country. To be a Chinese man in America is to be a victim of both racism and sexism. He was made to feel he was without strength, identity, and purpose. He was made to feel soft and weak, whose only job was to serve whites. Yes, ma, at one time I was ashamed of him because I thought he was "womanly". When those two white cops said, "Hey, fat boy, where's our meat?" he left me standing there on Grant Avenue while he hurried over to his store to get it; they kept complaining, never satisfied. . . . I didn't know that he spent a year and a half on Angel Island; that we could never have our right names; that he lived in constant fear of being deported; that, like you, he worked two full-time jobs most of his life; that he was mocked and ridiculed because he speaks "broken English". And Ma, I was so ashamed after that experience when I was only six years old that I never held his hand again. (Woo 1981: 145)

Reproductive Rights

There is a definitive association of women with a childbearing function—and that association cuts across racial lines, ethnic and religious lines, class lines, and most others as well. Yet, not all women can have children and not all women wish to.

There are also differences in the ways that women respond to reproduction and to what they assume are their reproductive rights. These issues are explored in greater detail in Part III. A few summary comments are offered here on three aspects of reproduction: controlling reproduction (birth control), halting reproduction (abortion), and the loss of an ability to reproduce (sterilization).

Women's views are quite divergent on these issues. There are differences along racial, class, and religious lines. And there are intensely emotional battles and even violence as some women and men on the political right attack and even bomb abortion clinics.

Certainly birth control is not an issue on which all US women are united. In addition to the official anti–birth control position mandated for women by the Catholic church, the Nation of Islam, and other religious groups, a widespread argument in several communities of color (Afro-American, Native American, and Puerto Rican especially) is that those who use or advocate birth control participate in a racist effort to limit or eliminate those populations. Regardless of the politics of today's advocates, birth control has been closely aligned with the eugenics movement and with other explicitly racist positions. As Angela Davis notes, the racism and class bias of the early birth control movement argued that it was a right for the privileged and a duty for the poor (Davis 1983).

Women are also divided over the question of abortion. Antiabortionists are quite capable of refusing abortions for themselves. What is at stake is their insistence on making a similar choice for all other women. And although the antichoice forces (men and women alike) push a single-issue line, in reality their position is about an all-encompassing, fundamentalist moral order with right wing politics and a definite place for women—as subservient as possible. Women who participate in this antifeminist, antiabortion backlash present a serious problem for those who argue that all women are sisters.

Legislative and judicial reversals in a woman's right to decide about her reproductive powers and the means to carry out her decision cause disproportionate suffering among women of color and poor women. In the years before abortion was legalized in New York State, for example, 80 percent of deaths from illegal abortions were among black and Puerto Rican women.

The most criminal assault on women's reproductive rights is forced sterilization. Once again, it is women of color, poor women, and most of all poor women of color who experience this unwanted loss of reproductive powers. In the 1970s an estimated 24 percent of all Native American women of childbearing age, and an estimated 35 percent of all Puerto Rican women of childbearing age had been sterilized. Of the women sterilized through federally subsidized programs, 43 percent were black. Although figures are not available on what percentage of these sterilizations were voluntary, those working in the antisterilization movement argue that the majority are clearly forced on women. Those who have organized and fought hardest against "la operación" are Puerto Rican women, Afro-American, Native American, and other women of color. That there has not been more active effort in this area from white women's groups is a source of bitterness among many women of color.

In the ongoing women's movement, questions of sexuality and reproduction remain at the heart of heated discussions, radical responses, divisions, and creative possibilities for change. Although when stripped to the most fundamental levels these issues are biological, the moment they are put into action, or even discussed, culture comes into play, and they become social issues. How, by whom, against whom they are put into action or denied expression becomes a matter of power, that is to say, politics.

Perhaps sexuality and reproduction are so controversial because of the pervasiveness with which ideology in mainstream U.S. culture has reduced women to sexual and reproducing objects. Large numbers of women, armed with a political movement, have fought against that

reductionism and sometimes used the very issues of sexuality and reproductive rights as methaphors for an all-encompassing liberation of
women.

This discussion illustrates the extent to which issues of sexuality
and issues of reproduction are subject to the duality of shared yet divergent experiences that characterize other spheres of women's lives.
In that sense, it may be better to speak of female sexualities and modes
of reproduction.

Religion

If asked to hold forth on the topic of "religion in the United States" a
response of many would be: "Which one?" Which one indeed? A listing
of what are called the world's "great religions" practiced in the United
States would bring the count to six: Buddhism, Christianity, Confus-
cianism, Hinduism, Islam, and Judaism. Such a listing does not include the traditional spiritual ways of Native Americans, nor the many
syncretized religions, combining, for example, traditional African religions with Christianity (Santeria among Cubans, Spiritualismo among
Puerto Ricans). And listing the so-called great religions practiced in the
United States does not begin to indicate the multitude of denominations, sects, and cults that exist within them.

The point is simply that on the question of religion in the United
States, most would begin with an assumption of diversity, rather than
an ecumenical approach which seeks to identify and build on points of
commonality among denominations and religions. Adding women to
the phrase—"women and religion in the United States"—conjures up
further images of diversity. Then what are the commonalities among
US women in the sphere of religion? There are two obvious ones. First,
in each of the "world religions" practiced in the United States the
proper place for women is defined, and it is on the whole a subservient
one. And second, women are the backbone of organized religions but
rarely serve as the leaders of the churches, synagogues, mosques, and
temples in which they are practiced.

Woman's Place

Through affirmations or challenges, religions reflect the dominant values in a society and in large measure mirror the social order. It is not
surprising then that in the major religions practiced in the United
States, the role of women in religious practice and in society is defined
in the holy religious writings as a subservient one.

Christians certainly disagree about the extent to which biblical passages defining women's second-class status should be taken literally. Yet, regardless of interpretation, such passages do not assign women an equal position with men. And as many feminists point out, when women are "praised" or given special attention, the Bible most often casts them in the role of mother.

In Judaism, there is an ongoing debate on women's roles in the synagogue and their responsibilities and rights as women of the Jewish community. In terms of synagogue services, one of the earliest issues raised in the mid-1970s was that of the mehitzah, the barrier which separates women and men during prayers. Another issue was that of counting women in the minyan (the prayer quorum). Many but not all Conservative synagogues voted to do so. Women as rabbis was yet another major issue, and in 1972 Sally Preisand became the first woman to be ordained a rabbi. Today both Reform and Reconstructionist movements have ordained well over seventy women rabbis, and the Conservative movement ordained its first twelve women in 1985.

But these changes have not come without conflict, and the debates continue. The Orthodox movement remains firmly opposed to allowing women to participate equally in religious life. Instead, women's special responsibilities in creating a Jewish home and raising the next generation of Jews are emphasized. According to an Orthodox rabbi, woman's role as mother is designed by God:

> It is not easy to form children in the Jewish mold and prepare them to become Jewish adults, and such a task would not have been primarily assigned to women had they not been especially prepared for it, physically, psychologically, intellectually, and spiritually, by Almighty God Himself. (Heschel 1983: xviii)

Women as the Backbone of Organized Religions

> Women are expected to sing in the choir, serve on the usher and stewardess boards, participate in the missionary society, cook in the kitchen, teach children in the Sunday School, and serve in all those positions that men regard as "women's work." But unlike men, women are not encouraged to enter the ministry. (Cone 1984: 132–133)

James Cone thus describes the specific situation in most black churches. But with a few variations here and there, it is a description applicable to religious bodies throughout the United States.

Casual observations and scholarly studies indicate the predominance of women in many religious activities. Black women represent more than 70 percent of the black church. Many hypotheses are offered to explain this phenomenon: it is women who are "in charge" of the morality of a community, and thus, they are in greater attendance in services; for many women religious services serve as something of a psychologically and sexually fulfilling experience; it is the one "public" activity which all groups encourage women to participate in, and on and on. It seems that the same explanation offered for the widespread involvement of black people in organized Christian churches can be applied to the question of why women are also there in great numbers. Despite the Bible's purported message to black people that as Ham's children they shall be the hewers of wood and the drawers of water, there is also the message that Jesus is the savior, and he shall set you free. Such a mixed message is also given to women: the Bible assigns a second-class status to women but also offers solace, comfort, and inspiration to them as an oppressed group.

While women are the "backbones" of churches, synagogues, and mosques, they are rarely the "heads." Throughout black history, some black women have served as preachers, but it was always an uphill battle as they often had to prove their call to the ministry to an extent not required of men. Women are still excluded from the ordained in some black churches.

Although fear of female leadership in organized religion is not often voiced in clear and unequivocal terms, it is possible to find such statements. For example, historian Lucy Dawidowicz remarks in reference to female leadership in synagogues:

> Women are efficient; they can organize, raise funds, bring order out of chaos. They can turn the shul into a Hadassah chapter. Not that I disapprove of Hadassah, its activites, of its ladies. But I do not like the idea of their taking over the synagogue. To my mind, the assumption by a woman of rabbinic or priestly function in the synagogue undermines the very essence of Jewish tradition. (Heschel 1983: xx)

Within the range of women's experiences in the sphere of religion, there is also a debate which echoes divisions we noted in the discussion on "the family." The women's movement has criticized organized religion for the role it plays in suppressing women. And, there is a call for radical changes by scholars who challenge the male-centered references to the deity, and the use of theological references to "keep women in their place" (Christ and Plaskow 1979; Daly 1973; Goldenberg 1979). In some cases, the call is for women to leave male-dominated organized religions and affiliate themselves with feminist spiritual groups.

The response of many women of color, as well as poor white women, is that the church for them is a shelter from economic and racial discrimination. Until those forms of discrimination end, or other institutions take over functions now carried out by these religious bodies, women will, it is argued, remain faithful to these traditional male-dominated religions.

Today, there are two movements which bring into sharp contrast how different women can be in their views of the spiritual world. On the one hand are the "born again" Christians, who adhere to a world view that calls for a return to "the old ways," to the most fundamentalist traditions in Christianity. On the other hand, there are women who, as a part of their feminist world view, call for a radical overhaul in the language, beliefs, and rituals of organized religions in order to remove the male bias at the very center of it all. This chasm between these two sets of women once again challenges us to recognize similarities without ignoring distinctions; to see differences without blurring commonalities.

Politics

In turning to politics, the final sphere of women's lives explored in this book, there is a sense in which we have come full circle. For "the woman question," whether discussed in the specifics of work, family, sexuality and reproductive rights, or religion, is at the base a question of power, and power is politics. In the broadest terms, we can say that women in the United States, in comparison with men, are defined as "other." From language to the highest political offices, men are the standard and women the other. Women have fewer choices about what they will do in the world of work. Women receive less pay for comparable work. Women are more often assigned secondary roles in public and religious activities. Women are challenged more in terms of their reproductive rights and sexual powers. And women are clearly more subject to sexual violence. The shorthand terms we use are that women are oppressed, or we speak of the need for women's liberation in connecting the status of women with a movement to change that status.

With all of the provisos noted earlier in terms of variations based on class, race, and other factors, the most striking commonality among US women is that as a group we do not wield political power comparable to that of men, especially white men of an affluent class. The areas of difference include perceptions of the specifics of our political status, actual differences in our respective political power, and our various views on how the status of women can be changed.

One way of looking at women's oppression in the political sphere is to note that nowhere in the United States are women represented in large numbers in sustained positions of leadership. The U.S. social order systematically excludes people of color, poor folks, and women from any significant degree of leadership and power.

But women are not totally powerless, for where there is oppression there is also resistance, and resistance is by its very nature the exertion of a degree of power. However, as far as organized political power is concerned, women are still a very long way from being proportionally represented. Geraldine Ferraro's vice presidential candidacy notwithstanding, there is still deep-seated discrimination against women in U.S. politics. Only about 10 percent of elected officials in the United States are women, and they are heavily concentrated in local government. Though women may be seen campaigning for political office, both Democratic and Republican parties are hesitant to nominate them for winable Congressional seats. Nine out of ten female Congressional candidates run against incumbents, and they are frequently served up as sacrificial lambs with very little financial or other support from their party.

Although sixty-five women ran for the U.S. House of Representatives in the 1984 election, the number in the House remained 22, the *only* black woman Representative being Cardiss Collins of Illinois. And the defeat of the Equal Rights Amendment, although a complex issue, is a symbol of women's lack of sufficient organized political power.

US women are bound by a common second-class status, yet, from an idea here and there to fully developed philosophies and ideologies, there is tremendous variation concerning *how* women's liberation is to be achieved. The many ideologies will be discussed more completely in the introduction to Part V. Here it is important to indicate the range of approaches.

The many different ways women seek to achieve gender equality are somewhat captured in this litany: feminism, radical feminism, cultural feminism, nationalist feminism, socialist feminism, feminist socialism, lesbian feminism, Third World lesbian feminism, feminist coalition politics, women in electoral politics, socialism, utopianism, indigenous traditionalism, indigenous socialism, and the list goes on and on.

How is the daily struggle viewed? A reading of the literature from the center of the women's movement indicates a range of responses, though, in general, the theoretical works speak of the struggle against patriarchy. The source of patriarchy is of course under dispute. Some argue a causal relationship with capitalism, others argue that patriarchy predates and antedates capitalism. A more straightforward rendition of this notion holds that the struggle of women is against all of the vestiges of male control and oppression of women—as expressed in attitudes and behavior which range from sexist language to male monopoly of political and economic power. From an activist perspective, the heart of the women's movement today is for greater participation and power in electoral politics; for equal pay for comparable work; for reproductive rights; and against pornography and all forms of sexual exploitation and violence.

It would be difficult to find a group of women of color who would argue against the need for each of these changes. However, while they would not deny the importance of these arenas of struggle, they would necessarily place them within the context of their daily lives. And within their lives, women of color are twice as likely to be unemployed as are white women; their life expectancy is years less than that of white women; they are fifteen to twenty-nine times more likely to live in substandard housing and receive no or inadequate health care; and their children are far more likely to receive a substandard education. Racism is the only explanation for why these conditions of women of color are so dramatically different. Thus, their struggle against sexism cannot be divorced from their struggle against racism. The history of the National Black Women's Club movement illustrates this point. As with the nineteenth-century women's movement, the club movement among Afro-American women was fundamentally organized by "middle-class" women. And at the same time that these black women in the 1900s addressed some of the same issues that were on the agenda of the women's movement of that era, there were other issues—racism being the most pronounced—which white women did not address in a consistent and frontal way. The continuation of black women's clubs and organizations today, and similar formations among other women of color, rests on the primacy which these women give to the continuing struggle against racial inequality. (For a discussion of the National Black Women's Club movement, see Giddings 1984: 95–117.)

At the center of the women's movement, there is the tendency to "level oppressions," that is, to suggest that all women are equally oppressed. Note this point in an historical context:

> As a prison house for the women themselves, the notion of Southern lady-hood was almost as effective as slavery. No one knew this better than Mary Chestnut. "All married women, all children, and girls who live on in their father's houses are slaves," she wrote with brutal finality. (Abbott 1983: 91–92)

There is no such "finality" in the view of many Afro-American women who know that the experience of their foremothers as slaves was brutally worse than that of the white Southern ladies who were their mistresses. In a modern day setting, "Poor women and women of color know there is a difference between the daily manifestations of marital slavery and prostitution because it is our daughters who line 42nd Street" (Lorde 1984: 112).

There is then a real danger in arguing that the oppression of every woman is equal to the oppression of every other woman. Yet there is also a danger in forcing every oppressive experience into a hierarchy such that it must be judged as more or less important than every other one and, therefore, more or less deserving of political action. Clearly, we need to find ways of acknowledging the various forms of women's oppression without losing sight of what are in fact differing degrees of exploitation. As Barbara Smith puts it:

> In a white dominated, capitalist economy, white skin, and if you have it, class privilege, definitely count for something, even if you belong at the very same time to a group or to groups that the society despises. Black women cannot help but resent it when people who have these privileges try to tell us that "everything is everything" and that their oppression is every bit as pervasive and dangerous as our own. From our frame of reference, given how brutally racism has functioned politically and historically against people of color in the U.S., such assertions are neither experientially accurate nor emotionally felt. (Bulkin et al. 1984: 76)

Of all the ways in which women's oppression—that is to say, women's powerlessness—is expressed, none is more blatant than the reality that, far beyond what is the case for men, women are potential victims of sexual harassment, sexual exploitation, and sexual violence. Battering, rape, and incest are the most physically violent forms. Sexual harassment involves sexual advances by men in a position to intimidate or unjustly exert their power in a job or classroom situation. Such advances are offensive, possibly psychologically damaging, and professionally disastrous to women. Sexual exploitation includes that form of prostitution in which a woman "agrees" to participate in sexual acts but does so because she has concluded that she has no alternative source of money, and pornography, which reduces women to their "sexual utility."

These various assaults against women are best characterized not as sexual acts but as acts of violence which dramatically signal women's powerlessness. These acts of psychological and physical violence cut across age lines. As recent exposés indicate, child molesting is not some isolated horror, but a widespread crime—which disproportionately affects little girls. And rape is among the special fears of older women in our cities. The increasing use of female children in pornographic movies and pictures is also an indication of the extremes of misogyny.

The severity of the physical and psychological pain which women suffer as a result of these various forms of sexual violence cannot be overstated. The conditions are such that most, if not all women, are in fear of such violence at some point in their lives. Susan Jacoby interviewed a group of women, all in their forties, most of whom grew up in first- and second-generation Jewish or Italian immigrant families. In their East Flatbush women's group, the following exchange took place:

> "I confess I don't feel much of a sense of sisterhood when I see pictures of Gloria Steinem with her streaked hair and slinky figure. I feel somehow that these people don't know how it is to be getting older with very little money and education. They have it a lot better than we do—it's not true that we're all in the same boat." Another woman disagreed: "Well, there's one thing that we all have in common—we're all afraid of muggers and rapists when we walk down a dark street at night. And that's something we have in common with the colored women who live right here in East Flatbush, even though most of us are better off financially than they are." (Baxandall et al. 1976: 388–389)

However, because *all* women in the United States live with the possibility that they will be sexually abused, harassed, raped, or battered does not mean that the actual experience with such violence is the same for all women.

It is tempting to say that all women are bound by the recurring suggestion, innuendo, or outright assertion that whatever sexual abuse they suffer, it is basically the woman's fault: "She shouldn't have been walking down that dark street"; or "If you wear a blouse like that you're asking for it." Yet throughout U.S. history, there has been a glaring exception to this "rule": it is the prevailing assumption that rape is most often committed by black men and that the victims are white women. In this case, blame is laid on the "oversexed" black male.

This use of the myth of black men's "super sexuality" as a coverup for other issues and problems is not new. Ida B. Wells, the great Afro-American antilynching warrior, found that of 504 black citizens lynched between 1896 and 1900, only 96 had ever been accused of rape. Thus, although rape was often the rationale for lynching black men, the charge brought against the accused was seldom rape. Rather, at the heart of the lynchings of black men was their "threat" to the labor market privilege of white men.

The myth is that white women are the victims of rape and black men are the rapists. The reality is that black women, other women of color, and particularly poor women of color are disproportionately the victims of this sexual violence. A study undertaken in Chicago indicated that black women are eighteen times more likely to be raped than white women (Joseph 1978: 3). And the reasons are clear.

> There are particular conditions that account for high incidents of rape— systematically sanctioned conditions—which are the results of institutional racism. Blacks are disproportionately over-represented in the lower socio-economic groups and the material conditions of their lives include poorly lighted and poorly policed living areas, exposures to the inse-

28

curities of public transportation, brutal family relations, and communities filled with the army of the walking wounded (the drug addicts, winos, superflies, and crazies). Since street crimes are by and large neighborhood crimes, these existing conditions account for the high incidence in intra-racial rape and other crimes. (Joseph 1978: 3)

Thus, women in the United States share a status of oppression, and perhaps the most traumatic expression of that status is in our potential victimization in sexual crimes. Yet once again, we note the tempering influence of race and class on women's experiences.

This exploration of five spheres of women's lives has made the point that on a certain level of generality, there are definite commonalities among US women; and on particular levels of specificity, there are differences among us of considerable importance. The oppression of women cuts across lines of class, race, ethnicity, age, religion, sexual orientation, region, and physical abilities. Yet, these same realities create the specific content of the oppression. The significance of this point is captured by Audre Lorde:

Certainly there are very real differences between us of race, age, and sex. But it is not those differences between us that are separating us. It is rather our refusal to recognize those differences and to examine the distortions which result from our misnaming them and their effects upon human behavior and expectations. . . .

Too often we pour the energy needed for recognizing and exploring differences into pretending those differences are insurmountable barriers, or that they do not exist at all. This results in a voluntary isolation or false and treacherous connections. Either way, we do not develop tools for using human differences as a spring board for creative change within our lives. (Lorde 1984: 115–116)

References Cited

Abbott, S.
1983 *Womenfolks: Growing Up Down South*. New York: Ticknor and Fields.

Bambara, T. C., ed.
1970 *The Black Woman: An Anthology*. New York: Signet.

Baxandall, R., L. Gordon, and S. Reverby.
1976 *America's Working Women: A Documentary History—1600 to the Present*. New York: Vintage.

Boucher, S.
1982 *Heartwomen: An Urban Feminist Odyssey Home*. New York: Harper & Row.

Bulkin, E., M. E. Pratt, and B. Smith, eds.
1984   *Yours in Struggle.* Brooklyn, N.Y.: Long Haul Press.

Christ, C. P., and J. Plaskow, eds.
1979   *Womanspirit Rising: A Feminist Reader in Religion.* San Francisco: Harper and Row.

Cone, J. H.
1984   *For My People: Black Theology and the Black Church.* Maryknoll, N.Y.: Orbis.

Daly, M.
1973   *Beyond God the Father: Toward a Philosophy of Women's Liberation.* Boston: Beacon Press.

Davis, A. Y.
1983   *Women, Race and Class.* New York: Vintage.

Fine, M., and A. Asch.
1981   "Disabled Women: Sexism Without the Pedestal." *Journal of Sociology and Social Welfare,* VIII(2): 233–248.

Fuentes, A., and B. Ehrenreich.
1983   *Women in the Global Factory.* Boston: South End Press.

Giddings, P.
1984   *When and Where I Enter.* New York: William Morrow.

Goldenberg, N. R.
1979   *Changing of the Gods: Feminism and the End of Traditional Religion.* Boston: Beacon Press.

Green, R.
1984   "Magnolias Grow in Dirt: The Bawdy Lore of Southern Women." In *Speaking for Ourselves,* M. Alexander, ed., pp. 20–28. New York: Pantheon.

Heschel, S., ed.
1983   *On Being a Jewish Feminist.* New York: Schocken.

Hohri, S.
1983   "Are You a Liberated Woman?" *East Wind: Politics and Culture of Asians in the U.S.* 2(1): 42–45. California: Getting Together Publications.

Hollibaugh, A.
1984   "The Sympathy of the Blood." *Village Voice,* June 26, 1984, pp. 22–25.

Hooks, B.
1984   *Feminist Theory: From Margin to Center.* Boston: South End Press.

Hune, S.
1982   Asian American Women: Past and Present, Myth and Reality. Unpublished manuscript prepared for conference on Black Women's Agenda for the Feminist Movement in the 80's, Williams College, Williamstown, Mass., November 12–14, 1982.

Joseph, G. I.
1978   Rape—Race—Rapism. Unpublished manuscript.

Leacock, E.
1979 "Women, Development and Anthropological Facts and Fictions" In *Women in Latin America: An Anthology from Latin American Perspectives*, pp. 7–16. Riverside, Calif.: Latin American Perspectives.

Levine, M. P., and R. Leonard.
1984 "Discrimination against Lesbians in the Work Force." *Signs* 9(4): 701–710.

Lord, S. B.
1979 "Growin' Up—Appalachian, Female, and Feminist." In *Appalachian Women: A Learning/Teaching Guide*, S. B. Lord and C. Patton-Crowder, eds., pp. 22–25. Knoxville, Tenn.: University of Tennessee.

Lorde, A.
1984 *Sister Outsider*. Trumansburg, N.Y.: Crossing Press.

Marable, M.
1983 *How Capitalism Underdeveloped Black America*. Boston: South End Press.

Ostrander, S. A.
1984 *Women of the Upper Class*. Philadelphia: Temple University Press.

Rapp, R.
1978 "Family and Class in Contemporary America: Notes Toward an Understanding of Ideology." *Science and Society* 42 (3, Fall): 278–300.

Rubin, L.
1976 *Worlds of Pain*. New York: Basic Books.

Shalala, D. E.
1983 Big Sister Is Watching You: A Feminist View of 1984. Unpublished speech prepared for delivery at the opening session of the 32nd Biennial Convention of the American Association of University Women, San Francisco Hilton and Tower Hotel, Saturday, June 25, 1983.

Stack, C.
1981 "Sex Roles and Survival Strategies in an Urban Black Community." In *The Black Woman Cross-Culturally*, F. S. Steady, ed., pp. 349–367. Cambridge, Mass.: Schenkman.

Valerio, A.
1981 "It's in My Blood, My Face—My Mother's Voice, the Way I Sweat." In *This Bridge Called My Back*, C. Moraga and G. Anzaldua, eds., pp. 41–45. Watertown, Mass.: Persephone Press.

Wolfe, A.
1976 "The Jewish Woman." In *Dialogue on Diversity*, B. Peters, and V. Samuels, eds., pp. 42–49. New York: Institute on Pluralism and Group Identity.

Woo, M.
1981 "Letter to Ma." In *This Bridge Called My Back*, C. Moraga and G. Anzalua, eds., pp. 140–147. Watertown, Mass.: Persephone Press.

PART I

WORK

$\mathbf{M}$OTHER Jones remarked, some sixty years ago, that women don't have careers . . . they have jobs. In doing their jobs, women share certain experiences. Women who work outside of their households tend to work in sex-segregated jobs, earn less than men, and receive less pay than men for doing comparable work. In traditional households, women do the housework. When they work outside their homes, women continue to be responsible for housework, thus putting them on the "double shift." Yet differences in their backgrounds and in the way society responds to those differences result in particular and sometimes very distinct experiences.

The articles in this section illustrate some of these commonalities and differences among women in the sphere of work. The articles address three very basic questions: Who are today's women workers? What kinds of work do women in the United States do? And what are the conditions women encounter at their workplaces?

Perhaps the most dramatic point concerning today's women workers is how many of us there are in the paid work force. In 1981, more than 52 percent of all working-age women (46.7 million) were in the labor force — up from 43 percent in 1970. As a result of that growth, women now constitute 43 percent of the paid labor force in the United

States and are responsible for nearly 60 percent of the country's economic growth since 1970 (Dion 1984: 7). Women, along with men of color, now make up a large majority of the U.S. working class. However, there is a reality not captured in these figures:

> In the last decades women entered the labor force in unprecedented and unexpected numbers, and the "typical" woman can now expect to spend most of her years, including those when her children are young, in the paid labor force. This typical woman is also a working class woman: she works for wages in clerical, service, manufacturing (and even some technical and professional) jobs that pay poorly and give her little possibility for advancement, little control over her work, and little decision-making power in her work. (Brodkin and Remy 1984: 15–16)

While this is not a very "pretty" picture, the near future for women workers is even less attractive. During a period of more general affluence, women could at least hope to lessen the gap between themselves and male workers. In the mid-1980s, however, "when working class men no longer hold their own against unemployment, union-management rollbacks, or even inflation, what hope is there for women to close the economic gap between the male and female worker?" (Snitow et al. 1983: 482). And of course, the limited chances a woman has to improve her work situation are further greatly affected by her class, race, ethnicity, physical condition, sexual orientation, age, and locale.

Today, as increasing amounts of work in the "information industry" involve various computerized processes, what will be the fate of the millions of women who sit at those keyboards from nine to five? With the same titles as the machines/programs they operate, "word processors," these women work under conditions which make them resemble sweatshop workers much more than the touted images of computer technicians. "Operators are seen as easily trained, replaceable, and interchangeable, not as highly trained, especially competent, or invaluable workers" (Brodkin and Remy 1984: 130). Because workers in these jobs must meet, or better yet, exceed "production quotas"—the new term for speedups—word processing may be one of the most stressful and physically damaging of today's jobs. We can predict that as the novelty of word processing wears off, wages for that work drop off, and more technologically advanced tasks develop, women of color will be increasingly slotted into the job of "word processor."

The history of women factory workers in the United States largely began with white women and girls from New England farms as the predominant work force in the region's burgeoning textile mills in the 1830s and 1840s. The Civil War, as with later wars, brought more women into factory work to meet expanded production needs and to replace men taken into the army. With the influx of millions of European immigrants in the late 1800s and early 1900s, the numbers of women and girls in the factory work force greatly increased.

It was in the garment industry that women predominated, and it was there that women were involved in intense union organizing for better pay and improved working conditions. Yet in 1983, there were as many sweatshops in New York City as in 1913. In those sweatshops, an individual's class is as evident as gender and race or ethnicity. Sweatshop exploitation now occurs in broader terms, for example, in the increasing amount of "homeworking" that women are doing, a practice that women workers at the turn of the century fought and put a stop to. For some women today—usually, although not always, middle class and often rural—it is argued that homework allows them to combine work and motherhood, creates more flexible hours, and hence offers greater opportunity for entrepreneurship or more schooling. Yet for others—poor and urban women particularly—the revived practice of homework reflects the same low pay, lack of benefits, long hours, poor working conditions, and other exploitative factors women workers fought against long ago.

The contradictions of gender, class, and work are such that it is conceivable that Nancy Reagan's high-fashion clothes may be "homemade." Her favorite designer, Adolpho, consigns his garment work to Ruth Fashions in Queens, New York, which farms out the work to homeworkers, women who do garment work in their homes. The New York Attorney General in 1982 cited Ruth Fashions as a chronic violator of laws prohibiting homework (Fuentes and Ehrenreich 1983: 52).

Certainly there are women in the United States who do not work for wages. And among these women, there are those who make the conscious decision not to work because they wish to "remain at home." Some women do not work outside of their homes because of a disability which prevents it or, more often, because of discrimination against those with the disability. The same holds true for older women, more of whom are capable and desirous of working than are permitted to do so. But the overwhelming majority of women work. Precisely because we are women, we clean, shop, launder, care for children, and do hundreds of other tasks involved in housework. For all of this work, women are not paid.

The debate in feminist circles on whether women should be paid for housework is a lively one. It is interesting to note the position argued by Angela Davis that paying "housewives" is not the solution: the large number of black South African men who work in mines at great distances from their families shows that capitalism can do without women's housework that reproduces workers and cares for others. The solution, argues Davis, is to abolish housework! (Davis 1983: 222–224).

Conforming to the domestic code, or what some have called the domestic ideology, society is said to consist of a public sphere and a private sphere. As if ordained or dictated by "natural law," men work in
the public sphere, where they compete and the most fit survive; women
work in the private sphere, where they love and care for others, and
clean. This code is so deeply embedded that when women enter the
paid "public sphere," the work of the private sphere remains our responsibility.

> All studies of unpaid domestic labor indicate that, despite "labor saving"
> commodities, women still spend as much time (though fewer calo-
> ries) now as they did in the 1920's on "housework." (Brodkin and Remy
> 1984: 32)

The work and stress of housework and being a mother are clearly
captured by Studs Terkel in the article about Jesusita Novarro, mother
of five, head of her household, and part-time worker who supplements
her very low wages with very low "welfare" payments.

Farm work was the single most common form of work for U.S.
women (in addition to housework) before the 1920s, reflecting the fact
that most people lived in the countryside or in towns with populations
under 2,500. Today, farm work is not even listed in most official government publications which categorize women's work. But for a small
number of US women the reality of farm work, painted by Katherine
Haynes in the second article by Terkel included here, remains. This
seventy-seven-year-old rural farm woman recalls her eighteen-hour
work days.

Four of the articles are about women who are paid for their labor
outside of their households as domestic workers, secretaries, shipyard
workers, and in the case of an upper-middle-class woman, as a corporate executive.

Drawing on extensive interviews and fieldwork in New York City,
Shellee Colen explores the motivations of Caribbean women to seek domestic work in the United States and conditions they face once employed by middle-class white women. While housework is the one job
that is common to women, it is paradoxically the job that most sharply
highlights differences among women in terms of race, ethnicity, and
class "for it is an occupation in which some women (poor, Black, ethnically subordinate) have worked for wages paid by other women (usually middle class, white, or ethnically dominant)" (Brodkin and Remy
1984: 80).

Domestic service has declined substantially since 1920, when it
was the single largest nonfarm occupation for women in the United
States. It became the dominant occupation for black women, though
by 1970 only 13 percent of black women workers were so employed.

Today, it is an occupation involving large numbers of immigrant women from the Caribbean, Latin and Central America, and Southeast Asia. Colen's article raises the question of the extent to which black women migrants from the Caribbean may, under some circumstances, share more in common with a woman migrant from Southeast Asia than with a black woman born in the United States.

In New York City, good weather finds large numbers of Latin women pushing youngsters in strollers and converging around Eighty-third Street and Riverside Drive—known as "Nannies Row." These women, like the Caribbean women described in Colen's article, often must leave their own children in the care of others in order to receive low wages for their roles as surrogate mothers (Geist 1984). The migrant status of many domestic workers complicates their situations substantially, as demands for greater respect and more reasonable wages are often met with threats of cancelling sponsorship or "turning in" to immigration authorities those who do not have their legal papers.

The dramatic decline in the number of U.S.-born black women doing domestic service occurred largely as a result of clerical jobs becoming more accessible. In 1980, 30.4 percent of U.S. women workers were listed in government statistics as involved in "administrative support, including clerical" work, meaning jobs that involve clerical, sales, and service work. Those which are exclusively female, or nearly so, are known as pink-collar jobs. Karen Kenyon describes the conditions of this work, which is not the blue-collar manual type done by unskilled factory workers or skilled trades*men*, nor is it at the pay and prestige levels of white-collar work. As Kenyon shows, pink-collar work has the unwritten requirement that the worker "look feminine" and do such things as make the coffee, pick up the gift for someone's birthday, and generally remain in the subservient position befitting the boss's "girl."

Just as a government and industry propaganda blitz during World War II urged large numbers of women—and for the first time there was room for women of color—to fill the factory places of men at war, another onslaught of propaganda after the war told women that it was time to give the jobs back to the men and return to their primary responsibilities in the home. The ideology of what is and what is not suitable work for women is deeply embedded in the culture of the skilled trades. Anne Braden's article on black and white Southern shipyard workers illustrates some of the intense prejudice which women must combat in order to do what is said to be "unladylike." The article also provides particular insight into what can be the powerful role of unionization in Southern workplaces, especially when the union women refuse to allow racism to divide and therefore conquer them.

At the top of the occupational ladder are women who work in professional and managerial jobs. A study by Hennig and Jardim (1978: 12) indicates that when women made up 39 percent of the work force, they constituted less than 5 percent of the individuals who earned more than $10,000 a year in the census category of Managers and Proprietors. The upper-middle-class woman who tells her story in the article by Elizabeth Oakes does not focus on the discrimination she has experienced because of her gender, but she does talk about the same typecasting and unequal pay scale that women at all occupational levels describe. The woman is independently moneyed, lives in an upper-middle-class country setting, and approaches her voluntary work and investments in stocks and bonds without the pressures of providing for her very own livelihood. That is a far cry from the conditions of millions of poor women, women of color, indeed of most working women in the United States.

Race and ethnicity are specifically addressed by Elaine Kim in the article on Asian American working women. With a higher work-force-participation rate than black or white female workers, the majority of Asian American women work in garment factories, electronics industries, and family-owned businesses. And contrary to the widespread notion that Asian Americans are "successful model minorities," "racial discrimination continues to play a major role in shaping the status of today's Asian American women" (Kim 1982: 129).

For all of the women who work at receiving welfare—and indeed it is *work* to become a recipient and even more work to somehow manage to make ends meet with low welfare payments—there is also a myth about their success. As the women who speak about welfare in a discussion with Louise te Boekhorst indicate, there is a myth that women on welfare are lazy women of color who use their payments to buy Cadillacs. The women interviewed by te Boekhorst, as is true of the majority of welfare recipients, are white women who are single mothers (as are 90 percent of those on welfare) and have two or fewer children (as is the case with 70 percent of all recipients). It may be somewhat atypical that these three women attend school and each is an honors student, but the difficulties they describe are most typical of ADC recipients.

The real trouble with welfare, as Barbara Ehrenreich puts it, is that it does not pay enough. Contrasting the $46,000 that Nancy Reagan reportedly spent on her inaugural wardrobe with the $4,600 a year which the average family on welfare receives (a sum being whittled down by inflation and social welfare cuts), it takes a lot of imagination to think of the women and children who barely make it on welfare as living in the lap of luxury (Ehrenreich 1985: C2).

There are a numerically small number of women who do live in the lap of luxury, the truly privileged upper class. One example of the domestic ideology's power is that the husbands of such women often fear their wives taking paid jobs because it would be considered evidence of the man's inability to provide financially for *his* family. Here is the myth of man the provider and, woman the homebody—roles which, because of their class orientation, are unnecessary.

In a recent work on upper-class women, Ostrander analyzes voluntarism. Although she does not present this charity work in a broad historical framework (see Capek 1985: 11), we do get a definitive sense of how, even at this level of affluence, whatever women do tends to be viewed as of less value than when it is done by men.

> For men of independent means, volunteering, even volunteering as a primary career, carries high prestige and considerable power. (It is elite males' volunteering—much more than wives or sisters, mothers or daughters—that maintains most of the perogatives of a dominant class structure. Men still dominate the boards of hospitals, churches, foundations, museums, schools and colleges: the more prestigious the board, the fewer the women appointed.) Upper class men seldom suffer from society's devaluing *their* "labor"—and they seldom make the distinction between paid and volunteer work, professional or volunteer service. (Ostrander 1984: 12)

But it is crucial to remember how great is the difference between "discrimination by privilege and protection, and discrimination by deprivation and exclusion" (Steady 1981: 28).

Taken as a whole, these articles concretely portray commonalities and differences among US women in terms of the work we do, the work we must do, and the work we are not permitted to do. A reality not directly addressed is the growing similarity in the conditions under which many women work around the world. As some multinational corporations "run away" to cheap labor supplies in Third World countries, with women workers often targeted as those whose substandard wages offer the companies the most profits, other companies head for the Southern United States, especially to areas hostile to unions, while still others reproduce these conditions at electronics factories in California and Massachusetts or sweatshops in New York. In response to this growing internationalization of capital, the struggles of women workers will necessarily become more international as well as more multiracial and multiethnic.

References Cited

Brodkin, S. and D. Remy, eds.
1984   *My Troubles Are Going to Have Trouble With Me.* New Brunswick, N.J.: Rutgers University Press.

Capek, M. E.
1985   "The Uses of Privilege." *The Women's Review of Books*, II(b): 11–12.

Davis, A. Y.
1983   *Women, Race and Class*. New York: Vintage.

Dion, M. J.
1984   *We, The American Women*. No. 2. U.S. Department of Commerce. Washington, D.C.: U.S. Government Printing Office.

Ehrenreich, B.
1985   "Hers." *New York Times*, February 14, 1985.

Fuentes, A., and B. Ehrenreich.
1983   *Women in the Global Factory*. Boston: South End Press.

Geist, W. E.
1984   "About New York: On the Job on 'Nannies Row.'" *New York Times*, October 17, 1984.

Hennig, M., and A. Jardim.
1978   *The Managerial Woman*. New York: Pocket Books.

Kim, E.
1982   *With Silk Wings: Asian American Women at Work*. Oakland, Calif.: Asian Women United of California.

Ostrander, S. A.
1984   *Women of the Upper Class*. Philadelphia: Temple University Press.

Snitnow, A., C. Stansell, and S.Thompson, eds.
1983   *Powers of Desire: The Politics of Sexuality*. New York: Monthly Review.

Steady, F. S.
1981   "The Black Woman Cross-Culturally: An Overview." In *The Black Woman Cross-Culturally*, F. S. Steady, ed. Cambridge, Mass.: Schenkman.

2

Jesusita Novarro

Studs Terkel

*She is a mother of five children: the oldest twelve, the youngest two. "I
went on welfare when my first husband walked out on me. I was swimming alone, completely cuckoo for a while. When I married this second
man, I got off it. When he started drinking and bringing no money
home, I had to quit my job and go on welfare again. I got something
with this welfare business and I don't like it."*

*She is working part-time as an assistant case aide at a settlement
house in the neighborhood. The director "says I'm doing real good and
can have a job upstairs with a little bit more money. It's only four hours,
because in the afternoon I want to be with my children. They're still
small."*

*She has just come home from the hospital where she was treated
for a serious illness. On this hot August afternoon—it is over a hundred
degrees—the blower in the kitchen isn't doing much good. The three
children in the house are more fascinated by technology—the tape
recorder—than the conversation, though they are listening . . .*

From *Working: People Talk About What They Do All Day and How They Feel About What
They Do*, by Studs Terkel. Copyright © 1972, 1974 by Studs Terkel. Reprinted by permission of Pantheon Books, a Division of Random House, Inc.

I start my day here at five o'clock. I get up and prepare all the children's clothes. If there's shoes to shine, I do it in the morning. About seven o'clock I bathe the children. I leave my baby with the baby sitter and I go to work at the settlement house. I work until twelve o'clock. Sometimes I'll work longer if I have to go to welfare and get a check for somebody. When I get back, I try to make hot food for the kids to eat. In the afternoon it's pretty well on my own. I scrub and can and cook and do whatever I have to do.

Welfare makes you feel like you're doing nothing. Like you're laying back and not doing anything and it's falling in your lap. But you must understand, mothers, too, work. My house is clean. I've been scrubbing since this morning. You could check my clothes, all washed and ironed. I'm home and I'm working. I am a working mother.

A job that a woman in a house is doing is a tedious job—especially if you want to do it right. If you do it slipshod, then it's not so bad. I'm pretty much of a perfectionist. I tell my kids, hang a towel. I don't want it thrown away. That is very hard. It's a constant game of picking up this, picking up that. And putting this away, so the house'll be clean.

Some men work eight hours a day. There are mothers that work eleven, twelve hours a day. We get up at night, a baby vomits, you have to be calling the doctor, you have to be changing the baby. When do you get a break, really? You don't. This is an all-around job, day and night. Why do they say it's charity? We're working for our money. I am working for this check. It is not charity. We are giving some kind of home to these children.

I'm so busy all day I don't have time to daydream. I pray a lot. I pray to God to give me strength. If He should take a child away from me, to have the strength to accept it. It's His kid. He just borrowed him to me.

I used to get in and close the door. Now I speak up for my right. I walk with my head up. If I want to wear big earrings, I do. If I'm overweight, that's too bad. I've gotten completely over feeling where I'm little. I'm working now. I'm pulling my weight. I'm gonna get off welfare in time, that's my goal—get off.

It's living off welfare and feeling that you're taking something for nothing the way people have said. You get to think maybe you are. You get to think, Why am I so stupid? Why can't I work? Why do I have to live this way? It's not enough to live on anyway. You feel degraded.

The other day I was at the hospital and I went to pay my bill. This nurse came and gave me the green card. Green card is for welfare. She went right in front of me and gave it to the cashier. She said, "I wish I could stay home and let the money fall in my lap." I felt rotten. I was just burning inside. You hear this all the way around you. The doctor doesn't even look at you. People are ashamed to show that green card. Why can't a woman just get a check in the mail: Here, this check is for you. Forget welfare. You're a mother who works.

This nurse, to her way of thinking, she represents the working people. The ones with the green card, we represent the lazy no-goods. This is what she was saying. They're the good ones and we're the bad guys.

You know what happened at the hospital? I was put in a nice room, semiprivate. You stay there until someone with insurance comes in and then you get pushed up to the fifth floor. There's about six people in there, and nobody comes even if you ring. I said, "Listen lady, you can put me on the roof. You just find out what's the matter with me so I can get the hell out of here."

How are you going to get people off welfare if they're constantly being pushed down? If they're constantly feeling they're not good for anything? People say, I'm down, I'll stay down. And this goes on generation to generation to generation. Their daughter and their daughter and their daughter. So how do you break this up? These kids don't ask to be born—these kids are gonna grow up and give their lives one day. There will always be a Vietnam.

There will always be war. There always has been. The way the world is run, yes, there will always be war. Why? I really don't know. Nobody has ever told me. I was so busy handling my own affairs and taking care of my children and trying to make my own money and calling up welfare when my checks are late or something has been stolen. All I know is what's going on here. I'm an intelligent woman up to a certain point, and after that . . . I wish I knew. I guess the big shots decided the war. I don't question it, because I've been busy fighting my own little war for so long.

The head of the settlement house wants me to take the social worker's job when I get back to work. I visit homes, I talk to mothers. I try to make them aware that they got something to give. I don't try to work out the problems. This is no good. I try to help them to come to some kind of a decision. If there's no decision, to live with it, because some problem doesn't have any answer.

There was one mother that needed shoes. I found shoes for her. There was another mother that needed money because her check was late. I found someplace for her to borrow a couple of dollars. It's like a fund. I could borrow a couple of dollars until my check comes, then when my check comes I give it back. How much time have mothers left to go out and do this? How many of us have given time so other mothers could learn to speak English, so they'll be able to work. We do it gladly because the Lord gave us English.

I went to one woman's house and she's Spanish speaking. I was talking to her in English and she wouldn't unbend. I could see the fear in her eyes. So I started talking Spanish. Right away, she invited me for coffee and she was telling me the latest news . . .

I would like to help mothers be aware of how they can give to the community. Not the whole day—maybe three, four hours. And get paid for it. There's nothing more proud for you to receive a check where you worked at. It's yours, you done it.

At one time, during her second marriage, she had worked as an assembler at a television factory. "I didn't care for it. It was too automatic. It was just work, work, work, and I wasn't giving of myself. Just hurry it up and get it done. Even if you get a job that pays you, if you don't enjoy it, what are you getting? You're not growing up. (Taps temple.) Up here."

The people from the settlement house began visiting me, visiting welfare mothers, trying to get them interested in cooking projects and sewing. They began knocking on my door. At the beginning, I was angry. It was just like I drew a curtain all around me. I didn't think I was really good for anything. So I kind of drew back. Just kept my troubles to myself, like vegetating. When these people began calling on me, I began to see that I could talk and that I did have a brain. I became a volunteer.

I want to be a social worker. Somebody that is not indifferent, that bends an ear to everybody. You cannot be slobberish. You cannot cry with the people. Even if you cry inside, you must keep a level head. You have to try to help that person get over this bump. I would go into a house and try to make friends. Not as a spy. The ladies have it that welfare comes as spies to see what you have. Or you gotta hide everything 'cause welfare is coming. There is this fear the social worker is gonna holler, because they got something, maybe a man or a boyfriend. I wouldn't take any notes or pens or paper or pencils or anything. I would just go into the house and talk. Of course, I would look around to see what kind of an environment it is. This you have to absorb. You wouldn't say it, but you would take it in.

I promised myself if I ever get to work all day, I'm going to buy me a little insurance. So the next time I go to the hospital I'll go to the room I want to go. I'm gonna stay there until it's time for me to leave, because I'm gonna pay my own bill. I don't like to feel rotten. I want my children, when they grow up, they don't have to live on it. I want to learn more. I'm hungry for knowledge. I want to do something. I'm searching for something. I don't know what it is.

3

Aunt Katherine Haynes

Studs Terkel

A worked-out mining town in eastern Kentucky, Blackey. It is near the Virginia border. The Cumberlands are in view; is it fog, smoke, or a heavy dust that causes them to appear more distant than they really are? The people of the town, population 350—the young have gone—are many of them, of Revolutionary War stock. Most are on welfare.

Along the superhighway, cutting through the mountains, gangs of men are casually engaged in road repair. All day trucks and half-trucks rumble by, kicking up clouds of coughing dust. During the trip to Blackey, there were glimpses of deep "hollers" and shacks; and an occasional person. Half-hidden by the mountain greenery were the ubiquitous small mountains of slag.

We're behind the mountains, deep in the hollow, Bull Creek. It's a long, winding, tortuous dirt road, some seven miles from Blackey.

Aunt Katherine Haynes is seventy-seven. She lives by herself in a cottage, on the rocks, at the foot of the mountains. It is surrounded by caterpillar tractors and bulldozers. On the wall, among olden photo-

graphs, is the legend: God Bless Our Home. It is a spare place, singularly neat: a folded umbrella in one corner, a homemade broom in another; an ancient brass bedstead is the one conspicuous piece of furniture.

She recalls the hollow of her small girlhood: "The road, a horse could travel it, but that was all. No cars, no wagons, or no nothin' back then. Then they went to have wagons and kinda widened the road up. Each man used to work six days a year, free labor. On the roads. If he wasn't out on the days the others was, why they laid him off a bigger piece to finish and he had to do that. That was the law. They always done it in the fall of the year.

"In the fall of the year, it's the prettiest place you've ever seen. When the leaves is colored . . . it's beautiful to see the hills when it's colored like that, brown and red and green and yeller. The pines always looks green and if the rest is all colored, the pines shows up.

"There was more big trees then, but the fields were cleaned up and tended. You can see there's nothin' cleaned up any more, 'cause I ain't able to do it . . . "

Housework and farmin' is all I done, never worked at nothin' else. Eighteen hours out of every twenty-four. Out-of-doors and then in the house at night. I have worked out in the fodder field and carry it in some time after dark. We'd stack it by moonlight Never got much rest on what little time I was in bed. (Laughs)

You usually didn't get much rest on Sunday, had to cook for ten children on Sunday. I've raised ten and I had eleven. Three meals a day I cooked on Sunday. I got so I couldn't cook like I used to. I used to be out here just runnin' and cookin' those meals in a few minutes and fillin' the table full. But my mind just jumps from here to there and I can't do that no more. Just hard work, that's all I ever knowed.

I can run circles around every girl I've got in the house today. I'm awful thankful for it, but I won't hold up much longer. I'm a gittin' down. Used to be I could stand and split wood all day long, but now I go out there and split a little while and it hurts the back of my legs to stoop over. But I done awful well I think.

I just don't know. I was just raised an old hillbilly and I'll die one. Radio, it's sittin' up there, but I can't hear too good. Don't have a television. I say there's too much foolishness on for me to watch. I hear a little about Vietnam. And I study a lot about it. But I have enough to worry on my mind without listenin' to that to worry more about. What was to be would be. No, I don't guess I have a grandson in Vietnam now. Terry's boy, I actually don't know if he's out of Vietnam or not.

They wasn't much to think on when you didn't have no education. I didn't get half through the third reader, so I've got no education at all. Only five months of school. I just quit out until we got the fodder saved. Then it got so cold, I couldn't go back. I'm just a flat old hillbilly. That's the only way I know to talk and the only way I'll ever try to talk.

There was fifteen in the family and we were raised in a log house. There wasn't a window in the house. If we seen how to do anything in the winter, we done it by firelight. There wasn't even a kerosene lamp. We had to keep the door open regardless of how cold it was. If you needed to work at somethin' we either done it by the light of the fire in the grate or opened the door. We always kept a good fire.

That was the way I learnt to write. I'd get me a piece of clay dirt out of the cracks and write on the side of the log house. I couldn't write a line when I was goin' to school. Now that's the truth.

4

"With Respect and Feelings"
Voices of West Indian Child Care and Domestic Workers in New York City

Shellee Colen

I'm not looking for them to shower us down with money, with clothes, but with a little respect and feelings. You know because they want full respect from us and at the same time they want to treat us like nothing. . . . A lot of West Indians are very insulted, but we do it because we have no choice.
Joyce Miller,[1] a thirty-one-year-old Jamaican woman in Brooklyn, discussed her past experiences as a domestic and child care worker in the New York City area.

It was a situation I resented. They had hampers and stuff like that, but when they undressed, they took [off] their clothes, they just walked out of them and left them on the bathroom floor. And I'd had enough. One Monday morning, I walked in and I said I'm not picking up any clothes today. (Laughs) I decided that I'm not picking up any CLOTHES today. . . . One

This article is for the West Indian women who generously gave of their limited time to share parts of their lives with me. For the thought and care they took in relating their experiences and for their patience with the whole process, I am deeply grateful. For creating this book and for her enthusiasm and editorial assistance, I want to express my gratitude to Johnnetta Cole. For her constant support and her editorial suggestions on an earlier draft of this article I thank Rayna Rapp. The article has benefitted from editorial suggestions by Annick Piant and from comments by Mindie Lazarus-Black, Helen Evers, Deborah D. Samuels, and Michael Landy made on a early draft of a related article. Copyright © 1985 Shellee Colen.

day I went on strike and she (the employer) said, "Well this is what the job requires and if you're going to hold the job, it's part. . . ." I didn't do it that day but the next day I [picked them up]. . . . Her argument is that she has always picked up after her husband and that's the way he is and she accepted him like that. Since she doesn't want to pick . . . up, I'm sure she hires somebody who will pick . . . up for her.
Monica Cooper, a twenty-seven-year-old former domestic worker from Jamaica, talked about an interchange with her suburban employer.

Whether or not the employer in the second incident resembles the 1980s media image of the working woman, professional, in skirt and tie, briefcase in hand, rushing from her apartment in a gentrified New York neighborhood or that of the affluent "housewife" giving parting instructions over her shoulder about picking up the kids from school and preparing dinner as she runs to meet friends and "go shopping," most working women's experiences are very different from hers. Whatever the current media image of women who work, the world of women's work is generally low paid, dead end, and undervalued. Nowhere is this truer than private household domestic and child care work. Within a sexual division of labor that assigns child care and domestic work to all women, private household workers take over these responsibilities for some women for pay. Shunned by men, this work becomes multiply devalued as it is passed from one woman to another along class, racial, ethnic, and migration lines, within the cash nexus.[2]

In this article, ten West Indian women currently or previously employed as private household child care and domestic workers in the New York City area speak of their experiences as domestic workers, as migrants, and as mothers.[3] They tell of how and why they do domestic work, what relationships exist with their employers, and how they balance their own family and household responsibilities with wage work. At times their voices could be those of other domestic workers over the last hundred or more years.[4] Sometimes their voices resemble those of other recent women migrants to the United States who have found themselves in the service sector of the economy. At other times, they echo the experiences of other working mothers.

Migration and Domestic Work

I am their only source of support . . . I thought about how the children are getting big and I wasn't working for the greatest salary. And I was thinking that there would come a time when I could just barely support the kids. So I need to make more money. So I just thought about coming to America. Maybe I'll be able to do it there.
Judith Thomas, a Vincentian mother of four, migrated in 1980 at twenty-nine years old.

Their responsibility for themselves, their children, or other kin moti-
vates their migration. Though all but one (who had just completed high
school) were employed prior to migration, some jobs were unsteady
while others offered little chance for mobility. For most, wages were
inadequate. They worked a range of jobs including primary school
teaching, police work, clerical and administrative assistant work in
government or the private sector, factory work, postal work, hig-
glering (petty trading), and servicing the tourist industry. Most had not
done domestic work before.

Like their relatives and friends before them,[5] these West Indian
women migrate to "better themselves." In New York they seek "opportunity," in employment and in education, for themselves and their children.[6] They are drawn, as well, by the availability of basic consumer
goods unaffordable at home and especially important to them as
mothers.

In spite of economic pressures and the expectations to migrate to
"better oneself," some women, like Janet Robinson and Dawn Adams,
postpone migration in order to remain with their children. Janet Robinson waitressed, did factory work and six months of domestic work
that paid "just a farthing," enough "to just get the baby milk and that's
it." Refusing several previous offers because she wanted to "watch my
daughter grow," in 1968, at thirty years old, she accepted an offer to go
to New York to do domestic work and support her twelve-year-old
daughter. Dawn Adams said she "always wanted to be there to bring
up my daughters. I didn't really have any thought of migrating." But
after several years of teaching, nurses' training, and four years on the
police force, the lack of opportunities to advance, to make better use of
her talents, and to better support her mother and daughters created
pressure on her to migrate in 1981 at the age of thirty-two, reluctantly
leaving her children and her mother.

While to be a good mother means to leave one's children and migrate, ironically, taking care of someone else's children is often their
first job in New York, especially for those without permanent residence status, the green card. Legal entrance to and residence in the
United States with permanent residence status is available primarily
to those sponsored by close relatives or by employers at the time of migration. Only a few in this group had this option. Most entered with
visitors' visas which they overstayed, becoming undocumented. To
achieve their goals, including reunion with their children, they needed
green cards. To get them, they turned to employer sponsorship in child
care and domestic work, the main route for West Indian women (other
than marriage to a permanent resident or a citizen, or sponsorship by
certain closely related permanent residents or citizens). None knew of
any West Indian woman (besides registered nurses, of whom there is a

shortage in New York) who had been sponsored by an employer outside of domestic work.[7]

Learning to Be "Maidish"

> This is not something I thought I would ever do for a living. If somebody had said to me "You're going to clean somebody else's house to make money," I'd say, "Come off it." I had an attitude about that but then after I really thought about it, I said if this is what I have to do, I'm going to make the best until the situation changes.

Monica Cooper spoke of her domestic work experience. She did general housekeeping and took care of two children for a suburban New Jersey family in which the husband owned a health care related business and the wife did not work outside the home. She describes her responsibilities:

> Everything. Meals, cooking, everything. Everything. And at that point [1976] I was making $80 a week [laughs] for 5 1/2 days, they call it. . . . [My] day off was Sunday and I had to be back by noon on Monday. . . . I decided to do it to get my sponsorship.

After three weeks on her first job here, Marguerite Andrews, a thirty-three-old former school teacher supporting four children, spoke of her adjustment. Although she had an "understanding," "good" employer, becoming a domestic worker and moving from the relative autonomy and high status of teacher to a subordinate, if not subservient, position was difficult.

> I'm not yet really adjusted to it. . . . She's not bossy or anything like that. But within myself I figure I should be more, I can't explain. . . . I don't like to use the word "maidish," but I should put myself all out to do everything. But you know this will have to take some time.

At that same time, Marguerite Andrews related an incident that took place in St. Vincent when Marguerite herself employed a domestic worker. When one of Marguerite's sons left his dirty clothes in a trail on the floor instead of placing them in the hamper, her employee refused to pick them up and wash them. Marguerite's son ordered the worker to do so, saying that she was paid to clean up after him. Although Marguerite took to heart the domestic worker's criticism of her son's manners, at that time, she shared his definition of the job. When Marguerite told me the story, she noted how her perspective on domestic work had changed and said she hoped that she would never receive such treatment. Ironically, with a change in jobs to new employers who demanded greater subservience, she has since experienced similar encounters from the subordinate position which has broadened her understanding of hierarchy from below.

Marguerite left this last job in which she had hoped to initiate sponsorship proceedings because "it is not humanly possible to stick it." Like Marguerite, others assess whether they can tolerate a particular job for the two or more years of sponsorship. Judith Thomas similarly assessed a potential sponsor job and left amicably before the procedure was begun: "I knew that the sponsor wouldn't work out with her, I couldn't last that long." Her next employers sponsored her.

Living In and the Sponsor Job

Everyone described sponsor jobs as the "worst," especially those which are live-in. Sponsored jobs on a live-in basis greatly exacerbate problems structural to domestic work. Although some employers seek to avoid exploitation and some are unaware of the impact of their behavior on the worker, many take advantage of the sponsorship situation, the workers' vulnerability, and their lack of experience with codes of behavior here. Exploitation may involve long hours, abysmal pay, a heavy work load, and particular attitudes and behaviors exhibited toward the worker.

Joyce Miller worked at her live-in sponsor job from 1977 to 1981. The couple for whom she worked, on the edges of suburban New Jersey, owned a chain of clothing stores. The wife worked part-time in the business and devoted the rest of her time to shopping for antiques, decorating, attending cooking classes, entertaining, traveling, and participating in her children's school. Joyce worked sixteen hours or more a day, was on call twenty-four hours a day, seven days a week, caring for the large house and three children for $90 a week ($110 at the time she quit). When she took a day off to see her lawyer, that day was deducted from her salary.

> The working situation there [was] a lot of work. No breaks. I work sometimes till 11 o'clock at night . . . I get up early in the morning and I get up at night to tend the baby. I wash, I cook, I clean.

As Joyce began to get "enlightened" (her words) to her own exploitation, her employer became upset.

When Dawn Adams, who was at the time undocumented, quit a short-lived suburban job, her employers threatened to report her to the Immigration and Naturalization Service. Others told of similar intimidation that plays on undocumented West Indian women's sense of vulnerability. This itself is heightened by occurences such as INS raids at the Port Authority bus terminal on Sunday nights and Monday mornings to "catch" undocumented domestic workers returning to suburban jobs from their day off.

Workers often felt trapped in sponsor jobs with no apparent end in sight. After four years in what was supposed to be her sponsor job, Monica Cooper got "restless and very depressed." She knew that her papers had passed the labor board but that her employers had said that they would not "bend over backwards" to help with her sponsorship.

> It started one week where I would just cry. Just cry period. And I was crying constantly for this week in question and Mrs. S., she would ask me what's the matter. Because I resented them but . . . I'd wipe my eyes and I'm smiling when they're around. But this week I couldn't do it anymore. I mean they'd go out and I'm there [alone] with the kids. It was like a total disadvantage. By the time I left there I was making $100 and I was with them for 4 1/2 years . . . And this week in question, I was just crying, and crying, crying. I couldn't tell her why I was crying. She said "Is it anything we did?" But . . . it was everything. By this time I could say it's all of you. But I told her no.

Soon after this tearful week, Monica Cooper retained a different lawyer, made new arrangements for her sponsorship (by a relative), and a few months later gave notice, quit, and found clerical work. In spite of the cost in money and time, some workers do quit unsatisfactory sponsor jobs and reinitiate the process with new employers.

Judith Thomas was sponsored by a woman who owned a cafe and whose husband worked in his family's textile business. She took care of their child and maintained their three-bedroom and three-bathroom apartment (though they hired someone else to do the "heavy" cleaning once a week). She remembered this experience:

> They just somehow figure because they're sponsoring you, they own you. And if they say jump, you should jump. And if they say sit, you should sit . . . when you start in at the beginning they tell you certain amount of . . . work and then as you go on they just keep on adding more and more. It was really a dedication. . . . I felt as if I wouldn't hold out. I couldn't make it. But then when I just think . . . that . . . I'd be better off staying here now and continuing, knowing that one day I'll get it all over with . . . And I think about my kids and just say regardless to what, I just have to do this. But I tell you it wasn't easy. There were some nights when I would just cry and cry and cry myself to sleep, and say, "God, how long it's going to be?"

With her green card, she has been firm about defining her job, pay, and working conditions in her current child care work for two lawyers. As she said, "I paid my dues when I wasn't legally here and I just believe that since I became legal, then every right of a legal person should be mine."

Isolation from kin, friends, and community is a painful consequence of many live-in jobs. Immersion into a foreign world aggravates
the loneliness and demoralization of many new migrants. Janet Robinson said that her first employer was good, "But I was very homesick
and lonely." Those in isolated suburban areas often fared the worst.
Those in the city and especially those who got away on days off to their
"own" community fared better. Marguerite Andrews squeezed just
enough out of her paycheck to escape from her Park Avenue live-in job
to a furnished room in Bedford-Stuyvesant every weekend. Joyce
Miller found that the isolation of a black woman living in a white
world had other consequences when people mistook her for a convict
from the nearby prison when she did the shopping in town. When faced
with a snowstorm on her day off, Monica Cooper paid several times her
normal bus fare to "get out" of her suburban live-in job and come to
New York. As she said, "There's no way on earth I'm going to have a
day off and stay in there."

Speaking of a short-lived, Park Avenue, potential sponsor, live-in
job, Marguerite Andrews asked,

> Is slavery really abolished? There is not much difference between work-
> ing in this situation and slavery. The working hours are the same, the ex-
> ploitation is the same. There is no human recognition. We eat the same
> food, live together in the same house, but we don't mingle. I am in it but
> not part of it.

While a (potential) sponsor live-in job may feel like "slavery," what it
resembles most closely is a form of legally sanctioned indentured ser-
vitude in which the worker performs until the green card is granted.

Despite the exploitation, several women feel gratitude toward
their employers for sponsoring them. As Joyce Miller said: "That's why
I give and take a lot of things. . . . A lot of things I let her get away with
because I feel endebted to her." Like several others, she has maintained relations with her former employers, especially to visit the children.

In discussing the role of immigrant workers in New York, Joyce
Miller said "they just want cheap labor . . . West Indians, or foreigners
or what they want to call it." She indicated many ways in which undocumented workers support the U.S. economy that include providing exploited labor, retaining immigration attorneys, and purchasing food,
clothing, and household items to send home regularly to kin.

Monica Cooper pinpointed racism as a major influence on immigration policy and procedure, noting the differential treatment of different immigrant groups:

> I do feel the system is set up to make it harder for black people coming
> here. It's . . . to a larger extent . . . people coming in from the black coun-

tries or [some of the] Third World countries . . . that sense that they have special quotas.

While not citing several political and economic factors, she compared the treatment of Korean and Haitian immigrants:

Look at the difference [between the treatment of the Haitians and the Koreans]. You don't have to know a lot about what's going on, current events, to be able to pick that out. Black people or people from the Third World . . . [Western] hemisphere, have a harder time gaining acceptance in this country than people from the East. . . . Their papers take longer. You go through everything that says you better go home. If you can stick it out then you're the better one and you *know* that people stick it out.

In spite of "everything that says you better go home" West Indian women do "stick it out." Visions of their children and families, letters from home, support from kin and friends in New York, and the determination to meet their goals empower them to overcome obstacles in their paths. Most must travel to their home islands for the final interview, a medical examination, and the granting of the green card.[8] They visit their children and kin, and with green cards in hand, many begin their childrens' "papers." Legal status permits them to visit home, but worsening economic conditions, including rampant inflation, often preclude long visits or returning to live. Joyce Miller, who after several years of "doing domestic" is a bookkeeper in a Manhattan real estate office, said, "A lot of Caribbean people come here and they are surprised. . . . They are disappointed. . . . They thought the life is easier. I think it's harder here than back home. In a certain way if we could get work back home as though we get it here, we would never stay."

Some leave private household work soon after receiving their green cards. Most who remain find "better" jobs with higher salaries which they command with their legal status. Most who have been in live-in positions find their own accommodations. Some remain in domestic work while preparing for other employment through further education and leave when they find other work. Fewer remain in domestic work indefinitely with "good" employers, often in spite of further education, for a variety of reasons.[9] The majority who leave private households, work in the "pink-collar" women's jobs, especially in clerical or health care occupations.[10]

"If people only knew what we went through to be here. I try to tell them but they don't hear," lamented Shirley Green. Remembering her sponsorship experiences, Joyce Miller said,

People don't understand how hard it is to get here. And we try to explain to them. It's terrible. And you think of all you go through. You go through all this paperwork and go through the lawyer and pay so much money and you get this blooming little piece of card, green paper. It's not even green.

The day when I got it I said, "This is IT?" They should have a better system than this.

Respect, The Asymmetrical Relations of "Doing Domestic"

I work hard. I don't mind working hard. But I want to be treated with some human affection, like a human being . . . I don't get any respect. . . . Since I came here this woman has never shown me one iota of, not even, go down to the smallest unit you can think, of human affection as a human being.
Marguerite Andrews discussed the treatment she received on a job.

While sponsored and live-in work are "the worst," carrying special meanings for the worker, they are exacerbations of problems possibly structural to domestic work. Although employers exhibit a range of behaviors, even with "good employers" some problems emerge which might be considered structural to the working conditions.

Low wages, lack of benefits, lack of formal contracts, lack of job ladders, low status, limited unionization, and personalized relations situate this work at the low levels of capitalism's tertiary sector framed by the asymmetrical relations of class, race, and sex. Beyond the low pay for repetitive and exhausting work, many women have difficulties with the asymmetrical social relations of the work. Like other relations mediated by a wage, these social relations mirror the dominant/subordinate class relations of capitalism. But they do so through the additional filters of sex, race, and migration which shape them in particular ways.

Within the contemporary sexual division of labor, child care and domestic work are assigned to women as extensions of women's supposedly "natural" nurturing and caregiving. "Naturalizing" the work implies that it is unskilled and not really worth wages, trivializing it. Devalued when passed from men to women in the society at large and within the same households,[11] the work is further devalued when passed from one woman who chooses not to do it and can pay for it, to another woman who performs it in someone else's household for the wages she needs to maintain her own household. The devaluation lends particular character to the dominant/subordinate relations between employee and employer.

The asymmetrical relations are further shaped by assigning this work, and much personal service work, to racially or ethnically distinct groups (either immigrant or native born) in the context of a society suffused with ideologies about racial and ethnic superiority and inferiority. The assignment of private household, personal service work to those with low status, by virtue of gender, and racial and ethnic hierarchies, reinforces the hierarchies.[12]

Class, sex, race, and migration have shaped the asymmetrical social relations for much domestic and child care work in the United States, from the first African house slaves to the Irish immigrant "servants" of one hundred years ago and to contemporary Salvadoran, West Indian, and other workers.[13] The worker is thus categorized as "other" (as defined by the dominant white male society), increasing the separation between employer and employee as well as the potential for exploitation. Marguerite Andrews states that "The racial thing really gets me down. I'm treated this way because of race. The only difference between us [Marguerite and her employers] is race." While race may be a major difference, it does not exist apart from sex, class, and migration for West Indian women of color in creating "otherness" which reflects and reinforces the particular asymmetrical social relations of the work.

The location of domestic work in the private household further influences the social relations of the work. While the nature of housework and its status as "productive" labor has been greatly debated,[14] work located in the home is often not recognized as work and is therefore devalued. In part, this is due to an ideological construct which paralleled the movement of much productive activity out of the home into a separate workplace during the process of capitalist industrialization in the West. The ideology strictly separated the workplace and the home, linking them to a parallel ideological separation between the genders which segregated women in the home.[15] In addition, the location of this work in the private household isolates and atomizes the worker and impedes the unionization of domestic work.

In discussing the asymmetrical relations, every woman spoke most about the lack of respect shown to her by employers. What the worker experiences as lack of respect often appears to be efforts to depersonalize the very personal relations involved in the work and to dehumanize the worker in a variety of ways. On one hand are the personalized relations of the work, the worker's intimate knowledge of her employers, her responsibility for maintaining and managing the household to free its members for other activities, her possible residence in the household, and her nurturance, guidance, and care, both physical and affective, for the children. On the other hand are the wage relations of the work, and the depersonalizing, dehumanizing treatment of the worker.

> The treatment here is terrible. . . . I think the employers should treat people much better because they're cleaning up after them to make the environment clean. They're helping them out. If they can do the work themselves, they [should] stay at their house or do the work themselves. Don't treat people like that.

Joyce Miller pointed out the unacknowledged need for the employee.
She spoke of how her twenty-four-hour responsibility for the children
and household freed her employers but at the same time was taken for
granted by them.

> She thought she had me there inevitably. She wanted me to be there for-
> ever. No one ever came there and stayed. Not because she's bad, but be-
> cause of the work. The responsibility. It was a lot. She doesn't like to stay
> home. She had her baby [third child] and like in the space of two weeks
> she's gone. She's not there at day. She's not there at night.

The employer worked short part-time hours at her husband's business,
"otherwise she got herself other activities. I mean hanging out with
friends for the day . . . shopping. . . . They don't give me anything extra
when they go on vacation [a few times a year]. Because I have the responsibility day and night." She added, "I'm not looking for them to
shower us down with money, with clothes, but with a little respect and
feelings. You know because they want full respect from us and at the
same time they want to treat us like nothing."

At times, Joyce Miller felt taken for granted by the employers for
whom she worked after getting her green card. They were a wealthy
couple with an elegant co-op on the Upper East Side of Manhattan. The
husband was a lawyer from a manufacturing family, while the wife,
from a New York real estate family, was an aspiring magazine writer
who was somewhat "spoiled" and very "untidy."

> The thing I hate, everytime I clean the house, you know that woman make
> a mess. She throw everything on the floor. She leave all the cabinets open,
> you bump your head everytime of the day. She leave all the drawers out.
> . . . I don't like things to be messed up. If I fix it, don't throw it down. If
> you use a thing, don't throw it on the floor. Put it in the hamper.

While picking up after people may be "part of the job," Janet Robinson, Dawn Adams, and others disliked finding a mess where they had
just tidied up and felt frustrated when they entered the apartment they
left spotless the evening before to "meet juice under the table, pieces of
bread on the floor, and the child's toys everywhere."

"Like a Human Being"

> The most important thing is to show the person that you know they are
> human too. Most important is how you treat them.
> *Beverly Powell commented on employers' behavior toward the worker.*

The low esteem for housework and for those who perform it was
noted by some women as the "worst part." As Beverly Powell said,

When people look down on you for cleaning up their messes, then it starts hurting. The worst thing is when they look at you as stupid, maybe not stupid, but as a damn fool. You should treat people exactly as how you want to be treated. We can't all be doctors or lawyers, someone has to clean up the dirt. I am a hard worker. I want a little consideration. If I'm paid $1,000 for work but treated like dirt, it will pay the bills, but forget it.

Like other West Indian domestic workers, Monica Cooper took pride in her housekeeping but resented her employers' distancing and denial of her as a person.

It was like because I am the employee, because of what I'm doing, somehow I was looked down on. I was a good housekeeper. Because that's how I am. Whatever it is I do, I love to do my best. And I did my best. . . . But . . . there is a blockage in between. It's like she and I are O.K., but if a friend comes by, you feel the difference: "Oh, now she's the housekeeper."

Whatever the relationship otherwise, it is depersonalized as it is presented beyond the household.

Clothing is one of the clearest forms of depersonalization. While for some women uniforms provide an inexpensive mode of dress that saved their own clothes for "after work," most who were asked to wear uniforms resented it. Judith Thomas "hardly ever wore the uniform because it was white" and therefore impractical for both child care and housework. She recounted a story which pinpoints a uniform's function. She accompanied her employer (a part-time grade school teacher whose husband was in business) to Miami to take care of the children. Judith said,

She wanted me to wear the uniform. She was really prejudiced. She just wanted that the maid must be identified. . . . She used to go to the beach every day with the children. So going to the beach in the sand and sun and she would have the kids eat ice cream and all that sort of thing. You know what a white dress would look like at the beach? . . . I tell you one day when I look at myself, I was so dirty, . . . just like I came out from a garbage can . . . I felt real upset.

That day, noting the condition of her uniform, she asked to wear jeans and a top and the employer agreed. The day she did, the employer's brother

came by the beach to have lunch with [the employer]. I really believe they had a talk about it, because in the evening, driving back from the beach, she said, "Well, Judith, I said you could wear something else to the beach other than the uniform, and I think you will have to wear the uniform because they're very formal on this beach and they don't know who is guests from who isn't guests."

In the context of racial segregation, uniforms function to unmistakably identify people of color as service workers, the only roles which would justify their presence in otherwise all white settings.

Food and eating are other arenas of dehumanization and depersonalization. Some employers left food for the worker to prepare for the children but none for the worker herself, though she might work an eight- to twelve-hour shift. One worker was accused of consuming "too much" of a particular food, milk, which she never drank. When one woman on a live-in job ate some pork chops which had been in the refrigerator for several days while her wealthy corporate executive employers dined out, she was informed that several pork chops were "missing" and that she should "find" them. With her own money, the worker replaced what she ate, and no comment was made. In other instances, the food that is left for the women to eat is inadequate for the amount of physical labor they perform. Janet Robinson remembered an early experience in which she was left a lunch of cottage cheese, which seemed practically inedible to her West Indian palate. Her reaction resembles that of the Barbadian domestic in Paule Marshall's story who exclaims, "as if anybody can scrub floor on an egg and some cheese that don't have no taste to it."[16]

Joyce Miller spoke of the classic situation in which, as a live-in worker for a young, wealthy family, she ate separately from the other members of the household.

> I couldn't eat with them at the table. . . . I have to eat after they finish eating. . . . And then I eat in the kitchen. There are a lot of people who do that because they want us to know that we are not equal. That's my point of view. You are the housekeeper. I think the only reason why I was in their house is to clean. . . . Like olden days. . . . That's the part I hate. I hate that part because it's showing me a lot of things. You need things from me, but when it comes down to sitting at the table with you, you are going to show me separation there. I just don't like it.

She contrasted this experience with her former New Jersey job in which she was underpaid but always included at the table. she said that if she went to sit by herself, they said to her, " 'No, no, no. You've got to come right here at the table.' . . . That was something she try to do all the time. That's one thing with her she was great about, I never felt left out."

While spatial segregation means that some women eat in the kitchen after others, some live-in workers are denied the privacy of their own rooms. Some share a room with children. Some with their own rooms regularly take in an agitated or sleepless child in the middle of the night.

Judith Thomas spoke of the depersonalization, trivialization, and lack of respect involved in being treated like a child on a live-in job.

It was another hard thing that as a woman, a mother, responsible for home, with a husband, and to come here to New York City and have to be living with people. . . . It was definitely hard for me. You know at times they would talk to you as though you were just some little piece of a girl. It was really humiliating at times. . . . Most of the time they wouldn't see me as that [fully adult] person. . . . A couple of times I really had to tell them that. I really had to say, "Well, I want to be treated as a full adult. You know, you all must remember that there was once I had a husband and kids and had the same responsibility as you all but because people go through different stages in life, here I am now in this situation. So, you know, don't forget that. You know, remember, I was once this responsible person. And don't treat me like a child or some little girl."

In contrast, women spoke of "good employers" who are "fair," who "understand," who "have genuine human affection" and who "treated me like a human being." Besides attempting to minimize the material exploitation and disrespect on the job, some employers helped out in medical and family crises and tried to assist in the worker's education or self-development. Dawn Adams' sponsor employers, a theatrical lighting designer and her photographer husband living in Greenwich Village, was "the best person to work for." She was "willing to help" Dawn attend college by offering to continue to pay her a full-time rate though Dawn would attend classes in the morning while the child, for whom Dawn was primarily responsible, attended nursery school. Another woman who worked for this employer concurred with Dawn. Janet Robinson spoke highly of several of her employers including her current ones, two lawyers. Beverly Powell likes her current employers, involved in theater, who pay her overtime and treat her well. Those whose employers are regularly absent from the home, especially for their own full-time employment, fare the best. However, rarely did anyone speak of any employer without ambivalence. Even when airing a complaint, many workers said something like "she has her good side. Regardless of everything else, I think she's O.K." The flip side is also true. As several women said, "Nobody's perfect." Joyce Miller was often "confused" by the very friendly relations with her sponsor employer who "told [her] everything," always included her in dining and most other activities, yet paid her poorly. The basic outlines of the job include the inherent contradictions of employer/employee relations, including lack of respect, in a personalized context.

"One of the Family": Manipulation, Trust, and Distrust

The highly personalized relations of domestic work, especially that which is live-in, produce such phrases as "like one of the family." As Monica Cooper said,

They never treated me in a way that I felt like, even though I'm working for them, that I'm family. 'Cause when you're living that close to someone for 4 1/2 years, if there is no bond between you, then something has to be radically wrong. I felt that I was just used for whatever they needed.

Joyce Miller said,

> whenever they want you to give your all in their favor, or anyway to feel comfortable to do what they want you to do, they use the words "we are family." That's the one I hate. "You are one of the family." That's not true. That's a password as sorry . . . if you're one of the family, don't let me eat after you. . . . They say it to make you feel O.K., but at the same time, they're not doing the right thing.

The ideology of family is used to manipulate the worker. Often used to explain why members of the *same* family should sacrifice for one another, here it is used to encourage people who are *not* family members to perform tasks or to tolerate treatment that may be exploitive. The image of family is called up to soften the edges of wage labor in personalized situations.

The image of family is most pervasive in child care. Most of the women in this group were hired primarily to care for children, which they preferred to their secondary housework responsibilities. Janet Robinson said "I love the kids" and was echoed by many others who take pleasure in their relationships with the children. They put a great deal of thought and caring into tending the children. When the child that she took care of misbehaved, Dawn Adams said,

> You know, it's not my child but I take care of her and I love her. I've been with her since she was three months old [she was then four years old]. And when she did it I was embarrassed myself.

Emotional vulnerability and exploitation are risks in child care situations, especially in conjunction with separation from one's own children. Some children received no parental discipline when they teased, hit, spit at, or were otherwise rude to the workers. When told that "Janet will clean it up," children learned to expect others to clean up after them. Several women mentioned that the parents were jealous of worker/child relationships. A jealous parent humiliated one worker by ordering her to her room when the employer's child sought comfort from the worker after being scolded by the parent. Relationships with the children often lead women to stay longer on jobs than they would otherwise; they sometimes return to visit children once they have left. The weekend after leaving a job, Beverly Powell lamented the end of a four-year relationship with the eight-year-old boy, who sometimes called her "mommy." While many women do keep in touch with the children, Beverly knew that the strained relations with the child's parents would prevent her from doing so.

I loved the kids and the kids loved me. They trusted me. . . . They could go on vacation far away and leave me with the kids and they'd call in because I was responsible enough for them to have confidence that "she's going to make them do what they're supposed to do."

Monica Cooper spoke about a major element in child care employment, trust. Beverly Powell's employers, a middle manager in a large corporation and her husband, a partner in a small import business, entrusted their son to her sole care twenty-four hours a day for five days a week at their country house each summer while they worked in Manhattan. However, the same employers who entrust their children to the worker may distrust the worker in other matters. Some women reported that the "thing she [the employer] hates most is to see me sitting down" as if the employers feared that the worker was cheating them by sitting down for a break. Though entrusting her with the care of their children for four years including while they were vacationing in the Caribbean, Monica's employers' trust vanished when she gave two-weeks notice.

Everything was O.K. For four years I was with them and they trusted me and . . . all of a sudden . . . they couldn't find this and they couldn't find that. . . . Now that I'm leaving they're going to miss a [gold] chain [necklace] and they're going to miss a slip, and they're going to miss everything else.

Balancing Babysitting and Barrels

The Responsibilities of Work and Family

Some of them don't even talk to you. They just want to know how their kid is or how the housework is going. They never one day ask you how you're feeling or anything else. . . . They're into their own little world and their own little life and leave you out, block you out like you're just nothing. And I think that really hurts a lot. Especially when people leave five, six kids in the West Indies and come here to do housework.

Joyce Miller, above, was joined by several others who said, "They don't ask how I am." This lack of consideration and denial of the worker's human identity beyond her role as child care or domestic worker contrasts with the ideology of family, a worker's intimate involvement in the household, and being entrusted with the care of children. A failure to recognize and respect her personhood makes an impact on her life off the job as well as on it. West Indian women juggle paid child care and domestic work with "the rest of their lives" to care for their own children.

While all wage-working mothers balance work and family responsibilities with some difficulty in contemporary capitalist society, child
care and household maintenance are stratified by class. The resources
on which women have to draw engender different ways of handling
their work and family duties. While both employer and employee may
work to support their households, the wages, working conditions, and
nature of kin and household responsibilties of these West Indian
women mean that they have to juggle a different set of responsibilities
in a different material and social context than their employers.

For example, the West Indian woman employed in domestic and
child care work must stretch her wages to support herself, her children, and usually other kin as well, across town and across oceans.
While wages range according to legal status, live-in or out, length of
employment and individual employers, they are generally low, and do
not include either medical benefits or overtime pay. Sometimes less,
current gross salaries generally range between $175 and $225 a week
for those with green cards. Although $300 a week was rumored to be
the highest salary available in 1985, no one in this group even approached this amount. Only Judith Thomas has medical insurance
paid by her employers. Several without insurance were paying off
large medical bills.

With their wages, women support at least two households, in full
or in part: their own in New York, and one or more composed of kin
(possibly including their children) in their home country. New York
housing takes the biggest bite out of their wages. Lawyers' fees, for
those who hire them for their own or their children's green cards, are
another major expense. Every woman sends remittances regularly.
Dawn Adams was not unusual in remitting at least half of her earnings
every other week to support her mother and two daughters, before her
daughters joined her. Like others, she sent both money, for living expenses and her daughters' school expenses, and barrels, packages
filled with food, clothing, and household goods, basic nonluxury items
either unavailable or exorbitantly priced in the home country. Due to
the high cost of basic items in Trinidad, Janet Robinson sends barrels
every few months to her daughter and grandson. The last one contained almost $800 worth of goods including three gallons of cooking
oil, forty pounds of rice, twenty pounds of detergent, flour, tea, cocoa,
toothpaste, and other items. Remittances of money (including school
fees for siblings and others) and goods may account for 20 to 75 percent of the domestic worker's income. Even after their children join
them, West Indian women send remittances as other kin depend on
them.

As Joyce Miller said, "We get paid less, they still take taxes, and at the same time we're buying the goods for the regular price. We don't get the price cheaper." Many reported working extra jobs at nights and on weekends to meet their financial responsibilities. Dawn Adams said, "You have to have your budget planned."

The lack of standardization, contracts, job security, or regular hours add to a worker's concern beyond the job. Beverly Powell was asked to change from her regular nine to six or seven, five-day shift, to take full twenty-four-hour responsibility for the eight-year-old boy from Sunday evening to Friday evening at the summer house while the parents worked in the city. She had to send her own daughter who joined her from Jamaica to live with Beverly's sister in Canada for the summer since Beverly could not be present to care for her. Her schedule became more irregular and unpredictable. For example, one Sunday morning she was requested to arrive several hours earlier than previously planned. This necessitated cancelling other plans and packing up to go immediately, though on arrival she found her employers lounging with afternoon drinks, as yet unready to depart. Many women spoke about the inconsiderateness of the unpredictably shifting schedules and the impact on their lives. Dawn Adams was regularly requested to remain late just as she prepared to leave, which often interfered with her "after work" plans. Several times her employers returned very late, which, for Dawn and other women, meant later and therefore longer and more dangerous subway rides home. As she said, "It seems as if it never bothered them [that] when they were in their house, I had to be on the streets." These schedule extensions left less time in which women could accomplish their own household and kin responsibilities, be with children, other kin, or friends, or just relax. As Beverly Powell said, "No matter how well paid I am, I want a little time to myself. . . . She doesn't even think of the child that I have. And then she talks about loyalty." As different women said: "They don't think that I have my family waiting for me." "They don't think about my child." "It's O.K. for them to ask me to stay extra time because they have their family together, but what about me?"

While child care arrangements across town were difficult, those across oceans were more so. These women with young children present paid a large part of their salaries to a local babysitter, often another West Indian, who took several children into her apartment. Many women reported a variety of problems that occur in this situation. Children left at home when a mother migrates are generally kept by kin, often a mother or sister, or friends. Although the mother provides as best she can, her children may feel emotionally or materially deprived, and the situation may be stressful for her, the children, and the caretakers.

This balancing is not without its emotional costs. The pain and loneliness of leaving children was central to these women's experiences. As Dawn Adams said, "What could be harder than me leaving my kids in St. Vincent and coming here to work, not seeing them. I don't see them for about two and a half years after that last night I slept in the house with them." When Beverly Powell described getting into bed at night and wondering if her daughter had been bathed and was asleep yet, she spoke for many women who reported crying themselves to sleep many nights, missing their children and wondering about their welfare. Joyce Miller was "so very, very lonely" for her son that she said, "I think I give them [her employer's children] more because I just think of them as my own. Just 'cause I was lonely, I gave them all I have." For other women, as well, employers' children became substitutes for their own. Being torn between affluent and poor material worlds is cause for more emotional balancing. The West Indian woman may work in a world of relative wealth in which she witnesses waste "that makes your heart bleed" and go home to another with her low wages where she confronts demands from a "third world" to send goods which she cannot afford.

Determination and Resistance

In answer to the question of what gets her through, Judith Thomas replied forcefully, "I think strong will. . . . I've always had . . . a determined mind." Drawing on their strength, determination, and networks of support, these West Indian women cope with and resist the exploitation they confront on the job. Their determination to achieve their goals for themselves and their children keeps them going. It is buoyed by letters from home saying "we're praying for you" and "if it wasn't for you, we couldn't make it."

They use strategies such as defining their own tasks and airing grievances on the job. Joyce Miller answered with "my name is Joyce" when addressed or referred to as "the maid" or "the girl." Dawn Adams, tired of risking another late night subway mugging, instructed her employers to hire a separate nighttime babysitter. None of these strategies eliminates the structural problems of the work which unionization, though difficult in domestic work, would begin to address. When exploitation is intolerable, quitting is the last option.

The support, pleasure, and meaning that they derive from other parts of their lives nourishes and renews them. Women spoke of the importance of relationships with their kin and friends, education, religious beliefs, and participation in church and community activities. Their ties to children and parents are primary. They seek out and re-create networks of kin and friends to ease their adjustment, provide companionship, and share housing, information, and jobs and services. Many exchange child care and household maintenance services with a friend or relative in the same household or between households. The conversations Dawn Adams had with the other babysitters in the park are reminiscent of Paule Marshall's description of a former generation of Barbadian domestic workers talking around the table after work "to reaffirm self-worth" and "overcome the humiliations of the work day."[17] Religious beliefs and activities provide crucial meaning and support for many women. Monica Cooper, who like many others "prayed a lot," also "set up school" for herself each night with her employer's college texts. School experiences benefit others. Active participation in West Indian church and community groups in New York empower and give pleasure to many women. Their identities derive primarily from these sources and not from their work.[18]

Leaving domestic work for the pink-collar ghetto may not seem to offer much, but it holds promise for many domestic workers. When Dawn Adams' $25 raise was rescinded a few months after it was given, because her employer, though a "good person to work for," had difficulty paying it, she had had enough. She found a bank teller job with regular hours, wages, and raises, and began college study toward a business and management degree. Though she took an initial pay cut, the job provides medical and dental benefits for herself and her children, who arrived in New York five months later. Judith Thomas, who earned her certification as a nursing aide, began looking for a job with medical and dental benefits for herself and her daughters soon after their arrival. No longer "frustrated" doing housework "because of circumstance," Monica Cooper expresses the optimism of many as she prepares for a singing career and does temporary clerical work: "Now I'm doing what I want to do because that's what I choose to do. At this point in my life, I'm not settling and doing anything that I don't want to do." Few are able to avoid doing things they do not want to do, but many are pleased to leave the particular constraints and exploitation of domestic work. Their balancing act as wage-working mothers continues as they enter another world of women's work.

Conclusion

While much domestic work resembles activities women do in their own families for love, it is in fact embedded in capitalist wage relations. While it resembles other work for wages, private household domestic work is fraught with contradictions: between its status as wage labor and the very personalized relations involved, between the framework of the cash nexus and the intimacies of child care, between the worker's involvement in a household and the peculiar forms of exploitation, depersonalization, and dehumanization she may experience.

These West Indian women share experiences with other women as mothers, workers, and migrants. While they balance kin and work responsibilities, they do so within a strikingly stratified system of child care and household maintenance. Their domestic work experiences most resemble those of other private household workers. Their obstacles and aspirations resemble those of other female migrants. Yet the particular interaction of gender, race, class, migration, and history makes their lives distinct.

Notes

1. I have assigned pseudonyms to protect the privacy of the women whose experiences are recounted here.

2. This article is based on ongoing doctoral dissertation research. It shares much data and analysis with the forthcoming dissertation and with my article entitled "Just a Little Respect: West Indian Domestic Workers in New York City," in a collection on domestic workers in Latin America and the Caribbean edited by Elsa M. Chaney and Mary Garcia Castro which is being published in Spanish and English under the tentative title of *El Trabajo de la Cuarta Parte: Servicio Domestico en América Latina y el Caribe.*

3. This article is based on four or more interviews of two to four hours each with ten West Indian (English-speaking Caribbean) women currently or previously employed in private household child care and domestic work. The interviews and numerous other conversations with the women are part of ongoing anthropological fieldwork. These ten women range from late twenties to late forties, with most in their early to mid-thirties. All are mothers whose children reside either with them in New York or with kin or friends in their home countries. Many of them related stories of friends or acquaintances which enabled me to get a broader sense of West Indian women's experiences. In addition, interviews with immigration lawyers, Department of Labor officials, and personnel from a variety of agencies and offices which offer services to the West Indian community provided other information for this article.

4. Where "domestic work" appears alone in the text, in reference to the current research, it should be understood to mean both child care and housekeeping within the private household. Child care was the primary job responsibility of most of the women, though many, especially those who were living in, were also responsible for domestic tasks. For immigration purposes, the official designation is domestic work of which child monitoring and housekeeping are two categories.

5. Each woman interviewed has kin or friends abroad who migrated before her to England, perhaps in the peak period of the 1950s and 1960s, or to Canada and the United States, where West Indian immigration has peaked since the early to middle 1960s. Migration has been ever present in the Caribbean experience, linked to Caribbean participation in an international capitalist system. From the forced migration of Africans into slavery to the most recent migrations for wage work, Caribbean people have migrated to work. The legacy of colonialism and the persistence of multinational-influenced dependency create conditions of underdevelopment and poverty. Women experience these as unemployment, underemployment, lack of educational opportunity, limited occupational mobility, and low standards of living which pressure them to migrate. Labor needs, immigration policies, and "opportunity" influence the destination. (See D. Marshall 1982 for an historical overview of Caribbean migration. See Prescod-Roberts and Steele 1980; Foner 1978; Davison 1962; and Philpott 1973 on migration to England. See Henry 1982 for an overview of migration to Canada, and Silvera 1983 on West Indian domestic workers in Canada. See Bryce-Laporte and Mortimer 1976; Mortimer and Bryce-Laporte 1981; Dominquez 1975; and Gordon 1979 on the recent migration to the United States.)

6. Many cite their own and their children's education as motivations to migrate. Sacrificing precious nights and weekends, all but the most recent migrants have furthered their education since migrating. Some are currently studying, and others plan to resume study, especially in business and health care fields. Planning for their children's college education, unaffordable in their home countries, is central to several women's plans.

7. Domestic work has become a fairly simple path to the green card through employer sponsorship. The Immigration and Naturalization Service and the Department of Labor have several requirements, including proof of a shortage of documented workers available to work for the "prevailing wage," currently (1985) just under $200 for a 44 1/2-hour week for live-in domestic workers. Most live in as requirements favor it. Legally workers are supposed to receive at least the minimum wage throughout the sponsorship and the prevailing wage at the time the green card is granted. Because no agency actually monitors compliance with guidelines for wages and working conditions, the sponsorship situation may result in exploitation of new immigrant women.

8. Joyce Miller estimates that 15 percent of the women who return to their home islands for their final interview for their green cards find themselves in the cruel situation in which they are either detained up to several months or denied the card entirely because of improper processing of their papers or failure of their medical exam (often because of conditions such as high blood pressure).

9. Often these are older women who may confront age discrimination in the labor market. They may also have benefits through another family member.

10. Pink-collar jobs are those jobs within a sex-segregated labor market which are filled primarily by women and which are characterized by low wages,

lack of unionization, little security, and few job ladders. Employed women tend to cluster in 20 out of 420 jobs as delineated by the Bureau of Labor Statistics, such as clerical, service, and sales work. (See Howe 1977 on pink-collar work.)

11. See Howe 1977 on the devaluation of women's work.

12. See Spellman 1981 for a discussion of the interaction of race, gender, and somatophobia in relation to personal service work.

13. Other than rural "help" in which young women of the same class, race, and ethnicity were sent to work alongside the members of a neighboring household, sex, race, class, and migration are integral to the history of domestic work in the United States. (See Dudden 1983, Katzman, 1978, Hamburger 1977, Glenn 1980, Dill 1979, Almquist 1979, Davis 1981, and others on this history.)

14. On housework, see Glazer-Malbin 1976, Gardiner 1975, Dalla Costa and James 1972, Howe 1977, Strasser 1982, and others.

15. The relegation of women to the home has another implication for the relationship between employer and employee. Though the child care and domestic workers in this group have been hired by a male and female couple, the bulk of the interaction is between the worker and the female employer who, while not performing the work herself, has been minimally assigned the management of those who do perform it.

16. P. Marshall 1983: 6.

17. P. Marshall 1983: 6.

18. This may derive from a "double consciousness" as well as from the "occupational multiplicity" of West Indians which Lowenthal discusses (Lowenthal 1972: 141).

References Cited

Almquist, E. M.
1979   *Minorities, Gender, and Work*. Lexington, Mass.: Lexington Books.

Bryce-Laporte, R. S., and D. M. Mortimer, eds.
1976   *Caribbean Immigration to the United States*. RIIES Occasional Papers 1. Washington, D.C.: Research Institute on Immigration and Ethnic Studies, Smithsonian Institution, pp.16–43.

Dalla Costa, M., and S. James.
1972   *The Power of Women and the Subversion of the Community*. Bristol, England: Falling Wall Press.

Davis, A. Y.
1981   *Women, Race, and Class*. New York: Vintage.

Davison, R. B.
1962   *West Indian Migrants: Social and Economic Facts of Migration from the West Indies*. London: Oxford University Press.

Dill, B. T.
1979 "Across the Boundaries of Race and Class: An Exploration of the Relationship between Work and Family Among Black Female Domestic Servants." Ph.D dissertation, New York University.

Dominquez, V. R.
1975 *From Neighbor to Stranger: The Dilemma of Caribbean Peoples in the United States.* New Haven: Antilles Research Program, Yale University.

Dudden, F. E.
1983 *Serving Women: Household Service in Nineteenth Century America.* Middletown, Ct.: Wesleyan University.

Foner, N.
1978 *Jamaica Farewell: Jamaican Migrants in London.* Berkeley: University of California Press.

Gardiner, J.
1975 "Women's Domestic Labor." *New Left Review* 89: 47–71.

Glazer-Malbin, N.
1976 "Housework: A Review Essay." *Signs* 1: 905–934.

Glenn, E. N.
1980 "The Dialectics of Wage Work: Japanese-American Women and Domestic Service, 1905–1940." *Feminist Studies* 6(3): 432–471.

Gordon, M. H.
1979 "Identification and Adaptation: A Study of Two Groups of Jamaican Immigrants in New York City." Ph.D dissertation, CUNY Graduate Faculty in Sociology.

Hamburger, R.
1977 "A Stranger in the House." *Southern Exposure* 5(1): 22–31.

Henry, F.
1982 "A Note on Caribbean Migration to Canada." *Caribbean Review* 11(1): 38–41.

Howe, L. K.
1977 *Pink Collar Workers: In the World of Women's Work.* New York: Avon.

Katzman, D. M.
1978 *Seven Days a Week: Women and Domestic Service in Industrializing America.* New York: Oxford University Press.

Lowenthal, D.
1972 *West Indian Societies.* London: Oxford University Press.

Marshall, D. I.
1982 "The History of Caribbean Migrations: The Case of the West Indies." *Caribbean Review* 11(1): 6–9, 52–53.

Marshall, P.
1983 "From the Poets in the Kitchen." In *Reena and Other Stories.* Old Westbury, N.Y.: Feminist Press, pp. 3–12.

Mortimer, D. M., and R. S. Bryce-Laporte, eds.
1981   *Female Immigrants to the United States: Caribbean, Latin American, and African Experiences.* RIIES Occasional Papers 2, Washington, D.C.: Research Institute on Immigration and Ethnic Studies, Smithsonian Institution.

Philpott, S. B.
1973   *West Indian Migration: The Montserrat Case.* London: Athlone Press.

Prescod-Roberts, M., and N. Steele.
1980   *Black Women: Bringing it All Back Home.* Bristol, England: Falling Wall Press.

Silvera, M.
1983   *Silenced.* Toronto: Williams-Wallace Publishers.

Spellman, E. Y.
1981   "Theories of Race and Gender: The Erasure of Black Women." *Quest: A Feminist Quarterly* 5(4): 36–62.

Strasser, S.
1982   *Never Done: A History of American Housework.* New York: Pantheon.

5

A Pink-Collar Worker's Blues

Karen Kenyon

More and more women every day are going out to work. A myth has grown around them: the myth of the "new woman." It celebrates the woman executive. It defines her look (a suit), and her drink (Dewar's or perhaps a fine white wine). It puts her "in charge." But it neglects to say whom she is in charge of—probably some other women.

The world still needs helpers, secretaries and waitresses, and the sad truth is that mostly woman fill these serving roles. Today more women hold clerical jobs than ever before (4 million in 1950 and 20 million in 1981). Wherever we look, we see the image of the successful woman executive but, in fact, most women are going out to become secretaries. The current totals: 3 million women in management and 20 million clerical employees. So for the majority of working women—the so-called "pink-collar workers"—liberation from home is no liberation at all.

Recently I took a job as a part-time secretary in a department office of a university. I thought the financial security would be nice (writers never have this) and I needed the sense of community a job can bring. I found there is indeed a sense of community among secretaries. It is, in fact, essential to their emotional survival.

Human Beings

I felt a bit like the author of "Black Like Me," a Caucasian who had his skin darkened by dye and went into the South, where he experienced what it was like to be black. Here I was, "a person," disguised as "a secretary." This move from being a newly published author to being a secretary made it very clear to me that the same people who are regarded as creative human beings in one role will be demeaned and ignored in another.

I was asked one day to make some Xerox invitations to a party, then told I could keep one (not exactly a cordial invitation, I thought.) The next day I was asked, "Are you coming to the party?" I brightened and said, "Well, maybe I will." I was then told, "Well, then, would you pick up the pizza and we'll reimburse you."

A friend of mine who is an "administrative assistant" told me about a campus party she attended. She was engaged in a lively, interesting conversation with a faculty wife. The wife then asked my friend, "Are you teaching here?" When my friend replied, "Well, no, actually I'm a secretary," the other woman's jaw dropped. She then said, "Don't worry. Nobody will ever guess."

I heard secretaries making "grateful" remarks like, "They really treat us like human beings here." To be grateful for bottom-line treatment was, I felt, a sorry comment.

We think we have freed our slaves, but we have not. We just call them by a different name. Every time people reach a certain status in life they seem to take pride in the fact that they now have a secretary.

It is a fact that it has to be written very carefully into a job description just what a secretary's duties are, or she will be told to clean off the desk, pick up cleaning and the like. Women in these jobs are often seen as surrogate wives, mothers and servants—even to other women.

Many times, when a secretary makes creative contributions she is not given her due. The work is changed slightly by the person in charge, who takes the credit. Most secretaries live in an area between being too assertive and being too passive. Often a secretary feels she has to think twice before stepping in and correcting the grammar, even when she knows her "superior" can't frame a good sentence.

Envy

When after three months I announced to my co-workers that I was quitting, I was met with kind goodbyes. In some I caught a glimpse of perhaps a gentle envy, not filled with vindictiveness at all, but tinged with some remorse. "I'm just a little jealous that someone is getting out of prison," admitted one woman. "I wish I'd done that years ago," said another.

Their faces remain in my heart. They stand for all the people locked into jobs because they need the money, because they don't know where else to go, afraid there's no place else, because they don't have the confidence or feel they have the chance to do anything else.

I was lucky. I escaped before lethargy or repressed anger or extreme eagerness to please took over. Before I was drawn over the line, seduced by the daily rewards of talk over coffee, exchanged recipes, the photos of family members thumbtacked to the wall near the desk, the occasional lunches to mark birthdays and departures.

I am free now, but so many others are trapped in their carpeted, respectable prisons. The new-woman myth notwtihstanding, the true tale of the woman on her own most often ends that way.

As I see it, the slave mentality is alive and well, It manicures its nails. It walks in little pumps on tiny cat feet. It's there every time a secretary says, "Yes, I'll do that. I don't mind" or finds ashtrays for the people who come to talk to someone else. The secretary has often forgotten her own dream. She is too busy helping others to realize theirs.

6

Shoulder to Shoulder

Anne Braden

In 1978, workers in the gigantic Newport News, Virginia, shipyard owned by Tenneco Corporation voted to be represented by the United Steelworkers of America. In 1979, after the company stalled negotiations, the workers struck for eighty-three days. In a major breakthrough for organized labor in the South, Local 8888 won a contract covering the yard's 16,000 workers.

Because of laws won by the civil rights movement, the shipyard began hiring women in traditionally male jobs in 1973. By the late seventies, one-third of the production and maintenance workers were women, and they have played an important role in the union. In the process, they have watched their lives and personalities change. Of the women quoted here, six are white—Paula Axsom, Nancy Crosby, Jan Hooks, Judy Mullins, Sandra Tanner, Ann Warren. Three are black— Cynthia (Cindy) Boyd, Peggy Carpenter, Gloria Council. "We got to know each other on the picket line," said Peggy Carpenter. "Oh, we may get mad now and then, but we say what we have to say, and we work together. We know who the enemy is. We stuck together, and it paid off."

Pages 98–105 in *Speaking for Ourselves: Women of the South* edited by Maxine Alexander. Reprinted by permission of the Institute for Southern Studies and Anne Braden.

ANN WARREN, MOTHER OF TWO SONS, NOW GROWN, STEELWORKER DELEGATE TO NEW-PORT NEWS CENTRAL LABOR COUNCIL: I was one of the first women ever to work on a ship. I hired in on October 4, 1973. I was separated from my husband; my sons were still little boys, and I knew I could not support them on a minimum-wage job. Then I saw a newspaper ad that the shipyard was going to hire a thousand women, so the next morning I was there. The government had told them that they had to hire a certain number of women to comply with EEOC [Equal Employment Opportunity Commission].

I hired in as a tack welder; now I'm classified as a mechanic in the shipfitters. We do very heavy work. I've worked with steel foundations that are bigger than a couch. I'll never forget that first day in the shipyard. They put me underneath a ship, held up by the big pillars. A young man was going to teach me; ten minutes later he leaves and for a half hour I sit there looking at that huge ship over my head, thinking, "God, don't let it fall."

At first I got a lot of static from the men. "This is no place for a woman, you ought to be outside taking care of your kids." I got angry one day, and I told one of the guys that I had to feed my damn kids just like he did, that's why I was there, and I never had too much trouble after that.

SANDRA TANNER, A PAINTER AND MEMBER OF LOCAL 8888'S SAFETY AND HEALTH COMMIT-TEE: I went to work in 1976, and there still weren't many women in the paint department where they put me. I'd never done anything like this before. I grew up in North Carolina; my father worked in a textile mill; my mother never worked outside the home. I did clerical work for W. T. Grant, worked up to management. They went out of business, and I came to the shipyard. I've always been the prissy type, and my brother said, "You'll never make it through the winter." It was cold, no heat anywhere on the ship; you had to eat outside or in the bottom of the ship because you had only twenty minutes, and you never knew whether your lunch would be there because a big rat might come and take it right out of your tool box. But I made it through the winter. Then my brother said, "You'll never make it through the summer, it's worse, it's so hot." But I made it through the summer, and I'm still there.

JAN HOOKS, TWIN SISTER OF ANN WARREN, MOTHER OF TWO DAUGHTERS, EDITOR OF LO-CAL 8888'S NEWSPAPER, THE VOYAGER: I'm a crane operator. The cranes fascinated me from the day I went in the shipyard. I had two daughters, no job, and had separated from my husband. I'm trained as a secretary, but I enjoy being outside. Ann was already working there and said come to the shipyard. My department is grunt-and-groan work; it's classified as an unskilled department— primarily uneducated black men. And I'll tell you those uneducated black men accepted me a whole lot quicker than anybody and went out of their way to help me. The white men in the age bracket from thirty to forty-five were the ones I had the biggest problem with. They seemed to feel the most threatened.

My first day in the yard I was sent to the bottom of a ship. They put me in a little hole, with no lights, and gave me a two-inch paint brush and a metal shovel and told me to clean this hole out. I was scared to death; it was hot as all get-out. But one woman working with me pulled me out, and she jumped all over the supervisor, told him no woman, no *worker*, was going in a tank by themselves without a light, or ventilation.

WARREN: When I first went there, they had only one bathroom for women in a six-block area. We raised Cain; six women fighting the whole shipyard. So they brought us two portable johns, and the men used them at night, and they stayed filthy. We got a padlock and locked them. One day it was real hot, and one of the girls was angry because the stench in the john made her gag. A construction supervisor—one of the biggest men in the shipyard—was down on the shipyards; she grabbed him by the hand, put him inside the toilet, and locked the door. She made him stay in there about ten minutes, and when he came out, he was heaving, he was so sick. Two days later we had the prettiest and brightest brand new toilet you've ever seen.

In 1976 five men formed a committee and asked the Steelworkers to help them organize. Women soon joined.

PEGGY CARPENTER, MOTHER OF A NINE-YEAR-OLD GIRL, A WELDING INSPECTOR, AND FINANCIAL SECRETARY OF LOCAL 8888: Before we had the union the supervisors felt they could talk to you any kind of way. And they would promote their girlfriends or women they liked; there was no seniority.

WARREN: Jan's and my father worked in the shipyard before he retired, and he was so proud of us both. He took us both out and bought us our work clothes when we first went in. He's always been ahead of his time—brought us up to show no partiality to anybody, black, white, man, woman. And he knew about unions because I remember walking a picket line with him when we were four years old. That was in the North Carolina mountains in the forties, at a big laundry. Jan and I went and asked our father what he thought about the union. He said yes, a union was probably the best thing that could happen at the shipyard, and if we wanted it to go after it. So we both did.

JUDY MULLINS, A MACHINIST AND A LEADER IN LOCAL 8888'S WORK FOR PASSAGE OF THE EQUAL RIGHTS AMENDMENT: It was different with me. Union is something I did not grow up with at all. My dad worked in the shipyard, but he said don't join the PSA [Peninsula Shipbuilders Association, the company-controlled union that then represented the workers]. He still considers the Steelworkers crime and corruption. But in the yard I listened to the men complain—I mean from day one, I heard them—about working conditions, low pay, lack of benefits, management pushing people around, unsafe conditions. And I knew a union was needed, here was a chance to change things a hundred percent.

GLORIA COUNCIL, A WELDER AND RECORDING SECRETARY OF LOCAL 8888: My sister was in the union before I was. The company made up things to fire her. But the union fought and got her her job back. So I saw what a union could do.

Local 8888 includes about as many office workers as production workers. Women who were pioneering in the heavy work on the shipways soon found allies among the women who worked in the offices, many of them on the highly technical computer jobs.

PAULA AXSOM, MOTHER OF TWO GROWN CHILDREN, NOW TIDEWATER COORDINATOR FOR RATIFICATION OF ERA: I'm a materials supply clerk; I monitor books for spare parts, a bookkeeping job. Those of us in the office were lowest on the totem pole in salary. Before we got our contract they were hiring clerical employees at minimum wage. I had been at the shipyard fifteen years, but production workers who had been there just a few years made more than I did, and I was topped out as to where I could go. All that has changed with the union.

CINDY BOYD, MOTHER OF TWO YOUNG CHILDREN, NOW CO-CHAIR OF LOCAL 8888'S COMPENSATION COMMITTEE: I work in the office, and actually I was doing pretty well before the strike. I'd been there seven years; my father was in service, and I worked summers during high school for the government, hoping I could someday be a clerk-typist. When I got the job at the shipyard, they trained us on computers, and I thought it was marvelous. The reason I went out on strike is that my husband works in the yard, and I knew what he was going through, being a black male in that shipyard. Not just him, but the women, too, with unsafe working conditions, no benefits. So we both came out on strike, and I was scared. We have two kids, and we didn't know if we would have a job again, but we decided to make that stand.

The computer operators put the company through a trick when we went out. We knew our jobs, we trained other workers, but we never wrote down procedures. We took that information out with us in our brains, and the supervisors didn't know how to get the work out; they really messed up the computer system.

When we got back, it was terrible. Harassment like I'd never heard of before. I had to go to a doctor and get medication. And they took away all the interesting duties we had, gave us menial tasks, and I finally asked for a transfer. Now I'm a materials supply clerk. I learned I had to fight because they weren't giving me anything. I used to cry when supervisors would harass me, but no more, I fight now just as hard as they fight me.

NANCY CROSBY, WHO, BEFORE THE UNION, WORKED ON A HIGHLY SKILLED JOB IN THE YARD'S COMPUTER CENTER: We all learned to be fighters. I worked in a highly secured area, very interesting work. Then my husband, Wayne, got active in the union and became president, and they took many of my duties away from me and finally transferred me, supposedly temporarily, to another job. They didn't trust me. I was in a salaried position and was not eligible for the union, but when the strike came, I went out, too—stayed out with the others, walked the picket line. After the strike I asked if I'd be put back in the computer center, but they said the job was no longer available. So now I have a clerical-type job in the design unit, where I belong to a different Steelworkers local, 8417. We've all given up some things for the union, but we've gained more. I learned about unions in Georgia where I grew up. I was one of eight children; my dad died when I was eleven, and we were very poor. I got a job as a store clerk to put myself through high school. But after I was married, Wayne and I worked together in a small Georgia can plant, and we helped organize a Steelworkers local there. Whether you are in an office job or on the shipways—I know that shipyard management has a lot more respect for those people they know will stand up to them.

WARREN: So we were all together. I'm an old shipyard worker, I stay dirty, and Cindy and Nancy and Paula, they're nice, working up there in the office. But there we were, working side by side, in the union hall, on the picket line, during the strike.

Local 8888's strike in 1979 was rough. Many strikers were arrested. State and local police attacked the strikers brutally on several occasions.

AXSOM: When the strike began the union organizer said he didn't want women on the picket line; he was afraid we'd get hurt. But the women went anyway.

WARREN: One of the first ones who got arrested was a woman. Police arrested her husband, and she made a flying leap and tackled the lieutenant to the ground. It took four of them to put her in the cop car. And we had a policeman with a camera; he'd harass the devil out of people, so we ganged up and covered one gate with fifty women, and every time that cop brought the camera up, we posed for him; we harassed him until they finally took him off the gates. Even the wives came out, mothers pushed babies in carriages on the line.

TANNER: Since the strike we've learned so much about our rights, about safety. That yard is a dangerous place. When I first went there, working in the paint department, they put me to busting rust—grinding rust off the ships' hulls so they can be painted. My supervisor never even showed me how to hook up my grinder. It has no guard, so not knowing how to use one you could cut your hand off. I busted rust for three days before I even knew what a respirator was. They had respirators, but they didn't educate the people. When we came off the ships you couldn't tell who was white or black, we were covered with rust.

But with the union we started having safety meetings once a week, and they educated us so much. I got to arguing with my supervisor all the time about how we needed ventilation and more safety equipment. I stayed in a lot of trouble, but I figured my lungs were worth it. I got so interested in safety that I've gone back to school part-time. I only finished high school before, but now I'm at the community college, studying occupational safety and health.

WARREN: None of us knew the rights we had under federal law. The state is not that much, but federal laws like EEOC, the Civil Rights Act, labor laws, our rights under OSHA, we learned all that.

COUNCIL: You always had the right to refuse to do dangerous work, but before the union there was no one to guarantee that right. Now there is. The main thing is that the company knows now that we are not afraid of them.

CARPENTER: I come from a struggling family of women. My mother and father separated; my mother worked in a chicken plant, plucking chickens, and went to school at night. She was a strong woman. I think I'm naturally like her, and the union brought out the real me. It game me a chance to use my abilities. I didn't go to college, but math was my favorite subject, so when I first went to the yard, I tried to get into clerical work. I'm glad now I didn't because I'm using my math as financial secretary for the union.

WARREN: That shipyard has always made the women, and the men, too, feel like they were stupid, ignorant. But they found out through the Steelworkers and our learning process that we are not ignorant people. For example, Jan had never worked with social services in her life, but she handled food stamps for the whole strike. She got to know everybody within a 200-mile radius who dealt with social services. Cindy is now one of our leaders, co-chair of workers' compensation. One of them, head of the compensation committee, went to Washington recently to testify on that. The shipyard has found out that we are not as stupid as they thought we were.

Women are fighting back against sexual harassment on the job now. One woman took a supervisor to court, and he was fired. She had asked for a raise and he said, all right, if you'll sleep with me, only he used cruder words. Now this was a white supervisor and a black woman—and she went back and asked him again, and he said the same thing. And she taped him.

CROSBY: So now they bar all tape recorders from the yard area.

TANNER: But the company is also turning it around and trying to use the sexual harassment thing to turn worker against worker. They're now telling our co-workers they'll get fired for sexual harassment.

HOOKS: The discrimination is still so rampant. In my department you see so many white guys that are supervisors, or specialists, and there's not a single woman above third-class mechanic. The work force in my department is 80 percent black, and I bet not two percent are above mechanic.

WARREN: As far as this company is concerned the people in that shipyard are either white men, or they are Southern white gentlewomen that don't have any business working, or they are niggers. And I mean they actually call them that, sometimes to their faces. Some women, white and black, have been made supervisors, but they are tokens. The government told the company to comply with EEOC, so they found women who scabbed. A decent supervisor who treats people right, man or woman, gets shafted. They want supervisors who will stay on people's backs all the time.

The women—along with union men—have gone into politics. In 1981, Local 8888 representatives, in coalition with several other unions, took over local Democratic conventions in Hampton and Newport News and elected most of the delegates to the state convention.

WARREN: We don't have anybody in office around here who will stand up for working people. Whether it be on the city council, in the House of Representatives, senators. And we figure we have to start here and put the people in that we need. The only way you can do that is to register to vote, and you'd be surprised how many people on the Steelworker rolls were not registered to vote.

AXSOM: So we ran a telephone bank. It's estimated that at least 2,500 people registered through those phone banks. Soon we'll be gearing them up again.

WARREN: Tenneco put on a campaign in the community for four years saying the Steelworkers were trouble with a capital *T*. So the whole area got against us, first because we were women in the shipyard, then because we were Steelworkers.

AXSOM: But I think we are turning that around now. Not totally, but people are coming around, people who were scared of us, they are knocking on the door, they are calling.

CARPENTER: This is something new for the South. And I think more unions, more working people, are going to get together, statewide, nationwide. We know what we want; we want a fair shake. We don't need to be rich or have a big Cadillac. We just want to be able to live and raise our children and not have to struggle every minute. I saw my mother struggle so, working in the poultry plant, and never have anything for it. Oh, we never went to bed hungry, she saw to that, but it was such a struggle for her.

WARREN: We've got to fight together, or we'll have nothing. One person can't do anything, but when you've got people behind you, you can accomplish things.

MULLINS: And for the betterment of everyone. Not just for us, but for everybody, try to make things better in our workplace and in our community. Because we are not going to make any changes in what's going on in this country until we can make changes in our own community. And that's what we're trying to do, make things better for everybody.

7

Economic Independence and Social Responsibility
The World of Upper-Middle-Class American Women

Elizabeth Oakes

Introduction

For the purpose of understanding the relationship between women and work, I interviewed an upper-middle-class American white woman. What follows are excerpts from those sections of the taped interview in which she speaks of some of the many facets of her life, facets which contribute to a world characterized by economic independence and social responsibility.

Through the words of Eleanor, the world of many upper-middle-class women is explored. It is a world of private girls' school, corporate wifery, suburban life, multiple residences, affluent living conditions as well as work, whether it is running a business, investing in the stock market, or fundraising.

While tempting, it is ill-informed to reduce these elite women to stereotypes of the suburban wife or business executive indistinguishable from her male counterparts. Their lives are as complex as the lives of women from any other class. They, too, have families and households, work and nonwork activities. The fact that they play the stock market or run a business tells us only part of the story; for it is equally important to understand these women's particular sense of social re-

sponsibility and their aesthetic sensibility. Each facet of their lives, such as their relationship to their husbands and servants, their homes and hobbies, contributes to a complete picture and reveals the specificity of their experience as upper-middle-class women. Their perception of society is shaped in part by the environment in which they live: a house in the country, traveling to Europe, gardening, etc.

Still, conflict is present in their lives. One such conflict stems from their economic and psychological isolation. This isolation stands in contrast to their deep social involvement with friends and community. They lead isolated lives in private schools, suburbia, and the nuclear family. Yet, at the same time, they develop long-lasting friendships with women of the same class, and they learn social responsibility to their community at an early age. They grow up to perform volunteer work and fundraise. However, their relationship to men—both fathers and husbands—is often distant.

Another conflict exists between their desire to "do for oneself" as opposed to "doing for others." There is tension between the desire to "put oneself first" and the commitment to "do for others"—kin and community.

Finally, this one life history reflects how deeply women of this class yearn for independence, whether it is economic, psychological, or physical.

Personal History and Background

Eleanor grew up in a family with one sister, one brother, a mother, and a father. She attended a girls' boarding school in Pennsylvania from the ninth grade until senior year. After graduating, she attended college for one year. She then left college and got married. She was nineteen. After ten years of marriage and giving birth to four boys, Eleanor and her professional husband divorced, leaving her as a single mother. She subsequently worked as a real estate broker and an airline executive. She then remarried. Currently, she tends to three residences, fundraises for various organizations, and travels with her husband on business. In the following section, she describes some of the experiences of her boarding school life, her interaction with boys, her first marriage, and life in suburbia.

I went to coed school through eighth grade and the rest of it was female. I was in a private girls' school. There were only a hundred girls—it was small. There were a hundred day students and a hundred boarders. This was outside of Philadelphia, Pennsylvania.

I was a boarder. And the day students (I had a very good friend who was a day student) would come to school with traces of lipstick on from the night before, but we were not allowed to wear lipstick; we had to wear uniforms. They had real natural, normal lives. When they were sixteen they would drive their own car to school and we were so envious we could hardly stand it. And they were outsiders as far as a lot of activities were concerned because being a boarding school, the boarding half had a lot of plays and things that you were involved in, in the evenings, that the day scholars were not part of.

It was unfortunate in many ways culturally. Besides the fact that every student was a girl, the faculty was all female. And the only time that we saw a man was when we went to church on Sunday, which was compulsory—the minister. Or maybe somebody who was working on the grounds or something like that. There was one social activity that they did have—it was kind of horsey country . . .

They had an activity called "beagling." The pack of beagles would go out . . . chasing the smell of rabbits. And they had sort of a Master of the Hounds of the beagles. And the beagles ran and you ran and you ran over fences and you ran and ran and ran. And it all would have been loathsome excepting for the fact that, number one, there was a superb hunt breakfast or tea.

And they're sniffing away and barking and hallooing and there was a lovely hunt tea afterwards and also there were some young men there.

After Boarding School

I went to college for one year and I was married at nineteen and I had my first child when I was twenty-one. I had four children by the time I was twenty-seven. I was the typical housewife. I wouldn't quite say suburban because we raised dogs and were much more apt to live in the country and our life, our times together, were spent with this common hobby of training and showing dogs and hunting. But, ah, so we did spend some time in the suburbs but very briefly. But it was the same kind of life. I mean, I would drive car pools and I was a Boy Scout den mother and I was active in the PTA and that kind of stuff, the usual activities.

Life Now

I'm apt to be in the country three weeks of a month and in the city one week a month. The life is complicated. It's running three places.

One (home) is an apartment in the city. One is a home in the country, and the other is a house in a summer resort area, which is rented
out a good bit of the time, but it takes a certain amount of organization. I would say we'd be lucky if we spent thirty days a year there. . . .
But it's an oasis for my husband. He really feels he is on an island, and
once you get on a ferry, you leave the rest of the country behind. It is
very important for him. It's where he relaxes best.

Work

*In the following section Eleanor describes the isolation of housework
and suburban nuclear family life. She then goes on to describe the different jobs she has held. In this section the relationship of Eleanor to
her work activities becomes evident. From housework to real estate
agent, the particularity of "work" to her class position is clear.*

One thing that is interesting about being a housewife. I think it's
the loneliest job in the world. And there is a certain amount of drinking
that is done that I've seen. That, I'm sure, is caused by the loneliness.

And when you take people into an isolated situation, even if it's a
two-acre isolation or a quarter-acre isolation, it's very hard. It's also, I
think, the job that you have to have the most self-discipline. There's nobody, there's no deadline usually, and there's nobody there, nobody to
watch you to see—like at work if you're sitting there with your feet on
the desk, everybody sees you doing nothing. It's very easy to do nothing
at home. You have to be, I think, extraordinarily well disciplined to
make life meaningful.

The first job I got since I had absolutely no training in anything
was with a small business that operates corporate aircraft. The corporation owned the aircraft and they hired the company that I worked
for to staff it and make sure that the aircraft was kept up and to make
all the arrangements for their travel all over the world wherever they
were going. And it was a very exciting job because it was the kind of job
with a lot of variety of activity for me. I never quite knew when I went
to work what I was going to be doing that day.

And I went on trips to Washington to help with my boss to see
about helping to get air routes. You had to go. I learned there that the
system of government when one has worked in a government agency,
whether it be the FAA, CAA, SEC, then you go into private practice and
you have a gold mine of a job because you're the person who knows the
ins and outs of it. And you never go to a lawyer or a person that has not
had training in the government agency in which you wish to get whatever you want. And it was just a big, long learning process. And I found
it fascinating.

I learned basically office procedures which I had never been exposed to. I didn't know how to file things. I didn't have to be in charge of the filing, the secretary did that, but I had to know how to find it. And, it was a very, very stimulating and interesting experience. It did not pay an awful lot.

And I started out with very prosaic jobs, keeping records of pilots' flying hours and learning a great deal about aircraft. How fast each airplane flew. How long it would take when the New York office calls and says, "Well, there are two guys who are flying to Detroit and they want to be there; they have to be there for a meeting at eleven. What time do they have to be at the airport?" Learn the times, make arrangements—more housewifery—to make sure that the limousine was waiting for them at the other end, that the motel rooms were ordered, make sure that the schedule fit, that the schedule of the aircraft fit their schedule.

As time went on I found that I was hiring stewardesses. And this was not for the corporate planes but we did also have an aircraft that flew commercially. I would get phone calls from India from the boss saying, "OK, we've arrived safely. What's new? Catch me up."

It was a fun aircraft. The steward spoke seven languages. He was a very handsome, dashing Swiss man and served five-course dinners on the plane flying across the Atlantic with the appropriate wine at each course. Oh, yeah, this particular airplane was the largest and fanciest corporate aircraft in the country. And this aircraft was taken down to Texas . . . where it got the interior . . . it was hard to imagine. It had gold fixtures in the bathroom. And it had a master bed . . . for the CEO, Chief Executive Officer—head of the company. And it had a crew of five, with the pilot, copilot, flight engineer, steward—he always had a steward, would never have a stewardess—and then a maintenance man who would go along. And they would go around the world so they were able to take care of the aircraft wherever they went.

The Corporate World Part I: The Corporate Wife

The following section describes the thoughts, feelings, and duties of corporate wives. It details the pushes and pulls on the woman who is forced to put the husband and his job first.

If You Take the Average Corporate Wife . . .

I think one of the reasons why the sacrifices are made to the corporations is 'cause that's where their money comes from—to live the way they want to live. I think that if the wife were financially independent and the income that they had together was enough to make them comfortable, there might be different choices. I think it's a marketplace choice.

The wife had to be a certain part of the functions and I think that I helped him get the job. . . . I had to be interviewed as well as he before he was given the job.

Well, it wasn't a formal interview in that way. I was invited down and the director of the hospital, who was not married at that time, had a dinner party where they had a number of senior-staff members there and their wives and it was a social go-through, I think, mainly, to see if I would be "one of the team."

They pump you about your life and what you are interested in and where you have lived and what you cared about. I think they just wanted to make sure that you didn't eat peas with your knife and things like that. I mean, there was a certain amount of that. That you could pass.

I felt like an IBM wife.

I think the key is, the real key is that the husband's job comes first and that has to be understood. In evaluating the family and the marriage in conjunction with the job, the husband comes first and the job comes first and then after that the family fits in. The IBM stands for "I've Been Moved."

You could never say, "I'm sorry, I like this community. And my children are happy in school. And we won't take the promotion and move." That was the sure path to mediocrity. So I think it doesn't matter what business it is, that is key. And I must say, as a wife, as a marital partner, if the man if not happy in his job I think it's very hard for a marriage to exist because there is nothing that a wife can do to supply the ego feedback the job does.

A good executive works hard and he plays hard too. What I've found is that the competition that is the food that they live on when they are working, they can't turn it off when they come home and it will go into the golf game or the tennis game or whatever it is. They do everything to win. There is no such thing in their lexicon as playing for fun.

But also along with it, I think, is that a good executive is very curious and is always learning and therefore an alive person.

The other thing is that the executive's social life is totally arranged by the wife. I mean, she may say, "Do you want to see so-and-so?" But if the wife were not there, there would be no social life. He does not call anyone and say, "Hey, do you want to go out to dinner Saturday night?"

Well, if it's a party that had to do with my husband's business, very often the people who are there, the majority of the men are in the same business and so the reason why we were invited is because of the fact that my husband is who he is in his field. So it is very easy to feel that you are a tagalong. But I have found on the whole that people are very open to talking to you even if you are a "woman not in the field."

... it's golf, and it's tennis, and it's bridge, and it's entertaining a great deal in the evenings, but there were people who did—I'm sure—volunteer work which was going on in one way or another.

And certainly in the suburb that I lived in, a lot of people became interior decorators, a lot became real estate brokers. And that was my first exposure because it was a suburb, bedroom community of New York, and everybody was married and two-by-two in New York. Divorce in the sixties was not half as prevalent as it is today. And a single woman was out-of-synch and a single working woman especially was out-of-synch with the rest of the community.

The Corporate World Part II: The Female Executive

In this section Eleanor describes female executives she knows as well as giving her opinions on sexism at the corporate level.

I went to a Board of Directors meeting once in a corporation that I own a few shares of stock. And the question came up, "Why don't you have any women on the Board of Directors?" And this man said, "As soon as there is a woman who is able enough to be on our Board of Directors, I will have her. But I am not going to have a token woman on this Board." And I couldn't agree with him more. I think it is a total disadvantage to any woman or minority member to Peter Principle them into something that they are not able to handle and it is bad for both sides.

Most women who are in my age group who have jobs of responsibility and who have "arrived" have fathers who treated them in the same way that they treated the son if they had sons. Or just treated them as an individual, not as a girl. And this is the way Joan (a friend of mine) was brought up by her father.

She is in the cosmetics world—she's a superb executive. She has a fantastic ability to have people work with her, for her, well. She's very sure of herself. She was, for a period of time, head of a company's international setting-up all over Europe—their cosmetic sales areas. They sent her to Harvard, paid for her to get a quicky MBA, which she did a couple of years ago. I think she's probably about fifty-five now at the most, max. And she is now in charge of their mergers and acquisitions. She is a very able woman. Very warm. Her life is very hectic. There is a vast amount of traveling. There is also a vast amount of what

I could consider time spent on trivia which is part of the business. And that is: "how things look," and entertaining, and "are the right people here," and making sure that all of the executives or whoever in whatever country are happy. That would absolutely send me up the wall. It is too much like being a housewife. I don't want to do it in business.

The woman executive does a great deal more interrelating with people than the man executive does. I think that a man is much more apt to make a decision on his own or discuss things with more people and the woman needs a little bit more, maybe, a feeling of support before she comes to a decision.

I would like to, also, be a real tough executive. I'd like to have a career goal from the time that I was very young, and devote a great deal of those energies to myself and that goal. Selfish—not selfish, self-centered. Self-confident. Well it isn't necessarily the tough executive, but it's the picture of a life where I really think about myself first. It would be a mind-blowing experience.

Investing: Toward Economic Independence

In this section of the interview, Eleanor describes the importance of women's financial independence to the maintenance of their self-respect. She describes how she invests in the stock market, enabling her to keep her independence from her husband. This independence is both psychological and economic.

And it's sad to say, but I think that very often in this world, money is power. It isn't as powerful as ideas, but if you get down below that— it is power—and this is what bugs me so about so many women my age. They say that the stock in the United States is owned at least 52 percent by women, not men, and they're probably a lot of them widows, and they just hand it over to some bank with some conservative policy and those bankers, I think, should go to jail for what they do with people's money. They don't pay any attention to them. They just stash it away in something that's safe and pays very little—and that's what the woman gets—and she pays for that service. It's cruel.

I think that specifically in marriages it's one of the ways that a woman can get out of the domination of a husband. If she has her own money, he can't boss her around in the same way 'cause she can tell him where to head. Whatever her dependency patterns are; I mean sometimes there's somebody who's got plenty of money, I guess, and is still dependent for other reasons. This is why the women in the work force today, I think, have much more of a sense of themselves, plus the power of being independent—and it gets rid of one crutch.

I don't say that I feel powerful. But I feel independent. And I also feel, even though it's slimy, that when one is in a position—if you go into a trust company or something like that—and you have some money—they're gonna treat you with a whole different respect than if you don't. Now it's nothing that—I mean I don't like it—but it's the truth.

When I first had some money after my father died, I could stop working if I wanted to. I knew I had this very good cushion and I knew darn well we were never going to starve and we were going to have a roof over our heads.

A woman friend of mine who—again divorced—went into the financial business world in New York City when she was fifty because there was a need—the investment companies finally realized that there was a need to have women there as counselors, money consultants, because there were some women who didn't want to talk to a man. She would start off with things like reading the financial pages every day, in the *Times* and the *Wall Street Journal*. Getting certain financial information services. Getting just a feel—doing dry runs, pretends—starting out by being safe—and diversifying and then, as you feel more confidence in yourself, you can grow, put more things in the fields that you believe in, and not have to be so conservative about it. But she was my teacher, and it was very nice of her to take the time.

I spend a considerable amount of time reading and keeping up on things in the financial world, so that I can make a little bit of money on the stock market. I would not be at all happy just handing what I have to somebody else and saying "do it." And if I have a particular goal, or something that I want money for, I'll knock myself out trying to find an option or something else that's gonna make it big.

Now recently I have invested in Kelly Services, the secretarial and other help, and the Reagan administration—what they're doing—and a lot of corporations—what they're doing—is cutting back on regular work force, because they have to pay so many benefits. And so if they have temps, they can pay the temp a little bit more per hour, but they don't have to pay all these extra benefits. So this is good for a temp company.

National Education is a company that specializes in trade schools and reeducation of adults, mostly, and a lot of it is correspondence courses. And with all the layoffs in the steel industry, and so much of the capital areas of the United States, reeducation is necessary to get these people jobs, and I felt that this was really the right thing at the right time. It did very well for a while and it has gone down. . . .

I really am much more apt to invest in a concept and then try and find a company within the concept that I find is doing its best. And I've come through reading *Megatrends*—the market is psychology. Eco-

nomics, pardon the expression, is not a science, and so I think if one
looks towards where you think—either because of demographics or
some other reason—there is a need, the person who supplies the need,
and supplies it best, is ready to go.

The computer age has made a wonderful thing—because if you
have a stock—every stock has a symbol and all you do is punch out the
symbol and that will tell you in today's world what it closed, yesterday
what it opened, what it is now, and then you can punch other little
things which will bring out any late report that the company has sent
out on any of its activities—whether it's on dividends or whatever. It's
a way you can follow up what the activity of the company is—in between the quarterly reports or the annual reports. And it's marvelous
to have that information close by.

I try not to make too many trades because it makes it difficult for
my husband's business.

I don't like to borrow money from men. I don't want to be dependent on a man and I don't mind being dependent on a woman.

Outside Interests

*This part of the interview is devoted to elucidation of some of Eleanor's
outside interests—gardening and traveling. In this section, she describes the importance of aesthetics in her life.*

I like to arrange flowers. It takes a certain amount of creativity.
And I'm very sensitive to color. Gardening is creative and a lawn is not
creative. It's a totally different thing. We do not have a lawn here other
than four little patches of lawn that can be mowed in twenty minutes.
The rest of it is in a semiwild state. A lawn isn't a garden. A garden is
creating paintings with different colors of things that you put together.
And it is a constantly growing thing. It also is a land of friendship. Because if you have perennials, anytime you have a garden, any friend
who has a garden and has some perennials, you always have to divide
them. So, they share and you share and you look at your garden and
you see your friends. It's very personal. I move things around every
year. I do a complete map of everything. Really, I'm getting old. I'm doing things that I wouldn't have thought about doing when I was
younger. Also there's the time to do it. But there is a map with every
perennial that is there in the beds that are drawn to scale and I put a
sheet of tissue paper over it every year and show exactly what is where
and what color it is and get the idea of how tall it is and then, if I don't
like the looks of it this year I will just divide in the spring and put
things in different places. It's just such fun.

I love to travel. . . . We started in England and since the four boys were not overly enthusiastic about going to cathedrals and art galleries and things, I tried to make sure that there were athletic things. So we went to Wimbledon, to see the tennis, and then we went over to France and then we spent a few days in Amsterdam and rented a V.W. van, and that was home for the summer, sort of. Then we went to Paris, stayed a few days, and through the Loire—and then we stayed in the south of France, on the Atlantic side, for three weeks, and they went swimming every day, and played tennis, and met French kids—and it took them away from the stress. Then we went to Pamplona to see the running of the bulls—and then went on to Italy—a week in Florence, a week in Rome, and then driving up through northern Italy to Austria and Germany, up through the Rhine, and up through Arles, and took the boat home. But it was fantastic. It exposed them to all kinds of cultures, and different foods and different people. I had wanted to go abroad since I was young, and I knew exactly what I wanted to see, first on my list, in every place. And it was just fabulous.

If I go as a tourist to Europe I'm interested in the history and the culture—and there's much more of it, frankly, there than there is in the Carib [Caribbean], for me. And if you can go with a meaningful purpose and study or be involved in something that's going on in the country— then it would be fascinating—but as a tourist it's very skin deep. I've been back many, many times. I've never been to the Far East which I want to do very badly. I'm either gonna have to do it alone or with a female friend, because my husband doesn't like to be gone out of the country that long—and there's no point in rushing over and rushing back in two weeks—so I won't do that very much. Well, we're going to London next summer, and that's business, but it's usually in this country.

But I love being by myself. And if I don't have a certain amount of time by myself, I get exhausted, drained. So I need recharging battery time. So I can go for a whole day without talking to anybody, just going around doing my thing, and be very happy.

Social Values, Social Responsibility: Volunteer Work

In this section, Eleanor describes her deep sense of community involvement and social responsibility. She describes the history of women's volunteer work and some of the drawbacks to contemporary forms of this work.

In another life I would like to be some sort of missionary, not a religious missionary. But I would like to have the training and be able to concretely help people.

It's the only kindness that you can do to help people who are, in that particular time, not in a position to help themselves. I wish I could do more. I wish I had the capability to offer more.

I just can't think of anything worse than somebody who is totally self-centered or cares only about themselves and their immediate friends and family. This is a great big world, and I would hate to be such a narrow person. There is always more pleasure in giving than receiving. It is much harder to receive than to give. And if you can do anything to help anybody, it's a double benefit. The old argument, with Freud, whether every "good" deed is selfishly driven, is great politically. Well the dichotomy of life is that you come into life and leave it alone; you're basically in the core. And on the other hand, you're a part of, a brother of everybody else on this earth and the caring has to go out . . . and finding out within your capabilities, your training, and your time is a very hard thing to find. If you find it, you'll find a happy person.

I was brought up by my mother to feel a strong commitment, a debt, to the community that you lived in. And you didn't just take, but within your capabilities you gave what you could.

She was very, very active. We were growing up in Virginia and she was very active with the Community Chest. She was the president of it at different times. She was terribly active in Planned Parenthood which was unheard of practically in the thirties. It was a nondiscussed subject, which did not bother her at all. She was very gung-ho for it. And in those days it was mostly volunteers. They didn't have paid staffs. She would be helping young women and older women. And she told me she was astonished at the number of women who didn't know "where babies came from."

The Junior League was one [volunteer organization] I suppose. The Junior League has changed a great deal from the time that I was a member, when I was first married . . . but it was sort of in. . . . My first job was working at a large mental hospital, a state mental hospital outside of Boston, and they thought it might be a good idea for the patients that were able to start a little newspaper and everything in it would be the work of the patients. And you volunteered so many hours a week, and that was what I did.

It [volunteer work] started in the olden days, for ladies to do social work. And, upper-middle-class, middle-class ladies . . . the programs they started—working as gray ladies in the hospitals. . . . There was a great deal more volunteer work in the olden days that there is now. . . . Now, there are very, very few things that volunteers can do. It has become much more professional. And so the volunteer person . . . it pushes them into a fundraising role, which is not really always satisfactory.

I find it awfully hard myself to ask for cash, and I think you have to be terribly sure that the agency that you're asking money for is doing a very fine job in order to get the push. I can be enthusiastic, but to be a good fundraiser you're supposed to say "We would like you to give *x* number of dollars if you could," and they always put it high, and I just find it distasteful to do that. I don't want to shame somebody into giving money. I want them to give because they want to give. I've had entertaining in the house for fundraising. I've had meals that people come and have music, and in two weeks we're going to have a cellist and a pianist play and have thirty people in the house for after dinner, at eight o'clock. . . .

The Gender Gap: Relations with Women, Not with Men

This last section is devoted to Eleanor's views on male-female and female-female relationships. She alludes to the distance women of her position feel toward men and how that is reinforced by society and upbringing. This contrasts starkly with the closeness she feels toward other women.

I had great arguments with my mother when I was a teenager, because—I think, maybe it was later, when I was having children—she always said men were totally different from women and it's just the miracle of the age that you ever get two people as opposite as men and women to live and to coexist in the same space.

I know practically no single men which I think on the whole is because men are very uncomfortable unmarried after a certain age. They're lonely, and they want somebody to come home to. And I think women can handle their loneliness much better than men.

I have found it impossible to be close to a man without having had some sexual feeling somewhere. I haven't had an asexual relationship with a man—there is just something there, there's some chemical something that is just part of the relationship. . . . So I just have never been lucky enough to have had that.

And one of the things that was interesting to me was that I was really quite scared of men. I was working for a company where the only other woman there was the secretary. And I had not been in the company of men all my life. And, ah, learning how to relate to them, making friends, was a new part of my life. And I treasure very dearly two or maybe three couples who would just invite me over to dinner. But almost everybody that I saw in my social life then at that time were women.

Friendship is very, very important to me. I've had certain key women friends in my life that have meant a great deal and I like them. And I particularly like women nowadays when more women are working and doing interesting things. They have more interesting things to say. Some of them are professors; some of them have to do with the field of law; some of them have to do with the field of business; and some are interior decorators in the world of design. And I think that they can be just as fascinating any day as, and sometimes much more so than, talking to a bunch of men.

I feel this very strongly, and it's because tangentially you can touch with every woman in every way—either just because of her sex, or shared experience, or there are any number of ways. You've got any number of togethers there when you need them.

8

With Silk Wings
Asian American Women at Work

Elaine H. Kim

Today's Asian American women are diverse in background and experiences, but we share common legacies and contemporary realities that give us a unique collective identity. Asian American women share with all women the problems of sex discrimination and stereotyping, and like other American women of immigrant origins, we have experienced the difficulties and triumphs of forging a new life in a nation of immigrants. But what distinguishes us from European immigrant women is the experience of American racism, which has been of primary importance in the shaping of the status and role of Asian women in the United States.

Because many Americans believed that Asians belonged to an inferior and "unassimilable" race, it was hoped that we would provide the labor needed to build the country and then return to our homelands instead of settling permanently in the United States. Although thousands of Asians were immigrating to America more than a century ago, our numbers were kept relatively small by racial immigration quotas and

Excerpted from *With Silk Wings: Asian American Women at Work* by Elaine H. Kim with Janice Otani. Reprinted by permission of Asian Women United of California.

legislation preventing marriage and inhibiting the development of new generations of American-born children. Furthermore, the integration of Asians into the mainstream of American life was impeded by social and economic segregation and by laws preventing naturalization as U.S. citizens with voting rights until after World War II. . . .

Contemporary Asian American Women

What distinguishes today's Asian American woman from her predecessors is the diversity of the contemporary population. In former years, Asian American communities were comparatively homogeneous and self-contained. Asian ethnic communities are still distinct, especially since recent immigration has breathed new life into urban Chinatowns and created new communities where none existed before. Moreover, most Asians in the United States are still concentrated in California and Hawaii, although populations are increasing in the Midwest, the South, and the East. Besides being more widely dispersed than before, Asian Americans are now working in occupations and capacities formerly closed to them and participating where their numbers are significant.

Although absolute social and economic segregation is a thing of the past for most Asian Americans, racial discrimination continues to play a major role in shaping the status of today's Asian American women.

Employment

Asian American women have never been casual workers in the American labor force. Today's Asian American woman is also a working woman. Nearly two-thirds, or 64%, of all adult Asian American women are in the work force, as compared with 58% of white women and 62% of black women.

While almost all women in America face the problem of sex discrimination in employment, Asian American women fare worse than their white sisters. According to the U.S. Department of Labor, women earn much less than their male counterparts in the same occupation, both in the professions and in unskilled work. In 1981, women earned only 64.7 cents for every dollar earned by a man, a gap that is the same as it was 30 years ago. Income levels of Asian American women, however, are even lower: in 1970, Filipino American women earned 47.5%, Japanese American women 43.7%, Chinese American women 39.6%, and Korean American women 37.0% of white men's income.[1] College-educated white women earn less than male high school graduates, but the disparity between education and income is wider for Asian American women, who have completed more years of school (12.7 years) than either white women (12.5 years) or white men (12.4 years).[2] Women in white collar jobs and professions face barriers in hiring and promotion: while 7 of every 10 teachers in America are female, one in 100 superintendents is a woman. Likewise, Asian American women are underrepresented in all levels of management and administration.

American-born Asian women continue to be clustered in low-profile, low-status, and low-paying occupations, mostly in the clerical ranks. Some scholars have suggested that personnel managers perceive Asian American women according to the racial stereotype of Asian Americans as "loyal, diligent, and attentive to detail"—all qualities of good subordinates.

There are many Asian immigrant women who came to this country with education and training in professional and technical occupations in recent years. Responding to the U.S. immigration policies established in 1965, women with backgrounds in medicine and nursing, dentistry, pharmacy, law, and other professions left their homelands only to find it difficult to practice their skills in the United States because of licensing and local training and experience requirements. Filipino women are better educated than males or females from any other population group in America—27% have college degrees—but many are underemployed. They are "hired at a lower level than their credentials might call for but assigned duties given to professionals," thereby saving money for their employers.[3]

Recent Immigrant Women

Most Asian immigrant women today are employed in traditional arenas as garment factory seamstresses, waitresses, cannery workers, and domestic servants or in newer, high-growth industries as electronics assembly workers and hotel room cleaners. In 1970, 57% of all Chinese American working women were seamstresses or food service workers.[4] In the same year, two-thirds of all garment factory workers and one-third of all private household domestics in the San Francisco-Oakland area were Asian American women.[5] Unaware of protective labor laws or even the terms of their union contracts, many women earn minimum or below-minimum wages and work 10 to 13 hours a day without overtime pay. In a 1976 television interview, one Korean immigrant seamstress said, "What could I learn about American life? I just sit here and sew. For me, to live is to swallow bitterness."[6]

During the last 10 years, Asian American social service agencies have attempted to address the needs of recent immigrants through bilingual social services in health, mental health, legal aid, and unemployment skills and language training programs. Unfortunately, federal cutbacks in social service programs and legal challenges to programs for minorities and women are resulting in a reduction in educational and employment options for immigrant minority women.

Without fluency in English and access to bilingual skills training, Asian immigrant women have little opportunity for career advancement. In 1979, 40% of the 6,000 employees in San Francisco's 36 major hotels were Asian American; of these, about one-third were women working as room cleaners, linen menders, kitchen helpers, or laundry workers. Commenting on their chances for promotion, a public relations director at one of the hotels said, "There's not much crossover amongst employees from one position to another in non-management positions. In fact, it doesn't exist. . . . In all honesty, I can't say that room cleaners very often get promoted. They stay at their entry level job."[7]

The tradition of family-owned business remains attractive to many recent Asian immigrants, who view long hours and unpaid or low-paid family labor in independent enterprises as preferable to entrapment in dead-end low-wage menial labor working for someone else. As in former days, Asian immigrant women are working beside their husbands in family enterprises like restaurants and grocery stores. But economic conditions are not now favorable for starting and maintaining small businesses: by October, 1982, the failure rate was higher than at any time since the Great Depression. Wage and price-cutting wars are a typical response to the keen competition among Asian-owned businesses, and business failure propels the immigrants back into menial labor again.

The problems facing Asian immigrant women in the workplace have not gone completely unchallenged. As traditional Asian concepts of benevolence and mutual obligation have proved unsuitable for the protection of workers in America, immigrant women are learning to utilize American-style litigation and collective bargaining practices to secure their rights and livelihoods. In 1980, thousands of Filipino, Chinese, Korean, and other immigrant hotel maids joined a month-long hotel workers' strike in San Francisco, winning a pay increase and staving off an increase in work load. In 1982, Chinese garment workers in New York City organized a march and a one-day strike that resulted in a union contract of far-reaching consequence to thousands of Chinese immigrant women workers.

When faced with limited employment opportunities, many immigrant mothers channel their energies into their children's education and futures.

I haven't had much of a life. My husband is a janitor, and I sew all day long, but I want my sons and daughters to go to college so that they can become engineers and doctors. Even my friends who own their own grocery stores don't want their children to operate the business. They want them to have professions.[8]

American-born Asian women, or women who have been at least partially educated in the United States, have been responsive to the pressures they feel because of their parents. As a rule, they have made important strides in employment during the last two decades, as a direct result of the Civil Rights legislation of the mid-1960s and subsequent affirmative action policies in both education and employment. More than half the 150 Asian American women interviewed by Asian Women United in 1981–82 found their current jobs as a direct result of affirmative action, particularly in the skilled trades and in professions like law and medicine. But as a group, Asian American women are drastically underrepresented in fields such as law and medicine, dentistry, architecture, and engineering, and few Asian American women are working anywhere as managers or administrators or in the skilled trades.[9]

In order to address their concerns, Asian American women need a greater voice and share in the leadership in institutions that affect their lives—community organizations, professional associations, labor unions, and governmental bodies, both in American society and within the Asian American communities. Asian American women must participate more actively in battles for equality. Chinese for Affirmative Action in San Francisco reports that of the many grievances and suits filed against discrimination, few have ever been initiated by Asian American women.[10] Clearly, it is not enough to let other minorities and women fight the battles for equality and justice and then sign up after a Consent Decree has been established. Through direct participation, Asian American women can learn what it means and what it takes to try to shape the factors that govern our lives. At the same time, we know from past history that strength and courage grow from struggle. Fifty-eight-year-old Korean American design engineer Helen Kim, whose seven-year sex discrimination grievance culminated in a 1980 victory that has profound implications for other women and minorities, attributes her phenomenal strength to her whole life of struggle.

My beginnings were really subhuman. Animals lived better than we did. I did everything—dug ditches, planted, hoed, weeded, cleaned toilets—you name it, I did it. But no matter how people tried to break me, they could not, because I have no fear. I was born to survive.[11]

For more than a century, Asian women in America have assumed roles as wives and mothers that included work on farms and in family businesses, labor which promoted the survival of the family unit and

the development of the Asian American communities as a whole. Today's Asian American woman is linked to the women of the past by her
commitment to her work, her family, her community, and her culture.
The paths she crosses today may differ from those of the past, but her
goals are the same: to realize her potentials and express herself as an
individual through creative work within the context of her identity as
an Asian American woman.

Notes

1. Gloria Kumagai, "The Asian Women in America," *Explorations in Ethnic
   Studies* 1:2 (July, 1978), p. 32.
2. Pauline Fong, "Economic Status of Asian Women," paper presented to the
   National Advisory Council on Women's Educational Programs, San Francisco, February, 1976.
3. Belen Andrada, "Occupational Profiles of Filipino Women in Minnesota,"
   in *Asian and Pacific American Experiences: Women's Perspectives*, ed. No-
   buya Tsuchida, Minneapolis: Asian/Pacific American Learning Resource
   Center, 1982, p. 145.
4. Betty Lee Sung, *Chinese Manpower and Employment*, Springfield, Va.:
   NTIS, 1975, pp. 90–92, 115–118.
5. Pauline Fong, *op. cit.*
6. "Asians Now," KTVU-2, Oakland , California, May, 1976.
7. *Oakland Tribune*, July 31, 1980.
8. Elaine Kim, interview with C.C., April, 1982.
9. "Selected Statistics on the Status of Asian-American Women," *Amerasia
   Journal* 4:1 (1977), pp. 138–139.
10. Elaine Kim, interview with Kathy Owyang Turner of Chinese for Affirma-
    tive Action, San Francisco, October 15, 1982.
11. Elaine Kim, interview with Helen Kim, December 29, 1981.

9

Working at Gettin' Yourself an Education

Louise te Boekhorst

This interview is excerpted from a two-hour taped conversation among four college friends. We have in common that we met as women returning to school to continue our formal education. Three of us (Ann, Barbara, and Carrie*) are welfare recipients as well as honor students, activists, mothers, and workers.

In this conversation, the women express a range of emotions and a conscious understanding of what it means to live on the razor's edge of survival. They share many of the same things, places, and feelings: powdered eggs, long welfare lines, and the frustration and anger of being restricted and delayed by forms, requirements, irrationalities, and injustices. Yet each woman speaks out of the particularities of her history, her perceptions, and her ways of surviving.

The importance of having and the injustice of being denied work, education, and public assistance is clear to these women. In highly creative ways, each has forged a strategy for living based on an interconnection among her need for work, her desire for education, and her right to public assistance. It is a tense, painful life, but there are also those moments when these women are empowered by understanding what is happening to them, and challenged by the possibility of changing what is done to them and millions of women like them.

*Fictitious names.

How do you manage to survive on welfare?

A: You shouldn't call it welfare because it isn't. It's called Public Assistance, P.A.

B: It shouldn't even be called P.A. It's not really assistance. You have to lie if you want to survive this system. You're lying about yourself and you feel it eventually. I hate to think of all the women who are sitting at home and don't know they could be going to school. I know a lot of women who don't want to do it because they just can't go through with the lying. There are women who are probably starving because they just don't want to lie. It's ridiculous and horrible if you think of all the things that go on.

A: If you're alive after being a year on P.A. that is prima facie evidence that you are cheating . . . because no other way could you be alive. Let's face it. If you're on P.A. and after a year you are not in the hospital suffering from malnutrition, you're not in a shelter, and you still have your kids (because if you don't have a place to live, they take your kids away from you because "you" are a neglectful parent), then you're a welfare cheat.

C: Well, I'm a former welfare cheat. Now I'm one of those people who are on the fringe; I have too much money to be on welfare, but not enough money to get any sort of assistance, like medical insurance and things like that. I still have to manipulate, to lie to survive.

B: I've been on welfare since 1973. I was off a couple of times, from '81 to '83, because my kids had to go to a foster home when I lost my apartment. Now that my youngest is eight, they've been sending me to WIN . . . the work incentive program. As soon as my case worker heard that I was going to school, she sent me to WIN. She said, "You have to go." I didn't know it at the time, but they cannot make you mess up school to go to WIN. They have to set your appointments up at another time. I found this out from my SEEK counselor. I was afraid they were going to make me drop out of school to go to work, but they wait 'til you're on summer vacation . . . that's why I'm going to summer school.

A: When I went downtown and told my case worker I had quit school because I just couldn't do it, she got this self-satisfied smile on her face and said, "Well, it's probably better this way. You're young, you're attractive, you can find a man." I stared at her and I said, "Look around this room. We are all here because we found a man." She didn't know what to say. But that's their idea— they want you to get married to get off welfare. They have no intention of your becoming economically self-supporting. As a matter of fact, they do everything within their power to make sure you don't. First of all, just bottom line: women need college educations just to be able to make what a man with an eighth-grade education makes. A B.A. degree might at least get you something that's above minimum wage. WIN trains you for minimum wage jobs. And guess what? Since 1981 there are no funds for training.

B: The welfare system really makes you feel bad about yourself.

C: Yeah, I'm sure I'd have a lot less self-confidence about speaking out about welfare if I hadn't got off of it. It's a major accomplishment for me. There was this real point in my life when I felt I now have control over my life and even then—even without the support of a community of women, even without having gone to school or anything, I felt so much pride that I had asked to be off of welfare. It was scary and everything but I had a job and I was making my minimum wage. It was just like I don't need this anymore and I felt so good. When it was suggested that I go back on getting foodstamps and getting the Medicaid, I just felt like I was dying. I got the forms and I tried to fill them out. There are so many questions, already it was like I have to start lying. Then knowing I'd have to go into that office and stand in line all day. I just couldn't face it. I just felt I'll be hungry, you know, I'd rather be hungry. I'll make it somehow. But, I have no medical insurance which is scary. Let's face it, that is very scary. I had to go to student loans to get money to go to the dentist and I have to pay that back but I am still going to the dentist. I'm going to get my eyes checked too. I'm doing that too.

B: I'm going to college now, but I could have gone to college twelve years ago. They could have told me twelve years ago. They don't ask you, do you want to go to school? Do you want a training program, do you want some kind of help with the kids? They never ask, "What do you want?" You know, I've known women who have been on welfare sixteen, twenty years and they could have gone to school. They didn't know it. You know, there's no reaching out to the welfare mothers, you're just like another number when you go in there and you're not a person. You're not a person that wants to do anything real for your children. They don't care.

C: I always felt there was a thing where they would give you just enough money to keep you hooked to coming in there but not enough money to really do anything. It's like a big bandaid.

B: You couldn't even go out to look for a job with the money you get from them.

A: No, but in fact when you sign up for WIN you sign a form that says you will provide the bus fare and clothing from your grant to look presentable and to get to any job interviews. And your grant is totally insufficient to even scrounge by anyway.

B: But I'm really in a bind now. After two years of college, I'm realizing that I need some type of work experience. I'm older than most college graduates will be and so I would like something to put on my resume. Not only that, I feel I would really benefit from some type of job. I know I would feel better about myself too. But I don't want to give up school to get a job. I would have to because I would have to get two jobs to support my three kids. You're really in a trap. Medicaid is crucial, absolutely crucial, with kids. I can't afford to lose it. There is no way that I can make more right now than what they are giving, including Medicaid. Just the dental bills would be outrageous. I can't feed my kids on $47 a week and I can't pay my rent on the $250 they budget me for rent. They know my rent is $450 a month. I get $500 a month total from welfare. My worker doesn't even want to know. She says, "You should really apply for housing [and I have, but it takes years to get it] 'cause I don't know how you pay for all this rent." But she doesn't ask how I'm paying it. Half my rent is paid by my mother and my grandmother. You're married to welfare.

A: Yeah, because they don't give you enough money! Forget the foodstamps. You're supposed to spend forty-three cents a meal! "Not impossible, you just don't know how to do it right!" But if you ever figure it out, you should get David Stockman's job. That should be one of the prerequisites for his job . . . to survive on welfare for two years with three kids.

B: The foster mother that had my kids got $200 for each kid. She owned her own house and got $600 a month to take care of my kids and feed them. I don't get that much and now I'm added to the case. I don't get that much a month for my kids.

A: But, the agency you see, that placed your kids in foster care got $20,000 to do that. Now, excuse me, but wouldn't it make so much more sense to give you $15,000. Cut out the administrative bullshit. Cut out what it is going to do to your kids. But it's the same thing they do if you don't have an apartment. They take your kids away from you because you're a neglectful parent if you can't afford to pay rent in N.Y.C. and you're on welfare. Ah, wait a second—there is no way you can pay rent.

B: There hasn't been a rent increase since like 1973.

A: Well they're talking about a ten-percent rent increase this period.

B: But that's nothing.

A: Ten percent of nothing. Do you know how much rents have gone up? Three hundred percent and the mayor wants to have two-party rent checks now.

Meaning that the rent goes directly to the landlord, even if basic services are not being provided.

A: You got it.

B: You have to put on an act—you have to be crazy, if you want anything to get done.

So what happens to women who for some reason can't do that?

C: They're starving.

A: First of all, what is there that we all have in common? Aside from that we're all in school, notice that we are all white—O.K.? When we put our hands out, there aren't as many people who are going to break our wrists. What is it that you notice about all these welfare women who are on the front pages of the *Post* who have killed their kids? It's really clear—its very very clear. I think there's also something about your background.

B: When I used to live down on the Lower East Side I used to hear people say look at those mutts—the black and Puerto Rican people—then they used to say, well as long as they kill themselves, we don't care, let them do it. This is the whole mentality—as long as they're killing each other—these are the same kind of people who say, when kids are killed, well, at least they killed black kids. This is a really sick world we live in—and people don't see what a sick world it is.

A: There is no sense in this country. To be black and female and on welfare you are not a human, period, the end. You are invisible and less than a human being. It's like a black woman with Medicaid going into a city teaching hospital: I can guarantee you this woman is going to lose vital organs. I try to tell women how to cheat, what to do, how to get day care if you are going to a four-year college. You have to share that stuff around when you're sitting in the WIN office, you have to spread stories around about how to get over—you have to do that—it's your duty. If you have found something that works it's your duty to pass that info on to everyone.

Do you feel that you get any kind of support, I mean emotional support?

C: When you're on welfare? None.

A: It's isolation.

C: It's totally isolated and you're ashamed. There is so much shame connected to it, you don't want to tell anybody. I like telling people about it now, you know. I like seeing the look on their faces.

B: Because you're not on welfare anymore.

C: Exactly, but it's also like . . . "WAKE UP!"

You mean like: This is who I am and these are my realities?

C: Yeah, like O.K. you're a welfare mother, you've gone through all this shit, you're doing this, you're doing the best you can. You've got this kid, when the kid hits adolescence it's been deprived for a lifetime, basically, of many basic necessities. You haven't been able to be there because you've been trying to get it together. Even if you end up going out to work after this initial period of living on welfare, the kid starts running with the wrong crowd 'cause that's the crowd it tends to associate with because that's the crowd where it feels it belongs. And your kid gets into trouble when it decides it's going to rob the neighborhood grocery or whatever—it gets into trouble. Then the kid is sent to a state run agency/home, whatever, for troubled children. They spend $70,000 a year—now its up to $90,000—to maintain your child in this place—this institution—meanwhile they haven't given you $70,000 for the entire life of the child.

A: And on top of it, they are paying $70K, $90K a year for the institution to abuse your child. If you did to your kid what the institution is doing to your kid—not only would you lose your kid, you'd be in jail.

B: And if they just gave you all the money that they spend on therapy, therapy for you, therapy for your kids. If I had all that money I don't think I would have as many problems dealing with the things I have to deal with—because I know I have problems with my kids that are directly related to them feeling like they don't have anything.

A: Sure, and when do you feel like you want to kill your kids—when you've got that garbage crawling up your back because you can't pay for this and you can't pay for that, that's when you want to kill your kids. That's what is neat about this course on child welfare. The first day of the course the question is raised: "How can we eliminate child abuse?" And people say stuff like—take the kids away from the parents, parents who abuse their children should be put in jail, we shouldn't be soft on them. At the end of the course—the last day of class, the same question is raised again: "How can we eliminate child abuse?" And the answers are: guaranteed annual income, more social services support for families at risk, more therapy with therapists who are interested in concrete reality—get rid of the psychiatrists—get rid of the experts—only welfare people should be directing policy that has to do with welfare. The answers are different once students are exposed to the facts. But they are so uninformed when they come in there. More day care centers—twenty-four hour day care centers—every kid should have a place in a day care center. If they didn't want us on welfare, the welfare system would not be set up the way it is. It's set up this way because the system wants people on welfare.

PART II

FAMILIES

"T HE American family" has a ring of authenticity, but to what and to whom does the phrase refer? In the introductory exploration of commonalities and differences in women's lives, we concluded that "family" refers to a multiplicity of forms in the United States today. Yet, if the concept has any meaning at all, it must refer to some shared set of functions carried out by various combinations of individuals.

Families, it is said, are concerned with reproduction and production. Or, families are in charge of the material and emotional well-being of a group of kinfolk. While various families do indeed fulfill these functions, such tasks can be and are carried out in other institutional settings, leading to the conclusion that even what families do, and perhaps do best, is not exclusively done by them. The value placed on families, however, is captured when we say that a group of unrelated people behaving in a certain way "are acting just like family."

Although a way of behaving is the most fundamental characteristic of "family," this complex set of behaviors and relations is often confused with a residential site, the household. While much of what is referred to as "family" activity takes place in a physical space shared by a group of related people, for many ethnic communities and classes, the group of individuals who regularly function as family are spread over some distance. In such cases, kinfolk are referred to as an extended family, in contrast to the smaller nuclear family unit.

Most would say family is that group of individuals one "comes home to," those who create a place of warmth and love and refuge from the outside world. The American Home Economic Association defines a family in these terms:

> Two or more persons who share resources, share responsibility for decisions, share values and goals, and have commitments to one another over time. The family is that climate that one "comes home to," and it is this network of sharing and commitments that most accurately describes the family unit, regardless of blood, legal ties, adoption or marriage.

The emphasis on sharing of tasks is far more ideal than real, for in that great majority of families where women are present, they are the individuals who hold a disproportionate responsibility for creating the climate called "home."

In outlining tasks associated with these families, the role of women is prominent. Firstly, within families, babies are born, children are nurtured physically and emotionally, and the basic material well-being of adults is provided. It is women who bear children, it is women who are the primary nurturers of the young, and it is women who, by and large, do the shopping, cooking, cleaning, and mending involved in the physical maintenance and well-being of adults. Secondly, within families, the young are socialized, taught the ways of the larger "American culture," as well as the ways of their particular racial and ethnic community, class, and gender. Although men may, and do, participate, it is unquestionably women who are in charge of these tasks, even the instruction of young boys about the ways of their gender.

Today, idealized notions of who constitutes family, and the respective roles and responsibilities of individuals therein, provide the foundation of a political view for the New Right and the battle cry for violent action, such as the bombing of abortion clinics by the most zealous. The 1984 Republican party platform accused welfare of shattering "family cohesion," both "by providing economic incentives to set up maternal households and by usurping the breadwinner's economic role in intact families." And it asserted, "the cruelest result was the maternalization of poverty, worsened by the breakdown of the family and accelerated by destructive patterns of conduct too long tolerated by permissive liberals."

The platform bemoans the loss of the family consisting of a man who works outside of the household, a woman who works *only* at home, and 2.5 children. This ideal, in its most exaggerated form, is reflected in the following statement from a John Birch Society pamphlet.

Traditionally a man's role as head of the family takes him away from the hearthstone. A woman is like many stones: she is the hearthstone from which warmth and light are reflected throughout the home; she is the decorative, exotic stones hedging and protecting precious and beautiful growth; she is graceful as marble, preserving culture and tradition; and, she is as hard as granite with anything that threatens her home and children. She is soapstone and pumice, ever-cleansing and smoothing. She is a touchstone; a close comfort to her mate and little ones. And she sometimes feels like a well-worn cobblestone, over which have passed the tribulations of all she holds dear. Woman is at once like the sunny sand that warms, and like the heart and sinew of the sandbags that keep the home secure from intruding torrents in crisis. She can be ruby-lipped, onyx-eyed, pearl-skinned, and topaz-tressed. But always she shines like the symbol of her marriage, the perfect diamond that will reflect her growth from bride to grandmother. (Wright 1978: 1)

The concern of the New Right and of many whose political perspective is far from conservative, is that "the American family" is declining, in trouble, or breaking up. Yet the reality is that a multiplicity of family forms have always existed in the United States and that, over time, these forms have remained relatively stable. What is new, however, are certain behaviors on the part of family members, especially women, and the effect of those changes on family life. Jane Flax noted four changes which have accelerated since 1970, corresponding to the period when the women's liberation movement became a visible public presence. These changes are the increases in the divorce rate, in families headed by women, in labor force participation by women, and in the number of "working mothers." Flax suggests that these phenomena are "among the most significant elements constituting the perceived 'decline' of the family, for they present at least the possibility of less patriarchal control over women and familial relations" (Flax 1983: 27).

The articles which follow address the traditional and changing situation of women in their families. These families and these women are, however, characterized as much by their diversity as by their similarities.

The families described by Betty Friedan in "The Problem That Has No Name" come the closest to what has been idealized as "the American family." Yet the situation Friedan describes is far from joyous for the women of those suburban families. By the time she writes "End of the Beginning," substantial changes have occurred but the result is not a new-found contentment.

In 1963, Betty Friedan wrote *The Feminine Mystique*, from which the first article in this chapter is taken. In 1966, along with several other women, she founded the National Organization for Women

(NOW). These were two important events in the modern feminist move-ment. But the families Friedan described and the women that NOW ap-pealed to were certainly not *all* "American" women. Indeed, one is struck by the total absence of women of color and working-class women in Friedan's description. Understanding the origin of her book explains its bias: she sent a questionnaire to her Smith College class-mates in 1957, and the responses she received led to *The Feminine Mys-tique*. Friedan spoke of these women's dissatisfaction with the life of a suburban housewife. With a fully employed husband, an attractive home, and busy children, these middle- and upper-middle-class white women dared to ask: Is this all there is to my life? Their discontent with the feminine mystique, the assumption of women's natural do-mesticity, demanded change.

Although the lives of these middle-class white women did change, the consequences of those changes led to a new "problem that has no name." In *The Second Stage*, from which her second article is taken, Friedan persistently focuses on one segment of U.S. womanhood. She argues that by reacting to definitions of women cast exclusively in terms of their relation to men—as wives, as mothers, and as home-makers—that is, in successfully reacting against the *feminine* mys-tique, a *feminist* mystique was created which denied "that core of women's personhood that is fulfilled through love, nurture, home." In *The Second Stage*, Betty Friedan once again speaks for women like her-self on the issues of family, home, marriage, and work. But once again she assumes that all or the majority of US women are like herself.

Contrast, for example, the problems without names described by Friedan, and the problems described by Kathy Alarid in the article by Elsasser, MacKenzie, and Texier. Alarid, a fifty-year-old Chicana who married at seventeen, reared eleven children, spent twenty years of her life as a housewife, and today is divorced and working full-time in a community service program. Her concluding lines on who are the "to-gether" Chicanas of today stand in sharp contrast to what Betty Friedan is seeking.

Any attempt to characterize the Chicano family is of course as risky as all such efforts to collapse heterogeneous human behavior into some homogenized sameness. As Mirande and Enriquez note, while there is no typical Chicano family but a number of family types, varying according to class, age, length of time in the United States, ed-ucation, region of residence, and other factors, it is nevertheless possi-ble to identify attributes more likely to characterize the Chicano than the Anglo family (Mirande and Enriquez 1979: 111). Among the attrib-utes they identify are a strong familistic orientation; deference to el-ders; respect, including special privileges and authority, for men; less value accorded to women/mothers despite their placement on a pedestal by males; separation of male and female roles; premarital chastity as the zenith of feminine virtue; and the view of the family as a place of warmth and support in an otherwise hostile and unrewarding environment (Mirande and Enriquez 1979: 111–112).

Friedan's description of the problems women encounter in middle-class, white, suburban families also stands in stark contrast to families that are not built around the relationship of heterosexual couples and heterosexual values. Audre Lorde, poet, essayist, and professor of literature, writes in an open and moving way about the relationship between herself, a black lesbian feminist, and her son. As she paints some of the tones of the relationship which her son has with his strong and feminist sister and with Lorde's lover, a white woman, we begin to sense the power of what anthropologists have observed: families, indeed all of kinship, is much more a matter of behavior than biology. Audre Lorde's straightforward and sensitive essay offers insight into how the tasks of nurturing and socializing the young are not absolute tasks, unaffected by the race, class, sexual preference, age, religion, and politics of the socializer.

Betty Friedan called the dissatisfaction of suburban white middle-class wives and mothers "the problem that has no name." Evelyn Torton Beck has described lesbian motherhood as "The Motherhood That Dare Not Speak Its Name."

> Between fifteen and twenty percent of all lesbians are mothers. The National Gay Task Force sets the actual numbers at between 1,430,000 and 2,000,000 in the United States alone. About two-thirds of these lesbians were married when their children were born; a substantial number were never married at all. Some lesbians become mothers by adopting children, while a small, but quickly growing number conceive as the result of artificial insemination, arranged privately or in clinics. Yet these lived realities have made little impact on the imagination of the dominant culture and have not kept the words *lesbian mother* from sounding to its ears like an absolute contradiction in terms, describing a non-existent creature, or at least one that should not exist. (Beck 1983: 8–11)

In ways that are quite powerful, Audre Lorde illustrates what it means to be a part of that motherhood that dare not speak its name, and to be so as a black woman in white America.

Privacy surrounds the world of upper-class women and their families. Indeed, it is as if seclusion and privacy are among the many things which the very rich can buy. Unlike the voluminous literature on the poor family, the ghetto family, the "broken" family, there is comparatively little information on how the upper one-ten-thousandth of the population lives.

The article by Rosabeth Kanter describes not the "super rich," but the wives of executives of an industrial corporation. Outlining the expected stages in the career of an executive's wife, from when her husband is on a premanagement level to when he is at the top of the organization or in a position representing it to the outside, Kanter offers information which illustrates ways in which the family lives of affluent women are antithetical to the lives of the masses of women in the United States. Yet she also illustrates ways in which the structural relationship of wealthy women to their husbands and children echoes the condition of so many other women.

It is the status of executive wives as unpaid workers which most clearly echoes the same old story. While there are, of course, particularities to the "two-person single career" of such families, the employer is still benefiting from the efforts of two people for one salary, and the woman's efforts are defined in terms of someone other than herself. But clearly the women in Kanter's article are not troubled by the range of issues which poor and working-class women must confront. What does it mean *not* to have to worry about enough cash to place a meal on the family table every evening? The executive's wife may indeed feel put upon by the demands of her husband's corporation, but at least she is not confronted by inadequate nutrition, unsatisfactory health care, poor educational facilities and curriculum for her children, and unsafe housing. The disparity between the material conditions of affluent and poor women cannot be wiped away by references to all women's oppression.

A common experience for all women, if their lives are long enough, is that of growing old. For although old age is a biological fate, it is a fate that varies according to culture, gender, race, ethnicity, class, family composition, and so forth. This point is vividly made in Melba Sánchez-Ayéndez's analysis of older Puerto Rican women in an urban U.S. community. The ways in which these women's cultural tradition defines and interprets relationships set the stage for how they use their social networks to secure the support they need. Specifically, Sánchez-Ayéndez focuses on two Puerto Rican cultural values: family interdependence and the differential nature and roles of women and men. Neither of these values is restricted to Puerto Rican families. Indeed, individuals of various racial and ethnic groups can recognize attitudes and behaviors which are familiar to them in their own families. Yet, the specific ways in which these values are acknowledged and experienced among the women in the community Sánchez-Ayéndez studied resonate with the richness and the particularities of an urban Puerto Rican culture in the United States.

It may be that the class and racial or ethnic group to which an aging woman belongs are the most important determinants of how she grows old. For example, the extended family structure and value systems of Afro-American, Asian American, Native American, and Latino communities may mitigate the isolation of older women. Economic necessity, however, is a part of what "requires" family members to do what they can to financially assist their elders, to help provide some protection from the dangers of crime in the city, and to manipulate the power structure to get needed services. As conditions for the poor grow increasingly harsh, and as programs for "minorities" are cut even more severely, the families of many older women may well face crises which are far beyond their ability to cushion.

Interrelationships among race/ethnicity, class, and gender are also key to understanding the situations of black families. The literature on black families suffers from two profound fallacies. First, the range of families among Afro-Americans is often reduced to pronouncements about *the* black family, with the impression given that *the* urban poor black family represents *all* black families. Second, the "explanation" for the plight of urban poor black families is usually simplistic, just plain wrong, or both. Much of what is written seems to ignore the pioneering work by Andrew Billingsley on the range of types of black families in the United States (Billingsley 1968) and the more recent work on black women within families by scholars such as Joyce Ladner (1971). Billingsley, Ladner, and other black social scientists have stressed the strengths of nontraditional families. But much of the study of black families continues to draw on the 1965 report of then Assistant Secretary of Labor Daniel P. Moynihan in which he described the state of black America as pathological, and blamed the "black matriarchy" for a good deal of that state in which Afro-Americans live.

There were many extraordinary statements in the Moynihan report, but two stand out and are still in vogue. Moynihan argued that although black men and women suffered under the weight of racial discrimination, black men suffered the most because "the very essence of the male animal, from the bantam rooster to the four-star general, is to strut" (Moynihan 1965: 16). And how could stability be achieved within black families? He argued that poverty would have to be eliminated among Afro-Americans and this would happen with full employment for black *men*. "The government should not rest until every able-bodied Negro man was working even if this meant that some women's jobs had to be redesigned to enable men to fulfill them" (Moynihan, quoted in Giddings 1984: 328).

Other studies "skip" the stage of blaming black women who head their households and go directly to poverty as the source of the condition of many black families. Harriette McAdoo's article brings into focus the importance of racism, not in isolation from economic conditions, but in conjunction with them, for an understanding of life in a range of Afro-American family settings: poor, working-class, middle-class, and affluent.

These factors of racism and class, in conjunction with gender, create a different reality for black women within their families. For example, the legacy of slavery and ongoing racism have created a condition whereby Afro-American women have a long-standing association with working outside of their households. One consequence of this is that they have a greater voice in family and household decisions. Another is greater flexibility in the roles of men and women within their families.

The article on Jewish women and families by Susan Schneider presents a number of points, some of which parallel the situation of women in other ethnic groups, some of which indicate the distinctiveness of Jewish families. Following McAdoo's article on black families, we note the extent to which extended family networks are also of real importance in Jewish families and cut across class lines. Part of the explanation of this pattern rests in understanding the structure of Judaism as a communal religion which "helped create and sustain what was in premodern times an extended family for Jews almost everywhere they lived." (Schneider 1984: 259) And among Jews, as with other ethnic minorities, families can serve as a place of refuge from discrimination.

Another parallel between Jewish and Afro-American families is the existence of negative stereotypes concerning women's roles in the family. How many unflattering stereotypic jokes exist about "the Jewish mother" and the daughter who is labeled a "Jewish American Princess"? Schneider sorts through the history behind these stereotypes, and provides a more accurate portrayal of the complexities of being Jewish and female in a family setting which continues to change in response to the world around it, while struggling to maintain religious and cultural traditions. Schneider is particularly insightful in posing questions as to why there is no Jewish American Prince stereotype and in exploring the relation of Jewish fathers to their daughters.

Schneider also argues that there are characteristics unique to the Jewish family, including the strong association of the mother with the survival and transmission of Jewish values. The mother is seen as infallible in her role as transmitter of Jewish identity and catalyst of change in the form of improvement of life from generation to generation (Schneider 1984: 260–261).

In the final article, "Out of the Stream: An Essay on Unconventional Motherhood," Shirley Glubka poses a number of fundamental questions about women and families through her description of the experiences, fears, guilt, and relief of a Midwestern-born Catholic white woman who gave up her child to another woman because she found motherhood to be work that she did not like or do well. The most important point in Glubka's article is that women do not automatically share either the experience of motherhood or the desire to nurture. This article raises a number of other questions, for example: How is the experience of ending a relationship of mother to one's child like and different from the more common experience of ending a conventional marriage? How does the decision to give up one's child contrast with the experience of lesbian women who are forced to give up their children? In what ways does the experience of closeting the reality of rejected motherhood compare with closeting one's sexual preference? If the biological act of giving birth does not inevitably create for women the desire to carry out the role of "mother," what are the possibilities that parenting can be more equally distributed between men and women?

From where do females receive messages about motherhood? This is a particularly important question in light of the ever-increasing rates of teenage pregnancy and motherhood. Among Afro-American teenagers, the rate is the highest in the world. Bell Hooks suggests that while a resurgence of interest in motherhood has positive implications, there are also some very disturbing ones. Hooks notes the perspective voiced by many white career women now choosing to bear children which says to masses of women that careers or work can never be as important or as rewarding as bearing children.

> This is an especially dangerous line of thinking, coming at a time when teenage women who have not realized a number of goals, are bearing children in large numbers . . . when masses of women are being told by the government that they are destroying family life by not assuming sexist-defined roles. . . . women are currently inundated with material encouraging them to bear children. Newspapers carry headline stories with titles like "motherhood is making a comeback"; . . . television talk shows do special features on career women who are now choosing to raise children. Coming at a time when women with children are more likely to live in poverty, when the number of homeless, parentless children increases by the thousands daily, when women continue to assume sole responsibility for parenting, such propaganda undermines and threatens feminist movement. (Hooks 1984: 136–137)

Finally, there is an issue not explicitly addressed in the following articles but underlying much of the discussion in women's studies and in public policy forums. The issue is that of the "feminization of poverty." This catchy phrase, sometimes inverted to the "pauperization of females," is supposed to capture the reality that women and their dependent children make up an increasing proportion of the poor in the United States.

According to some feminists, the feminization of poverty is important to the women's movement since it "offers a new bond which cuts across class, age, race and sexual preference because women are in fact just a husband away from poverty" (Democratic Socialists of America 1983). There are several fundamental distortions in this concept. It implies that gender—not class—has become the determinant of poverty (Burnham 1985), and that *all* women are equally vulnerable to the threat of poverty. This latter point is asserted in statements such as this: "Virtually all women are vulnerable—a divorce or widowhood is all it takes to throw many middle class women into poverty" (Ehrenreich and Stallard 1983: 9). The feminization-of-poverty notion de-emphasizes and therefore grossly distorts the importance of racism in setting the lines as to who will be poor in the United States. Not all poor people are people of color. But people of color are disproportionately represented among the poor. In Afro-American, Asian American, Chicano, Native American, and Puerto Rican communities, it is not just women who are poor—it is women, children, and men. Thus, the concept of the feminization of poverty underestimates the profound plight of black and other men of color. (An estimated 46 percent of all black men are jobless, including the unemployed, those not looking for work, those in correctional facilities or those unaccounted for [Burnham 1985: 18–23].)

The racial and class bias in the feminization-of-poverty concept must be recognized. At the same time, the reality of the situation among US women must be accurately and effectively addressed. In the past twenty years, the proportion of families headed by women has increased from 9.3 percent in 1960 to 15.4 percent in 1980. These families have a poverty rate that is between four and five times higher than those headed by men. In 1982, the proportion of poor families headed by women rose to 47 percent and two-thirds of all poor black families are maintained by women alone.

The nature and state of "the American family" cannot be understood without a recognition of the diversity of the groupings which bear the label of "family" and the varied, complex, and often contradictory place of women within them. The articles which follow portray that diversity in terms of the composition of values and mores within families and within the roles of women who are a part of them. But these articles also suggest that despite these differences, there are some fundamental tasks to be done—nurturing, socializing, and housekeeping, and at this point in history, primary (but in some cases secondary) responsibility for those tasks within families rests with US women.

References Cited

Beck, E. T.
1983   "The Motherhood That Dare Not Speak Its Name." *Women's Studies
        Quarterly*, XI(A): 8–11.

Billingsley, A.
1968 *Black Families in White America.* Englewood Cliffs, N.J.: Prentice Hall.

Burnham, L.
1985 "Has Poverty Been Feminized in Black America?" *Black Scholar: Journal of Black Studies and Research*, XVI(2): 14–24.

Democratic Socialists of America (DSA).
1983 Bay Area Newsletter, May.

Ehrenreich, B., and K. Stallard.
1983 *Poverty in the American Dream.* Boston: South End Press.

Flax, J.
1983 "Contemporary American Families: Decline or Transformation." In *Families, Politics and Public Policy*, I. Diamond, ed., pp. 21–40. New York: Longman.

Giddings, P.
1984 *When and Where I Enter.* New York: William Morrow.

Hooks, B.
1984 *Feminist Theory: From Margin to Center.* Boston: South End Press.

Ladner, J.
1971 *Tomorrow's Tomorrow: The Black Woman.* Garden City, N.Y.: Doubleday.

Mirande, A., and E. Enriquez.
1979 *La Chicana: The Mexican-American Woman.* Chicago: University of Chicago Press.

Moynihan, D. P.
1965 *The Negro Family: The Case for National Action.* Washington, D.C.: U.S. Department of Labor, Office of Policy Planning and Research.

Schneider, S. W.
1984 "Jewish Women in the Nuclear Family and Beyond." In *Jewish and Female*, S. W. Schneider, ed., pp. 255–286. New York: Simon and Schuster.

Wright, R.
1978 "A Man Looks At the Equal Rights Amendment." In *Sex, Family and the New Right*, L. Gordon and A. Hunter, eds., pp. 1–7. Somerville, Mass.: New England Free Press.

10

The Problem That Has No Name

Betty Friedan

The problem lay buried, unspoken, for many years in the minds of American women. It was a strange stirring, a sense of dissatisfaction, a yearning that women suffered in the middle of the twentieth century in the United States. Each suburban wife struggled with it alone. As she made the beds, shopped for groceries, matched slipcover material, ate peanut butter sandwiches with her children, chauffeured Cub Scouts and Brownies, lay beside her husband at night—she was afraid to ask even of herself the silent question—"Is this all?"

For over fifteen years there was no word of this yearning in the millions of words written about women, for women, in all the columns, books and articles by experts telling women their role was to seek fulfillment as wives and mothers. Over and over women heard in voices of tradition and of Freudian sophistication that they could desire no greater destiny than to glory in their own femininity. . . . They were taught to pity the neurotic, unfeminine, unhappy women who wanted to be poets or physicists or presidents. They learned that truly feminine women do not want careers, higher education, political rights—

Abridged from *The Feminine Mystique* by Betty Friedan by permission of W. W. Norton & Company, Inc., and the author. Copyright © 1983, 1974, 1973, 1963 by Betty Friedan.

the independence and the opportunities that the old-fashioned feminists fought for. . . .

By the end of the nineteen-fifties, the average marriage age of women in America dropped to 20, and was still dropping, into the teens. Fourteen million girls were engaged by 17. The proportion of women attending college in comparison with men dropped from 47 per cent in 1920 to 35 per cent in 1958. A century earlier, women had fought for higher education; now girls went to college to get a husband. By the mid-fifties, 60 per cent dropped out of college to marry, or because they were afraid too much education would be a marriage bar. Colleges built dormitories for "married students," but the students were almost always the husbands. A new degree was instituted for the wives—"Ph.T." (Putting Husband Through).

Then American girls began getting married in high school. And the women's magazines, deploring the unhappy statistics about these young marriages, urged that courses on marriage, and marriage counselors, be installed in the high schools. Girls started going steady at twelve and thirteen, in junior high. Manufacturers put out brassieres with false bosoms of foam rubber for little girls of ten. And an advertisement for a child's dress, sizes 3–6x, in the *New York Times* in the fall of 1960, said: "She Too Can Join the Man-Trap Set." . . .

In a New York hospital, a woman had a nervous breakdown when she found she could not breastfeed her baby. In other hospitals, women dying of cancer refused a drug which research had proved might save their lives: its side effects were said to be unfeminine. "If I have only one life, let me live it as a blonde," a larger-than-life-sized picture of a pretty, vacuous woman proclaimed from newspaper, magazine, and drugstore ads. And across America, three out of every ten women dyed their hair blonde. They ate a chalk called Metrecal, instead of food, to shrink to the size of the thin young models. Department-store buyers reported that American women, since 1939, had become three and four sizes smaller. "Women are out to fit the clothes, instead of vice-versa," one buyer said.

Interior decorators were designing kitchens with mosaic murals and original paintings, for kitchens were once again the center of women's lives. Home sewing became a million-dollar industry. Many women no longer left their homes, except to shop, chauffeur their children, or attend a social engagement with their husbands. Girls were growing up in America without ever having jobs outside the home. In the late fifties, a sociological phenomenon was suddenly remarked: a third of American women now worked, but most were no longer young and very few were pursuing careers. They were married women who held part-time jobs, selling or secretarial, to put their husbands through school, their sons through college, or to help pay the mortgage. Or they were widows supporting families. Fewer and fewer women were entering professional work. The shortages in the nursing, social work, and teaching professions caused crises in almost every American city. Concerned over the Soviet Union's lead in the space race, scientists noted that America's greatest source of unused brain-power was women. But girls would not study physics: it was "unfeminine." . . .

The suburban housewife—she was the dream image of the young American women and the envy, it was said, of women all over the world. The American housewife—freed by science and labor-saving appliances from the drudgery, the dangers of childbirth and the illnesses of her grandmother. She was healthy, beautiful, educated, concerned only about her husband, her children, her home. She had found true feminine fulfillment. As a housewife and mother, she was respected as a full and equal partner to man in his world. She was free to choose automobiles, clothes, appliances, supermarkets; she had everything that women ever dreamed of.

In the fifteen years after World War II, this mystique of feminine fulfillment became the cherished and self-perpetuating core of contemporary American culture. . . .

For over fifteen years, the words written for women, and the words women used when they talked to each other, while their husbands sat on the other side of the room and talked shop or politics or septic tanks, were about problems with their children, or how to keep their husbands happy, or improve their children's school, or cook chicken or make slipcovers. Nobody argued whether women were inferior or superior to men; they were simply different. Words like "emancipation" and "career" sounded strange and embarrassing; no one had used them for years. When a Frenchwoman named Simone de Beauvoir wrote a book called *The Second Sex*, an American critic commented that she obviously "didn't know what life was all about," and besides, she was talking about French women. The "woman problem" in America no longer existed.

If a woman had a problem in the 1950's and 1960's, she knew that something must be wrong with her marriage, or with herself. Other women were satisfied with their lives, she thought. What kind of a woman was she if she did not feel this mysterious fulfillment waxing the kitchen floor? She was so ashamed to admit her dissatisfaction that she never knew how many other women shared it. If she tried to tell her husband, he didn't understand what she was talking about. She did not really understand it herself. For over fifteen years women in America found it harder to talk about this problem than about sex. Even the psychoanalysts had no name for it. When a woman went to a psychiatrist for help, as many women did, she would say, "I'm so ashamed," or "I must be hopelessly neurotic." "I don't know what's wrong with women today," a suburban psychiatrist said uneasily. "I only know something is wrong because most of my patients happen to be women. And their problem isn't sexual." Most women with this problem did not go to see a psychoanalyst, however. "There's nothing wrong really," they kept telling themselves. "There isn't any problem."

But on an April morning in 1959, I heard a mother of four, having coffee with four other mothers in a suburban development fifteen miles from New York, say in a tone of quiet desperation, "the problem." And the others knew, without words, that she was not talking about a problem with her husband, or her children, or her home. Suddenly they realized they all shared the same problem, the problem that has no name. They began, hesitantly, to talk about it. Later, after they had picked up their children at nursery school and taken them home to nap, two of the women cried, in sheer relief, just to know they were not alone. . . .

Just what was this problem that has no name? What were the words women used when they tried to express it? Sometimes a woman would say "I feel empty somehow . . . incomplete." Or she would say, "I feel as if I don't exist." Sometimes she blotted out the feeling with a tranquilizer. Sometimes she thought the problem was with her husband, or her children, or that what she really needed was to redecorate her house, or move to a better neighborhood, or have an affair, or another baby. Sometimes, she went to a doctor with symptoms she could hardly describe: "A tired feeling . . . I get so angry with the children it scares me . . . I feel like crying without any reason." (A Cleveland doctor called it "the housewife's syndrome.") A number of women told me about great bleeding blisters that break out on their hands and arms. "I call it the housewife's blight," said a family doctor in Pennsylvania. "I see it so often lately in these young women with four, five and six children who bury themselves in their dishpans. But it isn't caused by detergent and it isn't cured by cortisone." . . .

A mother of four who left college at nineteen to get married told me:

> I've tried everything women are supposed to do—hobbies, gardening, pickling, canning, being very social with my neighbors, joining committees, running PTA teas. I can do it all, and I like it, but it doesn't leave you anything to think about—any feeling of who you are. I never had any career ambitions. All I wanted was to get married and have four children. I love the kids and Bob and my home. There's no problem you can even put a name to. But I'm desperate. I begin to feel I have no personality. I'm a server of food and putter-on of pants and a bedmaker, somebody who can be called on when you want something. But who am I?

A twenty-three-year-old mother in blue jeans said:

I ask myself why I'm so dissatisfied. I've got my health, fine children, a lovely new home, enough money. My husband has a real future as an electronics engineer. He doesn't have any of these feelings. He says maybe I need a vacation, let's go to New York for a weekend. But that isn't it. I always had this idea we should do everything together. I can't sit down and read a book alone. If the children are napping and I have one hour to myself I just walk through the house waiting for them to wake up. I don't make a move until I know where the rest of the crowd is going. It's as if ever since you were a little girl, there's always been somebody or something that will take care of your life: your parents, or college, or falling in love, or having a child, or moving to a new house. Then you wake up one morning and there's nothing to look forward to.

A young wife in a Long Island development said:

I seem to sleep so much. I don't know why I should be so tired. This house isn't nearly so hard to clean as the cold-water flat we had when I was working. The children are at school all day. It's not the work. I just don't feel alive.

In 1960, the problem that has no name burst like a boil through the image of the happy American housewife. In the television commercials the pretty housewives still beamed over their foaming dishpans and *Time's* cover story on "The Suburban Wife, an American Phenomenon" protested: "Having too good a time . . . to believe that they should be unhappy." But the actual unhappiness of the American housewife was suddenly being reported—from the *New York Times* and *Newsweek* to *Good Housekeeping* and CBS Television ("The Trapped Housewife"), although almost everybody who talked about it found some superficial reason to dismiss it. . . . Some said it was the old problem—education: more and more women had education, which naturally made them unhappy in their role as housewives. "The road from Freud to Frigidaire, from Sophocles to Spock, has turned out to be a bumpy one," reported the *New York Times* (June 28, 1960). . . .

Home economists suggested more realistic preparation for housewives, such as high-school workshops in home appliances. College educators suggested more discussion groups on home management and the family, to prepare women for the adjustment to domestic life. A spate of articles appeared in the mass magazines offering "Fifty-eight Ways to Make Your Marriage More Exciting." No month went by without a new book by a psychiatrist or sexologist offering technical advice on finding greater fulfillment through sex.

A male humorist joked in *Harper's Bazaar* (July, 1960) that the problem could be solved by taking away woman's right to vote. ("In the pre-19th Amendment era, the American woman was placid, sheltered and sure of her role in American society. She left all the political decisions to her husband and he, in turn, left all the family decisions to her. Today a woman has to make both the family *and* the political decisions, and it's too much for her.")

A number of educators suggested seriously that women no longer be admitted to the four-year colleges and universities: in the growing college crisis, the education which girls could not use as housewives was more urgently needed than ever by boys to do the work of the atomic age.

The problem was also dismissed with drastic solutions no one could take seriously. (A woman writer proposed in *Harper's* that women be drafted for compulsory service as nurses' aides and baby-sitters.) And it was smoothed over with the age-old panaceas: "love is their answer," "the only answer is inner help," "the secret of completeness—children," "a private means of intellectual fulfillment," "to cure this toothache of the spirit—the simple formula of handing one's self and one's will over to God."[1]

The problem was dismissed by telling the housewife she doesn't realize how lucky she is—her own boss, no time clock, no junior executive gunning for her job. . . .

The problem was also, and finally, dismissed by shrugging that there are no solutions: this is what being a woman means, and what is wrong with American women that they can't accept their role gracefully? As *Newsweek* put it (March 7, 1960):

> She is dissatisfied with a lot that women of other lands can only dream of. Her discontent is deep, pervasive, and impervious to the superficial remedies which are offered at every hand. . . . An army of professional explorers have already charted the major sources of trouble. . . . From the beginning of time, the female cycle has defined and confined woman's role. As Freud was credited with saying: "Anatomy is destiny." Though no group of women has ever pushed these natural restrictions as far as the American wife, it seems that she still cannot accept them with good grace. . . . A young mother with a beautiful family, charm, talent and brains is apt to dismiss her role apologetically. "What do I do?" you hear her say. "Why nothing. I'm just a housewife." A good education, it seems, has given this paragon among women an understanding of the value of everything except her own worth. . . .

The alternative offered was a choice that few women would contemplate. In the sympathetic words of the *New York Times*: "All admit to being deeply frustrated at times by the lack of privacy, the physical burden, the routine of family life, the confinement of it. However, none would give up her home and family if she had the choice to make again." . . .

The year American women's discontent boiled over, it was also reported (*Look*) that the more than 21,000,000 American women who are single, widowed, or divorced do not cease even after fifty their frenzied, desperate search for a man. And the search begins early—for seventy per cent of all American women now marry before they are twenty-four. A pretty twenty-five-year-old secretary took thirty-five different jobs in six months in the futile hope of finding a husband. Women were moving from one political club to another, taking evening courses in accounting or sailing, learning to play golf or ski, joining a number of churches in succession, going to bars alone, in their ceaseless search for a man.

Of the growing thousands of women currently getting private psychiatric help in the United States, the married ones were reported dissatisfied with their marriages, the unmarried ones suffering from anxiety and, finally, depression. Strangely, a number of psychiatrists stated that, in their experience, unmarried women patients were happier than married ones. . . .

Even so, most men, and some women, still did not know that this problem was real. But those who had faced it honestly knew that all the superficial remedies, the sympathetic advice, the scolding words and the cheering words were somehow drowning the problem in unreality. A bitter laugh was beginning to be heard from American women. They were admired, envied, pitied, theorized over until they were sick of it, offered drastic solutions or silly choices that no one could take seriously. They got all kinds of advice from the growing armies of marriage and child-guidance counselors, psychotherapists, and armchair psychologists, on how to adjust to their role as housewives. No other road to fulfillment was offered to American women in the middle of the twentieth century. Most adjusted to their role and suffered or ignored the problem that has no name. It can be less painful, for a woman, not to hear the strange, dissatisfied voice stirring within her.

It is no longer possible to ignore that voice, to dismiss the desperation of so many American women. This is not what being a woman means, no matter what the experts say. For human suffering there is a reason; perhaps the reason has not been found because the right questions have not been asked, or pressed far enough. I do not accept the answer that there is no problem because American women have luxuries that women in other times and lands never dreamed of; part of the strange newness of the problem is that it cannot be understood in terms of the age-old material problems of man: poverty, sickness, hunger, cold. The women who suffer this problem have a hunger that food cannot fill. It persists in women whose husbands are struggling interns and law clerks, or prosperous doctors and lawyers; in wives of workers and executives who make $5,000 a year or $50,000. . . .

It is no longer possible today to blame the problem on loss of femininity: to say that education and independence and equality with men have made American women unfeminine. I have heard so many women try to deny this dissatisfied voice within themselves because it does not fit the pretty picture of femininity the experts have given them. I think, in fact, that this is the first clue to the mystery: the problem cannot be understood in the generally accepted terms by which scientists have studied women, doctors have treated them, counselors have advised them, and writers have written about them. . . .

Are the women who finished college, the women who once had dreams beyond housewifery, the ones who suffer the most? According to the experts they are, but listen to these four women:

> My days are all busy, and dull, too. All I ever do is mess around. I get up at eight—I make breakfast, so I do the dishes, have lunch, do some more dishes and some laundry and cleaning in the afternoon. Then it's supper dishes and I get to sit down a few minutes before the children have to be sent to bed. . . . That's all there is to my day. It's just like any other wife's day. Humdrum. The biggest time, I am chasing kids.

> Ye Gods, what do I do with my time? Well, I get up at six. I get my son dressed and then give him breakfast. After that I wash dishes and bathe and feed the baby. Then I get lunch and while the children nap, I sew or mend or iron and do all the other things I can't get done before noon. Then I cook supper for the family and my husband watches TV while I do the dishes. After I get the children to bed, I set my hair and then I go to bed.

> The problem is always being the children's mommy, or the minister's wife and never being myself.

> A film made of any typical morning in my house would look like an old Marx Brothers' comedy. I wash the dishes, rush the older children off to school, dash out in the yard to cultivate the chrysanthemums, run back in to make a phone call about a committee meeting, help the youngest child build a blockhouse, spend fifteen minutes skimming the newspapers so I can be well-informed, then scamper down to the washing machines where my thrice-weekly laundry includes enough clothes to keep a primitive village going for an entire year. By noon I'm ready for a padded cell. Very little of what I've done has been really necessary or important. Outside pressures lash me through the day. Yet I look upon myself as one of the more relaxed housewives in the neighborhood. Many of my friends are even more frantic. In the past sixty years we have come full circle and the American housewife is once again trapped in a squirrel cage. If the cage is now a modern plate-glass-and-broadloom ranch house or a convenient

modern apartment, the situation is no less painful than when her grand-mother sat over an embroidery hoop in her gilt-and-plush parlor and mut-tered angrily about women's rights.

The first two women never went to college. They live in develop-ments in Levittown, New Jersey, and Tacoma, Washington, and were interviewed by a team of sociologists studying workingmen's wives.[2] The third, a minister's wife, wrote on the fifteenth reunion question-naire of her college that she never had any career ambitions, but wishes now she had.[3] The fourth, who has a Ph.D. in anthropology, is today a Nebraska housewife with three children.[4] Their words seem to indicate that housewives of all educational levels suffer the same feel-ing of desperation.

The fact is that no one today is muttering angrily about "women's rights," even though more and more women have gone to college. In a recent study of all the classes that have graduated from Barnard Col-lege,[5] a significant minority of earlier graduates blamed their educa-tion for making them want "rights," later classes blamed their educa-tion for giving them career dreams, but recent graduates blamed the college for making them feel it was not enough simply to be a house-wife and mother; they did not want to feel guilty if they did not read books or take part in community activities. But if education is not the cause of the problem, the fact that education somehow festers in these women may be a clue.

If the secret of feminine fulfillment is having children, never have so many women, with the freedom to choose, had so many children, in so few years, so willingly. If the answer is love, never have women searched for love with such determination. And yet there is a growing suspicion that the problem may not be sexual, though it must somehow be related to sex. I have heard from many doctors evidence of new sex-ual problems between man and wife—sexual hunger in wives so great their husbands cannot satisfy it. "We have made women a sex crea-ture," said a psychiatrist at the Margaret Sanger marriage counseling clinic. . . . Why is there such a market for books and articles offering sexual advice? The kind of sexual orgasm which Kinsey found in statis-tical plenitude in the recent generations of American women does not seem to make this problem go away.

On the contrary, new neuroses are being seen among women—and problems as yet unnamed as neuroses—which Freud and his followers did not predict, with physical symptoms, anxieties, and defense mech-anisms equal to those caused by sexual repression. And strange new problems are being reported in the growing generations of children whose mothers were always there, driving them around, helping them with their homework—an inability to endure pain or discipline or pursue any self-sustained goal of any sort, a devastating boredom with life. . . .

A White House conference was held on the physical and muscular deterioration of American children: were they being over-nurtured? Sociologists noted the astounding organization of suburban children's lives: the lessons, parties, entertainments, play and study groups organized for them. . . .

Can the problem that has no name be somehow related to the domestic routine of the housewife? When a woman tries to put the problem into words, she often merely describes the daily life she leads. What is there in this recital of comfortable domestic detail that could possibly cause such a feeling of desperation? Is she trapped simply by the enormous demands of her role as modern housewife: wife, mistress, mother, nurse, consumer, cook, chauffeur; expert on interior decoration, child care, appliance repair, furniture refinishing, nutrition, and education? . . . She has no time to read books, only magazines; even if she had time, she has lost the power to concentrate. At the end of the day, she is so terribly tired that sometimes her husband has to take over and put the children to bed.

This terrible tiredness took so many women to doctors in the 1950's that one decided to investigate it. He found, surprisingly, that his patients suffering from "housewife's fatigue" slept more than an adult needed to sleep—as much as ten hours a day—and that the actual energy they expended on housework did not tax their capacity. The real problem must be something else, he decided—perhaps boredom. Some doctors told their women patients they must get out of the house for a day, treat themselves to a movie in town. Others prescribed tranquilizers. Many suburban housewives were taking tranquilizers like cough drops. . . .

It is easy to see the concrete details that trap the suburban housewife, the continual demands on her time. But the chains that bind her in her trap are chains in her own mind and spirit. They are chains made up of mistaken ideas and misinterpreted facts, of incomplete truths and unreal choices. They are not easily seen and not easily shaken off.

How can any woman see the whole truth within the bounds of her own life? How can she believe that voice inside herself, when it denies the conventional, accepted truths by which she has been living? And yet the women I have talked to, who are finally listening to that inner voice, seem in some incredible way to be groping through to a truth that has defied the experts. . . .

I began to see in a strange new light the American return to early marriage and the large families that are causing the population explosion; the recent movement to natural childbirth and breastfeeding;

suburban conformity, and the new neuroses, character pathologies and sexual problems being reported by the doctors. I began to see new dimensions to old problems that have long been taken for granted among women: menstrual difficulties, sexual frigidity, promiscuity, pregnancy fears, childbirth depression, the high incidence of emotional breakdown and suicide among women in their twenties and thirties, the menopause crises, the so-called passivity and immaturity of American men, the discrepancy between women's tested intellectual abilities in childhood and their adult achievement, the changing incidence of adult sexual orgasm in American women, and persistent problems in psychotherapy and in women's education.

If I am right, the problem that has no name stirring in the minds of so many American women today is not a matter of loss of femininity or too much education, or the demands of domesticity. It is far more important than anyone recognizes. It is the key to these other new and old problems which have been torturing women and their husbands and children, and puzzling their doctors and educators for years. It may well be the key to our future as a nation and a culture. We can no longer ignore that voice within women that says: "I want something more than my husband and my children and my home."

Notes

1. See the Seventy-fifth Anniversary Issue of *Good Housekeeping*, May, 1960, "The Gift of Self," a symposium by Margaret Mead, Jessamyn West, *et al.*
2. Lee Rainwater, Richard P. Coleman, and Gerald Handel, *Workingman's Wife*, New York, 1959.
3. Betty Friedan, "If One Generation Can Ever Tell Another," *Smith Alumnae Quarterly*, Northampton, Mass., Winter, 1961. I first became aware of "the problem that has no name" and its possible relationship to what I finally called "the feminine mystique" in 1957, when I prepared an intensive questionnaire and conducted a survey of my own Smith College classmates fifteen years after graduation. This questionnaire was later used by alumnae classes of Radcliffe and other women's colleges with similar results.
4. Jhan and June Robbins, "Why Young Mothers Feel Trapped," *Redbook*, September, 1960.
5. Marian Freda Poverman, "Alumnae on Parade," *Barnard Alumnae Magazine*, July, 1957.

11

End of the Beginning

Betty Friedan

I did not intend to write another book on the woman question. I have already started a major new quest that is taking me way beyond my previous concerns, opening strange doors. I am tired of the pragmatic, earthbound battles of the women's movement, tired of rhetoric. I want to live the rest of my life.

But these past few years, fulfilling my professional and political commitments, and picking up the pieces of my personal life, for which the women's movement has been the focus for nearly twenty years, I have been nagged by a new, uneasy urgency that won't let me leave. Listening to my own daughter and sons, and others of their generation whom I meet, lecturing at universities or professional conferences or feminist networks around the country and around the world, I sense something *off*, out of focus, going wrong, in the terms by which they are trying to live the equality we fought for.

From these daughters—getting older now, working so hard, determined not to be trapped as their mothers were, and expecting so much, taking for granted the opportunities we had to struggle for—I've begun to hear undertones of pain and puzzlement, a queasiness, an uneasiness, almost a bitterness that they hardly dare admit. As if with all those opportunities that we won for them, and envy them, how can they ask out loud certain questions, talk about certain other needs they aren't supposed to worry about—those old needs which shaped our lives, and trapped us, and against which we rebelled?

• In California, in the office of a television producer who prides himself on being an "equal opportunity employer," I am confronted by his new "executive assistant." She wants to talk to me alone before her boss comes in. Lovely, in her late twenties and "dressed for success" like a model in the latest *Vogue*, she is not just a glorified secretary with a fancy title in a dead-end job. The woman she replaced has just been promoted to the position of "creative vice-president."

"I know I'm lucky to have this job," she says, defensive and accusing, "but you people who fought for these things had your families. You already had your men and children. What are we supposed to do?"

She complains that the older woman vice-president, one of the early radical feminists who vowed never to marry or have children, didn't understand her quandary. "All she wants," the executive assistant says, "is more power in the company." . . .

Mounting the barricades yet again in the endless battle for the Equal Rights Amendment—in Illinois, at the national political conventions—I also sensed a political bewilderment, a frustration, a flagging, finally, of energy for battle at all. It is hard to keep summoning energy for battles like ERA, which, according to all the polls and the public commitment of elected officials and political parties, should have been won long ago; or for the right to choose when and whether to have a child, and thus to safe, legal, medical help in abortion—won eight years ago and decreed by the Supreme Court more basic than many of the rights guaranteed in the Constitution and the Bill of Rights as it was written of, by, and for men—only to be fought over and over again, until even the Supreme Court in 1980 took that right away for poor women.

I sense other victories we thought were won yielding illusory gains; I see new dimensions to problems we thought were solved. As, for instance, the laws against sex discrimination in employment and education, and the affirmative action programs and class-action suits that have given women access to professions and executive jobs held only by men before. Yet, after fifteen years of the women's movement, the gap between women's earnings and men's is greater than ever, women earning on the average only fifty-nine cents to every dollar men earn, the average male high school dropout today earning $1,600 more a year than female college graduates. An unprecedented majority of women have entered the work force in these years, but the overwhelming majority of women are still crowded into the poorly paid service and clerical jobs traditionally reserved for females. (With the divorce rate exceeding 50 percent, it turns out that 71 percent of divorced women are now working compared to only 78 percent of divorced men; the women must be taking jobs the men won't touch.)

What will happen in the eighties as inflation, not just new aspirations, forces women to keep working, while unemployment, already reaching 7.8 percent, hits women the worst? Growing millions of "discouraged workers," who are no longer counted among the unemployed because they have stopped looking for jobs, were reported in 1980, two-thirds of them women.

It becomes clear that the great momentum of the women's movement for equality will be stopped, or somehow transformed, by collision or convergence with basic questions of survival in the 1980s. Is feminism a theoretical luxury, a liberal or radical notion we could toy with in the late soft age of affluence, in the decadence of advanced capitalist society, but in the face of 10 percent inflation, 7.8 percent unemployment, nuclear accident at home, and mounting terrorism from Right and Left abroad, something we must put aside for the grim new realities of economic and national survival? Or is equality itself becoming a question of basic human survival? . . .

In the state of New York, where I live now, a so-called "Equitable" Divorce Reform law was passed. Under this law a woman who has been a housewife for many years, or has not earned as much as her husband, will have to pay lawyers, appraisers and accountants to "prove" on ten counts the "equitability" of her contribution to their marriage. She has to prove this in economic terms in order to receive on divorce a decent share of whatever property or other assets were accumulated during the marriage, even if the house is in her name. The rhetoric of "women's lib" was used to justify the granting to such a divorced wife only "maintenance," as for an automobile, to be cut off, after one or two years of "rehabilitation," however long she might have been a housewife, however ill-equipped to earn, however unstable her job. The legislators ignored the census figures revealing 8 million female-headed households in 1979, a 46 percent increase since 1970, half existing on less than $10,000 a year, one third on less than $7,000. . . .

In that same period, I got a phone call asking me to speak at a "March Against Pornography," which was being billed by the media as the new frontier of feminism. I found myself snapping, "I'll be out of town." It seemed irrelevant, wrong, for women to be wasting energy marching against pornography—or any other sexual issue—when their very economic survival was at stake.

Also about that time, I found myself walking out in the middle of the monthly lunch of the Women's Forum, our "new girls" equivalent of the old boys' network, unable to sit through another corporate big-wig's tips on how women can get "real power" in the executive suite. Was this what the women's movement was all about?

Even in that "new girls" network of the women who've broken through to the executive suite and enjoyed the tokens of professional and political equality, I sense the exhilaration of "superwomen" giving way to a tiredness, a certain brittle disappointment, a disillusionment with "assertiveness training" and the rewards of power. Matina Horner, the high-powered president of Radcliffe, calls it a "crisis of confidence." . . .

Of course, the women's movement has for some years been the scapegoat for the rage of threatened, insecure housewives who can no longer count on husbands for lifelong support. Recently I've been hearing younger women, and even older feminists, blame the women's movement for the supposed increase of male impotence, the inadequacy or unavailability of men for the "new women." Some even suggest that the recent explosion of rape, "battered wives," "battered children" and violence in the family is a reaction to, or byproduct of, feminism.

The women's movement is being blamed, above all, for the destruction of the family. Churchmen and sociologists proclaim that the American family, as it has always been defined, is becoming an "endangered species," with the rising divorce rate and the enormous increase in single-parent families and people—especially women—living alone. Women's abdication of their age-old responsibility for the family is also being blamed for the apathy and moral delinquency of the "me generation."

Can we keep on shrugging all this off as enemy propaganda—"their problem, not ours"? I think we must at least admit and begin openly to discuss feminist denial of the importance of family, of women's own needs to give and get love and nurture, tender loving care. . . .

What worries me today is "choices" women have supposedly won, which are not real. How can a woman freely "choose" to have a child when her paycheck is needed for the rent or mortgage, when her job isn't geared to taking care of a child, when there is no national policy for parental leave, and no assurance that her job will be waiting for her if she takes off to have a child?

What worries me today is that despite the fact that more than 45 percent of the mothers of children under six are now working because of economic necessity due to inflation, compared with only 10 percent in 1960 (and, according to a Ford Foundation study, it is estimated that by 1990 only one out of four mothers will be at home full time), no major national effort is being made for child-care services by government, business, labor, Democratic or Republican parties—or by the women's movement itself. . . .

When I think back to the explosion of the women's movement at the opening of the decade—thousands of women marching down Fifth Avenue on August 26, 1970, in that first nationwide women's strike for equality, carrying banners for "Equal Rights to Jobs and Education," "The Right to Abortion," "24-Hour Child Care," "Political Power to the Women"—our agenda then seemed so simple and straightforward.

But on August 26, 1980, the women's movement was too tired from these endless, never finished real battles for equality to mount a nationwide symbolic march. NOW leaders were exhausted by their eighth unsuccessful attempt to get the ERA ratified in Illinois. The march of nearly 100,000 on Mother's Day, 1980, in Chicago, astounding in these days of apathy, greater than any Presidential candidate could summon, did not budge the Illinois state legislature. . . .

So, in 1980, the only battle against right-wing control of the Republican convention in Detroit was put up by women, and men, too, who protested in vain against repudiation by the Republican platform of their half-century endorsement of the Equal Rights Amendment. And the Republicans pledged instead to name only judges who would prosecute abortion as murder. Would Republican women then repudiate Reagan or keep their mouths shut and vote against their own interests as women? After all, just one state had ratified the ERA under the Democratic President who had said only "Life is not fair" when federal funding was barred for poor women needing abortion. . . .

This uneasy sense of battles won, only to be fought over again, of battles that should have been won, according to all the rules, and yet are not, of battles that suddenly one does not really want to win, and the weariness of battle altogether—how many women feel it? What does it mean? This nervousness in the women's movement, this sense of enemies and dangers, omnipresent, unseen, of shadowboxing enemies who aren't there—are they paranoid phantoms, and if so, why do these enemies always win? This unarticulated malaise now within the women's movement—is something wonderful dulling, dwindling, tarnishing from going on too long, or coming to an end too soon, before it is really finished?

Though the women's movement has changed all our lives and surpassed our dreams in its magnitude, and our daughters take their own personhood and equality for granted, they—and we—are finding that it's not so easy to *live*, with or without men and children, solely on the basis of that first feminist agenda. I think, in fact, that the women's movement has come just about as far as it can in terms of women alone. The very choices, options, aspirations, opportunities that we have won for women—no matter how far from real equality—and the small degree of new power women now enjoy, or hunger for, openly, honestly, as never before, are converging on and into new economic and emotional urgencies. Battles lost or won are being fought in terms that are somehow inadequate, irrelevant to this new personal, and political, reality. I believe it's over, that first stage: the women's movement. And yet the larger revolution, evolution, liberation that the women's movement set off, has barely begun. How do we move on? What are the terms of the second stage? . . .

What are the limits and the true potential of women's power? I believe that the women's movement, in the political sense, is both less and more powerful than we realize. I believe that the personal is both more and less political than our own rhetoric ever implied. I believe that we have to break through our own *feminist* mystique now to come to terms with the new reality of our personal and political experience, and to move into the second stage.

All this past year, with some reluctance and dread, and a strange, compelling relief, I've been asking new questions and listening with a new urgency to other women again, wondering if anyone else reads these signs as beginning-of-the-end, end-of-the-beginning. When I start to talk about them, it makes some women, feminists and antifeminists, uncomfortable, even angry.

There is a disconcerted silence, an uneasy murmuring, when I begin to voice my hunches out loud:

> *The second stage cannot be seen in terms of women alone, our separate personhood or equality with men.*
> *The second stage involves coming to new terms with the family—new terms with love and with work.*
> *The second stage may not even be a women's movement. Men may be at the cutting edge of the second stage.*
> *The second stage has to transcend the battle for equal power in institutions. The second stage will restructure institutions and transform the nature of power itself.*
> *The second stage may even now be evolving, out of or even aside from what we have thought of as our battle. . . .*

"How can you talk about the second stage when we haven't even won the first yet?" a woman asks me at a Catholic college weekend for housewives going back to work. "The men still have the power. We haven't gotten enough for ourselves yet. We have to fight now just to stay where we are, not to be pushed back."

But that's the point. Maybe we have to begin talking about the second stage to keep from getting locked into obsolete power games and irrelevant sexual battles that never can be won, or that we will lose by winning. Maybe only by moving into the second stage, and asking the new questions—political and personal—confronting women and men trying to live the equality we fought for, can we transcend the polarization that threatens even the gains already won, and prevent the ERA from being lost and the right to abortion and the laws against sex discrimination reversed. . . .

The women's movement didn't start with heroics, or even with the political rhetoric of revolution. For me, as for most others, it started with facing the concrete, mundane personal truth of my own life and hearing the personal truth of other women—the "problem that had no name" because it didn't quite fit the image of the happy suburban housewife we were all living in those days—that image of woman completely fulfilled in her role as husband's wife, children's mother, server of physical needs of husband, children, home. That image, which I called the "feminine mystique," bombarded us from all sides in the fifteen or twenty years after World War II, denying the very existence in women of the need to be and move in society and be recognized as a person, and individual in her own right.

We broke through that image. So for nearly twenty years now, the words written about and by and for women have been about women's need to be, first of all, themselves . . . to find themselves, fulfill themselves, their own personhood . . . to free themselves from submission as servants of the family and take control of their own bodies, their own lives . . . to find their own identity as separate from men, marriage and child-rearing—and to demand equal opportunity with men, power of their own in corporate office, Senate chamber, spaceship, ballfield, battlefield, at whatever price. . . .

I remain committed to these unfinished battles. We had to do what we did, to come out of the shadow of the feminine mystique, and into our personhood, as women. We had to fight for our equal opportunity to participate in the larger work and decisions of society and the equality in the family that such participation entails and requires. This was the essence of the women's movement—the first stage. It happened, not because I or any other feminist witch somehow seduced otherwise happy housewives by our words, but because of evolutionary necessity. . . .

The feminine mystique was obsolete. That's why our early battles were won so easily, once we engaged our will. It was, is, awesome—

that quantum jump in consciousness. A whole new literature, a new history, new dimensions in every field are now emerging, as the larger implications of women's personhood and equality are explored. The women's movement, which started with personal truth, not seen or understood by the experts, or even by women themselves, because it did not fit the accepted image, has, in the span of a single generation, changed life, and the accepted image.

But the new image, which has come out of the women's movement, cannot evade the continuing tests of real life. That uneasiness I have been sensing these past few years comes from personal truth denied and questions unasked because they do not fit the new accepted image—the *feminist* mystique—as our daughters live what we fought for. It took many centuries of social evolution, technological revolution, to disturb "the changeless face of Eve." That immutable, overshadowing definition of woman as breeder of the race, once rooted in biological, historical necessity, only became a mystique, a defense against reality, as it denied the possibilities and necessities of growth opened by women's new life span in advanced technological society.

Such is the accelerated pace of change today that it may take only a few years for the feminist image to harden into a similarly confining, defensive mystique. Does our feminist image already leave out important new, or old, dimensions of woman's possibility and necessity? I think the problem here is somehow to disentangle the basic truth of feminism from *reaction*—not just reaction against feminism, but the half-truth of *feminist reaction*. For insofar as the new feminist mystique is defined by reaction against the old feminine necessity, it could suppress important parts of our personhood—breeding a new "problem that has no name." It will not take long for younger daughters to rise against a mystique that does not truly open life for women. In another pendulum swing of reaction they could turn their backs again on the necessary, unfinished true battles of feminism, as some of us turned our backs on the life-serving core of feminine identity, along with the distorting, confining mystique. . . .

"I'm suffering from feminist fatigue," writes Lynda Hurst, a columnist on the *Toronto Star*, in a new non- or antifeminist sheet started in Canada in June 1980 called *Breakthrough*. "After the last dazzle of the [feminist] fireworks, there was deeper darkness. You are perhaps more enslaved now than you have ever been."

She says defiantly:

I've been letting sexist cracks slip past with barely a shrug. I haven't read *Ms.* magazine in months. I can sleep nights without worrying about my

lack of a five-year career plan. I can even watch "I Love Lucy" reruns
without tsk-tsking over the rampant sexism of the Ricardo marriage.

Don't get me wrong. It's not the women's movement I'm fed up with.
. . . It's the "feminist" label—and its paranoid associations—that I've
started to resent. I'm developing an urge to run around telling people that
I still like raindrops on roses and whiskers on kittens, and that being the
local easy-to-bait feminist is getting to be a bore.

I'm tired of having other people (women as well as men) predict my
opinion on everything from wedding showers to coed hockey. . . .

I don't want to be stuck today with a feminist label any more than I
would have wanted to be known as a "dumb blonde" in the fifties. The libber label limits and shortchanges those who are tagged with it. And the
irony is that it emerged from a philosophy that set out to destroy the
whole notion of female tagging.

I write this book to help the daughters break through the mystique
I myself helped to create—and put the right name to their new problems. They have to ask new questions, speak the unspeakable again, admit new, uncomfortable realities, and secret pains and surprising joys
of their personal truth that are hard to put into words because they do
not fit either the new or old images of women, or they fit them discon-
certingly.

These questions come into consciousness as personal ones, each
daughter thinking maybe she alone feels this way. The questions have
to be asked personally before they become political. Or rather, these
simple, heartfelt questions I've been hearing from young women all
over the country this past year seem to me to indicate a blind spot in
feminism that is both personal and political in its implications and
consequences. The younger women have the most questions:

"How can I have it all? Do I *really* have to choose?"

"How can I have the career I want, and the kind of marriage I
want, and be a good mother?"

"How can I get him to share more responsibility at home? Why do
I always have to be the one with the children, making the decisions at
home?"

"I can't count on marriage for my security—look what happened
to my mother—but can I get all my security from my career?"

"Can I make it in a man's world, doing it the man's way? What
other way is there? But what is it doing to me? Do I want to be like
men?"

"What do I have to give up? What are the tradeoffs?"

"Will the jobs open to me now still be there if I stop to have children?"

"Does it really work, that business of 'quality, not quantity' of time
with the children? How much is enough?"

"How can I fill my loneliness, except with a man?"

"Do men really want an equal woman?"

"Why are men today so gray and lifeless, compared to women? How can I find a man I can really look up to?"

"How can I play the sex kitten now? Can I ever find a man who will let me be myself?"

"If I put off having a baby till I'm thirty-eight, and can call my own shots on the job, will I ever have kids?"

"How can I juggle it all?"

"How can I put it all together?"

"Can I risk losing myself in marriage?"

"Do I have to be a superwoman?"

Among ourselves, the mothers, I also sense new uneasiness, new questions even harder to put into words lest they evoke those old needs, long since left behind, by us who fought so hard to change the terms of our own lives:

"I have made it, far beyond my dreams. If I put everything else aside, I can see myself as president of the company in ten years. It's not impossible for a woman now. But is that what I really want?"

"My marriage didn't work. I value my independence. I don't want to get married again. But how can I keep on taking care of my kids and myself, on what I earn, and have any kind of life at all, with only myself to depend on? All I do is work to pay the bills."

This is the jumping-off point to the second stage, I believe: these conflicts and fears and compelling needs women feel about the choice to have children now and about success in the careers they now seek—and the concrete practical problems involved (which have larger political implications). I believe daughters and mothers hold separate pieces of the puzzle. I think of my own uneasiness, being called "mother" of the women's movement—not because of modesty, but because of the way I felt about being a mother altogether. . . .

With my own daughter now, and so many others, I sense that we have begun to break some seemingly endless vicious cycle. "Another one like me!" "Don't let me be like her!" What we did, we had to do, to break that cycle. But it is not finished yet. It won't be finished until our daughters can freely, joyously choose to have children. They, and we, are beginning to be afraid—and some of our fears are false shadows of dangers past, and some are presently real—because the cycle we broke, and have to embrace again, is basic to life.

From their new place, the daughters can deny their fears and confusions until exaggerated dangers and unrecognized real problems turn them back. . . .

Daughters moving ahead where mothers could not go may be, in fact, not so much in danger of being trapped as their mothers were as they are in danger of wasting, avoiding life in unnecessary fear. But even the map we piece together from our bridged experience as women—our daughters and ourselves, moving proudly now as women through the first stage, breaking the chains that kept us out of man's world—is not enough for the next stage. For women may be in new danger of falling into certain deadly traps that men are now trying to climb out of to save their own lives. We can't traverse the next stage and reembrace the cycle of life as women alone.

I have been hearing from men this past year, warning signs of certain dead ends for women. Surprising clues of the second stage can be found in the new questions men are asking.

• A Vietnam veteran, laid off at the auto plant where he thought he was secure for life, decides: "There's no security in a job. The dollar's not worth enough any more to live your life for. I'll work three days a week at the garage and my wife will go back to nursing nights, and between us we'll take care of the kids." . . .

• A hotshot MBA in Chicago balks at the constant traveling and the sixty-to-eighty hour weeks he is expected to work, assigned to troubleshoot an aerospace company in Texas. "I'm supposed to leave Sunday night and get back Friday. My wife and I are getting to be strangers. Besides, I want to have a family. There are other things I want in life besides getting ahead in this company. But how can I say I won't travel like that when the other guys are willing to? They'll get ahead, and I won't. How can I live for myself, not just for the company?"

• A sales engineer in New Jersey, struggling to take equal responsibilities for the kids now that his wife has gone to work in a department store, says: "For ten years now, all you hear is women talking about what it means to be a woman, how can she fulfill herself as a woman, even forcing men to talk about women. It's over, the man sitting down with his paper, the wife keeping the kids out of his way. The women's movement forced us to think it through—the presumption that the house and the children were the women's responsibility, the shopping, the cooking, even if both were working. Now you're going to see more men asking, What am I doing with my life, what about my fulfillment, what does it mean being a man? What do I have but my job? I think you're going to see a great wave of men dropping out from traditional male roles. Our sense of who we are was profoundly based on work, but men are going to begin to define themselves in ways other than work. Partly because of the economy, partly because men are beginning to find other goodies at the table, like the children, where men have been excluded before. Being a daddy has become very important to me. Why shouldn't she support the family for a while and let *me* find myself?"

Are men and women moving in opposite directions, chasing illusions of liberation by simply reversing roles that the other sex has already found imprisoning? Maybe there are some choices we, they, don't want to face, or shouldn't have to face. Maybe they are not real choices—not yet, not the way society is structured now, or not ever, in terms of basic human reality. Do we have to transcend the very terms of these choices in the second stage?

I think we can only find out by sharing our new uncertainties, the seemingly insoluble problems and unremitting pressures, our fears and shameful weaknesses, and our surprising joys and strengths as we each have been experiencing them, the daughters, ourselves, and the men, as we begin to live the equality we fought for. Even though we know it's not really all that equal yet, even if we have some new thoughts about what equality really means—for women and men. We had better admit these feelings, or more and more women and men will lose heart and say they do not want equality after all.

I know that equality, the personhood we fought for, is truly necessary for women—and opens new life for men. But I hear now what I would not let myself hear before—the fears and feelings of some who have fought our movement. It is not just a conspiracy of reactionary forces, though such forces surely play up and manipulate those fears. . . .

There is a danger today in feminist rhetoric, rigidified in reaction against the past, harping on the same old problems in the same old way, leaving unsaid what's really bothering women and men in and beyond the new urgencies of personal economic survival. For there is a real backlash against the equality and the personhood of women—in America, as in Islam and the Vatican. Dangerous reactionary forces are playing to those unadmitted fears and yearnings with the aim of wiping out the gains of equality, turning women back to the old dependence, silencing women's new voice and stifling women's new active energy that threatens their own power in ways we do not yet clearly understand. In the name of the family, they would destroy the new equality that gives the family strength to resist dehumanizing forces that are emerging in the seeming impotence of capitalist America, in the resurgence of fundamentalist religion, in neofascism and in autocratic communism, and in the chaos of the Third World. We must ask new questions or we could lose, in the economic and emotional turbulence, the measure of equality that is essential to strengthen human life—and the future of the family. We could mistake, subvert, and betray the truly life-strengthening possibilities opened by the women's movement.

There is no going back. The women's movement was necessary.

But the liberation that began with the women's movement isn't finished. The equality we fought for isn't livable, isn't workable, isn't comfortable in the terms that structured our battle. The first stage, the women's movement, was fought within, and against, and defined by that old structure of unequal, polarized male and female sex roles. But to continue reacting against that structure is still to be defined and limited by its terms. What's needed now is to transcend those terms, transform the structure itself. Maybe the women's movement, as such, can't do that. The experts of psychology, sociology, economics, biology, even the new feminist experts, are still engaged in the old battles, of women versus men. The new questions that need to be asked—and with them, the new structures for the new struggle—can only come from pooling our experience: the agonies and ecstasies of our own transition as women, our daughters' new possibilities, and problems, and the confusion of the men. . . .

Saying no to the feminine mystique and organizing to confront sex discrimination was only the first stage. We have somehow to transcend the polarities of the first stage, and even the rage of our own "no," to get on to the second stage: the restructuring of our institutions on a basis of real equality for women and men, so we can live a new "yes" to life and love, and can *choose* to have children. The dynamics involved here are both economic and sexual. The energies whereby we live and love, and work and eat, which have been so subverted by power in the past, can truly be liberated in the service of life for all of us—or diverted in fruitless impotent reaction.

12

Kathy Alarid

Nan Elsasser, Kyle MacKenzie, and Yvonne Tixier y Vigil

We first met Kathy Alarid at the Albuquerque International Women's Year Conference. She moved from one small group of people to another, embracing old friends, smiling at new ones. "Sometimes I feel I've met everyone in Albuquerque," she said. "I've lived here all my life and what with working in the church, the PTA, the Brown Berets, and other Chicano groups, I must have at least one friend in every community group."

Kathy Alarid's experience of life in her fifty years has been diverse, and in many ways she personifies the changes that Hispanas of her generation have seen and felt. Married when she was seventeen, Kathy Alarid reared eleven children. The five youngest are still living with her. For twenty years she worked at home, a traditional housewife. Today she is divorced and working full-time at Ayuda, *a community service program. Here she talks about the gradual changes that have led to her present life.*

I grew up as an only child. My parents were divorced when I was a baby, and my mother married my stepfather when I was six. So I grew up in several places. I spent some time with my grandfather, some time with my grandmother, and other times with aunts and uncles, but I never really belonged anywhere.

Since I never had a home, I went to a bunch of different schools, sort of shuffled all over the place. After a while they put me in Harwood Girl's School. It was a Methodist boarding school here in town. I was a Catholic—I still am—but that didn't seem to make much difference. We were taught by missionaries and many of them tried to help me. I was a willful, stubborn child.

Then, when I was thirteen, I met Frankie, my husband. I fell in love with him right away. He was my first boyfriend, my first love, and I loved him like I'll never love another man.

Frankie was a year older than I was and he'd already quit school when I met him. He was kind of like an idol to me because he had a job and he was the first one in the neighborhood to get a car. He used to have all his suits custom-made because his family had money. They had a bar and a grocery store.

One day, after about a year, he fell in love with me and we started going around together. For me, that was just it. We went around together all the time after that.

When I was in the ninth grade, I quit Harwood and I started going to Albuquerque High. Then I quit that too, and got a job working in a curio shop. I was fifteen. I worked there for about two years.

Frankie and I were dating quite a lot. We were always together. It seemed we just couldn't leave each other alone. We were so much in love.

When I was sixteen, I got pregnant. Frankie and I got married. I was the happiest girl in the whole world. The two of us came to live with his family and I became like a *chinche*, a bed bug. I clung to his mother, his grandmother, his aunts, and they liked me a whole lot. They still do, even though we're divorced. I guess they liked me so much because I was such an apt pupil. I wanted to learn how to wash and iron, to sew and cook. And I did. I can sew. I can knit. I can crochet. I can embroider. I'm an excellent cook. I made all my baby clothes, and when my kids got married, I made their wedding clothes too.

In the early years, Frankie always had a good job, and I was always at home. I was pregnant fourteen times. Three of my babies died, and so I had eleven children. I got into the marriage but like nobody you've ever seen. It was so neat when the kids came home from school. I'd be cooking, the house always smelled of cookies or cakes or stuff. "Where's my mom?" Joseph would call. He's the oldest. Or I'd be lying in the bedroom nursing the new baby. "Where's my mom?"—that was just the neatest feeling for me.

All of my kids went to Saint John's school; and Frankie's mother had kids who were going there too. She turned me on to the PTA. I would go with her and help out selling bingo and working on the church bazaar, stuff like that. Bit by bit, I got really involved in the school and the church. I was president of the PTA year after year.

Frankie really loved the kids and he was really supportive with them. He used to play with them all the time, and he'd go to the school meetings with me. Our marriage, our family—it was good.

We're divorced now, and I won't ever marry again. I couldn't bring a man into this house or have him over my children. I couldn't do that to my children. I couldn't do that to the man. I couldn't do that to me— because I'll never love anybody like I loved Frankie.

We had been married about sixteen years and he started drinking. Well, he always drank. He was a basketball player, a good basketball player, but always after the games, the drinking. I didn't know what was happening, and neither did he. Gradually, I started going to the meetings at school and the church by myself. He would stay here and I would go. People would say, "Where's Frankie?" I'd say, "Well, he went to another meeting." And then you start the lying because you don't want people to know you're having problems. The kids were growing up, and the drinking got progressively worse. He missed a lot of work. Out of necessity, I had to become both father and mother.

Frankie would work some, and there would be enough money coming in to maintain the family. The older kids were working by then too. They'd give me the three dollars they got from raking leaves to buy bread and toilet paper, but it got to be really lean, even with his family helping out.

To supplement our income, I used to baby-sit for women on welfare, and I used to drive women to pick up their commodities. Before I knew it, I was driving to get my own commodities, because our income was so low we were eligible for commodities, too. I began to do housework, and I also worked as a maid at the American Bank from five to ten at night.

Finally Frankie got into Alcoholics Anonymous; and it saved his life. It was through the AA that I learned his drinking wasn't my fault. I'd gone through the whole guilt trip, but there I learned it wasn't me. We're contributing factors, but we're not the cause. I learned that Frankie had to do whatever he was going to do on his own. If it was doing away with himself, being found dead in an alley, or sobering up, he had to do it himself. I had to learn to let go, because they can't use us as crutches, and that's what I'd been. Frankie's been on AA for five years now and he hasn't touched a drop. He's been through a whole AA program. He's an advocate of it, and he gives talks all over the state.

But during the time he drank, we just grew apart. I'm talking about a span of ten years now. I became strong. I'd had it in me, but it hadn't come out, because, before, nothing was done without Frankie. He's *macho*. He's Mexican to the core. And strong, a very strong man. Now, though, I began getting strong.

At about this time, I got out of the PTA and the church and I went into social action. I just got into all sorts of community groups because of talking or speaking at meetings or at gatherings. I was on the advisory board of Head Start. I was on the board of directors of Model Cities. I worked as a volunteer with drug addicts and ex-cons.

Then Frankie sobered up one day and he wanted me to stop. He looked at me like he'd been asleep for ten years and then he woke up— and I wasn't the Kathy who said, "Well, if you don't want to go to the Mexican movie, I won't go. If you don't want to go to the picnic, I won't go." I was saying, "I'm going," and I wasn't asking permission. People would call me up on the phone asking about the meeting or the carnival and he would say, "You're not going," and I'd say, "I am."

That was about the time I got my job. I'd been doing volunteer work with a group called *Ayuda*. We had a grant from the state and we operated two hot lines for minority people. We gave information on what to do about runaway kids, girls getting pregnant, boys overdosing, Social Security, disability information. We were like a counseling service. That's when I met Dick, the guy from the welfare program. He'd seen me working at *Ayuda* and he said, "Kathy, we need you down here at welfare. We want to hire you. You don't need to type. You don't need to file. I just want you to be at the desk so when someone comes in here with a problem and they're not eligible for welfare, you let them walk out with a good feeling. You try to tell them where they can find help." I said, "I don't know if I can do it." I'd never been out of my home that much and I thought my kids needed me. He said, "You go home and you talk to your kids." So I came home, and I told the kids, and Joseph said to me, "Mom, if you don't take that job, I'll never speak to you again." So I took the job, and that's what I've been doing for the past five years, and I really enjoy it.

By now, living together was really intolerable for Frankie and me. I realized it. He realized it. Then one day, I just had to make a decision. It was like that movie, *The Way We Were*, because that's what happened. We still loved each other, but . . . We'd start in talking about unions. He'd start telling me that Chicanos have high-up positions at GE, and I'd tell him, "Name them on one hand." He'd say, "I don't want to talk to you because you're crazy." I'd say, "Well, you're stupid." It was just no good once we lost that respect for each other.

After the divorce, nobody swamped me with offers to take me out, except younger men. See, a Mexican man, a traditional Mexican male, does not like the type of woman that I am now. To the Chicanos my age, I'm an abomination. I talk too much. I'm too smart. I'm too strong.

The guy that I've been going with for the past three years is eighteen years younger than I am. He's a Puerto Rican from New York. I met him when he was going to college out here. I had never really been attracted to younger men, but Raul has taught me many things that I didn't know. I know that I have taught him, too. I've taught him tolerance and I've taught him patience.

If somebody would have told me three years ago that I'd be going through a trip like this, I'd have said, "You're crazy." Today, I'm often on TV and radio programs, talking about what the Chicana has to go through to be herself. First, she's got to go through the man. You find any Chicana that's into something, that's an activist, she's divorced.

13

Man Child
A Black Lesbian Feminist's Response

Audre Lorde

This article is not a theoretical discussion of Lesbian Mothers and their Sons, nor a how-to article. It is an attempt to scrutinize and share some pieces of that common history belonging to my son and to me. I have two children: a fifteen-and-a-half-year-old daughter Beth, and a fourteen-year-old son Jonathan. This is the way it was/is with me and Jonathan, and I leave the theory to another time and person. This is one woman's telling.

I have no golden message about the raising of sons for other lesbian mothers, no secret to transpose your questions into certain light. I have my own ways of rewording those same questions, hoping we will all come to speak those questions and pieces of our lives we need to share. We are women making contact within ourselves and with each other across the restrictions of a printed page, bent upon the use of our own/one another's knowledges.

The truest direction comes from inside. I give the most strength to my children by being willing to look within myself, and by being honest with them about what I find there, without expecting a response be-

From *Sister Outsider* by Audre Lorde, The Crossing Press, Trumansburg, N.Y., 1984.

yond their years. In this way they begin to learn to look beyond their own fears.

All our children are outriders for a queendom not yet assured.

My adolescent son's growing sexuality is a conscious dynamic between Jonathan and me. It would be presumptuous of me to discuss Jonathan's sexuality here, except to state my belief that whomever he chooses to explore this area with, his choices will be nonoppressive, joyful, and deeply felt from within, places of growth.

One of the difficulties in writing this piece has been temporal; this is the summer when Jonathan is becoming a man, physically. And our sons must become men—such men as we hope our daughters, born and unborn, will be pleased to live among. Our sons will not grow into women. Their way is more difficult than that of our daughters, for they must move away from us, without us. Hopefully, our sons have what they have learned from us, and a howness to forge it into their own image.

Our daughters have us, for measure or rebellion or outline or dream; but the sons of lesbians have to make their own definitions of self as men. This is both power and vulnerability. The sons of lesbians have the advantage of our blueprints for survival, but they must take what we know and transpose it into their own maleness. May the goddess be kind to my son, Jonathan.

Recently I have met young Black men about whom I am pleased to say that their future and their visions, as well as their concerns within the present, intersect more closely with Jonathan's than do my own. I have shared vision with these men as well as temporal strategies for our survivals and I appreciate the spaces in which we could sit down together. Some of these men I met at the First Annual Conference of Third World Lesbians and Gays held in Washington D.C. in October, 1979. I have met others in different places and do not know how they identify themselves sexually. Some of these men are raising families alone. Some have adopted sons. They are Black men who dream and who act and who own their feelings, questioning. It is heartening to know our sons do not step out alone.

When Jonathan makes me angriest, I always say he is bringing out the testosterone in me. What I mean is that he is representing some piece of myself as a woman that I am reluctant to acknowledge or explore. For instance, what does "acting like a man" mean? For me, what I reject? For Jonathan, what he is trying to redefine?

Raising Black children—female and male—in the mouth of a racist, sexist, suicidal dragon is perilous and chancy. If they cannot love and resist at the same time, they will probably not survive. And in order to survive they must let go. This is what mothers teach—love, survival—that is, self-definition and letting go. For each of these, the ability to feel strongly and to recognize those feelings is central: how to feel love, how to neither discount fear nor be overwhelmed by it, how to enjoy feeling deeply.

I wish to raise a Black man who will not be destroyed by, nor settle for, those corruptions called *power* by the white fathers who mean his destruction as surely as they mean mine. I wish to raise a Black man who will recognize that the legitimate objects of his hostility are not women, but the particulars of a structure that programs him to fear and despise women as well as his own Black self.

For me, this task begins with teaching my son that I do not exist to do his feeling for him.

Men who are afraid to feel must keep women around to do their feeling for them while dismissing us for the same supposedly "inferior" capacity to feel deeply. But in this way also, men deny themselves their own essential humanity, becoming trapped in dependency and fear.

As a Black woman committed to a liveable future, and as a mother loving and raising a boy who will become a man, I must examine all my possibilities of being within such a destructive system.

Jonathan was three-and-one-half when Frances, my lover, and I met; he was seven when we all began to live together permanently. From the start, Frances' and my insistence that there be no secrets in our household about the fact that we were lesbians has been the source of problems and strengths for both children. In the beginning, this insistence grew out of the knowledge, on both our parts, that whatever was hidden out of fear could always be used either against the children or ourselves—one imperfect but useful argument for honesty. The knowledge of fear can help make us free.

> *for the embattled*
> *there is no place*
> *that cannot be*
> *home*
> *nor is.**

For survival, Black children in America must be raised to be warriors. For survival, they must also be raised to recognize the enemy's many faces. Black children of lesbian couples have an advantage because they learn, very early, that oppression comes in many different forms, none of which have anything to do with their own worth.

To help give me perspective, I remember that for years, in the namecalling at school, boys shouted at Jonathan not—"your mother's a lesbian"—but rather—"your mother's a nigger."

*From "School Note" in *The Black Unicorn* (W. W. Norton and Company, New York, 1978), p. 55.

When Jonathan was eight years old and in the third grade we moved, and he went to a new school where his life was hellish as a new boy on the block. He did not like to play rough games. He did not like to fight. He did not like to stone dogs. And all this marked him early on as an easy target.

When he came in crying one afternoon, I heard from Beth how the corner bullies were making Jonathan wipe their shoes on the way home whenever Beth wasn't there to fight them off. And when I heard that the ringleader was a little boy in Jonathan's class his own size, an interesting and very disturbing thing happened to me.

My fury at my own long-ago impotence, and my present pain at his suffering, made me start to forget all that I knew about violence and fear, and blaming the victim, I started to hiss at the weeping child. "The next time you come in here crying . . .," and I suddenly caught myself in horror.

This is the way we allow the destruction of our sons to begin—in the name of protection and to ease our own pain. My son get beaten up? I was about to demand that he buy that first lesson in the corruption of power, that might makes right. I could hear myself beginning to perpetuate the age-old distortions about what strength and bravery really are.

And no, Jonathan didn't have to fight if he didn't want to, but somehow he did have to feel better about not fighting. An old horror rolled over me of being the fat kid who ran away, terrified of getting her glasses broken.

About that time a very wise woman said to me, "Have you ever told Jonathan that once you used to be afraid, too?"

The idea seemed far-out to me at the time, but the next time he came in crying and sweaty from having run away again, I could see that he felt shamed at having failed me, or some image he and I had created in his head of mother/woman. This image of woman being able to handle it all was bolstered by the fact that he lived in a household with three strong women, his lesbian parents and his forthright older sister. At home, for Jonathan, power was clearly female.

And because our society teaches us to think in an either/or mode—kill or be killed, dominate or be dominated—this meant that he must either surpass or be lacking. I could see the implications of this line of thought. Consider the two western classic myth/models of mother/son relationships: Jocasta/Oedipus, the son who fucks his mother, and Clytemnestra/Orestes, the son who kills his mother.

It all felt connected to me.

I sat down on the hallway steps and took Jonathan on my lap and wiped his tears. "Did I ever tell you about how I used to be afraid when I was your age?"

I will never forget the look on that little boy's face as I told him the tale of my glasses and my after-school fights. It was a look of relief and total disbelief, all rolled into one.

It is as hard for our children to believe that we are not omnipotent as it is for us to know it, as parents. But that knowledge is necessary as the first step in the reassessment of power as something other than might, age, privilege, or the lack of fear. It is an important step for a boy, whose societal destruction begins when he is forced to believe that he can only be strong if he doesn't feel, or if he wins.

I thought about all this one year later when Beth and Jonathan, ten and nine, were asked by an interviewer how they thought they had been affected by being children of a feminist.

Jonathan said that he didn't think there was too much in feminism for boys, although it certainly was good to be able to cry if he felt like it and not to have to play football if he didn't want to. I think of this sometimes now when I see him practising for his Brown Belt in Tae Kwon Do.

The strongest lesson I can teach my son is the same lesson I teach my daughter: how to be who he wishes to be for himself. And the best way I can do this is to be who I am and hope that he will learn from this not how to be me, which is not possible, but how to be himself. And this means how to move to that voice from within himself, rather than to those raucous, persuasive, or threatening voices from outside, pressuring him to be what the world wants him to be.

And that is hard enough.

Jonathan is learning to find within himself some of the different faces of courage and strength, whatever he chooses to call them. Two years ago, when Jonathan was twelve and in the seventh grade, one of his friends at school who had been to the house persisted in calling Frances "the maid." When Jonathan corrected him, the boy then referred to her as "the cleaning woman." Finally Jonathan said, simply, "Frances is not the cleaning woman, she's my mother's lover." Interestingly enough, it is the teachers at this school who still have not recovered from his openness.

Frances and I were considering attending a Lesbian/Feminist conference this summer, when we were notified that no boys over ten were allowed. This presented logistic as well as philosophical problems for us, and we sent the following letter:

Sisters:

Ten years as an interracial lesbian couple has taught us both the dangers of an oversimplified approach to the nature and solutions of any oppression, as well as the danger inherent in an incomplete vision.

Our thirteen-year-old son represents as much hope for our future world as does our fifteen-year-old daughter, and we are not willing to abandon him to the killing streets of New York City while we journey west to help form a Lesbian-Feminist vision of the future world in which we can all survive and flourish. I hope we can continue this dialogue in the near future, as I feel it is important to our vision and our survival.

The question of separatism is by no means simple. I am thankful that one of my children is male, since that helps to keep me honest. Every line I write shrieks there are no easy solutions.

I grew up in largely female environments, and I know how crucial that has been to my own development. I feel the want and need often for the society of women, exclusively. I recognize that our own spaces are essential for developing and recharging.

As a Black woman, I find it necessary to withdraw into all-Black groups at times for exactly the same reasons—differences in stages of development and differences in levels of interaction. Frequently, when speaking with men and white women, I am reminded of how difficult and time-consuming it is to have to reinvent the pencil every time you want to send a message.

But this does not mean that my responsibility for my son's education stops at age ten, any more than it does for my daughter's. However, for each of them, that responsibility does grow less and less as they become more woman and man.

Both Beth and Jonathan need to know what they can share and what they cannot, how they are joined and how they are not. And Frances and I, as grown women and lesbians coming more and more into our power, need to relearn the experience that difference does not have to be threatening.

When I envision the future, I think of the world I crave for my daughters and my sons. It is thinking for survival of the species—thinking for life.

Most likely there will always be women who move with women, women who live with men, men who choose men. I work for a time when women with women, women with men, men with men, all share the work of a world that does not barter bread or self for obedience, nor beauty, nor love. And in that world we will raise our children free to choose how best to fulfill themselves. For we are jointly responsible for the care and raising of the young, since *that* they be raised is a function, ultimately, of the species.

Within that tripartite pattern of relating/existence, the raising of the young will be the joint responsibility of all adults who choose to be associated with children. Obviously, the children raised within each of these three relationships will be different, lending a special savor to that eternal inquiry into how best can we live our lives.

Jonathan was three-and-a-half when Frances and I met. He is now fourteen years old. I feel the living perspective that having lesbian parents has brought to Jonathan is a valuable addition to his human sensitivity.

Jonathan has had the advantage of growing up within a nonsexist relationship, one in which this society's pseudo-natural assumptions of ruler/ruled are being challenged. And this is not only because Frances and I are lesbians, for unfortunately there are some lesbians who are still locked into patriarchal patterns of unequal power relationships.

These assumptions of power relationships are being questioned because Frances and I, often painfully and with varying degrees of success, attempt to evaluate and measure over and over again our feelings concerning power, our own and others'. And we explore with care those areas concerning how it is used and expressed between us and between us and the children, openly and otherwise. A good part of our biweekly family meetings are devoted to this exploration.

As parents, Frances and I have given Jonathan our love, our openness, and our dreams to help form his visions. Most importantly, as the son of lesbians, he has had an invaluable model—not only of a relationship—but of relating.

Jonathan is fourteen now. In talking over this paper with him and asking his permission to share some pieces of his life, I asked Jonathan what he felt were the strongest negative and the strongest positive aspects for him in having grown up with lesbian parents.

He said the strongest benefit he felt he had gained was that he knew a lot more about people than most other kids his age that he knew, and that he did not have a lot of the hang-ups that some other boys did about men and women.

And the most negative aspect he felt, Jonathan said, was the ridicule he got from some kids with straight parents.

"You mean, from your peers?" I said.

"Oh no," he answered promptly. "My peers know better. I mean other kids."

14

Wives

Rosabeth Moss Kanter

*Perpetual devotion to what a man calls his business, is only to be
sustained by perpetual neglect of many other things.*

—Robert Louis Stevenson, *Virginibus Puerisque*

Women are still expected to do things because of love or duty.

—Jessie Bernard, *Women and the Public Interest*

Some of the most important role-players at Industrial Supply Corporation were never seen on company premises. They were clearly outside
the official boundaries of corporate administration, listed nowhere,
paid nothing, and discouraged from visiting their husbands' offices
(even on weekends, because of security considerations). They are the
managers' wives. There was no employment relation between Indsco
and management wives, and no legitimate claims of one party on the
other. As in the bureaucratic theory that helped give rationale and

From *Men and Women of the Corporation* by Rosabeth Moss Kanter. © 1977 by Rosabeth Moss Kanter. Reprinted by permission of Basic Books, Inc., Publishers.

form to the modern corporate organization, men were presumed to leave their private relationships at the door to the company when they entered every morning. Wives stood on the other side of the door. At an off-site research meeting of junior executives and wives, paid for by their department, it was announced that only "Mr." should show on the hotel register; if "Mr. and Mrs." appeared, the manager footing the bill would need a letter from a vice-president.

Yet there were signs that the supposedly neat boundary between inside and outside the system marked by the legal employment relation was not so crystal clear. In Indsco offices were some obvious manifestations of the wives' involvement with the organization. Photographs of wives and children adorned men's offices so commonly that they seemed almost mandatory. Wives were automatically mentioned by name in articles in company newsletters about husbands' accomplishments: "Joseph Jones lives with his wife, Margaret, and their three children in Anytown Heights." Being a "family man" was a clear sign of stability and maturity and was taken into account in promotion decisions; sexual promiscuity on the part of Indsco's management men was frowned upon, despite a culture that joked about sexual pursuit. Wives were clearly seen by some of their husbands as a motivational factor in their careers, in answers to questions about why they worked at Indsco: "Providing for a family is a large reason why I work here. It gives me great gratification to know that I can give to my wife and kids at such a luxurious level." . . .

From the wives' perspective, the company was a critical part of their lives, defining how they spent their time and influencing what was possible in their relationships with their husbands. One wife in her mid-thirties, married to a rising manager, put it this way: "Until two years ago, when I thought about going back to school, I was an Indsco wife, married to the company as much as to Fred. No one ever demanded anything of me *per se* except going out to dinner with so-and-so. But in my own being, I was very dependent on Fred's experiences in Indsco. It chose the area we lived in. Our friends, except for a few neighbors, were Indsco friends, made *because* of the company. I always felt that our goal was to settle down, to set down roots when the kids were in junior high school. Now they are, and the company tells us to move, so we move, pushing that goal further ahead. . . . If Fred was doing well, I felt *I* was doing well. I'm the woman behind the man, I could take some pride in his achievements."

Young wives anticipated increasing sacrifices for the company as their husbands' careers progressed, pointing to effects on their marriages of the men's daily fatigue, travel, and evenings away, and demands that they play a growing role in official entertaining. "Husband-absence" also gave them exclusive child care responsibilities. Some wives considered themselves unpaid workers for the corporation, in the sense both of direct services and of opportunity costs for options in their own lives they had forgone. As wives saw it, then, they were very much inside the corporate system.

The existence of wives also had implications for women officially employed by the company. Just as the image of the secretary spilled over and infused expectations about other women workers, the image of the wife affected responses to career women at Indsco. Because corporate wives were generally seen to be content to operate behind the scenes and to be ambitious for their husbands rather than themselves and because they made use of social rather than intellectual skills in their hostess role, the image of women that emerged for some management men from knowing their own and other wives reinforced the view that career women were an anomaly, that they were unusual or could not really be ambitious, or that their talents must be primarily social and emotional rather than cognitive and managerial. . . .

Some of the expectations stemming from the existence of wives had another, more general, effect. Men could bring two people with them to the organization, and indeed, preferential hiring of married men and occasional attention to the wives' own characteristics frequently ensured that this was so. But career women, especially in the managerial ranks, did not have this advantage. There was no "corporate husband" role equivalent to that of corporate wife. Husbands of higher-ranking women who were not themselves part of Indsco sometimes resisted having anything at all to do with the company. . . .

Finally, concerns of the women outside the office were transferred directly to those inside. Wives' concerns about the sexual potential of office relationships occasionally pitted the two sets of women against each other as rivals. . . .

The competitive potential of office relationships was always there. Several saleswomen at Indsco felt, rightly or wrongly, that they were the targets of the sexual fantasies of male peers. Some said that men used them to taunt their wives, e.g., by making innuendos about going out on a sales call with one of the women. For this reason, many saleswomen felt it important they they establish good relations with the wives, giving women an additional task men did not have. Wives, in turn, not themselves directly participating in the work world, could fear what would happen when their husbands worked with women as peers, such as the Newton, Massachusetts, policemen's wives who protested the hiring of policewomen, giving as one reason the sexual potential of long shifts shared by men and women in patrol cars.[1] A few men played on these concerns and then used their wives' jealousies as reasons why women should not be hired for certain jobs, like those that involved travel with men.

For all of these reasons, wives cannot be ignored when looking at men and women in the administration of corporate bureaucracies. But at the same time, it is hard to know exactly where they do fit in the system or how to conceptualize their nature as both insiders and outsiders. They are sometimes directly involved with the organization, sometimes involved only with and through their husbands, and sometimes completely uninvolved.

Industrial Supply's Policy Dilemmas: What to Do About Wives

How to understand and take into account the position of wives is an intellectual task with relevance for both organization theory and organization policy. At Indsco, there was considerable debate over whether the organization should get involved in the family lives of managers at all, even in relatively innocuous ways like offering programs with serious educational content for wives dragged along to business conferences or running workshops on couple issues as an adjunct to career planning and development.

The "libertarian" position held that anything wives did was strictly voluntary, their own choice. Employees' private lives were—officially—their own business, and the company had no right to interfere. To think otherwise smacked of the worst kind of paternalism not in keeping with modern management, as in practices like wife-screening (never an explicit policy at Indsco) or company housing in company towns or the packaged social life complete with corporate country club provided by IBM. . . .

Yet, this "libertarian" position was also used to avoid the issue of how much Indsco was already constraining salesmen's and manager's families; it helped evade any organizational responsibility. To throw a party at an expensive restaurant for husbands and wives, for example, was considered within a manager's prerogative, but to spend the same amount of money to bring spouses on-site to teach them about company policies or what they husbands did all day long was inappropriate. The most recurrent complaint from Indsco wives had to do with the limits of the role they were given to play: on the one hand, faced with strong demands to be gracious, charming hostesses and social creatures, supporting their husbands' careers and motivating their achievements, with the boundaries of their own life choices set by the company; but on the other hand, kept away from opportunities to see, understand, and even participate in their husbands' jobs. They simultaneously wanted to be left alone to live their own lives *and* to be more involved in their husbands'.

Corporate policy and practices, then, were viewed by a second school of thought in the company as a source of marital tension and severe strain for wives which, in turn, had bearing on men's work performance. These people supported the idea that more attention be paid to work-family issues and that wives be seen as "inside" the company's boundaries. . . .

Clearly, then, understanding the corporate wife role and its appropriate connection to the organization is not a simple matter. It requires taking into account a number of circumstantial variations and developing a theoretical framework for identifying the constraints within which organization wives must operate.

Toward a Perspective on the Corporate Wife

Other writings on organization wives do not provide much help in advancing intellectual understanding. Most of them belong in the "wife-as-victim" category.

The corporate wife as a social role captured public attention in the early 1950s when William H. Whyte, Jr., wrote a series of articles in *Fortune* and elsewhere revealing the extent to which corporations looked over and made rules for wives of men they were considering for executive positions.[2] The corporate wife's acceptance of her fate was taken by Whyte as another sign of the rise of "groupmindedness," which he later documented in *The Organization Man*. Whyte's picture, as well as that presented by later journalists and psychiatrists, tended to show the corporate wife as a helpless casualty, even when a willing one. Moving from place to place frequently, subject to rules and constraints, excluded from the office world, stuck with almost exclusive household responsibilities, and lacking their husbands' opportunities for learning and adventure, corporate wives were portrayed as victims of a too-demanding system. And with reason. Alcoholism, unwanted pregnancies, divorce, and bouts of depression in women have all been attributed to features of the managerial life-style.[3] More recently, the suffering of wives of politicians was described in popular articles and books: Margaret Trudeau's emotional collapse, Joan Kennedy's mental distress, Abigail McCarthy's divorce, Angelina Alioto's runaway revolt. . . .[4]

The actual casualty rate among corporate wives has never been fully known, and at every wave of criticism and protest there was also a chorus of apparently contented wives waiting in the wings to insist that the advantages outweighed the disadvantages. However, no one disagreed that marriage to successful men was constraining, shaped role demands for wives, and often put the family last in the men's priorities. . . .

The second theme in the victim critique focused on economic exploitation: wives as unpaid workers. Some writers pointed to the direct and indirect services wives performed for their husbands' careers and organizations. Four kinds of task contributions were among those noted. *Direct substitution* involved the wife in work that could also be done by a paid employee; she substituted permanently, temporarily, or on an ad hoc basis, either at the office or at home. The wife might stuff envelopes, do some typing, answer phones, deliver packages, or keep accounts and records, like the wife of a consulting engineer mentioned in one report who kept his files and scrapbooks up to date and helped him make business contacts at conferences. The winners of one company's award for exceptional salesmanship (American Cyanamid Company's Golden Oval) all had wives without outside jobs, most of whom reported to an interviewer in 1973 that they spent a considerable amount of time helping their husbands with sales work. (In one case of a man who had won this award twice, his wife filled in when his secretary was on vacation, traveled with him on business, helped him entertain customers, and talked to him about his work even when *she* was bored.) *Indirect support* included those entertainment functions that were assumed to be part of the wife's "hostess" role, using her assumed skill as a relationship builder. Such services might be purchased if unavailable from a wife. *Consulting* involved discussion and advice on business matters, like those discussions that might be held with a management consultant. The wife acted as a business adviser, a psychotherapist, a listener, or even an "expert" on some part of her husband's work, helping him make decisions or choose between options. *Emotional aid* a part of the conventional housewife role, involved such services as "sending him off in a good frame of mind" and keeping him satisfied with his work. As Whyte summarized these latter functions, the wife was a "wailing wall, a sounding board, and a refuelling station."[5] She was an important adjunct to the company's motivational apparatus but was never rewarded directly by it for her services.

Though economic benefit supposedly came to the wife through the boost to the husband's career, a chord of protest was sounded by some critics and some wives, who found this situation unfair. As one wife complained, "I am paid neither in job satisfaction nor in cash for my work. I did not choose the job of executive wife, and I am heartily sick of it."[6] The argument was made that wives at least should be compensated for out-of-pocket expenses in their work for their husbands. The economic exploitation theme is also highlighted in recent feminist writings urging pay for housework, since work at home is involved in the "reproduction of labor power" and thus should be compensated by the work systems it benefits.

Corporate wives, in short, have been seen as outsiders, swallowed up by a greedy organization[7] that tries to absorb totally the lives of its managerial employees. . . .

The idea of a "career" for corporate wives points to a way to identify the particular dilemmas they face, the characteristic forces shaping their behavior. What the wife does, what she must contend with, is a function of the husband's career stage and the nature of managerial work in the large corporate bureaucracy. Thus, her role and the reasons for her implication in the organization at all are bound up with human issues in management itself: issues such as uncertainty, trust, and loyalty; internal company politics and external needs for legitimacy.

The Corporate Wife's Career Progression

Three phases can be identified in the career of a corporate wife in Industrial Supply Corporation and other industrial bureaucracies, each distinguished by a set of dilemmas and choices particular to it. The three phases partly overlap, and all three sets of functions may be performed simultaneously, but the distinctions between them reflect differences in the critical issues in the husband's career. The first is the *technical* phase, roughly corresponding to husbands' pre-management jobs and early rungs on management ladders, when the constraints on a wife flow directly from the husband's immediate job conditions, and any involvement on her part in his work is in the form of technical assistance or personal support directly to him. The most critical factor in husbands' careers is whether they can carry out the technical requirements of their jobs. At this point, wives form an anonymous mass, with little if any direct connection with the organization.

Then, as a husband enters middle and upper management, a second phase, the *managerial* phase, begins. Here the wife's role is shaped by the growing importance of the husband's involvement in company social networks. As he takes on "people-handling" tasks and becomes enmeshed in the informal political structure of the company, the wife adds social tasks that involve her more directly in a social network of other husbands and wives. The uncertainties in evaluation of managerial performance and the concomitant importance of such non-ability factors as trust, loyalty, and fitting in well in corporate society give shape to this phase. As the uncertainty factor increases in the husband's career, the visibility factor increases in the wife's. Entertaining and sociability, more or less private matters during the technical phase, may now receive official notice and scrutiny, taking on political meaning.

Finally, the *institutional* phase centers around the husband's location at the top of the organization or in a position where he must represent it to the outside. Diplomatic functions become important, for the organization seeks legitimacy and support from its environment (major suppliers, the immediate community, governmental agencies, the public-at-large) not only in formal ways but also through the persons of its leaders. At the very top, the wife-of-the-chief has an official role to play in the organization's diplomatic system: official hostess, link to the community, caretaker and mobilizer of other wives, and public relations professional. Wives-at-the-top are no longer hidden and officially excluded, and they may even have a budget for the conduct of their position. . . .

We can see in the "career progression" of a corporate wife, then, an increase in visibility with each shift in phase and a change in the principal orientation of the activities she might choose to perform. In the first phase, her activities take place primarily with respect to her husband; in the second, around a social network internal to the company; and in the third, around the organization itself. Each of these phases presents the wife with a set of decisions and dilemmas.

The Technical Phase: Handling Exclusion/Inclusion

The first dilemma faced by Industrial Supply Corporation wives revolved around *exclusion/inclusion*. Wives of men in sales and low-level management positions faced a system that shut them out officially of their husbands' job worlds, at the same time that job conditions limited their husbands' availability. Wives complained that there was too little left over after work: "His high at work made me angry. He was so involved there but under-involved at home. He'd be withdrawn and too democratic at home, completely abdicating any responsibility for what we shared, telling me that whatever I wanted was fine. He just didn't have any energy left."

Furthermore, the jargon-laden company culture created a communication problem—sometimes overtly denied by wives who would pretend to be interested while understanding little of what was said. At a research meeting, twelve wives whose husbands worked in the same unit generated a list of words and phrases they had heard their husbands use but that they could not define; it ran to 103 entries, before the group stopped for lack of time. Knowledge of their husbands as workers was minimal, and the wish was frequently expressed by both women and men that a wife have a chance to "see who he is when he is doing his job, to learn what it does to him." In keeping with the knowledge gap, the wife's-eye view of the corporation was a highly distorted one, with only bits and pieces of information filtering through. . . .

There were several ways in which this situation was handled. One option was to settle for total exclusion, with the wife choosing a path of her own that took her farther away from any direct involvement with her husband's job or with Indsco. Sometimes this occurred because she had a career of her own; if it were in a similar field, as for the psychologist wife of a counsellor in the personnel department, colleagueship could at least be maintained. But more often, in the early 1970s at Indsco, it took the form of diverging roles of husbands and wives, with the wife erecting an exclusionary barrier over her own technical domain of home and children and getting angry if the husband threatened her power there. She might want the husband to do some of the work of the household, but she also made clear that she was the boss, a pattern in several marriages of relatively young managers whom I observed at home. Such a choice set a vicious cycle in motion: The more the husband was away from the family system (through fatique, travel, work absorption, or excitement the wife did not share), the more the family operated without him, closing him out or punishing him on reentry for his absence, thereby intensifying any desire he had to get away. . . .

Attempts at inclusion were limited by the wife's position on the other side of official organization boundaries. Some who wished to render the kinds of job assistance mentioned earlier in the chapter found that they could do so in only limited and fairly menial ways (such as typing, running errands) that utilized relatively few of their talents and kept them distinctly subordinate. (The routinized tasks available to wives paralleled those menial jobs performed by official women's auxiliaries that spring up around public service organizations like hospitals.) . . .

But there were also those ambitious wives who refused to believe they could be left behind, who thought they could remain included in their husbands' jobs by dint of their own effort. One young wife said determinedly: "I don't feel that travel is a threat to our marriage. Indsco is no threat. What he doesn't tell me, I find out about myself. I go to his desk and read everything on it. *This chicken is going to learn.* I'm going to learn and know every aspect from A to Z. There's no such thing as an F in this school. When he comes home, it's bringing Indsco to me. I'm entitled to two hours of his time myself for me to learn." In reply, a more experienced Indsco wife said: "You can read, but you won't learn everything that your husband will. It's a unique experience." Retorted the first: "That's the way you interpret it; I might not." The second answered flatly: "You can't do it."

Tensions around inclusion/exclusion were translated into anger at the company for keeping the wives so separate and uninformed and for so constraining the wives' options for involvement. Those lavish social events to which wives were invited were seen as meaningless "bribes": "They're getting the little wife out of the kitchen for an evening so she won't feel left out," one wife said sarcastically. On the other hand, an experimental attempt to run an educational program for wives and husbands in one unit, part of a research effort, revealed how little wives felt it took to make them feel included. Four wives wrote: "Watching our husbands exercising the skills they have learned bridged the gap of corporate man and family man. Participating in some of the tasks that our husbands are involved in daily was very valuable. The entire experience enabled us to help them to cope with the intellectual, emotional, and physical demands made on them. It succeeded in bringing the company and its functions closer to us and helped to make us feel that we, too, are a part of Industrial Supply Corporation. When a wife is included, the corporation may not seem so large. All of this can result in nothing less than a wonderful sense of sharing between husband and wife in relation to what our men are doing all day, five days a week." Despite the wives' enthusiasm and increased commitment to Indsco, however, this event was not repeated, and their exclusion returned.

The Managerial Phase: Handling Instrumentality/Sentimentality

As a husband moved up the managerial ladder and became enmeshed in company politics, the wife's role with respect to the social network formed by the organization loomed larger, and she faced the issue of charting a course between instrumentality and sentimentality in her dealings with other people around Indsco. Choices revolved around the degree to which authenticity and feeling in relationships were subordinated to deliberate image manufacture and manipulation for political advantage.

In this phase, wives also became a large consideration in company policy, and the issue of whether wives would be judged as part of their husbands' evaluations began to be raised. Though Indsco had no formal wife-screening process, informally information about wives formed part of the scuttlebutt surrounding managers. . . .

Indsco wives of middle managers and top divisional managers were aware of the decisions highlighted by William Whyte's "organizational man" studies; at a certain point in their husbands' climb to the top, wives realized that friendships were no longer a personal matter but had business implications.[8] Social professionalism set in. The political implications of what had formerly been personal or sentimental choices became clear. Old friendships might have to be put aside because the organizational situation makes them inappropriate, as in the case of one officer husband who let his wife know it would no longer be seemly to maintain a social relationship with a couple to whom they had previously been very close because the first husband now far outranked the second. The public consequences of relationships made it difficult for some wives to have anything but a superficial friendship with anyone in the corporate social network. Yet, since so much of their time was consumed by company-related entertainment, they had little chance for other friendships, and reported considerable loneliness. A few wives complained about other costs to instrumentalism in relationships: having to entertain in their homes people they did not like and would not otherwise have invited, the need to be consistently cheerful and ready to be on display. Duplicity in relationships was one result. . . .

There were a number of reports of unfavorable comments about wives who failed to conform or fit in at Indsco, although no one admitted outright that wives' behavior affected husbands' careers. The wife seemed more important in field locations in smaller towns, where the corporate network might in fact become a closed social community. But all wives, even those living in the large and rather anonymous suburbs surrounding corporate headquarters, had to face the issue of how far to trade sentimentality for instrumentality. Some wives made instrumentality into a way of life—at least as seen by others, for part of the talent of such people was to retain the pretense of sentiment even in the most instrumental of dealings. Having operated politically in the rise of their husbands, they then claimed the right to "rule" the wives' network, standing, like the wives of ambassadors in the foreign service,[9] at the peak of a system of protocol that awarded them deference and gave them the right to scrutinize and comment on the lifestyle and manners of other wives. In exchange for helping their husbands, they demanded political influence. Instrumentality gave them an arena in which to wield power, even at the cost of superficiality, loneliness, and duplicity. Yet it was to gain public importance, something not possible in the technical phase or without a career of their own.

To choose sentiment, on the other hand, might mean opting out, a choice ill-afforded by those wives whose support and satisfaction were tied to their husbands' successes. Even for those desiring authenticity and feeling in their relationships, however, pure sentiment was no longer possible. Awareness of the operation of the social network meant that a degree of calculated choice had to enter into even fully sentimental ties. Wives and husbands alike could protest the unfairness of social network influences in career mobility, as many did; here wives were adamant in wishing they could live their own lives apart from social scrutiny. A few commented that the insidiousness of the gossip network in this respect lay in its insulation: gossip and gossip-carriers could not be confronted directly, since, in the official system, they were presumed not to exist.

The Institutional Phase: Handling Publicness/Privateness

It is one of the prevailing ironies of modern corporate life that the closer to the top of the organization, the more traditional and non-"modern" does the system look. As Max Weber noted, at this point more charismatic, symbolic, and "non-rational" elements come into play. . . .[10]

The dilemma that can confront people at this level is the issue of publicness/privateness. Both husband and wife can be made into public figures, with no area of life remaining untinged with responsibilities for the company. . . . One rising young Indsco executive felt that the following had to be considered the "modern risks" of corporate vice presidential and presidential jobs: traveling 80 percent of the time, getting shot at or kidnapped by radicals, prostituting yourself to customers, and opening your private life to scrutiny.

The higher executive's work spills over far beyond the limits of a working day. . . .[11] There may be no distinction between work and leisure. Activities well out of the purview of the organization's goals and defined as pleasure for other people (golf club memberships, symphony attendance, party-giving) are allowable as business expenses on income tax returns because the definition of what is "business" becomes so broad and non-specific. . . .

Fusion of business and private life also occurs around longer-term relationships. At the top, all friendships may have business meaning. Business relations can be made because of social connections. (One unlikely merger between two companies in very different fields was officially said to result from one company's need for a stock exchange listing held by the other, but off the record it was known to have been brought about by the friendship of the two presidents and their wives.) Charitable and community service activities, where the wife's role is especially pivotal, may generate useful business and political connections. Wives may meet each other through volunteer work and bring their husbands into contact, with useful business results. Stratification of the volunteer world paralleling class and ethnic differentiation in the society ensures that husbands and wives can pinpoint the population with which they desire connections by an appropriate choice of activity. As one chief executive wife wrote, "Any public relations man worth his salt will recognize the corporate wife as an instrument of communication with the community far more sincere and believable than all the booze poured down the press to gain their favor."[12]

The importance of the wife stems not only from her own skills and activities (which could be, and are, performed by paid employees) but also from the testimony her behavior provides, its clue to the character and personal side of her husband. The usefulness of this testimony, in turn, is derived from unique aspects of top leadership. Image, appearance, background, and likability are all commodities traded at the top of the system, where actors are visible and where they put pressure on one another to demonstrate trustworthiness. . . .

Furthermore, the capacities of an organization itself are unknown and cannot be reduced precisely either to history or to a set of facts and figures. Thus, the character of its leaders can become a critical guide to making a decision about a future relationship with it: whether to invest, to donate funds, to allow it into the community, to provide some leeway in the regulation of its activities. Indsco was always concerned about character in its managers. Company newspapers from field locations routinely stressed church leadership in articles about individual managers, and "integrity" and "acceptance of accountability" appeared on the list of eleven traits that must be possessed by candidates for officer level jobs. . . .

One way leaders can offer glimpses of their private beings is by bringing along their wives, by inviting others into their homes, and by making sure that their wives confirm the impression of themselves they are trying to give. By meeting in social circumstances, by throwing open pieces of private life for inspection, leaders try to convey their taste and their humanity. Wives, especially, are the carriers of this humanity and the shapers of the image of the private person. . . .

The wife is thus faced with an added task at the boundary of the public and the private: to make an event seem personal that is instead highly ritualized and contrived. She must recognize also the meanings conveyed by small acts (who sits next to whom, how much time she and her husband spend with each person, the taste implied by objects in the home, how much she drinks, who seem to be the family friends) and manage even small gestures with extreme self-consciousness. . . .

Private life thus becomes penetrable and not very private at the top. Wives face the demand to suppress private beliefs and self-knowledge in the interest of public appearance. As an instrument of diplomacy and a critical part of her husband's image, the corporate wife must often hide her own opinions in order to preserve a united front, play down her own abilities to keep him looking like the winner and the star. The women's intelligence and superior education—assets when the men looked for wives—give way to other, more social traits, such as gregariousness, adaptability, attractiveness, discretion, listening ability, and social graces. . . .

Stresses, choices, and dilemmas in the institutional phase, then, center around the tension between the public and the private. If wives at the top gained public recognition, they also lost private freedoms. The emotional pressure this entailed was too much for some wives, as literature in the corporate-wives-as-victims tradition made clear; but it should be pointed out, too, that emotional breakdowns and secret deviances could also reflect defiant independence, unobtainable in any other way under constraining role definitions. The wishes expressed by wives in this position were of two kinds. Some women said that if they were going to be used by the company anyway, they would like the opportunity to do a real job, exercise real skills—by which they meant take on official areas of responsibility. Others wanted merely to be able to carve out more areas of privacy and independence in an otherwise public existence.

Implications: The Organization and the Wife

There is much disagreement, among social scientists as well as Indsco employees and families, about the importance of wives to the organization or to their husbands' careers. Some writers have commented that a denial system operates to minimize attention to the contribution made by wives to their successful husbands. David Riesman noted that it was a male trait to claim individual credit for achievements and to forget the infrastructure that helped make them possible. Hanna Papanek argued that wifely collaboration in a husband's career was not openly acknowledged because of what she called the "fragility of male self-esteem."[13] But aside from any such masculinist biases, there were also organizational pressures to minimize the actual or reported role of wives in Indsco. Above all, the organization prided itself on "fairness," and its legitimacy among employees rested on belief in the attempt to create a just system that rewarded merit, even though it was known that internal politicking could not be completely eliminated. To admit to what one wife called "influence through the pillow" on decisions, or to acknowledge that someone other than an official employee was engaged in the company's work, would be to pose a challenge to legitimating ideologies. Thus, wives are relegated to the background and often accept this place. One wife of a high-ranking Indsco executive reported that both she and other executive wives of her acquaintance tended to deny that they played a part in their husbands' work—even when they knew they had been influential.

With respect to the corporation itself, the issue of the wife's importance is inextricably bound up with the notion that anything she does is voluntary, a matter of personal choice. Indeed, there *is* a degree of choice built into the roles wives play. There may be a wide range of options about when and how the wife participates, many of them negotiated privately between husband and wife. Many of the things a wife does would simply go undone if she were not there to perform them; organizations would be unlikely to replace most of a wife's services with that of a paid employee. The seeming voluntariness of the decisions of a wife to participate in her husband's career, along with the facts that some men do manage without a wife and that some wives have independent careers of their own, all help organizations to view the informal "women's auxiliary" as nothing more than a luxury. . . .

Whether or not the wife is important in the conduct of the corporation, however, the corporation is central in the conduct of her life. The behavior of wives, and the marital issues that arise, must be seen in the way we are viewing the behavior of all corporate workers: as a function of their location in the system, as a response to the role constraints within which they operated in the Industrial Supply Corporation of the 1970s. . . .

The very ambivalence of corporations toward the "wife problem" (William Whyte's label) indicates a fundamental tension in social life between the demands of organizational work and the pulls of family, at least in individualistic societies. Is the wife a helper to be embraced, or a danger to be minimized? Is she an unpaid worker, or a separate reality irrelevant to the organization—an independent person on whom the organization has no claims? From the corporation's perspective, is the family, the intimate tie, to be included in the organization to make more committed members, or is it to be discouraged, kept away, so that participants will feel no competing pulls?[14] Whose interests do the "women's auxiliaries" serve—their own, their husbands', the corporation's? What responsibilities do organizations have when their policies and practices impact on the family outside? These questions cannot be answered by default, by pretenses that wives are not part of the system. Issues remain: the nature of corporate responsibility; the limits on corporate greed—in this case, the organization's tendency to swallow up its members and consume them and their families.

From the perspective of individuals and *their* welfare, there are other problems organizations can address.[15] Some require delicate balancing: How to minimize wives' feelings of exclusion while permitting them independence. How to reduce the stresses of publicness and reduce image pressures. How to give families a voice in policies affecting them. Whether job pressures drive wedges between husbands and wives, and how these can be modified. How to help involve wives in husbands' work (and vice versa) without making them subordinated assistants. How to redefine success so as to minimize political manipulation and instrumentality. How to create positive relations between the women inside and the women outside the organization. Whether to compensate professional and managerial women for their lack of a "wife." As pressure mounts for more explicit national family policy, questions of the impact of forms of employment on family life cannot be avoided. . . .

Notes

1. Evelyn Keene, "Cruising on a Collision Course: Policeman's Wives Vs. Policewomen," *Boston Globe*, November 2, 1974.
2. William H. Whyte, Jr., "The Wives of Management," and "The Corporation and the Wife," *Fortune* (October 1951, and November 1951).
3. Robert Seidenberg, *Corporate Wives: Corporate Casualties?* (New York: Amacom, 1973); Harry Levinson, *Emotional Problems in the World of Work* (New York: Harper & Row, 1964); Myrna M. Weissman and Eugene S. Paykel, "Moving and Depression in Women," *Society*, 9(July–August, 1972): pp. 24–28. See also W. Lloyd Warner and James C. Abegglen, *Big Business Leaders in America* (New York: Harper and Brothers, 1955), p. 125.
4. Associated Press, " 'It's like being a prisoner,' says Trudeau's wife," *Boston Globe*, October 28, 1974; "The Relentless Ordeal of Political Wives," *Time*, October 7, 1974, pp. 15–22; Myra MacPherson, *The Power Lovers: An Intimate Look at Politicians and Their Marriages* (New York: Putnam, 1975).
5. John F. Cuber with Peggy Harroff, *The Significant Americans: A Study of Sexual Behavior among the Affluent* (New York: Appleton Century, 1965), p. 59; *New York Times*, April 29, 1973, cited in Seidenberg, *Corporate Wives*, p. 79; Whyte, "Wives of Management" and "The Corporation and the Wife"; Helena Z. Lopata, *Occupation: Housewife* (New York: Oxford University Press, 1971), p. 101.
6. Seidenberg, *Corporate Wives*, p. 86.
7. Lewis Coser uses this phrase, although he did not look at corporate wives. See *Greedy Organizations* (New York: Free Press, 1974).
8. Whyte, "The Wives of Management" and "The Corporation and the Wife."
9. Seidenberg, *Corporate Wives*, p. 30.
10. "Most bureaucratic structures are capped by a nonbureaucratic elite operating with greater freedom than the lower levels of the organization." Theodore Caplow, *The Sociology of Work* (Minneapolis: University of Minnesota Press, 1954), p. 66.
11. William H. Whyte, Jr., "How Hard Do Executives Work?", in *The Executive Life* (Garden City, New York: Doubleday, 1956), pp. 61–78; Peter Willmott, "Family, Work, and Leisure Conflicts Among Male Employees: Some Preliminary Findings," *Human Relations*, 2(December 1971), 575–84.

12. Of course, not all volunteer work is so instrumental; it is an important and often altruistic public service. The quote is from Dollie Ann Cole, "New Style of Corporate Wife," *New York Times*, December 2, 1973.

13. Hanna Papanek, "Men, Women, and Work: Reflections on the Two-Person Career," *American Journal of Sociology*, 78(January 1973), p. 100.

14. Theoretical issues are raised in Rosabeth Moss Kanter, *Commitment and Community* (Cambridge, Mass.: Harvard University Press, 1972), Chapter 4.

15. A large number of policy issues are raised in Rosabeth Moss Kanter, *Work and Family in the United States* (New York, Russell Sage Foundation, 1976). See also Bill Frupp, "Transfers and the Executive Rebellion," *Boston Globe*, November 13, 1975; and Samuel A. Culbert and Jean R. Renshaw, "Coping with the Stresses of Travel as an Opportunity for Improving the Quality of Work and Family Life," *Family Process*, 11(September 1972), pp. 321–22.

15

Puerto Rican Elderly Women
Shared Meanings and Informal Supportive Networks

Melba Sánchez-Ayéndez

Introduction

Studies of older adults' support systems have seldom taken into account how values within a specific cultural context affect expectations of support and patterns of assistance in social networks. Such networks and supportive relations have a cultural dimension reflecting a system of shared meanings. These meanings affect social interaction and the expectations people have of their relationships with others.

Ethnicity and gender affect a person's adjustment to old age. Although sharing a "minority" position produces similar consequences among members of different ethnic minority groups, the groups' diversity lies in their distinctive systems of shared meanings. Studies of older adults in ethnic minority groups have rarely focused on the cultural contents of ethnicity affecting the aging process, particularly of women (Barth 1969). Cultural value orientations are central to understanding how minority elders approach growing old and how they meet the physical and emotional changes associated with aging.

This article describes the interplay between values and behavior in family and community of a group of older Puerto Rican women living on low incomes in Boston.[1] It explores how values emphasizing family interdependence and different roles of women and men shape the women's expectations, behavior, and supportive familial and community networks.

Being a Woman Is Different from Being a Man

The women interviewed believe in a dual standard of conduct for men and women. This dual standard is apparent in different attributes assigned to women and men, roles expected of them, and authority exercised by them.

The principal role of men in the family is viewed as that of provider; their main responsibility is economic in nature. Although fathers are expected to be affectionate with their children, child care is not seen to be a man's responsibility. Men are not envisioned within the domestic sphere.

The "ideal" man must be the protector of the family, able to control his emotions and be self-sufficient. Men enjoy more freedom in the public world than do women. From the women's perspective, the ideal of maleness is linked to the concept of *machismo*. This concept assumes men have a stronger sexual drive than women, a need to prove virility by the conquest of women, a dominant position in relation to females, and a belligerent attitude when confronted by male peers.

The women see themselves as subordinate to men and recognize the preeminence of male authority. They believe women ought to be patient and largely forbearing in their relations with men, particularly male family members. Patience and forbearance, however, are not confused with passivity or total submissiveness. The elderly Puerto Rican women do not conceive of themselves or other women as "resigned females" but as dynamic beings, continually devising strategies to improve everyday situations within and outside the household.

Rosa Mendoza,[2] now sixty-five, feels no regrets for having decided at thirty years of age and after nine years of marriage not to put up with her husband's heavy drinking any longer. She moved out of her house and went to live with her mother.

> I was patient for many years. I put up with his drunkenness and worked hard to earn money. One day I decided I'd be better off without him. One thing is to be patient, and another to be a complete fool. So I moved out.

Although conscious of their subordinate status to their husbands, wives are also aware of their power and the demands they can make. Ana Fuentes recalls when her husband had a mistress. Ana was thirty-eight.

> I knew he had a mistress in a nearby town. I was patient for a long time,
> hoping it would end. Most men, sooner or later, have a mistress some-
> where. But when it didn't end after quite a time and everyone in the neigh-
> borhood knew about it, I said "I am fed up!" He came home one evening
> and the things I told him! I even said I'd go to that woman's house and
> beat her if I had to. . . . He knew I was not bluffing; that this was not just
> another argument. He tried to answer back and I didn't let him. He re-
> mained silent. . . . And you know what? He stopped seeing her! A woman
> can endure many things for a long time, but the time comes when she has
> to defend her rights.

These older Puerto Rican women perceive the home as the center
around which the female world revolves. Home is the woman's domain; women generally make decisions about household maintenance
and men seldom intervene.

Family relations are considered part of the domestic sphere and
therefore a female responsibility. The women believe that success in
marriage depends on the woman's ability to "make the marriage
work."

> A marriage lasts as long as the woman decides it will last. It is us who
> make a marriage work, who put up with things, who try to make ends
> meet, who yield.

The norm of female subordination is evident in the view that marriage
will last as long as the woman "puts up with things" and deals with
marriage from her subordinate status. Good relations with affinal kin
are also a woman's responsibility. They are perceived as relations between the wife's domestic unit and other women's domestic units.

Motherhood

Motherhood is seen by these older Puerto Rican women as the central
role of women. Their concept of motherhood is based on the female capacity to bear children and on the notion of *marianismo*, which
presents the Virgin Mary as a role model (Stevens 1973). *Marianismo*
presupposes that it is through motherhood that a woman realizes herself and derives her life's greatest satisfactions.

A woman's reproductive role is viewed as leading her toward more
commitment to and a better understanding of her children than is
shown by the father. One of the women emphasized this view:

> It is easier for a man to leave his children and form a new home with an-
> other woman, or not to be as forgiving of children as a mother is. They
> will never know what it is like to carry a child inside, feel it growing, and
> then bring that child into the world. This is why a mother is always will-
> ing to forgive and make sacrifices. That creature is a part of you; it nour-

ished from you and came from within you. But it is not so for men. To them, a child is a being they receive once it is born. The attachment can never be the same.

The view that childrearing is their main responsibility in life comes from this conceptualization of the mother-child bond. For the older women, raising children means more than looking after the needs of offspring. It involves being able to offer them every possible opportunity for a better life, during childhood or adulthood, even if this requires personal sacrifices.

As mother and head of the domestic domain, a woman is also responsible for establishing the bases for close and good relations among her children. From childhood through adulthood, the creation and maintenance of family unity among offspring is considered another female responsibility.

Family Unity and Interdependence

Family Unity

Ideal family relations are seen as based on two interrelated themes, family unity and family interdependence. Family unity refers to the desirability of close and intimate kin ties, with members getting along well and keeping in frequent contact despite dispersal.

Celebration of holidays and special occasions are seen as opportunities for kin to be together and strengthen family ties. Family members, particularly grandparents, adult children, and grandchildren, are often reunited at Christmas, New Year's, Mother's and Father's days, Easter, and Thanksgiving. Special celebrations like weddings, baptisms, first communions, birthdays, graduations, and funerals occasion reunions with other family members. Whether to celebrate happy or sad events, the older women encourage family gatherings as a way of strengthening kinship ties and fostering family continuity.

The value the women place on family unity is also evident in their desire for frequent interaction with kin members. Visits and telephone calls demonstrate a caring attitude by family members which cements family unity.

Family unity is viewed as contributing to the strengthening of family interdependence. Many of the older women repeat a proverb when referring to family unity: *En la unión está la fuerza.* ("In union there is strength.") They believe that the greater the degree of unity in the family, the greater the emphasis family members will place on interdependence and familial obligation.

Family Interdependence

Despite adaptation to life in a culturally different society, Puerto Rican families in the United States are still defined by strong norms of reciprocity among family members, especially those in the immediate kinship group (Cantor 1979; Carrasquillo 1982; Delgado 1981; Donaldson and Martínez 1980; Sánchez-Ayéndez 1984). Interdependence within the Puerto Rican symbolic framework "fits an orientation to life that stresses that the individual is not capable of doing everything and doing it well. Therefore, he should rely on others for assistance" (Bastida 1979: 70). Individualism and self-reliance assume a different meaning from the one prevailing in the dominant U.S. cultural tradition. Individuals in Puerto Rican families will expect and ask for assistance from certain people in their social networks without any derogatory implications for self-esteem.

Family interdependence is a value to which these older Puerto Rican women strongly adhere. It influences patterns of mutual assistance with their children as well as expectations of support. The older women expect to be taken care of during old age by their adult children. The notion of filial duty ensues from the value orientation of interdependence. Adult children are understood to have a responsibility toward their aged parents in exchange for the functions that parents performed for them throughout their upbringing. Expected reciprocity from offspring is intertwined with the concept of filial love and the nature of the parent-child relationship.

Parental duties of childrearing are perceived as inherent in the "parent" role and also lay the basis for long-term reciprocity with children, particularly during old age. The centrality that motherhood has in the lives of the older women contributes to creating great expectations among them of reciprocity from children. More elderly women than men verbalize disappointment when one of their children does not participate in the expected interdependence ties. Disappointment is unlikely to arise when an adult child cannot help due to financial or personal reasons. However, it is bound to arise when a child chooses not to assist the older parent for other reasons.

These older Puerto Rican women stress that good offspring ought to help their parents, contingent upon available resources. Statements such as the following are common:

> Of course I go to my children when I have a problem! To whom would I turn? I raised them and worked very hard to give them the little I could. Now that I am old, they try to help me in whatever they can. . . . Good offspring should help their aged parents as much as they are able to.

Interdependence for Puerto Rican older parents also means helping their children and grandchildren. Many times they provide help .

when it is not explicitly requested. They are happy when they can perform supportive tasks for their children's families. The child who needs help, no matter how old, is not judged as dependent or a failure.

Reciprocity is not based on strictly equal exchanges. Due to the rapid pace of life, lack of financial resources, or personal problems, adult children are not always able to provide the care the elder parent needs. Many times, the older adults provide their families with more financial and instrumental assistance than their children are able to provide them. Of utmost importance to the older women is not that their children be able to help all the time, but that they visit or call frequently. They place more emphasis on emotional support from their offspring than on any other form of support.

Gloria Santos, for example, has a son and a daughter. While they do not live in the same state as their mother, they each send her fifty to seventy dollars every month. Yet, she is disappointed with her children and explains why:

> They both have good salaries but call me only once or twice a month. I hardly know my grandchildren. All I ask from them is that they be closer to me, that they visit and call me more often. They only visit me once a year and only for one or two days. I've told my daughter that instead of sending me money she could call me more often. I was a good mother and worked hard in order for them to get a good education and have everything. All I expected from them was to show me they care, that they love me.

The importance that the older women attach to family interdependence does not imply that they constantly require assistance from children or that they do not value their independence. They prefer to live in their own households rather than with their adult children. They also try to solve as many problems as possible by themselves. But when support is needed, the adult children are expected to assist the aged parent to the degree they are able. This does not engender conflict or lowered self-esteem for the aged adult. Conflict and dissatisfaction are caused when adult children do not offer any support at all.

Sex Roles and Familial Supportive Networks

The family is the predominant source of support for most of these older women, providing instrumental and emotional support in daily life as well as assistance during health crises or times of need. Adult children play a central role in providing familial support to old parents. For married women, husbands are also an important component of their support system. At the same time, most of the older women still perform functional roles for their families.

Support from Adult Children

The support and helpfulness expected from offspring is related to perceptions of the difference between men and women. Older women seek
different types of assistance from daughters than from sons. Daughters are perceived as being inherently better able to understand their
mothers due to their shared status and qualities as women; they are
also considered more reliable. Sons are not expected to help as much
as daughters or in the same way. When a daughter does not fulfill the
obligations expected of her, complaints are more bitter than if the
same were true of a son: "Men are different; they do not feel as we feel.
But she is a woman; she should know better." Daughters are also expected to visit and/or call more frequently than are sons. As women are
linked closely to the domestic domain, they are held responsible for
the care of family relations.

Motherhood is perceived as creating an emotional bond among
women. When daughters become mothers, the older women anticipate
stronger ties and more support from them.

> Once a daughter experiences motherhood, she understands the suffering
> and hardships you underwent for her. Sons will never be able to under-
> stand this.

> My daughter always helped me. But when she became a mother for the
> first time, she grew much closer to me. It was then when she was able to
> understand how much a mother can love.

Most of the older women go to a daughter first when confronted by
an emotional problem. Daughters are felt to be more patient and better
able to understand them as women. It is not that older women never
discuss their emotional problems with their sons, but they prefer to
discuss them with their daughters. For example, Juana Rivera has two
sons who live in the same city as she and a daughter who resides in
Puerto Rico. She and her sons get along well and see each other often.
The sons stop by their mother's house every day after work, talk about
daily happenings, and assist her with some tasks. However, when a
physical exam revealed a breast tumor thought to be malignant, it was
to her daughter in Puerto Rico that the old woman expressed her worries. She recalls that time of crisis:

> Eddie was with me when the doctor told me of the possibility of a tumor. I
> was brave. I didn't want him to see me upset. They [sons] get nervous
> when I get upset or cry. . . . That evening I called my daughter and talked
> to her. . . . She was very understanding and comforted me. I can always
> depend on her to understand me. She is the person who better under-
> stands me. My sons are also understanding, but she is a woman and un-
> derstands more.

Although adult children are sources of assistance during the illnesses of their mothers, it is generally daughters from whom more is expected. Quite often daughters take their sick parents into their homes or stay overnight in the parental household in order to provide better care. Sons, as well as daughters, take the aged parent to the hospital or doctors' offices and buy medicines if necessary. However, it is more often daughters who check on their parents, provide care, and perform household chores when the parent is sick.

When the old women have been hospitalized, adult children living nearby tend to visit the hospital daily. Daughters and daughters-in-law sometimes cook special meals for the sick parent and bring the meals to the hospital. Quite often, adult children living in other states or in Puerto Rico come to help care for the aged parent or be present at the time of an operation. When Juana Rivera had exploratory surgery on her breast, her daughter came from Puerto Rico and stayed with her mother throughout the convalescence. Similarly, when Ana Toledo suffered a stroke and remained unconscious for four days, three of her six children residing in other states came to be with her and their siblings. After her release from the hospital, a daughter from New Jersey stayed at her mother's house for a week. When she left, the children who live near the old woman took turns looking after her.

Most adult children are also helpful in assisting with chores of daily living. At times, offspring take their widowed mothers grocery shopping. Other times, the older women give their children money to do the shopping for them. Daughters are more often asked to do these favors and to also buy personal care items and clothes for their mothers. Some adult offspring also assist by depositing Social Security checks, checking post office boxes, and buying money orders.

Support from Elderly Mothers

The Puerto Rican older women play an active role in providing assistance to their adult children. Gender affects the frequency of emotional support offered as well as the dynamics of the support. The older women offer advice more often to daughters than to sons on matters related to childrearing. And the approach used differs according to the children's gender. For example, one older woman stated,

> I never ask my son openly what is wrong with him. I do not want him to think that I believe he needs help to solve his problems; he is a man. . . . Yet, as a mother I worry. It is my duty to listen and offer him advice. With my daughter it is different; I can be more direct. She doesn't have to prove to me that she is self-sufficient.

Another woman expressed similar views:

Of course I give advice to my sons! When they have had problems with
their wives, their children, even among themselves, I listen to them, and
tell them what I think. But with my daughters I am more open. You see, if
I ask one of my sons what is wrong and he doesn't want to tell me, I don't
insist too much; I'll ask later, maybe in a different way; and they will tell
me sooner or later. With my daughters, if they don't want to tell me, I insist. They know I am a mother and a woman like them and that I can understand.

Older mothers perceive sons and daughters as in equal need of
support. Daughters, however, are understood to face additional problems in areas such as conjugal relations, childrearing, and sexual harassment, due to their status as women.

Emotional support to daughters-in-law is also offered, particularly when they are encountering marriage or childrearing problems.
Josefina Montes explains the active role she played in comforting her
daughter-in-law, whose husband was having an extramarital affair.

I told her not to give up, that she had to defend what was hers. I always
listened to her and tried to offer some comfort. . . . When my son would
come to my home to visit I would ask him "What is wrong with you? Don't
you realize what a good mother and wife that woman is?" . . . I made it my
business that he did not forget the exceptional woman she is. . . . I told
him I didn't want to ever see him with the other one and not to mention
her name in front of me. . . . I was on his case for almost two years. . . . All
the time I told her to be patient. . . . It took time but he finally broke up
with the other one.

When relations between mother and daughters-in-law are not friendly,
support is not usually present. Eulalia Valle says that when her son
left his wife and children to move in with another woman, there was
not much she could do for her daughter-in-law.

There was not much I could do. What could I tell him? I couldn't say she
was nice to me. . . . Once I tried to make him see how much she was hurting and he replied: "Don't defend her. She has never been fond of you and
you know it." What could I reply to that? All I said was, "That's true but,
still, she must be very hurt." But there was nothing positive to say about
her!

Monetary assistance generally flows from the older parent to the
adult children, although few old people are able to offer substantial financial help. Direct monetary assistance, rarely exceeding fifty dollars, is less frequent than gift-giving. Gift-giving usually takes the form
of monetary contributions for specific articles needed by their children or children's families. In this way the older people contribute in-
directly to the maintenance of their children's families.

The older women also play an active role in the observance of special family occasions and holidays. On the days preceding the celebration, they are busy cooking traditional Puerto Rican foods. It is expected that those in good health will participate in the preparation of foods. This is especially true on Christmas and Easter when traditional foods are an essential component of the celebrations.

Cooking for offspring is also a part of everyday life. In many of the households, meals prepared in the Puerto Rican tradition are cooked daily "in case children or grandchildren come by." Josefina Montes, for example, cooks a large quantity of food everyday for herself, her husband, and their adult children and grandchildren. Her daughters come by after work to visit and pick up their youngest children, who stay with grandparents after school. The youngest daughter eats dinner at her parents' home. The oldest takes enough food home to serve her family. Doña[3] Josefina's sons frequently drop by after work or during lunch and she always insists that they eat something.

The older women also provide assistance to their children during health crises. When Juana Rivera's son was hospitalized for a hernia operation, she visited the hospital every day, occasionally bringing food she had prepared for him. When her son was released, Doña Juana stayed in his household throughout his convalescence, caring for him while her daughter-in-law went off to work.

The aged women also assist their children by taking care of grandchildren. Grandchildren go to their grandmother's house after school and stay until their parents stop by after work. If the children are not old enough to walk home by themselves, the grandparent waits for them at school and brings them home. The women also take care of their grandchildren when they are not old enough to attend school or are sick. They see their role as grandmothers as a continuation or reenactment of their role as mothers and childrearers.

The women, despite old age, have a place in the functional structure of their families. The older women's assistance is an important contribution to their children's households and also helps validate the women's sense of their importance and helpfulness.

Mutual Assistance in Elderly Couples

Different conceptions of women and men influence interdependence between husband and wife as well as their daily tasks. Older married women are responsible for domestic tasks and perform household chores. They also take care of grandchildren, grocery shopping, and maintaining family relations. Older married men have among their chores depositing Social Security checks, going to the post office, and buying money orders. Although they stay in the house for long periods, the men go out into the community more often than do their wives. They usually stop at the *bodegas*,[4] which serve as a place for socializing and exchange of information, to buy items needed at home and newspapers from Puerto Rico.

Most married couples have a distinctive newspaper reading pattern. The husband comments on the news to his wife as he reads or after he has finished. Sometimes, after her husband finishes reading and commenting on the news, the older woman reads about it herself. Husbands also inform their wives of ongoing neighborhood events learned on their daily stops at the *bodegas*. Wives, on the other hand, inform husbands of familial events learned through their daily telephone conversations and visits from children and other kin members.

The older couple escort each other to service-providing agencies, even though they are usually accompanied by an adult child, adolescent grandchild, or social worker serving as translator. An older man still perceives himself in the role of "family protector" by escorting the women in his family, particularly his wife.

Older husbands and wives provide each other with emotional assistance. They are daily companions and serve as primary sources of confidence for each other, most often sharing children's and grandchildren's problems, health concerns, or financial worries. The couple do not always agree on solutions or approaches for assisting children when sharing their worries about offspring. Many times the woman serves as a mediator in communicating her husband's problems to adult children. The men tend to keep their problems, particularly financial and emotional ones, to themselves or tell their wives but not their children. This behavior rests upon the notion of men as financially responsible for the family, more self-sufficient, and less emotional than women.

Among the older couples, the husband or wife is generally the principal caregiver during the health crises of their spouse. Carmen Ruiz, for example, suffers from chronic anemia and tires easily. Her husband used to be a cook and has taken responsibility for cooking meals and looking after the household. When Providencia Cruz's husband was hospitalized she spent many hours each day at the hospital, wanting to be certain he was comfortable. She brought meals she had cooked for him, arranged his pillows, rubbed him with bay leaf rubbing alcohol, or watched him as he slept. When he was convalescing at home, she was his principal caregiver. Doña Providencia suffers from osteoarthritis and gastric acidity. When she is in pain and spends the day in bed, her husband provides most of the assistance she needs. He goes to the drugstore to buy medicine or ingredients used in folk remedies. He knows how to prepare the mint and chamomile teas she drinks when not feeling well. He also rubs her legs and hands with ointments when the arthritic pain is more intense than usual. Furthermore, during the days that Doña Providencia's ailments last, he performs most of the household chores.

While both spouses live, the couple manages many of their problems on their own. Assistance from other family members with daily chores or help during an illness is less frequent when the woman still lives with her husband than when she lives alone. However, if one or both spouses is ill, help from adult children is more common.

Friends and Neighbors as Community Sources of Support

Friends and neighbors form part of the older women's support network. However, the women differentiate between "neighbors" and "friends." Neighbors, unlike kin and friends, are not an essential component of the network which provides emotional support. They may or may not become friends. Supportive relations with friends involve being instrumental helpers, companions, and confidants. Neighbors are involved only in instrumental help.

Neighbors as Sources of Support

Contact with neighbors takes the form of greetings, occasional visits, and exchanges of food, all of which help to build the basis for reciprocity when and if the need arises. The establishment and maintenance of good relations with neighbors is considered to be important since neighbors are potentially helpful during emergencies or unexpected events. Views such as the following are common: "It is good to get acquainted with your neighbors; you never know when you might need them."

Josefina Rosario, a widow, has lived next door to an older Puerto Rican couple for three years. Exchange of food and occasional visits are part of her interaction with them. Her neighbor's husband, in his mid-sixties, occasionally runs errands for Doña Josefina, who suffers from rheumatoid arthritis and needs a walker to move around. If she runs out of a specific food item, he goes to the grocery store for her. Other times, he buys stamps, mails letters, or goes to the drugstore to pick up some medicines for her. Although Doña Josefina cannot reciprocate in the same way, she repays her neighbors by visiting every other week and exchanging food. Her neighbors tell her she is to call them day or night if she ever feels sick. Although glad to have such "good neighbors," as she calls them, she stresses she does not consider them friends and therefore does not confide her personal problems to them.

Supportive Relationships Among Friends

Although friends perform instrumental tasks, the older women believe that a good friend's most important quality is being able to provide emotional support. A friend is someone willing to help during the "good" and "bad" times, and is trustworthy and reserved. Problems may be shared with a friend with the certainty that confidences will not be betrayed. A friend provides emotional support not only during a crisis or problem, but in everyday life. Friends are companions, visiting and/or calling on a regular basis.

Friendship for this group of women is determined along gender lines. They tend to be careful about men. Relationships with males outside the immediate familial group are usually kept at a formal level. Mistrust of men is based upon the women's notion of *machismo*. Since men are conceived of as having a stronger sexual drive, the women are wary of the possibility of sexual advances, either physical or verbal. None of the women regards a male as a confidant friend. Many even emphasize the word *amiga* ("female friend") instead of *amigo* ("male friend"). Remarks such as the following are common:

> I've never had an *amigo*. Men cannot be trusted too much. They might misunderstand your motives and some even try to make a pass at you.

The few times the women refer to a male as a friend they use the term *amigo de la familia* ("friend of the family"). This expression conveys that the friendly relations are not solely between the woman and the man. The expression is generally used to refer to a close friend of the husband. *Amigos de la familia* may perform instrumental tasks, be present at family gatherings and unhappy events, or drop by to chat with the respondent's husband during the day. However, relations are not based on male-female relationships.

Age similarity is another factor that seems to affect selection of friends. The friendship networks of the older women are mainly composed of people sixty years of age and older. Friends who fill the role of confidant are generally women of a similar age. The women believe that younger generations, generally, have little interest in the elders. They also state that people their own age are better able to understand their problems because they share many of the same difficulties and worries.

Friends often serve as escorts, particularly in the case of women who live alone. Those who know some English serve as translators on some occasions. Close friends also help illiterate friends by reading and writing letters.

Most of the support friends provide one another is of an emotional nature, which involves sharing personal problems. Close friends entrust one another with family and health problems. This exchange occurs when friends either visit or call each other on the telephone. A pattern commonly observed between dyads of friends is daily calls. Many women who live alone usually call the friend during the morning hours, to make sure she is all right and to find out how she is feeling.

Another aspect of the emotional support the older women provide one another is daily companionship, occurring more often among those who live alone. For example, Hilda Montes and Rosa Mendoza sit together from 1:00 to 3:00 in the afternoon to watch soap operas and talk about family events, neighborhood happenings, and household management. At 3:00 P.M., whoever is at the other's apartment leaves because their grandchildren usually arrive from school around 4:00 P.M.

Friends are also supportive during health crises. If they cannot come to visit, they inquire daily about their friend's health by telephone. When their health permits, some friends perform menial household chores and always bring food for the sick person. If the occasion requires it, they prepare and/or administer home remedies. Friends, in this sense, alleviate the stress adult children often feel in assisting their aged mothers, particularly those who live by themselves. Friends take turns among themselves or with kin in taking care of the ill during the daytime. Children generally stay throughout the night.

Exchange ties with female friends include instrumental support, companionship, and problem sharing. Friends, particularly age cohorts, play an important role in the emotional well-being of the elders.

The relevance of culture to experience of old age is seen in the influence of value orientations on the expectations these Puerto Rican women have of themselves and those in their informal supportive networks. The way a group's cultural tradition defines and interprets relationships influences how elders use their networks to secure the support needed in old age. At the same time, the extent to which reality fits culturally-based expectations will contribute, to a large extent, to elders' sense of well-being.

Notes

1. The article is based on a nineteen-month ethnographic study. The research was supported by the Danforth Foundation; Sigma Xi; the Scientific Research Society; and the Delta Kappa Gamma Society International.

2. All names are fictitious.
3. The deference term *Doña* followed by the woman's first name is a common way by which to address elderly Puerto Rican women and the one preferred by those who participated in the study.
4. Neighborhood grocery stores, generally owned by Puerto Ricans or other Hispanics, where ethnic foods can be purchased.

References Cited

Barth, F.
1969 Introduction to *Ethnic Groups and Boundaries*, F. Barth, ed. Boston: Little, Brown.

Bastida, E.
1979 "Family Integration and Adjustment to Aging Among Hispanic American Elderly." Ph.D. dissertation, University of Kansas.

Cantor, M. H.
1979 "The Informal Support System of New York's Inner City Elderly: Is Ethnicity a Factor?" In *Ethnicity and Aging*, D. L. Gelfand and A. J. Kutzik, eds. New York: Springer.

Carrasquillo, H.
1982 "Perceived Social Reciprocity and Self-Esteem Among Elderly Barrio Antillean Hispanics and Their Familial Informal Networks." Ph.D. dissertation, Syracuse University.

Delgado, M.
1981 Hispanic Elderly and Natural Support Systems: A Special Focus on Puerto Ricans. Paper presented at the Scientific Meeting of the Boston Society for Gerontological Psychiatry, November, Boston, Mass.

Donaldson, E. and E. Martínez.
1980 "The Hispanic Elderly of East Harlem" *Aging* 305–306: 6–11.

Sánchez-Ayéndez, M.
1984 "Puerto Rican Elderly Women: Aging in an Ethnic Minority Group in the United States." Ph.D. dissertation, University of Massachusetts at Amherst.

Stevens, E. P.
1973 "Marianismo: The Other Face of Machismo in Latin America." In *Female and Male in Latin America*, A. Pescatello, ed. Pittsburgh: University of Pittsburgh Press.

16

Societal Stress
The Black Family

Harriette P. McAdoo

A group of Black parents were discussing their children's experiences of racism. One father said, "When Marcia was three, we were at a shopping plaza and an older white child taunted her about being Black. Marcia didn't know what to say, and walked off. When we talked to her about it, she seemed to feel better, and I had hoped she would forget all about it. But she didn't—it still bothers her, she still remembers it." Another parent said, "I know my kids aren't treated the same as whites at school. Somehow, you know, teachers seem to expect less from Black kids. The kids feel it, and wonder why they're treated differently."

These parents are painfully aware of the stress of racism in their lives and their children's lives. Being a member of a minority group in America means being treated differently, and this societal stressor places huge demands on family life.

Until recently, both family scholars and the public have attributed racial differences in family life to the poverty in which many Black families live. Once Blacks were better educated and upwardly mobile,

Chapter 12 in *Stress and the Family* edited by Hamilton McCubbin and Charles R. Figley copyright 1983. Reprinted by permission of Brunner/Mazel, Inc.

so the theory went, these differences would disappear. But the civil rights movement and the development of group consciousness among people of color brought to reality the fact that Blacks were not being allowed to melt into a single white American culture. They were actively affirming their pride in their unique African-American heritage and demanding an end to racial discrimination. Although some assimilation has occurred, differences persist in religion, music, and language, pointing to the basic soul-searching role that cultural heritage plays in the maintenance of positive self-identity and positive mental health. These cultural differences tend to persist even when Black families become part of the middle class (McAdoo, 1979).

Of course, Black families share many characteristics and problems with white families: The developmental changes in children and parents as they grow and age; the problems of single parents or dual-employed families; the stressors of inflation, unemployment, war or natural disasters . . . all have relevance for Black families. But they must be seen in context: A racist environment changes and intensifies the meaning and impact of these normative and catastrophic sources of stress. Black families are not able to have the same opportunities and experiences as white families, and these differences are important reasons for considering their special stressors and coping patterns.

The focus of this chapter is on the societal stressors of racism on Black families, and how these families remain strong and responsive as they cope with these stressors. This chapter will sketch some of the stressors of racism by discussing the concept of mundane extreme environmental stress and by looking specifically at how this environment affects the economic situation of Black families. The second part of the chapter deals with how the special strengths of Black families contribute to their ability to cope with these stressors; the reliance on the extended family and community for support and the flexibility of roles in the family are two such strengths.

Stressors of Racism: The Mundane Extreme Environment

Chester Pierce, a Black psychiatrist, has compared the stress on Blacks in the United States with the harsh physical stress on those who live in extreme climates. Just as the day-to-day demands of coping with severe cold and scarce food supply define life for the Eskimo people in the Arctic, so severe racial prejudice defines life for Blacks. Pierce (1975), borrowing a term from anthropologists, calls this racist "climate" a *mundane extreme environment*. In this case the extreme environment is not a physical, geographic one, but a social one; it provides the entire context for people's lives and expectations (Peters, 1981).

The "extreme" difficulties which white society imposes on Black people by denying their identity, their values, and their economic opportunity are not unusual or extraordinary but "mundane," daily pressures for Blacks.

The concept of a mundane extreme environment suggests vividly how racism is a pervasive, daily reality for Black families. This reality goes beyond the single interactions with non-Blacks in the neighborhood or with strangers on the way to school or work, when a Black child or adult may be treated differently than one who is non-Black. It even goes beyond the cross burnings that are increasing and the actual violence that occurs more frequently than we would like to admit. Rather, the reality for Black individuals is affected most seriously by the negative perceptions that are held about them by whites. These negative images are part of the American culture and difficult to escape, for they are projected continuously throughout the culture— through TV, through pictures in school books, in ethnic jokes, and from personal experiences when the different racial groups come into contact with each other. These attitudes come to the surface when there is a lack of acceptance for those with cultural differences, or when teachers do not expect as much from their Black children and, therefore, are given less in return. It occurs also when employers do not consider Blacks to be capable of doing a job regardless of their individual abilities or training.

It is important to see that the subordinate social position of Black Americans is supported and maintained by social institutions such as schools or the social welfare system (Ogbu, 1978). We must avoid "blaming the victims" of this pervasive, extremely stressful environment. While degrees of racial oppression vary with each situation, the potential for being devalued and put down is *always* present, dangling constantly over Blacks, beyond their control.

Economic Stressors

One of the most basic ways this stressful environment affects families is in the denial of economic opportunities. This denial manifests itself in the inadequate education, job discrimination, and higher unemployment rates, all resulting in lower incomes for Black families.

Unemployment

The editors of these volumes have chosen to classify the stressors of unemployment as a "catastrophe"; however, unemployment for Black urban youth is such a common experience that it is often seen in the Black community as a "normative" stressor. While the white unemployed youth can be confident that the catastrophe of unemployment is for a limited time, the Black youth in the same situation knows that he probably will face it for an extended time. Due to the problems of poor education and limited employment opportunities, families of color in all social classes have, in general, lower incomes than white families, even when they have college degrees. Forty-one percent of Black children live in families with poverty level incomes, many headed by single mothers (Pearce & McAdoo, 1981). Some say that all of these conditions are the result of things that are wrong with Blacks themselves. A more accurate analysis reveals these stressful conditions to be the result of a long continuing history of inequities that have fostered the development of groups who do not develop the skills or who lack the social and personal connections that would allow them to be able to help themselves out of their impoverished situations.

One cannot help but respond in amazement that there still exists the energy among Blacks to attempt to be self-sufficient, when there have been so many barriers placed before them. For example, one of the strongest values that Black families have had is faith that education would improve their situation (McAdoo, 1978). During the first years of elementary school, the parents have high expectations of their children and high dreams for them. While the parents are dreaming of their children bettering their lives and having less stress than they themselves have had, others are viewing these high expectations as "unrealistic." What happens is that teachers really do not expect their students in urban schools to achieve and send them the unspoken messages that they really are not expected to achieve. As a result, the students live up to the lowered expectations and another class of students becomes unable to compete in the labor market.

Although minority enrollment in colleges and universities has risen dramatically in the last ten years, most minority students in school beyond high school have been enrolled in terminal or community college programs. Blacks have traditionally been denied access to higher education related to technology, business, and sciences in four-year universities, and thus, to the higher-paying jobs that follow. Even now, most minority students are concentrated in a few two-year colleges, while whites go to universities (Institute for the Study of Educational Policy, 1980). Black students withdraw from these institutions at a much higher rate than do whites. Few Blacks go into the engineering or other technical fields which command the highest salaries on graduation (McAdoo, 1982a).

But even with a degree, racial discrimination on the job is a reality. Minority college graduates can expect to earn only 85% of what white men with similar backgrounds earn. A 1980 *Wall Street Journal* article reports that Black middle managers feel that racism continues to bar them from promotions and the accompanying higher salaries (Kaufman, 1980). In one study of middle-class Black families, many parents reported experiencing insidious or overt discrimination at work which hindered job advancement (McAdoo, 1979).

The national unemployment rate for Blacks is twice the rate for whites (McAdoo, 1982a). For young Black men in urban areas, the situation is desperate; recent data indicate the national youth unemployment rate among Blacks is nearly 60%. Even this number, appalling as it is, is probably too low, for it only counts those who consistently look for jobs; millions of young people have simply given up. According to Jones (1971), these teenagers have become permanent members of the underclass, whose prospects are worse now than they were for anyone during the Great Depression of the 1930s. These young men will enter middle adulthood with no work experience; this extended unemployment will permanently affect their earning potential.

White youth who are unemployed for periods of time probably live at home where at least one parent has a job. Black youth, in contrast, often live in a one-parent household with a mother who is under economic stress. U.S. Census and Department of Labor data show that 40% of these unemployed youth have no relative who is working. Not only do they not have a job, but many are also without a realistic role model of an actively employed adult.

Another factor in explaining the generally lower income levels of Black families is the higher proportion of single-parents and thus single wage-earner families. Half of all Black families are single-parent families headed by women, partly because there are fewer men than women, and partly because of the increase in divorces and teen pregnancies. Many of these women-headed Black families have incomes below the poverty line; Black single mothers are less likely than whites to be collecting child support or alimony, and far fewer have jobs (McAdoo, 1982a). Yet the majority of Black parents are self-supporting and not dependent on public support.

Housing

The lower economic status of Blacks has potentially stressful ripple effects for families. The cost of housing, for example, may restrict them to living in high-crime neighborhoods or public housing projects. For example, Ruby Jones and her three children live in a two-story cement block apartment building in a housing project built in the 1950s. It was built in an industrial area near the center of the city. Two years ago, some of the units were torn down when the state widened the freeway, and the roar of the traffic goes on all the time. "It's a messed-up place to live," says Ruby. "There is a shooting or fire here almost every week, sometimes two or three a week. My kids can hear the shots and sirens when they are doing their homework or trying to sleep at night. I'm embarrassed to say we live here." Although Ruby likes her neighbors and has a brother living nearby, she wishes she could earn enough money to afford a better home for her kids, but rents are too high everywhere else.

Health Care

Reduced income for minority families also affects the quality of health care for Black families. Poor families avoid the expenses of preventative health care, and as inflation hits middle-income families harder, they begin to shift priorities too (General Mills American Family Report, 1979). Concentrated in low-level jobs with poor benefits, Black families are less likely than whites to have adequate health insurance; surveys of Black families indicate that they tend to feel that their health care is poor (McAdoo, 1982b). The infant mortality rate for Blacks is 21.7 per 1000 births, as compared to 12.3 for whites. This higher rate probably indicates poor health care during pregnancy, resulting in low birth weights and more birth defects. The proportion of Black children who have not been immunized against infectious diseases has risen recently, leading to fears of renewed outbreaks of these diseases. The overall mortality rate for Blacks has been consistently higher than for whites, and a recent survey of Black parents found that many partially attributed this higher death rate to the psychological and social pressures of racism in their everyday environment (McAdoo, 1982b).

These stressors, both overt and covert, form the most difficult barrier preventing Blacks from living without a high degree of stress. The stressors of discrimination and of lower economic status result in living conditions that are unhealthy, but these environments are blamed upon the persons who are really the victims, rather than the sources of these stresses. The mundane stressful environments are the result of discrimination that interacts with people who have been made to feel that there is only limited hope for bettering their lives, and thus this environment is perpetuated.

Coping with the Stressors of Racism

These stressors of racism and economic disadvantage do indeed create an extreme environment for Black families. Yet it would be wrong to view these families as totally unhealthy or inadequate because of these stressors. In fact, the family has remained a strong and responsible institution for Black people throughout their history, even during the slavery era (Staples, 1971).

The most functional and effective coping strategies for Blacks come from the strength and support they find within their own families and kin networks. The strengths we will discuss here are the reliance on the help-exchange network of family and friends, and the flexibility of family roles in Black families.

The Help-Exchange Network of Family and Friends

William, age 32, and Gloria Robinson, age 28, live in a large midwestern city near her parents and four of her six brothers and sisters. They have two small children. William is a carpenter, although he has been laid off for the past two months. His unemployment checks sometimes do not quite cover expenses, and he is sometimes depressed that he can't find another job. When their car broke down last month, they borrowed the money for the repair bill from William's brother. Gloria herself has been able to pick up some temporary work, mostly through an employment agency. While she is working and William is not, the kids stay with Gloria's sister Donna. The two sisters often help each other with child-care responsibilities. Last year Gloria's sister Jane and Jane's daughter lived with William and Gloria for several months while Jane looked for a new job and apartment. Gloria sees her sisters often, sometimes two or three times a week, and the whole family gets together at her parents' house almost every weekend. When she is worried about money or has an argument with William, she turns to her sisters and her mother.

In Gloria's case, her family is her main source of social support, with some help from William's family. They help when her nuclear family needs money, when she needs a babysitter, or when she just wants someone to talk to. The family members see one another frequently, and Gloria gives help as well as receiving it. Sociologists term this arrangement a "kin help-exchange network." In Gloria's case "kin" refers to her parents and siblings. For other Black families the term can include more distant relatives, as well as family friends or neighbors (Stack, 1975; Staples, 1971). Census data indicate that Black families take in relatives to live in their households for a time much more often than white families (Billingsley, 1968; Hill, 1971). Black parents report feeling more protective of their children than white parents do. They often act as a buffer between their children and the racism of teachers or other whites. Black childrearing patterns reflect this "buffering"; parents actively promote their children's psychological well-being in the face of omnipresent stressors (Nobles, 1974; Richardson, 1981). To cope with a hostile society, Black families have turned to the resources within their families and among their friends.

Nor is this reliance on support from kin merely a response to poverty. A study of stress and coping patterns of middle-class Black families found that almost every family gave and received help from their kin network (McAdoo, 1982b). This help took the form of child-care, loans of money in emergencies, emotional support, and exchange of help with repairs or chores. Those who were under more stress relied on kin the most.

These middle-class parents were aware of the sacrifices their families had made to put them through school and help them succeed, and they regarded their own success as an achievement shared with the wider kin group. They felt, in turn, that offering help and support was "what is done in families" and valued their extended family relations very highly. Although few actually shared housing with extended family members, most lived close by. This study revealed that these families showed a strong preference for handling stress within the family and would turn to an outside agency only when they had exhausted their internal resources (McAdoo, 1979).

The strong commitment to the success of their children and the pride in educational accomplishments which the subjects of McAdoo's study felt in their families and which other studies have found (Peters, 1976) may reflect a coping strategy. Hope for the future of the children may help parents to maintain optimism in the face of current difficulties or hardships. As one parent said, "My parents struggled to put us through school; it seemed to make up for the choices they never had" (McAdoo, 1979).

Black families also get support from the broader Black community. Although religion is less important than it used to be for many families, churches do provide spiritual, psychological, and material help. Pride in the Black heritage is another functional coping strategy, in that it strengthens self-esteem; families develop a positive sense of the value of their diverse African-American experiences and try to pass this on to their children (McAdoo, 1978; Staples, 1971). The study of middle-class family stress and coping found that parents under greater stress were more likely to be involved in integrated or all-white social groups; lower-stressed parents were more active in all-Black social activities (McAdoo, 1982b). Parents who cope most successfully seem to maintain a balance between their economic aspirations, found in the white world, and their roots in the Black community. This necessary *duality* of Black life is experienced by many as another source of stress.

Flexibility of Family Roles

In white families, the roles of each parent and of the children are clearly and, until recently, rigidly defined: father was the breadwinner, while mother tended to care for the home and children. But in Black families, both parents have always had to work outside of the home just to make ends meet; the dual-employed couple is not a new phenomenon among Blacks. Both parents share the task of earning a living and share the domestic and childrearing tasks as well.

For example, George Bradley is an assistant city clerk. His wife Mary works the second shift at a large computer manufacturing company. While she sees the children off to school, she still has time to take care of the shopping and do some housecleaning before she leaves for work. George gets dinner for the kids, helps them with their homework, and enjoys watching TV with them before he puts them to bed. Larry, their 16-year-old, is in charge if George must work late, and the other two have their assigned chores around the house.

This pattern is becoming familiar in many white families too. But George and Mary grew up in households like this and are comfortable with these flexible roles. Research into Black families shows that most marriages are egalitarian; that is, husband and wife share authority to make decisions and share family responsibilities (Hill, 1971; Hyman & Reed, 1969; Mack, 1971). Black men are not threatened by the fact that their wives work outside of the home as some white men are; that is the pattern they expect and are accustomed to (Peters, 1976; Tenhouten, 1970). This role flexibility and shared decision-making ease strains in dual-employed and dual-career families. Moreover, Black women are less "helpless" if they are divorced or widowed and are better able to deal with the role changes required in the transition to a single-parent family or stepfamily. This flexibility of roles, too, serves to complement the support of the extended family; for example, it allows for entrance of other relatives into the nuclear family unit.

Conclusion

In this chapter, the stressors of the "mundane extreme environment" generated by racism are discussed briefly, with an emphasis on those associated with the economic disadvantages many Blacks face. But the strengths and coping strategies of Black families have helped them to handle this "extreme environment." Reliance on family and friends— the help-exchange kin network—and the capacity for flexibility in family roles are two such strengths that have been among the most effective coping strategies.

These aspects of Black family stress and coping have important implications for public policy, as well as for family stress theory and research. Social service agencies should try to increase and support the existing helping networks rather than replace them. One example of how this has been encouraged were the tax reforms that permitted deductions for child-care payments to grandparents. At the same time, policymakers should not assume the Black families will "take care of their own" so well that they do not need services. They should, rather, be aware of the great diversity of experiences and needs in Black families and avoid stereotyping—even stereotyping that is positive (McAdoo, 1979).

Obviously, a serious commitment to work with Black families, or with minority families in general, calls for interventions at what Melson . . . calls the exosystem (the Black community and the larger social context), as well as the microsystem (the Black family unit and kin). The roots of social discrimination and mundane stressors must be attacked and eliminated and, therefore, need to be targets of social policy and concern, even though the fruits of our interventions will not be seen for at least another decade. Concomitantly, we need to advance our understanding of family coping within the family-kin network, with the expectation that such knowledge can be used to strengthen Black families now and in the future.

References

Billingsley, A. *Black families in white America*. Englewood Cliffs, NJ: Prentice-Hall, 1968.

General Mills American Family Report. *Family health in an era of stress*. Minneapolis, MN: General Mills, 1979.

Hill, R. *The strengths of the Black family*. Washington, DC: National Urban League, 1971.

Hyman, H., & Reed, J. Black matriarchy reconsidered: Evidence from secondary analysis of sample surveys. *Public Opinion Quarterly*, 1969, *33*, 346–354.

Institute for the Study of Educational Policy. *Minorities in two-year colleges*. Washington, DC: Howard University, 1980.

Jones, L. *Great expectations: America and the baby boom generation*. New York: Coward, McCann & Geohagan, 1971.

Kaufman, J. Black managers. *Wall Street Journal*, 9 July 1980, 1.

Mack, D. Where the Black matriarchy theorists went wrong. *Psychology Today*, January 1971.

McAdoo, H. Factors related to stability in upwardly mobile black families. *Journal of Marriage and the Family*, November 1978, *40*, 762–778.

McAdoo, H. Black kinship. *Psychology Today*, May 1979, 67–69.

McAdoo, H. Demographic trends for people of color. *Social Work*, 1982, *27*: 1, 15–23. (a)

McAdoo, H. Levels of stress and family support in black families. In H. McCubbin, E. Cauble, & J. Patterson (Eds.), *Family stress, coping and social support.* Springfield, IL: Charles C. Thomas, 1982. (b)

Nobles, W. African root and American fruit: The Black family. *Journal of Social and Behavioral Sciences*, 1974, *20*, 66–77.

Ogbu, J. *Minority education and caste.* New York: Academic Press, 1978.

Pearce, D., & McAdoo, H. *Women and children: Alone and in poverty.* Washington, DC: National Advisory Council on Economic Opportunity, September 1981.

Peters, M. *Nine Black families: A study of household management and childrearing in Black families with working mothers.* Unpublished doctoral dissertation, Harvard University, 1976.

Peters, M. "Making it" Black family style: Building on the strength of Black families. In N. Stinnett, J. DeFrain, K. King, P. Knaud, and G. Rowe (Eds.), *Family strengths 3: Roots of well-being.* Lincoln, NE: University of Nebraska Press, 1981.

Pierce, C. The mundane extreme environment and its effect on learning. In S. C. Brainerd (Ed.), *Learning disabilities: Issues and recommendations for research.* Washington, DC: National Institute of Education, 1975.

Richardson, B. *Racism and child rearing.* Unpublished doctoral dissertation, Claremont College, 1981.

Stack, C. *All our kin.* New York: Harper & Row, 1975.

Staples, R. *The Black family: Essays and studies.* Belmont, CA: Wadsworth Publishing Company, 1971.

Tenhouten, W. The Black Family: Myth and reality. *Psychiatry*, May 1970, *2*, 145–173.

17

Jewish Women in the Nuclear Family and Beyond

Susan Weidman Schneider

Jewish Women and the Jewish Family

Feminism and the Family

The Jewish family has been labeled pathogenic and supportive, cruel and kind; the women in it have been the butt of jokes, the material of stereotypes, and the basis for invective and caricature. Any attempt to demythologize the lives of Jewish women must talk about the institution in which we relate to those we live with most intimately and whose expectations shape both our identity and our behavior. Though so-called "family issues"—marriage, childbearing, and child rearing, the division of domestic labor, and so forth—should certainly not be the exclusive concern of the women, at present they occupy more space in the lives of women than of men.

How Jewish women see themselves in the context of their own families—and how Jewish men and women interact in families—is important beyond the confines of the immediate family itself. All members of the group—in this case, Jews—are perceived as extended family. A New York editor, asked why he works in a Jewish institution, replies, "It's *mishpocha* [family]." This means that our relationships with other Jews, even outside any connection with our "real" families, are colored by the roles and the expectations we learn in our family interactions.

No matter how "the" Jewish family has been defined, the traditional role of the wife/mother has been fairly constant: she is responsible for the management of the household, for the socialization and "domestic" education of the girl children, and sometimes for part of the family's income as well. Although fewer and fewer Jewish daughters, wives, or mothers are living in anything resembling the two-parent nuclear families of previous generations, the families we were born into or which we've chosen to create with spouses, children, friends, or lovers remain the context for relating to those we're closest to. Examining these changing forms of family life and their implications for all Jews, Jewish organizations have for the past decade sponsored numerous conferences and publications and brainstorming sessions on issues that relate to how Jews live in families.[1] And while they have been active for more than a hundred years in some communities, the numerous Jewish organizations which exist to counsel and provide support services for families and children find themselves now in the limelight. Suddenly Jewish family life (by which is usually meant Jewish *women's* role in family life) is hot news.

The uncertainty of Jewish life (threatened from without by oppression and from within by assimilation) contributes to the heavy emphasis on "family." Because the historical threat has been so real, it's hard for women to redefine roles in the family, or redefine the family itself, without encountering a great deal of resistance from those who would create a false polarization between feminism and the family. Thus the women's movement, with its reevaluation of traditional male-female roles within the family, may have been perceived as a special threat to some Jews, despite (or because of) the fact that many Jewish women were highly visible in the movement.

In contrast, there are those who actually see Jewish identity endangered by any further changes in the definition of the Jewish family. Sociologist Chaim I. Waxman says that the family "is the *central institution* for defining and transmitting the identity and identification without which the Jewish ethnoreligious community could not exist."[2] And Blu Greenberg gives family life more credit than it usually receives, except when under attack. She says, "The Jewish home has been more significant in transmitting religious values than the synagogue."[3]

While's it's tempting to believe that women's domestic role (which is what's usually meant by the euphemism "home") has been an important vehicle for Jewish continuity, this belief also puts an immense burden on Jewish women who are eager to move into other spheres of influence as well.

Why all the emphasis *now* on the importance of family in Jewish life? With appropriate uneasiness, Jewish feminists suggest that the hue and cry is a reaction to the emergence of Jewish women into the labor force from their typical roles in the American Jewish family of the past forty years. They point out that when Jewish men moved into the mainstream of American life from the 1920s to 1945, no one called a conference to examine how *their* actions were subverting the traditional Jewish male values of study and religious observance. "This talk of 'family' all sounds to me like a push to keep women at home having babies," says Ann G. Wolfe, a New York social worker long active as a professional in Jewish life.

Aside from the legitimate accusation that the present concern for Jewish families is a backlash against the women's movement and has to do only with wanting to keep Jewish women at home (well shod but pregnant), there is another factor explaining the potent mythology of Jewish family life. Family may be much more important to a group that perceives itself as easily threatened by outside forces. We suspect that because "Jews, more than any other group of white Americans, are . . . more apt to be discriminated against; feelings of security and well-being may entail greater emphasis on family ties . . . than is generally true of others."[4]

In the 1970s the contemporary women's liberation movement sparked redefinitions of what women's roles could be. Jewish women's discussion groups, for instance, focused on new roles and new directions: entry or reentry into the workplace, greater options for women in religious Judaism, a reevaluation of volunteerism. By contrast, the action in the 1980s is in the family arena.

Now the conferences are entitled "Jewish Family Network" and "The Effect of the Women's Movement on the Jewish Family," and so on. The issues are the same so-called "women's" issues, but the difference in focus is very important. With the rubric now "family" and not "new roles for Jewish women," we return to an analysis of a woman's behavior based on her relation to others. Her needs as an individual are no longer at center stage. And yet even though the current focus on "family" issues is troublesome, it may not be all bad, especially if it prefigures the provision of more services to women, men, and children.

Attacking the hardy myth that the Jewish family is the one institution that keeps us all happy and Jewish, psychologist Phyllis Chesler speculates on the frailty of the family as it tries to service the needs of all its members:

> Ask yourself, how effective is the Jewish family in dealing with Jewish poverty in America—and in Israel? With the problems of the Jewish aged, of Jewish youth and with the problems of the Jewish woman? Has the Jewish family been able to eliminate wife-beating, wife abandonment, female depression, sexual frigidity, insecurity and a pathological degree of female dependency and self-sacrifice for men and small children? Has the Jewish family been able to teach women how to mother and nurture daughters and each other as they do sons? To show compassion for female suffering?[5]

This is not only the radical feminist position; Rabbi Gerson Cohen, Chancellor of the Jewish Theological Seminary, concurs:

> The Jewish family never sustained the Jew. That is a myth that is being perpetrated by people who are dissatisfied with the synagogue and find themselves failures. The family, as a unit in a strongly organized community, had very little to do except to generate, feed, and clothe kids. The community educated them. Where? In the street, in the marketplace, in the synagogue, in the house of study, in the assembly hall. The family today is being asked to do things which it can't possibly do. It is called upon to replace community, to provide leisure, love, respect, satisfaction, fulfillment. But that's impossible, because we can't do these things in isolation. We can do them only as a community.[6]

Perhaps the very structure of Judaism as a communal religion helped create and sustain what was in premodern times an extended family for Jews almost everywhere they lived. The community was another extension of the family. After all, with most prayers requiring the minimum of ten adults (all male in those days, and in many places today), Jews *could not* live in isolation from one another. Even where civil law would have permitted Jews to own tracts of land and live on isolated farms, the religious structure of Judaism mandated proximity to other Jews, fostering communities that were geographically as well as spiritually close. Understanding this, we have already driven one wedge into the myth that it was the tireless effort of the Jewish mother, with her enabling and her cooking, that held Jews together. The *minyan* (prayer quorum), and not the nuclear family, may have been the cell for Jewish continuity.

Historian Paula Hyman has analyzed the myths surrounding the Jewish family: "It can be argued that . . . the nature of the Jewish community served to preserve the traditional Jewish family rather than that the Jewish family preserved Judaism. . . . The theory that women are culture bearers is one which may women are inclined to accept without challenge, despite its inaccuracy, because it is flattering. It connotes power and a recognition of the value of the mothering role."[7]

Aside from the classic association of the mother with the survival and transmission of Jewish values, there are other characteristics unique to the Jewish family. Change, in the form of improvement of life from generation to generation, is what most of us have come to see as the "Jewish" way. Jews "want better" for their children. It's hard to imagine a situation in a Jewish family that would echo the story of one Italian-American family. Joe Brancatelli tells that his father gave up a promising legal career to return to the family shoe-repair business because *his* father said he was needed there. He was a "good son." The author describes himself as the "bad son" in the story, because he aspired to something different. He quotes his father: "You can't be a writer. You're a Brancatelli, you sell shoes."[8] It's almost impossible to imagine this scene being played out—or accepted as the norm—in an American Jewish family, where children who have before them the prospect of "bettering" themselves are held up as models for all to admire.

Upward economic mobility, in addition to geographic mobility, has left Western Jews with the sense that it's natural for children to live lives different from their parents'. The problem with this is ensuring religious and cultural continuity within the change. The essence of this concern comes through in a conversation overheard after a conference on Jewish women and the family. One woman said, "I wasn't religious, but I raised my kids with Jewish values and good politics. They're Jewish now, but who knows what the future will bring?" Her companion answered, "Look, I raised my son to understand that he's Jewish because of his connection to Jewish history. But do I know if my grandchildren will be Jewish?" Neither woman had any faith at all in her own role as a transmitter of Jewish identity to her children. The myth of the Jewish mother's infallibility in this regard was obviously no comfort. . . .

Keeping the Kinship Ties Tied

In Jewish family structure the extended family has always been important. For example, in Yiddish there are specific words to denote the relationship between the sets of parents of a married couple. They are *machutunim* to one another, the mother-in-law on the other side is the *machuteneste*, and the father-in-law on the other side is a *machutan* to the father-in-law on your side. A network of family ties is drawn tight even through language. The close connection between the present generation and any and all recorded ancestors is known in Yiddish as *yichus*, or proud family line.

Jewish families have many more kinship ties than other families, with relatives often staying in or near the same geographic area. In one study, 78 percent of the Jews (as compared to 14 percent of the Protestants) say that they have "regular interactions" with at least five households of these relatives.[9] What may be a uniquely Jewish way of keeping the kinship ties tied is the "cousins' club," meeting regularly to create a family network that reinforces every member's sense of belonging, of having a reference group or "home room" even in adulthood.[10]

For women the security that can come from having a sense of belonging to a family is especially valid. We've been accustomed to taking on the names of the men we are married to, sometimes losing even our first names in the process. Cousins' clubs serve the purpose for women of providing a kind of primary identity—family are the people who will love you—or at least stand by you—no matter what you do and no matter what your name.

And being cousins, members of the extended family circle are less likely to drive you crazy than siblings, parents, or children, while still providing the warm glow—or backbiting or blood feuds—of family connectedness. Especially when family ties are becoming more complicated because of divorce and remarriage, and at a time when women with children worry about how/when the children will connect with *their* families, it's good to remind ourselves that *we* count too, and that the people we were once connected to in a primary way (as daughters, nieces, cousins) can be a source of pleasure in our lives again, regardless of our marital status. Especially now that Jewish families are having fewer children, relationships with cousins are very important—for adults and for kids—as a substitute for friendship with siblings.

The very practical advantages of family kinship networks have been explored too. Contrary to commonly held beliefs of social scientists that close family ties are most often associated with lower-class populations, for Jewish families there's a correlation between extended family ties and middle-class status.[11] The sharing of resources—skills or cash—among family members who had similar values and social and residential bonds was instrumental in bringing the family to this status and in maintaining it. . . .

With changing circumstances, the ways in which Jews relate to their extended families may change also. Smaller families mean fewer siblings and, later, fewer cousins, while the rising incidence of Jewish events for females (such as baby-naming ceremonies and Bat Mitzvahs) provide new opportunities for ritual celebrations where family members can meet.

In the Jewish extended family, women's nurturing role has meant

that women spend a great deal of time as cooks and organizers, which
has at least one advantage. Since Jewish life-cycle events and holiday
celebrations often feature special foods, women, almost always the
providers of the food, have had a private realm for *schmoozing** and intimacy, a context in which they can get to know one another.

For Jewish women, especially Orthodox women, even synagogue
life is an opportunity to be in a collectivity of women—in the women's
gallery, usually totally divided from the men's section. This division of
women and men takes place in some home-bound ceremonies and gatherings as well, with women not eating with men in the succah, or staying in a separate room during the *brit milah*,† or during the Saturday
night *melave malke* (ushering out of the Sabbath). At Orthodox weddings there may be separate dancing rooms for men and for women,
and in Syrian Jewish homes, even in America, a Saturday-afternoon
sibbit (a praying, studying, singing, feasting celebration of a birth, engagement, or other simcha) has the men all sitting at a large table with
all the women serving them.

These separations from men do create an opportunity for women
to support one another, at least momentarily free from other obligations. The question logically arises as to how much of our admiration
of female bonding in this context is appropriate, and how much is mere
apology for a caste system which defines women as enablers and
shunts them aside.

Mothers and Daughters from a Feminist Perspective

When we consider relationships within the Jewish family, we risk getting caught in a tangled web of myths and damaging stereotypes about
Jewish women. The contradictory myths—that the second-generation
American Jewish mother appears to be all self-sacrifice while covering
a hard core of manipulation; that her daughters are demanding and aggressive and are eternally tethered to a shallow materialism—don't
take into account the historical realities that have shaped these stock
characters. Some mothers may fit the Yiddishe Mama stereotype, just
as some daughters cannot feel that they are worthwhile people without
the trappings of material success. But the constant associations of
"Mama" and "Princess" with being Jewish deny the history behind the
stereotypes (the survival value of Mama's concern for her children; the
ornamental value of having a dolled-up daughter as a symbol of the
newly successful American Jewish man) while perpetuating the ugly
implications of the stereotypes themselves.

Even if we are never mothers, we have all been daughters some-

*Editor's note: talking, chatting.
†Editor's note: the ceremony of circumcision of a male child.

time. And although we learn about mothers and sons in the Torah—starting with Eve and Cain and Abel, going on to Sarah and Isaac and many more—mothers and daughters are markedly scant, both in the Torah and in subsequent Jewish writings. The traditional Jewish material on mothers and daughters comes from folklore rather than serious literature, leaving women to the mercy of the popular culture.

The unattractive, ubiquitous and essentially anti-Semitic stereotyping of Jewish women[12] either as Yiddishe Mamas or Princesses has a message for anyone trying to understand Jewish mother-daughter relations. These stereotypes are really opposite sides of the same coin. The all-sacrificing mother, denying her own needs while intrusively involved in the perceived needs of her children, contrasts vividly in every way with the selfish daughter, self-absorbed, demanding, too interested in the events of her own life to be sympathetic to others, and certainly unwilling to submit to male authority. There are many ironies in this juxtaposition, not the least of which is that the Princess is expected to become the Mama as soon as possible after she marries and/or has children of her own. . . .

This Jewish mother is strictly a creation of American Jewish writing (and thinking) and the manifestation of the leap into prosperity that allows women the luxury of being "overinvolved" with their children, even if only in myth. Some of the realities behind the stereotype were there all along—the self-sacrifice of the mother who did without in order to feed her children, for example, or the mother's concerns for her children's safety during sieges, pogroms, and famines. . . .

It's time to move beyond these images—noting first that they originated in certain needs that Jews have had—and look at the realities of Jewish family life for women. . . .

. . . When American Jewish men began to enjoy a degree of financial success, many tried to assimilate to a more "American" style of behavior and thinking. This included accepting the prevailing neo-Victorian notion that woman's place was in the home, that she was a fragile creature who needed protection from the outside world. Thus upward social mobility caused the world of the American Jewish woman to shrink![13] What a shock this must have been to women whose image of themselves, and of their mothers and grandmothers before them, had been of hardy, active people. The real roles of Eastern European Jewish women included helping support the family, making decisions, and having (at least in much of family and community life) shared responsibilities with their husbands. . . .

For women finding themselves suddenly remanded to the home front because new prosperity made their wages unnecessary and their husband's status required an at-home wife, there was no other choice but to put the same energies into the raising of children that previously had gone into paid labor *plus* home responsibilities. Like their non-

Jewish sisters, many Jewish women (especially after the Second World War, with prosperity and a houseful of labor-saving devices), threw themselves into their maternal role. The difference for Jewish women was the tremendous influence of the family in Jewish life (or at least the perception of its influence) and the sense that the children were both a way of ensuring Jewish continuity and one of the only sanctioned ways in which the mother could express herself. It was also through her performance of the maternal role that the Jewish woman was judged and judged herself.

What effect has this Jewish mother's involvement with home life had on her daughter? The daughter seems more distressed by Mama's self-sacrifice than by her manipulative power—seeing her, for example, deprive herself and give to her offspring. The mama who is rumored to have no drives of her own isn't a useful role model for the daughter who today is trying to synthesize the work and achievement goals of her father and brothers (and perhaps her grandmother) with her mother's investment in the domestic scene.

When our mothers are also our models for future versions of ourselves, their feeding us and starving themselves presents a terrifying, sacrificial model that may have nothing to do with present-day cupboard realities, where abundance is more likely than want, but may reflect the vivid psychological reality of a woman who can't afford to have any needs of her own. This sacrificial feed-the-others mentality of Jewish women is not a matter of individual pathology—it is so widespread that we have to recognize it as a vestigial survival skill. . . .

The messages we picked up about women, the image transmitted to us, was often of self-sacrifice and self-abnegation. Many of us also learned that no parallel sacrifices were ever expected of men. "There were seven children in my family, plus my parents," reminisces a woman now in her late sixties. "When we were growing up on the Lower East Side of New York my mother would go down every morning and buy eight rolls for breakfast. She would cut and butter them all, giving one to each child and one to my father. Then she would gather up the crumbs on the board, sweep them with one hand into the cupped palm of the other, and put the crumbs into her coffee. That was *her* breakfast."

Our earliest identification suggests that we will base much of our behavior on that of the adults present in our childhood, most likely our mothers. We sometimes see this as a frightening model. Perhaps because we know that, despite the pseudopowerful image of a Sophie Portnoy, our mothers, like most women, have been largely powerless to shape their own lives, to make their own choices. Psychiatric and popular literature abound with references to women of achievement who identify with their fathers' power rather than with what they perceive as their mothers' passivity. Despite the emergence of a feminist analysis of family roles which recognizes some of our mothers' strengths, we must still contend with our early perceptions that our mothers are simultaneously all-powerful in our juvenile world and often victims of circumstance in the larger sphere.[14]

And so we grow up—all women, and not just Jewish women—torn between the passive model (waiting to be *chosen*, whether by husbands or employers) and striving for a more active role in shaping our own lives. With self-sacrifice the dominant mode for at least some Jewish mothers, Jewish daughters seeking to assert themselves must first understand the anger and disappointment many feel toward their most important role models. "I still have an enormous amount of anger towards my mother for the fact that she hasn't asserted her needs or her rights all these years. I understand her feelings of helplessness, but they make me angry, and frighten me. I think that that's why I'm so outspoken myself. I'm not going to let anyone make a *shmatte* out of me," says a woman of forty who is still trying to overcome the desire to fight her mother's battles for her. . . .

A somewhat complicitous helpmeet/ally relationship between many Jewish daughters and mothers may derive from the fact that the women shared an exclusion from aspects of Jewish ritual life, may have sat together and away from the men in synagogue, and shared also a domestic reality that men—even within the same family—often had no part in. Many mothers who didn't work outside their homes felt a companionship void that they looked to their daughters to fill. Older women, speaking honestly, admit that they didn't want to tell any "secrets" to anybody—even close friends—outside their family circle. Their daughters, presumably witnesses to some of the secrets anyway, were safe ears.

The anecdotes of these Jewish daughters reveal both closeness and conflict with their mothers and a tension between an intimate dependency and the yearning for independence continuing unresolved even into adulthood. A New York journalist in her forties describes her own relationship: "My mother always wanted to be my best friend, and always criticized every friend I ever had, letting me know that She could be counted on for undying loyalty, but not Them."

The emotional closeness of Jewish families was certainly echoed in the family structures of the other two groups of women (Slavic and Italian) that Dr. Corinne Azen Krause has studied.[15] But Jewish women tend not to live in the same houses, or even in the same neighborhoods, as their mothers. There seems to be a conscious effort for daughter to get some distance from mother (and mother from daughter), despite expressed feelings of closeness.

Responding to Krause's study, a business manager in her thirties describes how she plans to deal with her own mother's aging: "She isn't going to be able to lay a guilt trip on me. I would tell her, 'Look,

Mother, I'll be happy to provide care for you at any expense, to arrange for whatever is necessary. But it is just *impossible* for you to come and live with me.'"

There are exceptions to this pattern, of course. One clear difference is among daughters of Holocaust survivors, who, like their brothers, tend to maintain very close geographic bonds to their parents, often living at home long after their peers have struck out on their own. Another is in both Orthodox and Syrian American Jewish communities, where daughters marry young and often deliberately choose to live in the same neighborhood as their mothers. But both Orthodox and Syrian families tend to have many more children than the Jewish average, so the relationship between mother and daughter may not be perceived as so close, or so confining, as that between mothers and daughters in smaller families.

Not only geography, but also significant life-style differences between adult Jewish daughters in the 1980s and their mothers have created a veritable "tradition of change" over the past three generations:

1. The way the daughter generation interprets life is different from what came before. *Grandmothers*, whether Jewish, Italian or Slavic, according to Krause's study, acted out of survival needs. Whatever they did, occupationally or within the family, they knew they were ensuring sheer physical survival and comfort for their families and themselves. Their daughters (the *mother* generation of the study) did what was expected of them by others. For Jewish women, especially, this conclusion must ring true. Remember that middle generation of Jewish women who were told that if they worked outside their homes it would bring shame upon their husbands, impugning the men's reputations as adequate providers? For the *daughter* generation there are choices. Serve one's own needs? Serve the needs of one's own family? Work full time? Part time? In short, the social climate, at least for middle-class women, has changed in such a way as to place very different meanings on the ways we live.

2. The shape of the lives of the daughter generation is different. Jewish women, if they do choose to have children, are having them later in life than women of other ethnic groups. Perhaps this reflects our greater level of education and consequently our greater career opportunities. Whatever the cause for the postponement, as Jewish women put off childbearing or don't have children at all, the pattern of the daughters' lives differs radically from those of their mothers and grandmothers; at certain ages we are in different phases from those of previous generations at the same age. . . .

3. Different generations may have very different goals for their own offspring. The at-home, nonworking mother may prolong her chil-

dren's dependency, so she will be raising children who are different in certain ways from the generation of sons and daughters produced by working mothers. Current realities—with the majority of mothers of preschool children out to work—are producing offspring in some ways more self-sufficient than their parents.

Has the women's movement changed any of our negative feelings toward our own mothers? Has it healed any of the wounds we've received or inflicted? In the safe context of the women's movement many women have begun to examine for the first time the complexities of this relationship—as daughters still connected to our mothers by a knot tied with love, pain, and guilt.

Part of the new respect women are showing their mothers is in recording oral histories of older women. Certainly part of the search and discovery is the quest for our *own* usable past, but some is—especially for Jewish women—homage to a generation of women (particularly immigrant women) whose own lives gave them opportunities for courage and fortitude, flexibility and strength, that we, largely middle-class daughters, haven't had the opportunities to be tested on.

The women's movement has given us some of the intellectual tools and the support necessary to effect a reconciliation with our mothers which might in earlier generations have taken place almost biologically, as a natural evolution from being daughters to being mothers ourselves. But for a daughter faced with caring for an aged mother the situation may be especially poignant. With earlier conflicts sometimes still unresolved, the daughter must become care-giver to her mother. Women, whether as daughters or daughters-in-law, have traditionally been the ones responsible for care of the elderly and infirm, a situation now causing enormous pressure in the lives of middle-aged daughters, caught between the often irreconcilable demands of younger and older generations. . . .

The characteristic plaint of the older woman—"I would rather die than be a burden to my children"—bespeaks a terror at an impending loss of control over one's own life in the face of a world turned upside down, a world in which someone whose own life has been devoted to caring for others now needs caring for. There is a more chilling aspect of the Jewish mother's expressed reluctance to be a burden to her children: perhaps the mothers feel that the burden won't be shouldered! In her studies of depressed middle-aged women Pauline Bart discusses the phenomenon of older Jewish parents who live frugally in order to make sure they'll have a nest egg to use if illness or disability should strike. Bart comments that these parents are reluctant to be in need of help from their children for fear of putting the relationship "to the test which it may not survive."[16]

Part of the way this is enacted may be in the willingness of older Jewish parents to relocate to "Sun Belt" communities, leaving their *children* behind. (In fact, this southward shift in the population of older Jews is, along with the declining birthrate, the most crucial Jewish demographic finding of the early 1980s) . . .

"Respect" is the key word for daughters as they and their mothers age—respect for the older woman, and for the reasons behind behavior that might otherwise be puzzling. The Jewish concept of *Derech Eretz* (literally, the way of the land) means that an extra measure of understanding is due to those who are much older than we. To our mothers it may mean that we question them sympathetically about their own lives, that we try to show that their experience, however radically different from our own, has value. (Sometimes this is impossible for daughters but possible between granddaughter and grandmother, in which case the ties of guilt and responsibility are not drawn so tightly.) . . .

One way of opening up a new relationship between daughters and older mothers is by discussing—if you can—the idea of an ethical will. Judaism has always had a tradition of passing along parental values to children in the form of a written will, setting out what values, what ethical precepts, what spiritual guidance parents want to leave children. Needless to say, most of these in the past were written by men. In fact, The *Encyclopedia Judaica* describes them as "a *father's* last words to his children" (italics added). You or your mother may at first consider this ghoulish, but there's a case to be made for helping your mother to see that she has given more to her children—and therefore has more to leave them—than an accumulation of property. . . .

The conflicts between mother and daughter in Jewish families take a different turn in the relationship between daughters-in-law and mothers-in-law. The focus here is usually not so much on the dynamics between the two women as on the man who connects them. An exception to this is the classical Biblical tale of mother-in-law and daughter-in-law: Naomi and Ruth. These women nurture each other when the men in the family have died; the story highlights not only the special friendship and love between the women but also the fact that it takes place in the conspicuous absence of the son/husband who provides the link between them.

When the son is present we certainly have examples of hostility in the traditional mother-in-law/daughter-in-law relationship. One of these is the "broiges-tants"—the "dance of enmity" that the bride and her mother-in-law would perform at an Eastern European Jewish wedding. The dance and some of the proverbs about the relationship between these two women are precursors to the mother-in-law jokes (always told by men), an expression of the fear men have of a bonding between these two women.

Some of the hostility women express has to do with shifting expectations. The mother-in-law expects that her son will marry and continue to be taken care of as she has taken care of him. After his marriage she fears that the treasure she has cherished will not be as highly valued by his wife as he is by his mother. Now that daughters-in-law (like daughters) have aspirations of their own, they aren't able to give the kind of care to their husbands that many mothers-in-law would like to think is their son's due.

Many cultures have anti-mother-in-law jokes and tales. What is particularly problematic in the relationship between Jewish mothers- and daughters-in-law is the higher value traditionally placed on Jewish male offspring. The mother-in-law really does believe that she is turning over a treasure to a stranger's keeping. One woman tells, with some anger: "My mother-in-law is always telling me to remind my husband to get a haircut, to dress warmly, to have his good suit cleaned before the family Bar Mitzvah. This man is past fifty. But my mother-in-law still feels that if he looks untidy it reflects badly on *her*."

Empirical evidence suggests a kind of infantilization of the son/husband, in which both his mother and his wife are complicitous. Both women have a great deal invested in what the man does. Miriam, the wife of Rabbi Small in the *Friday the Rabbi* . . . mystery-story series, worries about what he will eat and recalls that his mother warned her that it was best to keep the courses coming without interruption, otherwise David would stop eating. How many times have you heard a woman say of her husband, "It's like having another child"? Some wives, and some mothers, feel more comfortable in the role of maternal care-giver to a man; it's one way of seizing, or taking back, power in the dyad.

Daughters and Fathers

An essay contest with the subject "My Jewish Mother" elicits entries from Hebrew school students who have very clear ideas about what makes their mothers Jews:[17] "She always cooks a lot of food for the holidays," wrote one. It's hard to imagine a parallel essay contest on the Jewish father; there's very little to differentiate him from "Jew" since we have been taught to respond to the word "Jew" by thinking of a man.

Unlike the image of the Jewish mother in popular culture, there's no single, stereotyped view of the Jewish father. This is not to say that we don't have certain notions about Jewish fathers too. We are accustomed to thinking that there are certain things he is *not*, among them that he is not selfish in regard to his children. When *Ms.* magazine ran an article in the late seventies about fathers and food—fathers holding the family purse strings; men deciding what kind of food the family would eat and what eating-out relief the mother would get; and, in primitive cultures, which teeth women would have removed or sawed down in the name of beauty (leaving them unable to chew the choice meats, which the men then ate)—Jewish women responded: "Well, that's certainly not the Jewish model. Jewish fathers aren't like that. Jewish fathers *sacrifice* for their children." . . .

The Father and the Princess

With material success in America, Jewish men's distance from their children increased. No longer a figure sitting in synagogue or in a study hall, or working in the neighborhood and appearing regularly for three meals a day in the family kitchen, he removed himself from the domestic scene by hard work, hard play, and plenty of male bonding. Sociologist Rela Geffen Monson notes: "Thus, the father who was concerned with *kashrut** in the home, the quality and quantity of Jewish learning of his children and in their emotional, ethical and intellectual growth as Jews, was replaced by the one who provided the money so that secondary institutions and surrogate teachers and models could do this job for him, under the direction and coordination of the mother."[18]

The one single trait in any composite portrait of the assimilated, non-Orthodox North American Jewish father would be desire for his daughter to reflect his success. In a horrible poster of the "JAP" advertised in stationery-store windows across the country in 1979, a conspicuously consuming young woman is pictured in diamond stud earrings, a gift from Daddy when she stopped smoking. (The poster also shows her with a cigarette in one hand and the warning "Don't tell Daddy.") She is his pride and joy, his ornament. Legend has it that he can refuse her nothing.

Always younger and sometimes more attractive in an "American" way than her mother, embellished with material goods and even cosmetic surgery, this daughter can be the most successful female object in the house, the best symbol of the father's having made it. If his son goes to an Ivy League school, perhaps the son's own efforts have been involved in some way. If a daughter dresses well and wears costly ornaments, only the father's wealth is responsible. Unlike what the popular wisdom posits, a young woman's father may be more responsible for the indulged-princess image than her mother.

Fathers without sons appear to be more supportive of their daughters' academic and other accomplishments. Those women—and there are a few—who describe sitting and studying Talmud with their European-born scholarly fathers are all women without brothers! Par-

*Editor's note: observance of the Jewish dietary laws.

allel to this are the women who learned business skills from their fathers, or were groomed to take over a family business (a more recent
phenomenon).

With Jewish women having access to first-rate professional training now, perhaps a daughter's career achievements will be the new
pride-and-pleasure factor for fathers, making their daughters even better ornaments. Careerist daughters often describe their fathers as crucial models and their mothers as more shadowy, background figures to
the drama on center stage. . . .[19]

Female and Male

In every patriarchal society there are marked differences in the way
male and female children are raised, since parents assume that they
arc socializing them for very different role as adults. Girls of almost
every ethnic and religious group thus lead lives that are more circum-
scribed than those of their brothers.

As we know, in the relations between Jewish brothers and sisters
two messages are transmitted very early. The first is that sons are valued more than daughters. The second is that the education of sons is
more important than that of daughters.

From the very birth of a male child there's rejoicing and ritual celebration. Until recently (the past ten years or so) a girl child, at best,
got her name called out in synagogue the Sabbath after her birth—if
her parents were regular synagogue-goers. (Things are being equalized
somewhat now with the proliferation of welcoming ceremonies for
newborn Jewish daughters. . . .

In some societies it's assumed that the children will sacrifice for
the parents. Jewish families, among others, expect that parents will
usually be willing to sacrifice for children. However, a dimension
unique to the Jewish family, and to the relationships fostered within it,
is the assumption that sisters will sacrifice themselves for their brothers. A non-Jewish Bostonian married to a Jewish doctor puts it this
way: "My husband was raised like a pasha. His sisters were expected
to wait on him hand and foot. Everything he did was important. And
my sisters-in-law were raised to believe that they themselves were
worthless." . . .

In light of situations like these, it is no wonder that the studies of
high-achieving women show that they almost invariably come from
families in which there were no male siblings and in which they were
treated like the missing son.

Yet somehow, despite the documentation that boys are favored in
Jewish families, Jewish daughters are the children thought of as
spoiled or demanding or self-absorbed. Why, since Jewish sons are

raised with material advantages comparable to those of their sisters, is there no comparably widespread "prince" stereotype? The answer is that the daughter is still a two-dimensional object, whereas the son has a real, authentic life. It's acceptable for a Jewish young man to think well of himself, to feel worthy of all that he possesses or achieves, to strive openly for excellence. The core anxiety for his sister, often victimized by the demanding-princess stereotype, is that she is only the sum of her parts: what she possesses or wears or achieves, or whom she marries. There is no parallel objectification of her brother. . . .

Notes

1. For an overview of some of the recent cross-cultural research into family life, see Andrew J. Cherlin and Carin Celebuski, *Are Jewish Families Different?* (New York: The William Petschek National Jewish Family Center, American Jewish Committee, 1982). The monograph states, "the premise that Jewish family life is different, or distinctive, does not rest on a solid empirical foundation."

2. *Single-Parent Families: A Challenge to the Jewish Community* (New York: American Jewish Committee, 1981).

3. At a conference, "Women's Roles and the Family," 1980.

4. Judith G. Rabkin and Elmer L. Struening, in *Ethnicity, Social Class and Mental Illness* (New York: American Jewish Committee, 1976).

5. "An Exclusive Interview with Dr. Phyllis Chesler," *Lilith* #2, Winter 76/77, pp. 26–27.

6. From an address delivered at the 1979 Jewish Educators Assembly convention.

7. From a speech before the American Jewish Congress in the mid-1970s.

8. "The Ties that Choke [sic]," *Perspectives*, U.S. Commission on Civil Rights Quarterly (Spring 1980), pp. 39–43.

9. Marshall Sklare, *America's Jews* (New York: Random House, 1971), p. 95.

10. For an analysis of the unique patterns American Jews have developed for connecting with their relatives, see William E. Mitchell, *Mishpokhe: A Study of New York City Jewish Family Clubs* (The Hague: Mouton, 1978).

11. Myrna Silverman, "Jewish Family and Kinship in Pittsburgh," Ph.D. thesis, Univ. of Pittsburgh, 1976.

12. Anti-Semitic because certain general characteristics are defined simultaneously as negative and Jewish.

13. For expansion of the subject of the changes immigrant and second-generation Jewish women have gone through, see Charlotte Baum, Paula Hyman, and Sonya Michel, *The Jewish Woman in America* (New York: Dial, 1976).

14. See Shulamit Firestone's astonishing, brilliant essay *The Dialectic of Sex* (New York: Bantam, 1972) for an analysis of how daughters and sons betray their mothers as they grow up.

15. *Grandmothers, Mothers and Daughters* (New York: American Jewish Committee, 1978).
16. Harold J.Wershow, "The Older Jews of Albany Park—Some Aspects of a Subculture of the Aged and Its Interaction with a Gerontological Research Project," *The Gerontologist*, 4 (1964), pp. 198–202, cited in Bart, "Depression in Middle Aged Women: Some Sociocultural Factors," Ph.D. thesis, UCLA, 1967.
17. "What is a Jewish Mother?" *Lilith* #4, Fall/Winter 77/78, pp. 18–20.
18. *Women's League Outlook* (Spring 1982), p. 7. See also a 1977 discussion guide published by the American Jewish Committee, "Changing Roles of Men and Women in the Jewish Family."
19. See Margaret Hennig and Anne Jardim, *The Managerial Woman* (Garden City, N.Y.: Doubleday, 1977).

18

Out of the Stream
An Essay on Unconventional Motherhood

Shirley Glubka

As I started this piece for the sixth or seventh time, I wondered how far back I would have to go to understand my unusual relationship to motherhood. Beyond my own life, I knew—to my mother and my grandmothers and aunts and great-aunts and generations of women behind them. I thought about those generations and was struck by a vision: I saw a swollen stream of women, all taking on the role of mother without the least sign of rebellion. I saw myself leaping out of this stream and landing hard, alone and disoriented, flopping like the proverbial fish out of water. Quite a sad scene.

Then I remembered reality. In my family there were plenty of good Catholic mothers with the mandatory five to seven children trailing them through aisles of grocery stores. But there were also others: the one who never married, never had children, and cleaned houses for a living; the one who did marry, never had children, and worked in the college cafeteria; the one who had children and, when the last one came along, suggested to her husband that this child might be better

This article is reprinted from *Feminist Studies*, Volume 9, no. 2 (1983): 223–234, by permission of the publisher *Feminist Studies*, Inc., c/o Women's Studies Program, University of Maryland, College Park, MD 20742.

raised by someone else, someone who was not tired of starting over with baby after baby. The husband would not hear of such a thing and the woman stayed in the stream of conventional mothers—but not without rebellion. Those others stand in my personal history as surely as those women who seem to have taken on the role of mother without a qualm.

How peculiar, then, that I should have such a strong and immediate image that all the women before me were mothers, compliant in their role. On the other hand, how understandable that I should be assaulted by such an image. I, who left the conventional role of mother years ago, have no more protection from the myths surrounding motherhood than any other woman. In fact, I might be more vulnerable than most. Like the outcast, I sometimes imagine that all other women belong to an inner circle of mothers, a circle full of warmth and goodness, the locus of satisfying and productive activity.

I severed whatever connection I might have had to that imagined inner circle ten years ago when my son Kevin was three years old and I was thirty. At that time, Kevin and I were separated, by my choice. Kevin acquired a new mother in the form of Gretchen Ulrich, who was a teacher in his daycare center.

If I believed in such things, I would regard Gretchen as one of the more enduring and beneficent apparitions of my life. She appeared as if by magic in my living room one day (actually, we were having an unscheduled parent-teacher conference) and by the end of several hours of conversation, we had come to an agreement. She would try being Kevin's mother and I would try something that was not quite not being his mother. He would live with her, I would live alone, and occasionally he and I would visit with each other. We determined a trial period which was to last one month; but we knew quite well by the end of our conversation that the arrangement would be permanent.

I had begun my experience with motherhood in a conventional enough way: inside the institution of marriage, a little haphazardly (through a failure of birth control that did not unduly distress either my husband or me—we had planned to have children eventually, why not now?) and, all in all, quite happily. When Kevin was eight months old, I left my husband, taking Kevin with me. For all practical purposes, that was the end of our involvement with my ex-husband. I had become a single mother.

I had also become a feminist, a critic of the status quo on many fronts, committed to finding sensible, humane, nonsexist ways to live. I tried communal living in what seemed to be an ideal situation—with other women from my consciousness-raising group, other children, and a few politically aware, thoroughly sincere men. We based our experiment on feminist principles. All work, including childcare, was divided equally among us. The experiment was a success—for a year. The reasons for the disintegration of any living situation are, to say the least, hard to catch hold of. I could say we had personality conflicts; I could say it was extremely difficult to maintain a way of living that was unsupported by society at large. Both the purely personal and the social/political explanations would be true and even taken together they are not all of the truth. For whatever complex combination of reasons, our collective household split apart.

I continued to seek and find ways to break the isolation of single motherhood. I found excellent daycare, neighbors with preschoolers who wanted to exchange babysitting, friends both female and male who volunteered days, evenings, nights, and even whole weekends of their time caring for Kevin. Compared with most single mothers, I was superbly supported; yet I felt constantly burdened. It was becoming clear that I did not like the role of mother. Specifically, I did not like the kind of work involved in being a mother.

Having written this, I stop to think. And the voices come—among them one that sounds suspiciously like my own: "You didn't like the work? You left your child because you didn't *like* the *work*?" And the images come of irresponsible mothers abandoning their children for no reason: lazy, flighty, selfish, or just plain *bad* women—loose women in garish green silky dresses with long slits up the leg, tossing their babies into garbage cans and going out for a good time. . . . When my fantasy reaches this height of stereotyped ridiculousness it becomes easier to deal with. No mother separates from her child lightly. Yes, I left the mother role because in a radical way I did not like the job of being a mother; and because I believed that Kevin would be better off if he were raised by someone who wanted to do that kind of work; and because, by some miracle, that person appeared in my life.

It would be a simplification to say that I liked nothing about the mother role. That role is complex—and one of its complexities is that it changes radically again and again as time passes. I rather liked the work of mothering during Kevin's infancy—all the holding, the nursing, washing him, even changing his diapers was fine with me. I was good at it, I was playing out a lifelong fantasy, and he was an "easy baby." When I went to women's liberation meetings, I held him in my lap. If he cried, I nursed him. When he fell asleep I put him down on the carpet beside me and went on participating in the meeting. I could write when he was a baby, too. He would play quietly and I would type. When I took a break I would go and cuddle him—then return to typing. Easy, I thought.

By the time he was a year-and-a-half old it wasn't easy any more. He didn't stay put. He was developing into a person who would not be cuddled and ignored. He would *not* be ignored—and I didn't want to pay attention. Much of the work of mothering a small child (especially if you have only one) consists in being present for another, being ready to respond to emergencies, being ready to appreciate accomplishments, being there for long periods of time with nothing, really, to do— except watch and wait. During these times (which, if they were not in our living room, seem always to have been in some park or other) I would try to read or write, try to keep my mind active, try to keep my sense of myself. But I never managed the trick of being with myself and being ready to respond to Kevin at the same time. I vacillated between two approaches. For a while I would try shutting him out, focusing on my reading or writing or thinking; and I would feel abruptly invaded by any small demand he made. Then I would try the opposite tack and hold myself in a state of dull readiness, trying to forget my own mind, my own need to be with myself, trying to be ready for whatever he needed without anger, without that painful sense of violation. Neither worked well, of course. I was trying to do work for which I was not suited.

Not everyone responds this way to the demands of mothering a small child. There are women who amaze me with their skills. Like jugglers (I have always been in awe of jugglers) they seem able to keep track of many simultaneous movements. They can balance their own lively consciousness with the activities and needs of their children— without losing themselves in the complicated, ever-changing pattern. On good days they even make beauty and fun out of the juggle. I have often wondered at least half-seriously if my simple inability to pay attention to two things at once might lie at the core of my problems with mothering.

I don't know if my difficulties with the mother role were made more or less painful by the fact that I found Kevin to be the most attractive child I had ever met. I liked him very much. He was bright and beautiful. I liked being related to him, was proud to be his mother. My affection for him was powerful, tender, and could well up in tears easily and often. It was not Kevin I disliked; it was the work of being his mother day by day.

Many aspects of that work were difficult for me. I was overwhelmed, for example, to find myself responsible for the physical existence of a little person who could suddenly move about under his own power. How could I know when he might step in front of a moving car, climb high and fall to his death, swallow poison? I could not lose the feeling that Kevin was at every moment vulnerable to a multitude of dangers. It was as if I were on guard duty, constantly vigilant, never fully relaxed.

Many mothers feel that when their infants become toddlers the job of being mother becomes easier and more rewarding—especially after the development of language and the completion of toilet training. In contrast, I felt the job expand into a complexity that I could hardly handle. Suddenly, for example, I was to pass on values to a malleable young soul. "Pass on" was, in my case, quite a euphemism. My own ethical stance and value system were still in the process of being reconstructed after the blitz of the late sixties. I felt absolutely inadequate to the task of building a strong structure for a preschool child. I struggled painfully with every situation that called for a decision about values: should I teach him nonviolence or the art of self-defense? Should I encourage him to question my commands or respect my need to have things done in certain ways? Should I demand that he maintain order in his room or allow him a measure of chaos? Every decision seemed to matter immensely—and to present unresolvable difficulties. I knew too much to opt simply for a highly structured universe on the one hand, or an existence that would trust to benign natural spontaneity on the other. And I was too confused to create a complex, workable blend of both.

The fact that I was now spending hour upon hour with a person who was verbal but not very good at being verbal was also difficult for me. I am the sort of person who can concentrate easily in the presence of jackhammers and roaring highway traffic, but let the most routine whispered conversation start up and I become totally distracted. When Kevin talked, whether to me or to one of his beloved stuffed animals, my whole mind swerved in his direction. But I was not good at child-level conversation and not particularly appreciative of the verbal gems of a three-year-old. I was, in fact, bored. I have often envied friends who take an easy delight in the speech of the very young. Not only do they enjoy the spontaneous comments of children; they also have mysterious ways of eliciting the most peculiar and interesting responses from them. Gretchen is one of these people and in the last ten years she has shared with me many instances of Kevin's verbal brilliance. Oddly enough, I have often taken special pleasure in hearing Gretchen tell me what Kevin has said. It is as if her appreciation of his words has provided a setting in which I can enjoy them.

Gretchen and I have always seemed to fit together like two radically different pieces adjacent in the same puzzle. I did a very good job of mothering during Kevin's infancy and then entered the painful period that taught me I did not want to go with the mother role. When I looked ahead I saw the grade school years as a severe challenge and if I imagined Kevin's adolescence I shuddered. Gretchen, on the other hand, got queasy at the thought of diapers and had no desire to be a mother to a small helpless nonverbal specimen of humanity; she liked a child she could talk to and she even, to my amazement, liked the fact that the child would become a teenager; she wanted to be a mother through that whole long growing process. More specifically, she wanted to be Kevin's mother. And so we made the change.

There is a stubborn, clear-headed part of me that has never doubted the rightness of my decision. With that part I know that Kevin, Gretchen, and I all have more satisfying lives because I made that decision. With that part I have organized groups for women who, like me, have left the mother role. With that part I fight the demons of the night.

There are two of these demons, both expert tormentors. One springs from reality, the other from myth. They are given to impersonating each other, like clever twins. I have spent many hours trying to pin down their identities, and I get a little better at it as time goes on. The first demon is decidedly unpleasant, but necessary. It is the caretaker of all the genuine pain that comes from giving up a child. That pain rises and subsides through the months and years. It feels demon-controlled because it comes without warning, without apparent cause, and most often in the middle of the night.

In the beginning, soon after Kevin and I separated, this demon of genuine pain was quite distinct, not readily confused with the second tormentor. I remember one night especially well. It was as if all the pain had gathered to a single point in time and I must experience it in a sort of purity. I felt as if Kevin and I had been surgically separated. The pain felt physical, deep, radical—and I knew it would lessen with time. That I had *chosen* the separation and believed it was going to be good for both Kevin and me must have determined the kind of pain I felt—pain that could be so accurately described by the image of surgery. When I think of the thousands of women who have been forcibly separated from their children—because they were black and slaves and sold in separate lots, because they were lesbians and considered by that fact unfit, because they made their living by prostitution and were therefore put in prison, or for whatever reason—when I think of those women I imagine a pain that is not the clean and chosen pain of surgery but instead the ragged, uncontrollable pain of flesh torn at random which heals slowly into an ugly scar and which hurts terribly even though new flesh has formed.

The second demon is not only unpleasant, but also unnecessary. It is the demon of myth and illusion and it is part of what is now being called the institution of motherhood.[1] The foundation stone of that institution and the constant message of its demon is this: *children are meant to be raised by their natural (that is, biological) mothers.*

I grew up in the all-white, working-class world of the small town Midwest and went to Catholic schools in the forties and fifties. I did not routinely encounter challenges to this basic tenet of the institution of motherhood. On the contrary, I absorbed the precept into my being.

I imagined I would someday be Mother Supreme. With infinite patience, good humor, and wisdom, I would faithfully raise not one child, but twelve. Having read *Cheaper by the Dozen* and *Jo's Boys*, I had decided to fill my life with wonderful, wacky children. I planned to have a few of my own, but the majority would be homeless waifs, "abandoned" by their mothers who were too poor or too ill to take care of them. With me a child would have a secure home.

That sort of self-image does not dissolve easily. In some very old part of my soul I still believe that I am a superior mother. I also still believe, with that same anachronistic part of my soul, that all children are best raised by their natural mothers. I have learned that neither of these beliefs is true, but in weak moments I forget what I have learned and thus open the door to the demon of myth and illusion. Like the demon of genuine pain, this creature comes most often at night. I know he has come when I find myself lying awake and nursing the terrible feeling that I have deprived my child of the most blessed of relationships; that my child is denied the special depth of bonding that could only come between him and me; that if I had stayed with him, he and I would have a full, clear, honest, tension-free relationship. I can remain in the grip of this demon for hours, colluding with society against myself.

But at some point I break free. I remember reality. I did not like the mother role. As long as I continued in it, I was doing something that aroused in me boredom, anxiety, depression, anger, and at times a fear that I would lose my sanity; it aroused in me also a deep fear that I would do violence to my child; at its best it turned me into a highly responsible, joyless, rather rigid person. Out of such things, great relationships are not made. I am not the best person to raise my child; only a powerful myth can make me think that I am.

The demon of myth and illusion has a strong grip which is not broken entirely by the act of remembering my own experience. I have also been faced with the task of sorting through distortions in my vision of Kevin's experience. The demon would paint the child as abandoned, damaged, a tragic figure. In my effort to correct this portrait I have sometimes drawn my own false picture: the child who moved easily from one mother to the next, happily relieved and blessedly unhurt. Somewhere between the demon and my own wishful thinking the truth hides. My memory, when it clears, tells me that Kevin's experience was as complex as mine, a mixture of pain and benefit.

I will never know all that Kevin felt during the time of transition, but two scenes come to my mind and I suspect that each is a hint and an essence, a clue to the nature of his first days and nights in Gretchen's house. One scene is painful, the other quietly delightful.

About a week after the separation I visited Kevin in his new house—our first visit. What I remember is saying good-bye. Gretchen held him, standing on the edge of the porch. I told him I was leaving and hugged him while she still held him. He got his arms around me like a vice, would not let go, and sobbed out all the loss, powerlessness, frustration, and pain that he felt. After a while we pried him loose from me and I turned and went down the porch steps crying and drove home crying. Gretchen called me a couple of hours later to say that he had gotten calm before too long and had had a quiet, happy game before bedtime.

The second scene that comes to mind was at the beginning of one of those early visits. Kevin and Gretchen were in their living room and had not heard me coming. For several minutes, which is a very long time, I did the thing that anyone in my position would dearly want to do: I spied on them. I was the mouse in the corner. I had the privilege of seeing my child and his new mother in a spontaneous moment. Classical music was playing on the stereo, one of those pieces of music that is subtle and engaging and moves like water in rough country with swift clarity and little falls and still places following on each other over and over. Gretchen sat with Kevin on her lap and their hands pantomined what I later found out were two alligators who talked and kissed and then fiercely ate each other up; which caused much laughing in Kevin and the familiar lump in my throat.

So he must have felt pain and he must have felt joy, too, in having a mother now who was as overflowing with energy for being his mother as I had been drained of it. It must have been confusing for quite a while to want to be with me and to be having such a good time with Gretchen. He got attached to her quickly. He began to express pride in the fact that he had two mothers—this made him special. But he was torn; he liked living with Gretchen and at the same time he wanted to live with me. Sometime during the first year he came up with the perfect solution for his dilemma: he proposed that we should all live together, he, Gretchen, and I. An intelligent idea, certainly; just the thing from his point of view. Needless to say, being only four, he did not have the power to transform his idea into reality.

Mixed with the pain, relief, fun, and confusion Kevin felt during those early days of the transition was at least one more set of feelings: frustration, impatience, irritation, anger. Anger was not a new thing in Kevin's life. His anger and mine had mixed and grown together for some time before our separation. Several months before Gretchen appeared and changed our lives, Kevin found a way to express that building rageful energy: he took a new name. He called himself Fire. With great seriousness he instructed everyone he met to call him Fire, his name was no longer Kevin. A month or so after our separation, he issued new instructions: we were all to stop calling him Fire; his name was Kevin.

Kevin's stay in the angry realm of Fire was relatively brief, I think. The fact that he was separated not only from me, but also from my anger, must have had something to do with that. But the separation could not, by itself, have dissolved his rage. In fact, it must have generated new anger. Gretchen's obvious abundant good feeling about Kevin and about her new job as mother did much to help him toward resolution of his feelings. In addition, he had invaluable assistance from the staff at his new daycare center (to which he was moved when Gretchen became his mother and decided she should not also be his teacher). Presented not only with his unusual name, but also with more tangible evidence of his anger (biting, kicking, and so forth), they reacted with intelligence and creativity—and patience. They taught him how to be angry without being destructive. The central character in this lesson on anger was Fred. Fred was life-sized, stuffed, and beat-up-looking—with good reason, since the point of his existence was to be an object of punching, biting, kicking, verbal assault and any other manner of attack a creative preschooler might invent. Kevin, I am told, learned to use Fred as no other child in the center ever had.

The fact that Kevin was encouraged to express his rage must have something to do with its disappearance. As far as I can tell, he is not now a particularly angry person; and he does not seem to have any resentment (at least at this point in his life) about having been required to leave me and adopt a new mother.

I can say this with some confidence because one recent spring (Kevin was eleven) I found the precise mixture of relaxation, courage, and support from other people in my life that allowed me, finally, to ask The Question. The setting was an A & W Restaurant situated on a busy road along with K-Mart, G.I. Joe's, and quite a number of auto dealers. Kevin and I were having hamburgers and root beer. In the middle of my hamburger, I asked him, "So, Kevin, what do you think about the fact that I am your real mom and we don't live together?"

He was quite ready with his answer and considerably calmer than I was. He had a theory: he supposed that I had not been able to afford having a child and so had given him to Gretchen. (Other children in Kevin's situation have expressed similar theories. It seems that children who do not live with their parents are likely to come up with an explanation of their situation that absolves both them and their parents of responsibility for the separation. In Kevin's case it was lack of money; in another child's it was immigration laws that required the parent to leave. In neither case did the external force actually have anything to do with the separation.) I told Kevin that money had not been a problem and talked a little about the real reason for my decision. Then I held my breath.

His response was calm and thoughtful. He said it was a good thing I had given him to Gretchen, he was sure the job of being a mother would have gotten harder and harder for me, and Gretchen was a good mom. He added, clearly not ready to abandon a well-thought-out theory, that he supposed I would have had financial problems if I had kept him.

Before that day in the A & W, I had a recurring fantasy that Kevin would, sometimes in his thirties, go to a psychotherapist and, hour by expensive hour, unearth his anger at me for "giving him away." Perhaps he will do just that, I cannot know. But the fantasy does not come to me now. I have asked the crucial question, which is really many questions: is it all right? do you hate me? were you damaged? And I have received the gift of a calm answer from a child who seems to believe his life is just fine.

Still, the demons come. Worry, guilt, romantic notions of what-might-have-been, a deep sense of loss—all mix together in the middle of the night. In the daytime, out in the world, I am bothered by another tangle of difficulties: I feel vulnerable to the judgments of others, isolated, different; I am afraid and I hide the fact that I am a mother; I cultivate a habit of cautious speech; I deny an aspect of my being. Any gay person will recognize this syndrome. It is called living in the closet.

I have lived partly in and partly out of the closet ever since I gave up my child. I told my family and close friends as soon as I made the decision, but for the first five years I did not talk about it with anyone who had left the mother role. I assumed there were hardly any of us. I did know of one woman, a friend of friends, but I avoided meeting her. Then I decided to do some intensive dealing with this huge fact in my life. I wrote my master's thesis on the experience of giving up my child. I organized a couple of groups for women who had left the mother role—groups that were a sort of coming out for me, complete with highs and lows, moments of clarity and confusion, and a sense that my life was changing. And I am still closeted. There are many people from whom I have hidden the fact of my motherhood: bosses, coworkers, neighbors, the families of my friends, any casual acquaintance. I feel the power of the institution of motherhood too clearly to take the revelation of my status lightly.

On the other hand, as the existence of this essay demonstrates, I feel compelled to tell the world about the experience of giving up my child. This is cathartic for me. Every time I wrestle anew with my mothering experience and get it pinned down for a while to a (somewhat) solid floor of words, I feel both relief and a fresh sense of control. I get my reward. But this is the most difficult writing I ever tackle, and I do not do it for pleasure. I do it because it needs doing and has been so little done.[2] In these days when the threat of a "Family Protection Act" hangs over us like some sharp and dangerous appendage to the institution of motherhood, it seems more important than ever to speak about alternative ways of raising our children. We must make it clear that many women cannot or will not be forced into the mold of happy motherhood; and this includes many women who already have children. Mothers—and fathers, too—who need to give up their children must be able to do so with dignity, without stigma, not only for their own sake, but also (and perhaps especially) for the sake of the children.

If ever I were to lose my conviction about this (and I could, in one of those sloppy, sentimental nights when a soft glow surrounds the image of the Mother Supreme), the morning news would quite likely help me remember reality. In the past month my local radio station has reported the murders of two young children—one by the father while the mother looked on, one by the mother. These murders are hardly unusual. I happen to have the statistics from 1966. In that year, 496 children were murdered by their parents in the United States. I am convinced that if it were an acceptable option to decide not to continue in the parenting role, at least some of these children would still be alive. Some battered children, too, would escape the bruises, the broken bones, the burns. Other children, less obviously abused, would find themselves released from the subtle prison of their parents' tension, anger, and unhappiness. They would find themselves being raised by someone who wanted to do the job. And that, I believe, would make all the difference.

Notes

1. The institution of motherhood is, by my definition, a system of customs, laws, ideals, and images that (1) determines how the *work* of mothering is generally defined, organized, and performed in a society; (2) powerfully influences the form and quality of the mother-child *relationship* in that society. For an excellent description of the working of this institution, see Adrienne Rich's *Of Woman Born: Motherhood as Experience and Institution* (New York: W.W. Norton & Co., 1976).

2. For more writing by women who have given up their children, see the following: Louise Billotte, "Mothers Don't Have to Lie," *Mother Jones*, May 1976: 22–25; *The Living of Charlotte Perkins Gilman: An Autobiography* (n.p., Katharine Beecher Stetson Chamberlain, 1935; reprint, New York: Harper & Row, 1963); Martha Jane Cannary Hickok, *Calamity Jane's Letters to Her Daughter* (n.p., Dr. Nolie Mumie, n.d., limited ed.; n.p., Don C. Foote

and Stella A Foote, n.d., limited ed.; reprint, San Lorenzo, Calif: Shameless Hussy Press, 1976); Patricia Preston, "Parenting in Absentia," *Branching Out*, May/June 1977; 8–10; Judy Sullivan, *Mama Doesn't Live Here Anymore* (New York: Pyramid Books, 1974); Lucia Valeska, "If All Else Fails, I'm Still a Mother" *Quest* 1 (Winter 1975); 52–63.

PART III

SEXUALITY AND REPRODUCTION

Biology sets certain outer limits beyond which we humans cannot operate. Yet, within those fairly far-flung boundaries, socially constructed meanings shape and sculpt exactly how each of us reacts, experiences, and changes. This point is very clear when we focus on gender and sexuality.

Anatomical and hormonal characteristics—in short, biology—initially label us as females. One look at the newborn and the pronouncement can be made: "it's a girl" (or, "it's a boy"). But that pronouncement is not some "value-free" statement of biology, for in this social context, it already says something about who this creature is. Research indicates that from the very moment the gender of an infant is known, those around that baby react in accordance with how boys or girls are to be treated, as defined by the mores and traditions of the society. Thus, in our society girl and boy babies are not slapped with equal force to get them breathing outside the mother's womb.

The only point of debate is how quickly—seconds or minutes—culture and society more than biology begin to define who this newborn is. For it is fairly quickly after birth (and increasingly before birth, now that sex can be so easily determined in the uterus) that bio-

229

logical sex is transformed into a socially constructed set of meanings: gender. There is far more controversy as to when one's sexual preference(s) is first determined or chosen. At one end of the continuum of views, it is assumed that our sexuality is some

> innate, unchanging essence that is covered over with layers of social and personal proscriptions and could, or should, under some circumstances be uncovered or released. (O'Brien 1981: 20)

At the other end of the continuum it is argued that our sexuality, including biological components, is socially molded from early childhood. This view sees sexuality as a learned relationship to the world, with an important but not a determinate biological component.

> In sexuality, there is a real biological substrate for a range of sexual responses that involve the brain, hormones, muscles, and blood vessels—tinglings, flutterings and flushes, engorgements, secretions, and muscular contractions—and are elicited for any individual only by certain stimuli: a particular person or type of person, a scent, a scene, a sound; a physical experience, a psychological situation; violence or pornography. But whatever or whoever arouses us, as well as our biological responses to arousal, are, I believe, individual characteristics that develop from childhood as part of one's history of experiences and interactions with the external world. ... there is nothing about desire, arousal, orgasms, or feelings of transcendent oneness that "comes naturally." (Bleier 1984: 167)

Looking at the history of "sexualities" in the United States demonstrates the extent to which their very existence and definitions are as much matters of social and cultural meanings as biology. For example, male *homosexuality* and *lesbianism* as sexual types were not classified in the United States until the late nineteenth century, when "capitalism and urban development made it possible for individuals to exist beyond the sphere of the extended family as a productive and reproductive unit" (Vance 1984: 8). Certainly same-sex intimacy not only took place but was punished in earlier periods of European rule in North America and was considered to result from the kind of carnal lust that anyone was subject to—not the sexual behavior of a particular individual known as a *homosexual*. By the twentieth century, two women who shared a deep friendship and a bed would be defined as *lesbians*.

As noted in the first essay in this book, there is an ideology which reduces women to sexual and reproductive objects, often setting up a conflicting ideal of "woman" as a man's Playboy bunny by night and his children's nurturing mother by day. The women's movement challenged this ideology and in some quarters sanctioned a range of ways for women to express their sexuality and approach reproduction (from celibacy to polygamy, from heterosexuality to homosexuality, from conventional motherhood to artificial insemination).

Perhaps it was a strong reaction against this view of women as sexual and reproductive objects that led some in the women's movement to perceive the "liberation" of women through the total disassociation from sexual relations with men. According to this view, lesbianism becomes not only a sexual preference but a necessary political condition for the liberation of every woman. The influence of this perspective is such that one professor of women's studies and sociology observed, while preparing to teach a course, that there were serious gaps in information about female sexuality in feminist literature, namely, the absence of positive descriptions of heterosexual intimacy and orgasm. Yet most women, including feminists, are practicing heterosexuals (Gardetto 1984).

Until recently, there has been very little attention to the sexuality and sexual activities of older women. Indeed, there was widespread discomfort and disbelief that old people continue to be sexual beings. Increasing sensitivity to the sex roles and sexual lives of older women in the United States springs in part from sheer demographics. People are living longer and more of these folks are women: today, women in the United States outlive men by nearly eight years.

However, there is a double standard whereby men are said to grow more distinguished looking as they age. For some men, career accomplishments of later life make them more attractive. Women, on the other hand, are generally said to become increasingly less attractive as they age. Despite biological findings, which indicate that sexual capacity in terms of frequency of arousal and vigor declines earlier in men than in women, older women tend not to be as sexually active as older men. This fact may reflect, in part, the extent to which a woman's sexual appeal is so often equated with her physical attractiveness; older women are generally not considered to be as attractive as younger women and, therefore, not as sexy. There is still too little recognition of this important part of the lives of aging women.

The women's movement that began in the 1960s and 1970s developed during a period when contraceptives could negate the automatic association of sexual relations between females and males with reproduction. Relationships among lesbians as well as among old people also challenged the association of sexual relations with reproduction. In turn, the new ideas of the women's movement permitted and, in some cases, encouraged more open attitudes about different kinds of sexual relationships and practices. And the idea of sex as pleasurable was raised for discussion.

Some individuals and groups do not welcome these new ideas. Indeed, the struggle to retie sexuality with reproduction in the most traditional of knots is central to the New Right's domestic program. This political force of constituencies headed by Jerry Falwell, Phyllis Schlafly, Jesse Helms, and others, with the tacit support of the president of the United States, seeks not only to eliminate the right to abortion but to reassert every possible patriarchal form of family structure and male dominance.

The women's movement, and the lesbian and gay movement, had a significant role in politicizing the issues and breaking down the historic status quo which the New Right seeks to put back together again. Who is going to engage in sexual relations with whom, in what ways, and with what consequences for reproduction are questions that have become more openly political and economic than ever before. After the Supreme Court passed its historic decision legalizing abortion, the New Right began a well-financed and well-organized campaign, the ultimate goal of which is a "human life" amendment to the U.S. Constitution which would ban all abortions. As an indication of the success of the New Right campaign, by the spring of 1979, twenty "human life" amendments with forty-four cosponsors were introduced in the House of Representatives, and two with seventeen cosponsors were introduced in the Senate. Different versions of this constitutional amendment continue to appear before Congress. In 1980 the Supreme Court upheld the Hyde Amendment (an amendment to a congressional bill which puts a severe obstacle in the way of poor women's receiving funds for abortions). Since 1980, thirty-seven states have adopted their own versions of that amendment.

While funding for abortions is being systematically cut, especially funds available for poor women and women on welfare, the federal government is paying 95 percent of the costs for their sterilization. It cannot go unnoticed that women of color—and through them peoples of color—are disproportionately victimized by fundamentalist and white New Right forces which simultaneously seek to block one-time cessation of reproductive powers while supporting the eternal loss of such powers.

The article by Angela Davis documents the long-standing racial and class biases of much of the movement for women's reproductive rights. Current federal support of sterilization of women of color, and to a lesser extent, of working-class women generally, recalls the eugenics movements of the nineteenth and early twentieth centuries. Davis also reminds us that within the women's movement there is insufficient attention to those "women's issues" which most dramatically and negatively affect women of color. The antipornography movement, for example, is visibly white and middle class, while women of color and working-class women are more involved with issues such as sterilization abuse, health care, and welfare. Such differential involvements may flow from the realities of who is affected, but this disparity among groups of women deeply challenges the very notion of a unified women's movement. As Audre Lorde wrote in an open letter to Mary Daly:

> Surely you know that for nonwhite women in this country, there is an 80 percent fatality rate from breast cancer; three times the number of unnecessary eventiations, hysterectomies and sterilizations as for white women; three times as many chances of being raped, murdered, or assaulted as exist for white women. These are statistical facts, not coincidences nor paranoid fantasies. (Lorde 1984: 70)

These figures indicate differences in the frequency and intensity with which women of different racial groups experience assaults on their sexuality and reproductive rights. The attitudes of women of various groups concerning these matters are more difficult to define. Yet, three of the following articles offer very definite views on the attitudes, perceptions, and experiences of at least some working-class women in heterosexual marriages, some Afro-American women of various ages and household statuses, and some women of various Latino heritages, nationalities, and classes.

When Lillian Rubin wrote *Worlds of Pain: Life in the Working Class Family*, the lives of the white working class in the United States had recently been affected by the civil rights, student, antiwar, and women's movements. As Rubin notes, the same period in the 1970s brought "The Pill" and a sexual revolution, a sharply rising divorce rate, and a concern for the future of the family. This was the historical context in which she interviewed women and men of blue-collar families about their marriages and sexual relations. Although some of the same strains and conflicts which helped shape their lives then remain today, and others have receded, the current era presents its own set of struggles for white working-class couples—struggles which emanate from the work people do, their relationships within their families, and very importantly, connections between the two. The people who speak in Rubin's article are among the fifty white working-class families she interviewed.

> They are all intact families, neither husband nor wife has more than a high-school education, the husband works in what is traditionally defined as a blue-collar occupation, the wife was under forty at the time of the study, and there was at least one child of elementary-school age (under twelve) still in the home. (Rubin 1976: 9).

She also interviewed twenty-five professional middle-class families whose characteristics matched the working-class group in all but education and occupation. The strength of Rubin's work is in the direct comparisons she makes between the two kinds of families—for the women appear to be more different in attitudes about marital sex than in behavior.

In Rubin's very sharp accounts, there are many important points about attitudes and behavior in the sexual and reproductive lives of the white working and middle class. Two points warrant emphasizing here because they address profound commonalities in the experiences of US women . . . and men. Sexual behavior, Rubin reminds us, is a mirror of socialization, of power, of submissiveness. In fact, sex and sexuality may well be the most commonly used and widely accepted arenas where many important issues of our lives are addressed, more often symbolically and metaphorically than in literal ways. These include issues of submissiveness and dominance; issues of control and vulnerability.

The second commonality suggested by Rubin's discussion is the sexual ever-readiness associated with men. This may be a complex, compensatory response to socialization that constricts the development of the emotional side of the male personality in all but sexual expression. Women, on the other hand, are socialized "to be emotional," especially over males, but punished for being so when it comes to themselves.

Whereas Rubin focused on groups of women who share a given class, Oliva Espín's article highlights similarities and differences among various women of "Hispanic ethnicity." Espín argues that four major factors affect the development of sexuality among Latinas in the United States. These factors, while played out with variations in the lives of specific women, nevertheless are common to all: historical influences, immigration, language, and the psychological effects of oppression. Espín illustrates the influence of a generalized Hispanic culture on Latino lesbians, for whom "coming out" may be harder than for Anglo women, and may hurt their chances of working in the Latino community.

In a particularly insightful passage, Espín, a practicing psychotherapist, develops the point that Latino women experience a "unique combination of power and powerlessness which is characteristic of the culture" (Espín 1984: 155). Their power is expressed in the role of grandmother; the ways that women are trusted and looked to for advice (while it is assumed that men are not to be depended on nor trusted); the greater status enjoyed by older Hispanic women than by their Anglo counterparts; and the role of health and spiritual healer carried out by many Latino women. However, these expressions of power are counterbalanced by the message that Latinas should be "submissive and subservient to males in order to be seen as 'good'" (Espín 1984: 156). Espín then traces the direct line from being a "good woman" to the shunning of sexual pleasure as proof of one's goodness.

It is especially interesting to compare the article by Espín with
that by Gloria Joseph, which is based on several open discussions on
sexual matters among black women of various ages and backgrounds.
Espín's portrayal of Latino cultural mores suggests that the openness
with which the black women in Joseph's article discussed their sexual
relations would not happen as easily among Latinas. The point can be
suggested that sexuality, despite its biological base, is still affected by
culture, and within a particular culture by factors of race, ethnicity,
class, age, and so forth.

Joseph begins with a call for honest discussions of sexuality between black men and women. Certainly, since the 1960s there has been
a continuous, but not always productive, debate on the range of issues
involving Afro-American women and men: heterosexual relations; interracial dating and marriage; female heads of households; relationships between individuals of different classes; homosexuality and he-
terosexism. The open discussions of these black women may make
more of a contribution to this ongoing debate than all of the attacks
and counterattacks so prevalent in black magazines and journals.

Two points stand out in the far-ranging discussions of the black
women: a clear ambivalence felt about black men, and an openness to
exploring themselves and understanding others' explorations of different sexual patterns and experiences. The ambivalence, it seems, grows
out of black women's awareness, from early in their lives, that black
men are oppressed in the United States by one of the same forces that
they are: racism. These ambivalent feelings clearly differ from what
many white women see as a distinction between themselves as the oppressed (because of their gender) and white men as the oppressor (because of their gender). The words of James Baldwin echo this important point.

A black gay person who is a sexual conundrum to society is already, long
before the question of sexuality comes into it, menaced and marked because he's black or she's black. The sexual question comes after the question of color; it's simply one more aspect of the danger in which all black
people live. I think white gay people feel cheated because they were born,
in principle, into a society in which they were supposed to be safe. The
anomaly of their sexuality puts them in danger, unexpectedly. Their reaction seems to me in direct proportion to the sense of feeling cheated of the
advantages which accrue to white people in a white society. There's an element, it has always seemed to me, of bewilderment and complaint. Now
that may sound very harsh, but the gay world as such is no more prepared
to accept black people than anywhere else in society. It's a very hermeti-
cally sealed world with very unattractive features, including racism.
(Goldstein 1984).

It is instructive to reread these words, substituting white women for white gay people in Baldwin's analysis.

The second point which the women in Joseph's piece state so clearly is that these are times when black women are open to a range of expressions of sexuality, and appreciate that sexuality is not a concrete, never-shifting constant, but changes and revolves. These black women, of working, middle, and professional classes, single and married, with and without children, discuss their fears and their intrigues, their suspicions and their interests in celibacy, interracial dating and marriage, lesbianism, female bonding, along with male sexual intimacies, bisexuality, and polygamy. Growing interest combined with honest confrontations of fears concerning differences in sexualities may, in fact, characterize far more women—of all races—than those who speak so clearly here.

Amber Hollibaugh's piece is ostensibly about her return home to a family who years earlier had rejected her sexual preference for women and, thus, had rejected her. Yet as Hollibaugh shares this journey, suggesting that maybe one can go home again, we learn that the break with her family was as much over her position on the Vietnam war and her politics in general as it was about her lesbianism. In a passage that clearly speaks of the fear of differentness and worship of homogeneity in U.S. society, Hollibaugh makes her point.

> Their fear of my queerness came as much from my moving outside the expectations of our family as it did from sex. They generated their dignity, lives, through the power of the family and a sympathy of the blood. It was their sense of my betrayal I most wanted to speak to. (Hollibaugh 1984: 2)

This passage warns us against those simplistic divisions of ourselves and of others according to our sexual preferences as opposed to our politics, our feelings about family, and our jobs.

It is in the areas of gender, sexuality, and reproduction that US women may appear to share the most. Are we not all of the female gender? And biologically, regardless of our sexual preference, is it not we, and we alone, who are capable of giving birth to our species? But gender and sexuality are more socially constructed than biologically given. As Ruth Hubbard notes, how we express gender and how we play out our particular sexuality develops out of our different life situations, with factors such as class and race, constrained by what we can imagine as permissible, correct behavior (Hubbard 1984: 2–5).

One of the consequences of the women's movement is that there is greater openness about and experimentation with what is indeed possible and permissible in the areas of sexuality and reproduction. But there are also countervailing forces which seek, under an ultraconservative agenda, to narrow choices and stifle human diversity in these areas. The very issues of sexuality and reproduction become, then, important arenas where women, along with men, will continue to struggle over respect for differences versus imposed uniformity.

References Cited

Bleier, R., ed.
1984   *Science and Gender: A Critique of Biology and Its Theories on Women.* New York: Pergamon.

Espín, O. M.
1984   "Cultural and Historical Influences on Sexuality in Hispanic/Latin Women: Implications for Psycho-Therapy." In *Pleasure and Danger: Exploring Female Sexuality*, C. Vance, ed., pp. 149–164. Boston: Routledge and Kegan Paul.

Gardetto, D. C.
1984   "Heterosexuality and Silence." *Sojourner*, October, pp. 13–14.

Goldstein, R.
1984   " 'Go the Way Your Blood Beats.' Interview with James Baldwin." *Village Voice*, June 26, 1984, pp. 13–16.

Hollibaugh, A.
1984   "The Sympathy of the Blood." *Village Voice*, June 26, 1984, pp. 22–25.

Hubbard, R.
1984   "Reflections of a Feminist Biologist on Human Sexuality and Reproduction." *Women's Studies Quarterly*, 12 (4): 2–5.

Lorde, A.
1984   *Sister Outsider*. Trumansburg, N.Y.: Crossing Press.

O'Brien, M.
1981   "The Politics of Reproduction." Boston: Routledge and Kegan Paul. In *Science and Gender: A Critique of Biology and Its Theories on Women*, R. Bleier, ed., pp. 165–166. New York: Pergamon.

Rubin, L.
1976   *Worlds of Pain*. New York: Basic Books.

Vance, C. S., ed.
1984   *Pleasure and Danger: Exploring Female Sexuality*. Boston: Routledge and Kegan Paul.

19

Racism, Birth Control and Reproductive Rights

Angela Y. Davis

When nineteenth-century feminists raised the demand for "voluntary motherhood," the campaign for birth control was born. Its proponents were called radicals and they were subjected to the same mockery as had befallen the initial advocates of woman suffrage. "Voluntary motherhood" was considered audacious, outrageous and outlandish by those who insisted that wives had no right to refuse to satisfy their husbands' sexual urges. Eventually, of course, the right to birth control, like women's right to vote, would be more or less taken for granted by U.S. public opinion. Yet in 1970, a full century later, the call for legal and easily accessible abortions was no less controversial than the issue of "voluntary motherhood" which had originally launched the birth control movement in the United States.

Birth control—individual choice, safe contraceptive methods, as well as abortions when necessary—is a fundamental prerequisite for the emancipation of women. Since the right of birth control is obviously advantageous to women of all classes and races, it would appear that even vastly dissimilar women's groups would have attempted to

From *Women, Race & Class*. Reprinted by permission of Random House, Inc.

unite around this issue. In reality, however, the birth control movement has seldom succeeded in uniting women of different social backgrounds, and rarely have the movement's leaders popularized the genuine concerns of working-class women. Moreover, arguments advanced by birth control advocates have sometimes been based on blatantly racist premises. The progressive potential of birth control remains indisputable. But in actuality, the historical record of this movement leaves much to be desired in the realm of challenges to racism and class exploitation.

The most important victory of the contemporary birth control movement was won during the early 1970s when abortions were at last declared legal. Having emerged during the infancy of the new Women's Liberation movement, the struggle to legalize abortions incorporated all the enthusiasm and the militancy of the young movement. By January, 1973, the abortion rights campaign had reached a triumphant culmination. In *Roe* v. *Wade* (410 U.S.) and *Doe* v. *Bolton* (410 U.S.), the U.S. Supreme Court ruled that a woman's right to personal privacy implied her right to decide whether or not to have an abortion.

The ranks of the abortion rights campaign did not include substantial numbers of women of color. Given the racial composition of the larger Women's Liberation movement, this was not at all surprising. When questions were raised about the absence of racially oppressed women in both the larger movement and in the abortion rights campaign, two explanations were commonly proposed in the discussions and literature of the period: women of color were overburdened by their people's fight against racism; and/or they had not yet become conscious of the centrality of sexism. But the real meaning of the almost lily-white complexion of the abortion rights campaign was not to be found in an ostensibly myopic or underdeveloped consciousness among women of color. The truth lay buried in the ideological underpinnings of the birth control movement itself.

The failure of the abortion rights campaign to conduct a historical self-evaluation led to a dangerously superficial appraisal of Black people's suspicious attitudes toward birth control in general. Granted, when some Black people unhesitatingly equated birth control with genocide, it did appear to be an exaggerated—even paranoiac—reaction. Yet white abortion rights activists missed a profound message, for underlying these cries of genocide were important clues about the history of the birth control movement. This movement, for example, had been known to advocate involuntary sterilization—a racist form of mass "birth control." If ever women would enjoy the right to plan their pregnancies, legal and easily accessible birth control measures and abortions would have to be complemented by an end to sterilization abuse.

As for the abortion rights campaign itself, how could women of color fail to grasp its urgency? They were far more familiar than their white sisters with the murderously clumsy scalpels of inept abortionists seeking profit in illegality. In New York, for instance, during the several years preceding the decriminalization of abortions in that state, some 80 percent of the deaths caused by illegal abortions involved Black and Puerto Rican women.[1] Immediately afterward, women of color received close to half of all the legal abortions. If the abortion rights campaign of the early 1970s needed to be reminded that women of color wanted desperately to escape the back-room quack abortionists, they should have also realized that these same women were not about to express pro-abortion sentiments. They were in favor of *abortion rights*, which did not mean that they were proponents of abortion. When Black and Latina women resort to abortions in such large numbers, the stories they tell are not so much about their desire to be free of their pregnancy, but rather about the miserable social conditions which dissuade them from bringing new lives into the world.

Black women have been aborting themselves since the earliest days of slavery. Many slave women refused to bring children into a world of interminable forced labor, where chains and floggings and sexual abuse for women were the everyday conditions of life. A doctor practicing in Georgia around the middle of the last century noticed that abortions and miscarriages were far more common among his slave patients than among the white women he treated. According to the physician, either Black women worked too hard or

> as the planters believe, the blacks are possessed of a secret by which they destroy the fetus at an early stage of gestation. . . . All country practitioners are aware of the frequent complaints of planters (about the) . . . unnatural tendency in the African female to destroy her offspring.[2]

Expressing shock that "whole families of women fail to have any children,"[3] this doctor never considered how "unnatural" it was to raise children under the slave system. The previously mentioned episode of Margaret Garner, a fugitive slave who killed her own daughter and attempted suicide herself when she was captured by slavecatchers, is a case in point.

> She rejoiced that the girl was dead—"now she would never know what a woman suffers as a slave"—and pleaded to be tried for murder. "I will go singing to the gallows rather than be returned to slavery!"[4]

Why were self-imposed abortions and reluctant acts of infanticide such common occurrences during slavery? Not because Black women had discovered solutions to their predicament, but rather because they were desperate. Abortions and infanticides were acts of desperation, motivated not by the biological birth process but by the oppressive conditions of slavery. Most of these women, no doubt, would have expressed their deepest resentment had someone hailed their abortions as a stepping stone toward freedom.

During the early abortion rights campaign it was too frequently assumed that legal abortions provided a viable alternative to the myriad problems posed by poverty. As if having fewer children could create more jobs, higher wages, better schools, etc., etc. This assumption reflected the tendency to blur the distinction between *abortion rights* and the general advocacy of *abortions* The campaign often failed to provide a voice for women who wanted the *right* to legal abortions while deploring the social conditions that prohibited them from bearing more children.

The renewed offensive against abortion rights that erupted during the latter half of the 1970s has made it absolutely necessary to focus more sharply on the needs of poor and racially oppressed women. By 1977 the passage of the Hyde Amendment in Congress had mandated the withdrawal of federal funding for abortions, causing many state legislatures to follow suit. Black, Puerto Rican, Chicana and Native American Indian women, together with their impoverished white sisters, were thus effectively divested of the right to legal abortions. Since surgical sterilizations, funded by the Department of Health, Education and Welfare, remained free on demand, more and more poor women have been forced to opt for permanent infertility. What is urgently required is a broad campaign to defend the reproductive rights of all women—and especially those women whose economic circumstances often compel them to relinquish the right to reproduction itself.

Women's desire to control their reproductive system is probably as old as human history itself. As early as 1844 the *United States Practical Receipt Book* contained, among its many recipes for food, household chemicals and medicines, "receipts" for "birth preventive lotions." To make "Hannay's Preventive Lotion," for example,

> [t]ake pearlash, 1 part, water, 6 parts. Mix and filter. Keep it in closed bottles, and use it, with or without soap, immediately after connexion.[5]

For "Abernethy's Preventive Lotion,"

> [t]ake bichloride of mercury, 25 parts; milk of almonds, 400 parts; alcohol, 100 parts; rosewater, 1000 parts. Immerse the glands in a little of the mixture. . . . Infallible, if used in proper time.[6]

While women have probably always dreamed of infallible methods of birth control, it was not until the issue of women's rights in general became the focus of an organized movement that reproductive rights could emerge as a legitimate demand. In an essay entitled "Marriage," written during the 1850s, Sarah Grimke argued for a "right on the part of woman to decide *when* she shall become a mother, how often and under what circumstances."[7] Alluding to one physician's humorous observation, Grimke agreed that if wives and husbands alternatively gave birth to their children, "no family would ever have more than three, the husband bearing one and the wife two."[8] But, as she insists, "the *right* to decide this matter has been almost wholly denied to woman."[9]

Sarah Grimke advocated women's right to sexual abstinence. Around the same time the well-known "emancipated marriage" of Lucy Stone and Henry Blackwell took place. These abolitionists and women's rights activists were married in a ceremony that protested women's traditional relinquishment of their rights to their persons, names and property. In agreeing that as husband, he had no right to the "custody of the wife's person,"[10] Henry Blackwell promised that he would not attempt to impose the dictates of his sexual desires upon his wife.

The notion that women could refuse to submit to their husbands' sexual demands eventually became the central idea of the call for "voluntary motherhood." By the 1870s, when the woman suffrage movement had reached its peak, feminists were publicly advocating voluntary motherhood. In a speech delivered in 1873, Victoria Woodhull claimed that

> (t)he wife who submits to sexual intercourse against her wishes or desires, virtually commits suicide; while the husband who compels it, commits murder, and ought just as much to be punished for it, as though he strangled her to death for refusing him.[11]

Woodhull, of course, was quite notorious as a proponent of "free love." Her defense of a woman's right to abstain from sexual intercourse within marriage as a means of controlling her pregnancies was associated with Woodhull's overall attack on the institution of marriage.

It was not a coincidence that women's consciousness of their reproductive rights was born within the organized movement for women's political equality. Indeed, if women remained forever burdened by incessant childbirths and frequent miscarriages, they would hardly be able to exercise the political rights they might win. Moreover, women's new dreams of pursuing careers and other paths of self-development outside marriage and motherhood could only be realized if they could limit and plan their pregnancies. In this sense, the slogan "voluntary motherhood" contained a new and genuinely progressive vision of womanhood. At the same time, however, this vision was rigidly bound to the lifestyle enjoyed by the middle classes and the bourgeoisie. The aspirations underlying the demand for "voluntary motherhood" did not reflect the conditions of working-class women, engaged as they were in a far more fundamental fight for economic survival. Since this first call for birth control was associated with goals which could only be achieved by women possessing material wealth, vast numbers of poor and working-class women would find it rather difficult to identify with the embryonic birth control movement.

Toward the end of the nineteenth century the white birth rate in the United States suffered a significant decline. Since no contraceptive innovations had been publicly introduced, the drop in the birth rate implied that women were substantially curtailing their sexual activity. By 1890 the typical native-born white woman was bearing no more than four children.[12] Since U.S. society was becoming increasingly urban, this new birth pattern should not have been a surprise. While farm life demanded large families, they became dysfunctional within the context of city life. Yet this phenomenon was publicly interpreted in a racist and anti-working-class fashion by the ideologues of rising monopoly capitalism. Since native-born white women were bearing fewer children, the specter of "race suicide" was raised in official circles.

In 1905 President Theodore Roosevelt concluded his Lincoln Day Dinner speech with the proclamation that "race purity must be maintained."[13] By 1906 he blatantly equated the falling birth rate among native-born whites with the impending threat of "race suicide." In his State of the Union message that year Roosevelt admonished the well-born white women who engaged in "willful sterility—the one sin for which the penalty is national death, race suicide."[14] These comments were made during a period of accelerating racist ideology and of great waves of race riots and lynchings on the domestic scene. Moreover, President Roosevelt himself was attempting to muster support for the U.S. seizure of the Philippines, the country's most recent imperialist venture.

How did the birth control movement respond to Roosevelt's accusation that their cause was promoting race suicide? The President's propagandistic ploy was a failure, according to a leading historian of the birth control movement, for, ironically, it led to greater support for its advocates. Yet, as Linda Gordon maintains, this controversy "also brought to the forefront those issues that most separated feminists from the working class and the poor."[15]

> This happened in two ways. First, the feminists were increasingly emphasizing birth control as a route to careers and higher education—goals out of reach of the poor with or without birth control. In the context of the whole feminist movement, the race-suicide episode was an additional factor identifying feminism almost exclusively with the aspirations of the

more privileged women of the society. Second, the pro-birth control feminists began to popularize the idea that poor people had a moral obligation to restrict the size of their families, because large families create a drain on the taxes and charity expenditures of the wealthy and because poor children were less likely to be "superior."[16]

The acceptance of the race-suicide thesis, to a greater or lesser extent, by women such as Julia Ward Howe and Ida Husted Harper reflected the suffrage movement's capitulation to the racist posture of Southern women. If the suffragists acquiesced to arguments invoking the extension of the ballot to women as the saving grace of white supremacy, then birth control advocates either acquiesced to or supported the new arguments invoking birth control as a means of preventing the proliferation of the "lower classes" and as an antidote to race suicide. Race suicide could be prevented by the introduction of birth control among Black people, immigrants and the poor in general. In this way, the prosperous whites of solid Yankee stock could maintain their superior numbers within the population. Thus class-bias and racism crept into the birth control movement when it was still in its infancy. More and more, it was assumed within birth control circles that poor women, Black and immigrant alike, had a "moral obligation to restrict the size of their families."[17] What was demanded as a "right" for the privileged came to be interpreted as a "duty" for the poor.

When Margaret Sanger embarked upon her lifelong crusade for birth control—a term she coined and popularized—it appeared as though the racist and anti-working-class overtones of the previous period might possibly be overcome. For Margaret Higgens Sanger came from a working-class background herself and was well acquainted with the devastating pressures of poverty. When her mother died, at the age of forty-eight, she had borne no less than eleven children. Sanger's later memories of her own family's troubles would confirm her belief that working-class women had a special need for the right to plan and space their pregnancies autonomously. Her affiliation, as an adult, with the Socialist movement was a further cause for hope that the birth control campaign would move in a more progressive direction.

When Margaret Sanger joined the Socialist party in 1912, she assumed the responsibility of recruiting women from New York's working women's clubs into the party.[18] *The Call*—the party's paper—carried her articles on the women's page. She wrote a series entitled "What Every Mother Should Know," another called "What Every Girl Should Know," and she did on-the-spot coverage of strikes involving women. Sanger's familiarity with New York's working-class districts was a result of her numerous visits as a trained nurse to the poor sections of the city. During these visits, she points out in her autobiography, she met countless numbers of women who desperately desired knowledge about birth control.

According to Sanger's autobiographical reflections, one of the many visits she made as a nurse to New York's Lower East Side convinced her to undertake a personal crusade for birth control. Answering one of her routine calls, she discovered that twenty-eight-year-old Sadie Sachs had attempted to abort herself. Once the crisis had passed, the young woman asked the attending physician to give her advice on birth prevention. As Sanger relates the story, the doctor recommended that she "tell (her husband) Jake to sleep on the roof."[19]

> I glanced quickly to Mrs. Sachs. Even through my sudden tears I could see stamped on her face an expression of absolute despair. We simply looked at each other, saying no word until the door had closed behind the doctor. Then she lifted her thin, blue-veined hands and clasped them beseechingly. "He can't understand. He's only a man. But you do, don't you? Please tell me the secret, and I'll never breathe it to a soul. Please!"[20]

Three months later Sadie Sachs died from another self-induced abortion. That night, Margaret Sanger says, she vowed to devote all her energy toward the acquisition and dissemination of contraceptive measures.

> I went to bed, knowing that no matter what it might cost, I was finished with palliatives and superficial cures; I resolved to seek out the root of evil, to do something to change the destiny of mothers whose miseries were as vast as the sky.[21]

During the first phase of Sanger's birth control crusade, she maintained her affiliation with the Socialist party—and the campaign itself was closely associated with the rising militancy of the working class. Her staunch supporters included Eugene Debs, Elizabeth Gurley Flynn and Emma Goldman, who respectively represented the Socialist party, the International Workers of the World and the anarchist movement. Margaret Sanger, in turn, expressed the anti-capitalist commitment of her own movement within the pages of its journal, *Woman Rebel*, which was "dedicated to the interests of working women."[22] Personally, she continued to march on picket lines with striking workers and publicly condemned the outrageous assaults on striking workers. In 1914, for example, when the National Guard massacred scores of Chicano miners in Ludlow, Colorado, Sanger joined the labor movement in exposing John D. Rockefeller's role in this attack.[23]

Unfortunately, the alliance between the birth control campaign and the radical labor movement did not enjoy a long life. While Socialists and other working-class activists continued to support the demand for birth control, it did not occupy a central place in their overall strat-

egy. And Sanger herself began to underestimate the centrality of capitalist exploitation in her analysis of poverty, arguing that too many
children caused workers to fall into their miserable predicament.
Moreover, "women were inadvertently perpetuating the exploitation
of the working class," she believed, "by continually flooding the labor
market with new workers."[24] Ironically, Sanger may have been encouraged to adopt this position by the neo-Malthusian ideas embraced in
some socialist circles. Such outstanding figures of the European socialist movement as Anatole France and Rosa Luxemburg had proposed a "birth strike" to prevent the continued flow of labor into the
capitalist market.[25]

When Margaret Sanger severed her ties with the Socialist party
for the purpose of building an independent birth control campaign, she
and her followers became more susceptible than ever before to the
anti-Black and anti-immigrant propaganda of the times. Like their
predecessors, who had been deceived by the "race suicide" propaganda, the advocates of birth control began to embrace the prevailing
racist ideology. The fatal influence of the eugenics movement would
soon destroy the progressive potential of the birth control campaign.

During the first decades of the twentieth century the rising popularity of the eugenics movement was hardly a fortuitous development.
Eugenic ideas were perfectly suited to the ideological needs of the
young monopoly capitalists. Imperialist incursions in Latin America
and in the Pacific needed to be justified, as did the intensified exploitation of Black workers in the South and immigrant workers in the
North and West. The pseudo-scientific racial theories associated with
the eugenics campaign furnished dramatic apologies for the conduct
of the young monopolies. As a result, this movement won the unhesitat-
ing support of such leading capitalists as the Carnegies, the Harrimans
and the Kelloggs.[26]

By 1919 the eugenic influence on the birth control movement was
unmistakably clear. In an article published by Margaret Sanger in the
American Birth Control League's journal, she defined "the chief issue
of birth control" as "more children from the fit, less from the unfit."[27]
Around this time the ABCL heartily welcomed the author of *The Rising
Tide of Color Against White World Supremacy* into its inner sanctum.[28]
Lothrop Stoddard, Harvard professor and theoretician of the eugenics
movement, was offered a seat on the board of directors. In the pages of
the ABCL's journal, articles by Guy Irving Birch, director of the American Eugenics Society, began to appear. Birch advocated birth control
as a weapon to

> prevent the American people from being replaced by alien or Negro stock,
> whether it be by immigration or by overly high birth rates among others
> in this country.[29]

By 1932 the Eugenics Society could boast that at least twenty-six states had passed compulsory sterilization laws and that thousands of "unfit" persons had already been surgically prevented from reproducing.[30] Margaret Sanger offered her public approval of this development. "Morons, mental defectives, epileptics, illiterates, paupers, unemployables, criminals, prostitutes and dope fiends" ought to be surgically sterilized, she argued in a radio talk.[31] She did not wish to be so intransigent as to leave them with no choice in the matter; if they wished, she said, they should be able to choose a lifelong segregated existence in labor camps.

Within the American Birth Control League, the call for birth control among Black people acquired the same racist edge as the call for compulsory sterilization. In 1939 its successor, the Birth Control Federation of America, planned a "Negro Project." In the Federation's words,

> (t)he mass of Negroes, particularly in the South, still breed carelessly and disastrously, with the result that the increase among Negroes, even more than among whites, is from that portion of the population least fit, and least able to rear children properly.[32]

Calling for the recruitment of Black ministers to lead local birth control committees, the Federation's proposal suggested that Black people should be rendered as vulnerable as possible to their birth control propaganda. "We do not want word to get out," wrote Margaret Sanger in a letter to a colleague,

> that we want to exterminate the Negro population and the minister is the man who can straighten out that idea if it ever occurs to any of their more rebellious members.[33]

This episode in the birth control movement confirmed the ideological victory of the racism associated with eugenic ideas. It had been robbed of its progressive potential, advocating for people of color not the individual right to *birth control*, but rather the racist strategy of *population control*. The birth control campaign would be called upon to serve in an essential capacity in the execution of the U.S. government's imperialist and racist population policy.

The abortion rights activists of the early 1970s should have examined the history of their movement. Had they done so, they might have understood why so many of their Black sisters adopted a posture of suspicion toward their cause. They might have understood how important it was to undo the racist deeds of their predecessors, who had advocated birth control as well as compulsory sterilization as a means of eliminating the "unfit" sectors of the population. Consequently, the young white feminists might have been more receptive to the suggestion that their campaign for abortion rights include a vigorous condemnation of sterilization abuse, which had become more widespread than ever.

It was not until the media decided that the casual sterilization of two Black girls in Montgomery, Alabama, was a scandal worth reporting that the Pandora's box of sterilization abuse was finally flung open. But by the time the case of the Relf sisters broke, it was practically too late to influence the politics of the abortion rights movement. It was the summer of 1973 and the Supreme Court decision legalizing abortions had already been announced in January. Nevertheless, the urgent need for mass opposition to sterilization abuse became tragically clear. The facts surrounding the Relf sisters' story were horrifyingly simple. Minnie Lee, who was twelve years old, and Mary Alice, who was fourteen, had been unsuspectingly carted into an operating room, where surgeons irrevocably robbed them of their capacity to bear children.[34] The surgery had been ordered by the HEW-funded Montgomery Community Action Committee after it was discovered that Depo-Provera, a drug previously administered to the girls as a birth prevention measure, caused cancer in test animals.[35]

After the Southern Poverty Law Center filed suit on behalf of the Relf sisters, the girls' mother revealed that she had unknowingly "consented" to the operation, having been deceived by the social workers who handled her daughters' case. They had asked Mrs. Relf, who was unable to read, to put her "X" on a document, the contents of which were not described to her. She assumed, she said, that it authorized the continued Depo-Provera injections. As she subsequently learned, she had authorized the surgical sterilization of her daughters.[36]

In the aftermath of the publicity exposing the Relf sisters' case, similar episodes were brought to light. In Montgomery alone, eleven girls, also in their teens, had been similarly sterilized. HEW-funded birth control clinics in other states, as it turned out, had also subjected young girls to sterilization abuse. Moreover, individual women came forth with equally outrageous stories. Nial Ruth Cox, for example, filed suit against the state of North Carolina. At the age of eighteen—eight years before the suit—officials had threatened to discontinue her family's welfare payments if she refused to submit to surgical sterilization.[37] Before she assented to the operation, she was assured that her infertility would be temporary.[38]

Nial Ruth Cox's lawsuit was aimed at a state which had diligently practiced the theory of eugenics. Under the auspices of the Eugenics Commission of North Carolina, so it was learned, 7,686 sterilizations had been carried out since 1933. Although the operations were justified as measures to prevent the reproduction of "mentally deficient persons," about 5,000 of the sterilized persons had been Black.[39] According to Brenda Feigen Fasteau, the ACLU attorney representing Nial Ruth Cox, North Carolina's recent record was not much better.

> As far as I can determine, the statistics reveal that since 1964, approximately 65% of the women sterilized in North Carolina were Black and approximately 35% were white.[40]

As the flurry of publicity exposing sterilization abuse revealed, the neighboring state of South Carolina had been the site of further atrocities. Eighteen women from Aiken, South Carolina, charged that they had been sterilized by a Dr. Clovis Pierce during the early 1970s. The sole obstetrician in that small town, Pierce had consistently sterilized Medicaid recipients with two or more children. According to a nurse in his office, Dr. Pierce insisted that pregnant welfare women "will have to submit (sic!) to voluntary sterilization" if they wanted him to deliver their babies.[41] While he was "tired of people running around and having babies and paying for them with my taxes,"[42] Dr. Pierce received some $60,000 in taxpayers' money for the sterilizations he performed. During his trial he was supported by the South Carolina Medical Association, whose members declared that doctors "have a moral and legal right to insist on sterilization permission before accepting a patient, if it is done on the initial visit."[43]

Revelations of sterilization abuse during that time exposed the complicity of the federal government. At first the Department of Health, Education and Welfare claimed that approximately 16,000 women and 8,000 men had been sterilized in 1972 under the auspices of federal programs.[44] Later, however, these figures underwent a drastic revision. Carl Shultz, director of HEW's Population Affairs Office, estimated that between 100,000 and 200,000 sterilizations had actually been funded that year by the federal government.[45] During Hitler's Germany, incidentally, 250,000 sterilizations were carried out under the Nazis' Hereditary Health Law.[46] Is it possible that the record of the Nazis, throughout the years of their reign, may have been almost equaled by U.S. government-funded sterilizations in the space of a single year?

Given the historical genocide inflicted on the native population of the United States, one would assume that Native American Indians would be exempted from the government's sterilization campaign. But according to Dr. Connie Uri's testimony in a Senate committee hearing, by 1976 some 24 percent of all Indian women of childbearing age had been sterilized.[47] "Our blood lines are being stopped," the Choctaw physician told the Senate committee, "Our unborn will not be born. . . . This is genocidal to our people."[48] According to Dr. Uri, the Indian Health Services Hospital in Claremore, Oklahoma, had been sterilizing one out of every four women giving birth in that federal facility.[49]

Native American Indians are special targets of government propaganda on sterilization. In one of the HEW pamphlets aimed at Indian people, there is a sketch of a family with *ten children* and *one horse* and another sketch of a family with *one child* and *ten horses*. The drawing are supposed to imply that more children mean more poverty and fewer children mean wealth. As if the ten horses owned by the one-child family had been magically conjured up by birth control and sterilization surgery.

The domestic population policy of the U.S. government has an undeniably racist edge. Native American, Chicana, Puerto Rican and Black women continue to be sterilized in disproportionate numbers. According to a National Fertility Study conducted in 1970 by Princeton University's Office of Population Control, 20 percent of all married Black women have been permanently sterilized.[50] Approximately the same percentage of Chicana women had been rendered surgically infertile.[51] Moreover, 43 percent of the women sterilized through federally subsidized programs were Black.[52]

The astonishing number of Puerto Rican women who have been sterilized reflects a special government policy that can be traced back to 1939. In that year President Roosevelt's Interdepartmental Committee on Puerto Rico issued a statement attributing the island's economic problems to the phenomenon of overpopulation.[53] This committee proposed that efforts be undertaken to reduce the birth rate to no more than the level of the death rate.[54] Soon afterward an experimental sterilization campaign was undertaken in Puerto Rico. Although the Catholic Church initially opposed this experiment and forced the cessation of the program in 1946, it was converted during the early 1950s to the teachings and practice of population control.[55] In this period over 150 birth control clinics were opened, resulting in a 20 percent decline in population growth by the mid-1960s.[56] By the 1970s over 35 percent of all Puerto Rican women of childbearing age had been surgically sterilized.[57] According to Bonnie Mass, a serious critic of the U.S. government's population policy,

> if purely mathematical projections are to be taken seriously, if the present rate of sterilization of 19,000 monthly were to continue, then the island's population of workers and peasants could be extinguished within the next 10 or 20 years . . . [establishing] for the first time in world history a systematic use of population control capable of eliminating an entire generation of people.[58]

During the 1970s the devastating implications of the Puerto Rican experiment began to emerge with unmistakable clarity. In Puerto Rico the presence of corporations in the highly automated metallurgical and pharmaceutical industries had exacerbated the problem of unemployment. The prospect of an ever-larger army of unemployed workers was one of the main incentives for the mass sterilization program. Inside the United States today, enormous numbers of people of color—and especially racially oppressed youth—have become part of a pool of permanently unemployed workers. It is hardly coincidental, considering the Puerto Rican example, that the increasing incidence of sterilization has kept pace with the high rates of unemployment. As growing numbers of white people suffer the brutal consequences of unemployment, they can also expect to become targets of the official sterilization propaganda.

The prevalence of sterilization abuse during the latter 1970s may be greater than ever before. Although the Department of Health, Education and Welfare issued guidelines in 1974, which were ostensibly designed to prevent involuntary sterilizations, the situation has nonetheless deteriorated. When the American Civil Liberties Union's Reproductive Freedom Project conducted a survey of teaching hospitals in 1975, they discovered that 40 percent of those institutions were not even aware of the regulations issued by HEW.[59] Only 30 percent of the hospitals examined by the ACLU were even attempting to comply with the guidelines.[60]

The 1977 Hyde Amendment has added yet another dimension to coercive sterilization practices. As a result of this law passed by Congress, federal funds for abortions were eliminated in all cases but those involving rape and the risk of death or severe illness. According to Sandra Salazar of the California Department of Public Health, the first victim of the Hyde Amendment was a twenty-seven-year-old Chicana woman from Texas. She died as a result of an illegal abortion in Mexico shortly after Texas discontinued government-funded abortions. There have been many more victims—women for whom sterilization has become the only alternative to the abortions, which are currently beyond their reach. Sterilizations continue to be federally funded and free, to poor women, on demand.

Over the last decade the struggle against sterilization abuse has been waged primarily by Puerto Rican, Black, Chicana and Native American women. Their cause has not yet been embraced by the women's movement as a whole. Within organizations representing the interests of middle-class white women, there has been a certain reluctance to support the demands of the campaign against sterilization abuse, for these women are often denied their individual rights to be sterilized when they desire to take this step. While women of color are urged, at every turn, to become permanently infertile, white women enjoying prosperous economic conditions are urged, by the same foces, to reproduce themselves. They therefore sometimes consider the "waiting period" and other details of the demand for "informed consent" to sterilization as further inconveniences for women like themselves. Yet whatever the inconveniences for white middle-class women, a fundamental reproductive right of racially oppressed and poor women is at stake. Sterilization abuse must be ended.

Notes

1. Edwin M. Gold *et al.*. "Therapeutic Abortions in New York City: A Twenty-Year Review" in *American Journal of Public Health*, Vol. LV (July, 1965), pp. 964–972. Quoted in Lucinda Cisla, "Unfinished Business: Birth Control and Women's Liberation," in Robin Morgan, editor, *Sisterhood is Powerful: An Anthology of Writings from the Women's Liberation Movement* (New York: Vintage Books, 1970), p. 261. Also quoted in Robert Staples, *The Black Woman in America* (Chicago: Nelson Hall, 1974), p. 146.

2. Herbert Gutman, *The Black Family in Slavery and Freedom, 1750–1925* (New York: Pantheon Books, 1976), pp. 80–81 (note).

3. *Ibid.*

4. Herbert Aptheker, "The Negro Woman" in *Masses and Mainstream*, Vol. 11, No. 12, February, 1948, p. 12.

5. Quoted in Rosalyn Baxandall, Linda Gordon, Susan Reverby, editors, *America's Working Women: A Documentary History—1600 to the Present* (New York: Random House, 1976), p. 17.

6. *Ibid.*

7. Gerda Lerner, *The Female Experience: An American Documentary* (Indianapolis: Bobbs-Merrill, 1977), p. 91.

8. *Ibid.*

9. *Ibid.*

10. "Marriage of Lucy Stone under Protest" appeared in *History of Woman Suffrage*, Vol. 1. Quoted in Miriam Schneir, *Feminism: The Essential Historical Writings* (New York: Vintage Books, 1972), p. 104.

11. Speech by Victoria Woodhull, "The Elixir of Life." Quoted in Schneir, *op. cit*, p. 153.

12. Mary P. Ryan, *Womanhood in America from Colonial Times to the Present* (New York: Franklin Watts, Inc., 1975), p. 162.

13. Melvin Steinfeld, *Our Racist Presidents* (San Ramon, California: Consensus Publishers, 1972), p. 212.

14. Bonnie Mass, *Population Target: The Political Economy of Population Control in Latin America* (Toronto, Canada: Women's Educational Press, 1977), p. 20.

15. Linda Gordon, *Woman's Body, Woman's Right: Birth Control in America* (New York: Penguin Books, 1976), p. 157.

16. *Ibid.*, p. 158.

17. *Ibid.*

18. Margaret Sanger, *An Autobiography* (New York: Dover Press, 1971), p. 75.

19. *Ibid.*, p. 90.
20. *Ibid.*, p. 91.
21. *Ibid.*, p. 92.
22. *Ibid.*, p. 106
23. Mass, *op. cit*, p. 27.
24. Bruce Dancis, "Socialism and Women in the United States, 1900–1912," *Socialist Revolution*, No. 27, Vol. VI, No. 1 (January–March, 1976), p. 96.
25. David M. Kennedy, *Birth Control in America: The Career of Margaret Sanger* (New Haven and London: Yale University Press, 1976), pp. 21–22.
26. Mass, *op. cit*, p. 20.
27. Gordon, *op. cit*, p. 281.
28. Mass, *op. cit*, p. 20.
29. Gordon, *op. cit*, p. 283.
30. Herbert Aptheker, "Sterilization, Experimentation and Imperialism," *Political Affairs*, Vol. LIII, No. 1 (January, 1974), p. 44.
31. Gena Corea, *The Hidden Malpractice* (New York: A Jove/HBJ Book, 1977), p. 149.
32. Gordon, *op. cit*, p. 332.
33. *Ibid.*, pp. 332–333.
34. Aptheker, "Sterilization," p. 38. See also Anne Braden, "Forced Sterilization: Now Women Can Fight Back," *Southern Patriot*, September, 1973.
35. *Ibid.*
36. Jack Slater, "Sterilization, Newest Threat to the Poor," *Ebony*, Vol. XXVIII, No. 12 (October, 1973), p. 150.
37. Braden, *op. cit.*
38. Les Payne, "Forced Sterilization for the Poor?" *San Francisco Chronicle*, February 26, 1974.
39. Harold X., "Forced Sterilization Pervades South," *Muhammed Speaks*, October 10, 1975.
40. Slater, *op. cit.*
41. Payne, *op. cit.*
42. *Ibid.*
43. *Ibid.*
44. Aptheker, "Sterilization," p. 40.
45. Payne, *op. cit.*
46. Aptheker, "Sterilization," p. 48.
47. Arlene Eisen, "They're Trying to Take Our Future—Native American Women and Sterilization," *The Guardian*, March 23, 1972.
48. *Ibid.*
49. *Ibid.*
50. Quoted in a pamphlet issued by the Committee to End Sterilization Abuse, [CESA], Box A244, Cooper Station, New York 10003.

51. *Ibid.*
52. *Ibid.*
53. Gordon, *op. cit.*, p. 338.
54. *Ibid.*
55. Mass, *op. cit.*, p. 92.
56. *Ibid.*, p. 91.
57. Gordon, *op. cit.*, p. 401. See also pamphlet issued by CESA.
58. Mass, *op. cit.*, p. 108.
59. Rahemah Aman, "Forced Sterilization," *Union Wage*, March 4, 1978.
60. *Ibid.*

20

The Marriage Bed

Lillian Breslow Rubin

I suppose the problems and conflicts you've had have played themselves out in your sexual adjustment?

A chorus of yes's greets the question. Not one couple is without stories about adjustment problems in this difficult and delicate area of marital life—problems not just in the past, but in the present as well. Some of the problem areas—such as differences in frequency of sexual desire between men and women—are old ones. Some—such as the men's complaints about their wives' reluctance to engage in variant and esoteric sexual behaviors—are newer. All suggest that there is, in fact, a revolution in sexual behavior in American society—a revolution that runs deep and wide, a revolution in which sexual behaviors that formerly were the province of the college-educated upper classes now are practiced widely at all class and educational levels.

The evidence is strong that more people are engaging in more varieties of sexual behavior than ever before—more premarital, post-marital, extra-marital sex of all kinds. In 1948, for example, Kinsey

From *Worlds of Pain: Life in the Working-Class Family* by Lillian Breslow Rubin. © 1976 by Lillian Breslow Rubin. Reprinted by permission of Basic Books, Inc., Publishers.

found that only 15 percent of high-school-educated married men ever engaged in cunnilingus, compared to 45 percent of college-educated men. But the world changes quickly. Just twenty-five years later, a national survey shows that the proportion of high-school-educated men engaging in cunnilingus jumped to 56 percent.[1] And among the people I met, the figure stands at 70 percent.

But to dwell on these impressive statistics which tell us what people *do*, without attention to how they *feel* about what they do is to miss a profoundly important dimension of human experience—that is, the *meaning* that people attribute to their behavior. Nowhere is the disjunction between behavior and attitude seen more sharply than in the area of sexual behavior. For when, in the course of a single lifetime, the forbidden becomes commonplace, when the border between the conceivable and the inconceivable suddenly disappears, people may *do* new things, but they don't necessarily *like* them.

For decades, novelists, filmmakers, and social scientists all have portrayed working-class men as little more than boorish, insensitive studs—men whose sexual performance was, at best, hasty and perfunctory; at worst, brutal—concerned only with meeting their own urgent needs. Consideration for a woman's needs, variety in sexual behaviors, experimentation—these, it is generally said, are to be found largely among men of the upper classes; working-class men allegedly know nothing of such amenities.[2]

If such men ever lived in large numbers, they surely do no longer. Morton Hunt's *Playboy* study, which does not control for class but does give data that are controlled for education, provides evidence that men at all educational levels have become more concerned with and more sensitive to women's sexual needs—with the greatest increase reported among high-school-educated men. Comparing his sample with the 1948 Kinsey data on the subject of foreplay, for example, he notes that Kinsey reported that foreplay was "very brief or even perfunctory" among high-school-educated husbands, while college-educated husbands reported about ten minutes. Twenty-five years later, Hunt found that the median for non-college and college-educated husbands was the same—fifteen minutes. Similar changes were found in the variety of sexual behaviors, the variety of positions used, and the duration of coitus—with especially sharp increases reported among high-school-educated men.

Not surprisingly, it is the men more often than the women who find the changing sexual norms easier to integrate—generally responding more positively to a cultural context that offers the potential for loosening sexual constraints. For historically, it is men, not women, whose sexuality has been thought to be unruly and ungovernable—

destined to be restrained by a good (read: asexual) woman. Thus, it is
the men who now more often speak of their wish for sex to be freer and
with more mutual enjoyment:

> I think sex should be that you enjoy each other's bodies. Judy doesn't care
> for touching and feeling each other though.

. . . who push their wives to be sexually experimental, to try new things
and different ways:

> She thinks there's just one right position and one right way—in the dark
> with her eyes closed tight. Anything that varies from that makes her
> upset.

. . . who sometimes are more concerned than their wives for her orgasm:

> It's just not enjoyable if she doesn't have a climax, too. She says she
> doesn't mind, but I do.

For the women, these attitudes of their men—their newly expressed wish for sexual innovation, their concern for their wives'
gratification—are not an unmixed blessing. In any situation, there is a
gap between the ideal statements of a culture and the reality in which
people live out their lives—a time lag between the emergence of new
cultural forms and their internalization by the individuals who must
act upon them. In sexual matters, that gap is felt most keenly by
women. Socialized from infancy to experience their sexuality as a negative force to be inhibited and repressed, women can't just switch "on"
as the changing culture or their husbands dictate. Nice girls don't!
Men *use* bad girls but marry good girls! Submit, but don't enjoy—at
least not obviously so! These are the injunctions that have dominated
their lives—injunctions that are laid aside with difficulty, if at all. . . .

We need only to look at our own responses to two questions to understand how vital the double standard remains. When we are asked,
"What kind of woman is she?", we are likely to think about her sexual
behavior; is she "easy" or not. But the question, "What kind of man is
he?" evokes thoughts about what kind of work he does; is he strong,
weak, kind, cruel? His sexual behavior is his private business, no concern of ours.

Whether these issues are especially real for working-class women,
or whether women of that class are simply more open in talking about
them than their middle-class counterparts, is difficult to say. Most of
these middle-class women came to their first sexual experiences at college where, during the early-to-middle 1960s, they suddenly entered a
world where sexual freedom was the byword. . . .

. . . one thing is clear. Among the people I spoke with, working-
class and middle-class couples engage in essentially the same kinds of

sexual behaviors in roughly the same proportions. But working-class wives express considerably more discomfort about what they do in the marriage bed than their middle-class sisters.

Take, for example, the conflict that engages many couples around the issue of oral-genital stimulation. Seventy percent of the working-class and 76 percent of the middle-class couples engage in such sexual activity. A word of caution is necessary here, however, because these gross figures can be misleading. For about one-third of each group, engaging in oral-genital stimulation means that they tried it once, or that it happens a few times a year at most. Another 30 percent of the middle-class couples and 40 percent of the working-class couples said they have oral sex only occasionally, meaning something over three times but less than ten times a year. Thus, only about one-fourth of the working-class couples and one-third of the middle-class couples who engage in oral sex use this sexual mode routinely as a standard part of their repertoire of sexual techniques. Still, fewer of the working-class women say they enjoy it unreservedly or without guilt. Listen to this couple, married twelve years. The husband:

> I've always been of the opinion that what two people do in the bedroom is fine; whatever they want to do is okay. But Jane, she doesn't agree. I personally like a lot of foreplay, caressing each other and whatever. For her, no. I think oral sex is the ultimate in making love; but she says it's revolting. [*With a deep sigh of yearning.*] I wish I could make her understand.

The wife:

> I sure wish I could make him stop pushing me into that (ugh, I even hate to talk about it), into that oral stuff. I let him do it, but I hate it. He says I'm old-fashioned about sex and maybe I am. But I was brought up that there's just one way you're supposed to do it. I still believe that way, even though he keeps trying to convince me of his way. How can I change when I wasn't brought up that way? [*With a pained sigh.*] I wish I could make him understand.

Notice her plaintive plea for understanding—"I wasn't brought up that way." In reality, when it comes to sex, she, like most of us, wasn't brought up *any* way. Girls generally learn only that it's "wrong" before marriage. But what that "it" is often is hazy and unclear until after the first sexual experience. As for the varieties of sexual behavior, these are rarely, if ever, mentioned to growing children, let alone discussed in terms of which are right or wrong, good or bad, permissible or impermissible. . . .

Even those women who do not express distinctly negative feelings about oral sex are often in conflict about it—unsure whether it is really all right for them to engage in, let alone enjoy, such esoteric sexual behavior, worrying about whether these are things "nice girls" do. One twenty-eight-year-old mother of three, married ten years, explained:

> I always feel like it's not quite right, no matter what Pete says. I guess it's not the way I was brought up, and it's hard to get over that. He keeps telling me it's okay if it's between us, that anything we do is okay. But I'm not sure about that. How do I know in the end he won't think I'm cheap.

> Sometimes I enjoy it, I guess. But most of the time I'm too worried thinking about whether I ought to be doing it, and worrying what he's *really* thinking to get much pleasure.

"How do I know he won't think I'm cheap?"—a question asked over and over again, an issue that dominates these woman and their attitudes toward their own sexuality. Some husbands reassure them:

> She says she worries I'll think she's a cheap tramp, and she doesn't really believe me when I keep telling her it's not true.

Such reassurances remain suspect, however, partly because it's so hard for women to move past the fears of their own sexuality with which they have been stamped; and partly because at least some men are not without their own ambivalence about it, as is evident in this comment from one young husband:

> No, Alice isn't that kind of girl. Jesus, you shouldn't ask questions like that. [*A long, difficult silence.*] She wasn't brought up to go for all that [*pause*] fancy stuff. You know, all those different ways and [*shifting uncomfortably in his chair, lighting a cigarette, and looking down at the floor*] that oral stuff. But that's okay with me. There's plenty of women out there to do that kind of stuff with. You can meet them in any bar any time you want to. You don't have to marry those kind.

As long as that distinction remains, as long as men distinguish between the girls they marry and the girls they use, many women will remain unconvinced by their reassurances and wary about engaging in sexual behaviors that seem to threaten their "good girl" status.

Those assurances are doubly hard to hear and to believe when women also know that their husbands are proud of their naïveté in sexual matters—a pride which many men take little trouble to hide:

> It took a long time for me to convince her that it didn't have to be by the books. She was like an innocent babe. I taught her everything she knows.

Even men whose wives were married before will say with pleasure:

> It's funny how naïve she was when we got married. She was married before, you know, but still she was kind of innocent. I taught her just about everything she knows.

For the women, the message seems clear: He wants to believe in her innocence, to believe in the special quality of their sexual relationship, to believe that these things she does only for him. She is to be pupil to his teacher. So she echoes his words—"He taught me everything I know." Repeatedly that phrase or a close equivalent is used as women discuss their sexual behavior and their feelings about it. And always it is said with a sure sense that it's what her husband wants and needs to believe, as these incongruent comments from a woman now in her second marriage show:

> One thing I know he likes is that he taught me mostly all I know about sex, so that makes him feel good. It also means that I haven't any habits that have to be readjusted to his way or anything like that.

That seems a strange thing to say when you were married for some years before.

Startled, she looked at me, then down at her hands uncomfortably.

> Yeah, I guess you'd think so. Well, you know, he likes to feel that way so why shouldn't he, and why shouldn't I let him?

Given that knowledge, even if it were possible to do so on command, most women would not dare risk unleashing their sexual inhibitions. From where a woman stands, the implicit injunction in her husband's pride in her innocence is that her sexuality be restrained. And restrain it she does—a feat for which she is all too well trained. The price for that training in restraint is high for both of them, however. He often complains because she doesn't take the initiative:

> She never initiates anything. She'll make no advances at all, not even subtleties.

She often replies:

> I just can't. I guess I'm inhibited, I don't know. All I know is it's very hard for me to start things up or to tell him something I want. Maybe that comes from back when women weren't supposed to enjoy sex. Now that's supposed to be changed, but I don't know.

On the other hand, not infrequently when women put aside that restraint and take the initiative, they may find themselves accused of not being feminine enough:

> It isn't that I mind her letting me know when she wants it, but she isn't very subtle about it. I mean, she could let me know in a nice, feminine way. Being feminine and, you know, kind of subtle, that's not her strong point.

Sensitive to the possibility of being thought of as "unfeminine" or "aggressive," most women shy away from any behavior that might bring those words down upon their heads. For it is painful for any woman of any class to hear herself described in these ways:

> I don't like to think he might think I was being aggressive, so I don't usually make any suggestions. Most of the time it's okay because he can usually tell when I'm in the mood. But if he can't, I just wait.

These, then, are some of the dilemmas and conflicts people face around the newly required and desired sexual behaviors. Among working-class women, isolation and insulation compound their problems. It is one thing to read about all these strange and exotic sexual behaviors in books and magazines, another to know others like yourself who actually do these things:

> He keeps trying to get me to read those books, but what difference would it make? I don't know who those people are. There's a lot of people do lots of things; it doesn't mean I have to do them.

If the books aren't convincing, and it's not culturally acceptable to discuss the intimate details of one's sex life with neighbors, friends, co-workers, or even family, most women are stuck with their childhood and adolescent fears, fantasies, and prohibitions. Small wonder that over and over again during my visit the atmosphere in the room changed from tense anxiety to exquisite relief when subjects such as oral sex were treated casually, with either the implicit or explicit understanding that it is both common and acceptable sexual practice:

> Jim keeps telling me and telling me it's okay, that it's not dirty. But I always worry about it, not really knowing if that's true or not. I read a couple of books once, but it's different. I never talked to anyone but Jim about it before. [Smiling, as if a weight had been lifted from her shoulders.] You're so cool about it; talking to you makes it seem not so bad.

... Sexual conflicts in marriage are not always constellated around such exotic issues, however; nor, as I have said, are any of them the exclusive problem of a particular class. Thus, although what follows rests on material taken from my discussions with working-class couples, much of it applies to the professional middle-class as well. True, the middle-class couples more often are able to discuss some of their issues more openly with each other. But despite the current, almost mystical, belief in communication-as-problem-solving—talk doesn't always help. True, middle-class couples much more often seek professional help with these problems. But sexual conflicts in a marriage are among the most intractable—the recent development and proliferation of sex therapies notwithstanding. Those therapies can be useful in dealing with some specific sexual dysfunction—prematurely

ejaculating men or nonorgasmic women. But the kinds of sexual conflicts to be discussed here are so deeply rooted in the socio-cultural
mandates of our world that they remain extraordinarily resistant regardless of how able the psychotherapeutic help we can buy. . . .

In fact, the earliest sexual problems rear their heads with the
couple's first fight. Regardless of what has gone before, at bedtime,
he's ready for sex; she remains cold and aloof. Listen to this couple in
their mid-to-late-twenties, married nine years. The wife:

> I don't understand him. He's ready to go any time. It's always been a big
> problem with us right from the beginning. If we've hardly seen each other
> for two or three days and hardly talked to each other, I can't just jump
> into bed. If we have a fight, I can't just turn it off. He has a hard time un-
> derstanding that. I feel like that's all he wants sometimes. I have to know
> I'm needed and wanted for more than just jumping into bed.

The husband:

> She complains that all I want from her is sex, and I try to make her under-
> stand that it's an expression of love. I'll want to make up with her by mak-
> ing love, but she's cold as the inside of the refrig. Sure I get mad when that
> happens. Why shouldn't I? Here I'm trying to make up and make love, and
> she's holding out for something—I don't know what.

The wife:

> He keeps saying he wants to make love, but it just doesn't feel like love to
> me. Sometimes I feel bad that I feel that way, but I just can't help it.

The husband:

> I don't understand. She says it doesn't feel like love. What does that mean,
> anyway? What does she think love is?

The wife:

> I want him to talk to me, to tell me what he's thinking about. If we have a
> fight, I want to talk about it so we could maybe understand it. I don't want
> to jump in bed and just pretend it didn't happen.

The husband:

> Talk! Talk! What's there to talk about. I want to make love to her and she
> says she wants to talk. How's talking going to convince her I'm loving her.

In sex, as in other matters, the barriers to communication are
high, and the language people use serves to further confuse and mys-
tify. He says, "I want to make love." She says, "It doesn't feel like
love." Neither quite knows what the other is talking about; both feel
vaguely guilty and uncomfortable—aware only that somehow they're
passing each other, not connecting. He believes he already has given

her the most profound declaration of love of which a man is capable. He married her; he gives her a home; he works hard each day to support her and the children:

> What does she want? Proof? She's got it, hasn't she? Would I be knocking myself out to get things for her—like to keep up this house—if I didn't love her. Why does a man do things like that if not because he loves his wife and kids? I swear, I can't figure what she wants.

This is one time when *she* knows what she wants:

> I want him to let me know in other ways, too, not just sex. It's not enough that he supports us and takes care of us. I appreciate that, but I want him to share things with me. I need for him to tell me his feelings. He keeps saying no, but to me, there's a difference between making love and sex. Just once, I'd like him to love me without it ending up in sex. But when I tell him that, he thinks I'm crazy.

For him perhaps, it *does* seem crazy. Split off, as he is, from the rest of the expressive-emotional side of himself, sex may be the one place where he can allow himself the expression of deep feelings, the one place where he can experience the depth of that affective side. His wife, on the other hand, closely connected with her feeling side in all areas *but* the sexual, finds it difficult to be comfortable with her feelings in the very area in which he has the greatest—sometimes the only—ease. She keeps asking for something she can understand and is comfortable with—a demonstration of his feelings in non-sexual ways. He keeps giving her the one thing he can understand and is comfortable with—his feelings wrapped up in a blanket of sex. Thus do husbands and wives find themselves in an impossibly difficult bind—another bind not of their own making, but one that stems from the cultural context in which girls and boys grow to adulthood.

I am suggesting, then, that a man's ever-present sexual readiness is not simply an expression of urgent sexual need but also a complex compensatory response to a socialization process that *constricts the development of the emotional side of his personality in all but sexual expression.* Conversely, a woman's insistent plea for an emotional statement of a nonsexual nature is a response to a process that *encourages the development of the affective side of her personality in all but sexual expression.*[3]

Such differences between women and men about the *meaning* of sex make for differences between wives and husbands in frequency of desire as well—differences which lead to a wide discrepancy in their perceptions about the frequency of the sexual encounter.[4] Except for a few cases where the women are inclined to be more sexually active than the men, he wants sex more often than she. To him, therefore, it seems as if they have sex less often than they actually do; to her, it seems more often. But the classical caricature of a wife fending off her husband's advances with a sick headache seems not to apply among working-class women. Once in a while, a woman says:

I tell him straight I'm not in the mood, and he understands.

Mostly, however, women say:

I don't use excuses like headaches and things like that. If my husband wants me, I'm his wife, and I do what he wants. It's my responsibility to give it to him when he needs it.

Whether she refuses outright or acquiesces out of a sense of duty or responsibility, the solution is less than satisfactory for both partners. In either case, he feels frustrated and deprived. He wants more than release from his own sexual tension; he wants her active involvement as well. Confronted with his ever-present readiness, she feels guilty:

I feel guilty and uncomfortable when he's always ready and I'm not, like I'm not taking care of him.

. . . coerced:

I feel like it hangs over my head all the time. He always wants it; twice a day wouldn't be too much for him. He says he doesn't want me just to give in to him, but if I didn't he'd be walking around horny all the time. If we waited for me to want it, it would never be enough for him.

. . . and also deprived:

Before I ever get a chance to feel really sexy, he's there and waiting. I'd like to know what it feels like sometimes to really want it that bad. Oh, sometimes I do. But mostly I don't get the chance.

Thus, she rarely has the opportunity to experience the full force of her own sexual rhythm, and with it the full impact of her sexuality. It is preempted by the urgency and frequency of his desires.

Finally, there is plenty of evidence that the battle between the sexes is still being waged in the marriage bed, and in very traditional ways. Several couples spoke of their early sexual adjustment problems in ways that suggest that the struggle was not over sex but over power and control. Often in the early years, when she wants sex, he's tired; when he wants sex, she's uninterested. For many couples, the pattern still repeats itself once in a while. For about one fifth of them, the scenario continues to be played out with great regularity and sometimes with great drama, as this story of one early-thirties couple illustrates.

In six months of premarital and ten years of marital coitus, the
woman had never had an orgasm:

> We had sex four or five times a week like clockwork all those years, and I
> just laid there like a lump. I couldn't figure out what all the noise was
> about.

Asked how he felt about her passivity during that period, her
husband—a taciturn, brooding man, whose silence seemed to cover a
wellspring of hostility—replied:

> If she couldn't, she couldn't. I didn't like it, but I took what I needed. [*After
> a moment's hesitation.*] She's always been hard to handle.

A year ago, attracted by ideas about women's sexuality that
seemed to her to be "in the air," she began to read some of the women's
literature on the subject. From there, she moved on to pornography
and one night, as she tells it:

> The earth shook. I couldn't believe anything could be so great. I kept won-
> dering how I lived so long without knowing about it. I kept asking Fred
> why he'd never made me understand before. [*Then, angrily.*] But you'll
> never believe what happened after that. My husband just lost interest in
> sex. Now, I can hardly ever get him to do it anymore, no matter how much
> I try or beg him. He says he's too tired, or he doesn't feel well, or else he
> just falls asleep and I can't wake him up. I can hardly believe it's happen-
> ing sometimes. Can you imagine such a thing? I even wonder whether
> maybe I shouldn't have made such a big fuss about it. Maybe it scared him
> off or something.

Her husband refused my attempts to explore the issue with him, insist-
ing that all is well in their sex life, but adding:

> She's always asking for something or hollering about something. I don't
> have any control around this house anymore. Nobody listens to me.

It would seem, then, that as long as he could "take what I needed,"
he could feel he was asserting some control over his wife and could remain sexually active and potent. When she unexpectedly became an assertive and active participant in the sex act, the only possibility for retaining control was to move from the active to the passive mode. Thus,
he fell impotent. His wife, now acutely aware of her sexual deprivation, is left torn between anger, frustration, and the terrible fear that
somehow she is responsible for it.

A dramatic story? Certainly. But one whose outlines are clear in 20
percent of these marriages, where three women complained about their
husbands' impotence and seven about sexual withholding—not surprisingly, a problem most of the men were unwilling to talk about. In

the three cases where the husband did address the issue at all, either he denied its existence, "It's no problem; I'm just tired;" or blamed his wife, "She doesn't appeal to me," or "She's too pushy." The last has been a subject of recent concern expressed publicly by psychologists and widely publicized in the mass media. The performance demands being laid on men are extraordinary, we are told, and women are cautioned that their emergent assertiveness—sexual and otherwise— threatens the sexual performance of their men. The time has come, these experts warn, to take the pressure off.

Nowhere, however, do we hear concern about the effects of the performance demand on women. Yet never in history have heavier demands for sexual performance been laid on them. Until recently, women were expected to submit passively to sex; now they are told their passivity diminishes their husbands' enjoyment. Until recently, especially among the less-educated working class, orgasm was an unexpected gift; now it is a requirement of adequate sexual performance.[5] These new definitions of adequacy leave many women feeling "under the gun"—fearful and anxious if they do not achieve orgasm; if it does not happen at the "right" moment—that is, at the instant of their husbands' ejaculation; or if they are uncomfortable about engaging in behaviors that feel alien or aberrant to them.[6] If anxiety about one's ability to perform adequately has an untoward effect on the male orgasm, is there any reason to believe it would not inhibit the female's as well? . . .

While it is undoubtedly true that more women have more orgasms more often than ever before—and that most of them enjoy sex more than women in earlier generations—it is also true that there are times when their husbands' wish for their orgasm is experienced as oppressive and alienating—when it seems to them that their orgasm is more a requirement of his pleasure than their own. We may ask: How rational are these thoughts? And we may wonder: Why should it be a matter of question or criticism if, in the course of pleasuring their wives, men also pleasure themselves? When phrased that way, it should not be questioned! But if we look at the discussion around female orgasm or lack of it a little more closely, we notice that it is almost invariably tied to male pleasure. If a woman doesn't have an orgasm, it is a problem, if not for her, then because both her man's pleasure and his sense of manhood are diminished. Can anyone imagine a discussion of male impotence centering around concern for women? In fact, when we talk about the failure of men to achieve erection or orgasm, the discourse takes place in hushed, serious, regretful tones—always in the context of concern about how those men experience that failure. How many of us have ever thought, "What a shame for his woman that he can't have an erection." Any woman who has shared that experience with a man knows that her concern was largely for him, her own frustration becoming irrelevant in that moment. Any man who has experienced impotence knows that his dominant concern was for the failure of his manhood.

It is not surprising, therefore, that several of the women I talked to were preoccupied with their orgasm, not because it was so important to them, but because their husbands' sense of manhood rested on it. Holding her head, one woman said painfully:

> I rarely have climaxes. But if it didn't bother my husband, it wouldn't bother me. I keep trying to tell him that I know it's not his fault, that he's really a good lover. I keep telling him it's something the matter with me, not with him. But it scares me because he doesn't believe it, and I worry he might leave me for a woman who will have climaxes for him.

With these final words, she epitomizes the feelings of many women, whether orgasmic or not, at least some of the time: *her orgasm is for him, not for her.* It is his need to validate his manhood that is the primary concern—his need, not hers. For women of the working class, who already have so little autonomy and control over their lives, this may well be experienced as the ultimate violation.

To compound the anxiety, now one orgasm is not enough. One woman, having read that some women have multiple orgasms, worried that her husband would soon find out:

> It's really important for him that I reach a climax, and I try to every time. He says it just doesn't make him feel good if I don't. But it's hard enough to do it once! What'll happen if he finds out about those women who have lots of climaxes?

. . . It is both sad and ironic now to hear men complain that their wives are too cautious, too inhibited, or not responsive enough in bed. Sad, because the deprivation men experience is real; ironic, because these are the costs of the sexual limitations that generations of their forebears have imposed on women. Changing such historic patterns of thought and behavior will not be easy for either men or women. For certainly, many men are still not without ambivalence about these sexual issues with reference to their women—a subtlety that is not lost on their wives. But even where men unambivalently mean what they say about wanting their wives to be freer in the marriage bed, it will take time for women to work through centuries of socially mandated denial and repression:

> All I know is, I can't just turn on so easy. Maybe we're all paying the price now because men didn't used to want women to enjoy sex.

... and probably will require their first being freer in other beds as well:

> I was eighteen when we got married, and I was a very young eighteen. I'd never had any relations with anybody, not even my husband, before we were married. So we had a lot of problems. I guess I was kind of frigid at first. But you know, after all those years when you're holding back, it's hard to all of a sudden get turned on just because you got married. I know it's not right, but sometimes I think we should have had sex before we were married. Then maybe it wouldn't have been so much trouble after.

Yes, it is "hard to all of a sudden get turned on just because you got married." And as long as women's sexuality continues to be subjected to capricious demands and treated as if regulated by an on-off switch—expected to surge forth fully and vigorously at the flick of the "on" switch and to subside quietly at the flick of the "off"—most women will continue to seek the safest path—in this case, to remain quietly someplace between "on" and "off."

Notes

1. Hunt's (1974) study, conducted for *Playboy* magazine, included a representative sample of urban and suburban adults, of whom 982 were men and 1,044 were women. Seventy-one percent of the sample were married (not to each other), 25 percent were never married, and 4 percent had been married.
2. For a good description of this stereotype, see Shostak (1971). See also Komarovsky (1962:82–111) who, while noting that the stereotype applies to "only a small minority" of the families she studied, found that only 30 percent of the women said they were very satisfied with their sexual relations. And some of the data she presents do, indeed, validate the stereotype more forcefully and very much more often than among my sample where it is practically nonexistent.
3. Cf., Simon and Gagnon (1969:733–752) and Gagnon and Simon (1973), whose work is a major contribution toward understanding the differences in male-female sexuality as an expression of the differential socialization patterns for women and men, and who also point to the masculine tendency to separate love and sex and the feminine tendency to fuse them. They suggest, in fact, that the male "capacity for detached sexual activity, activity where the only sustaining motive is sexual . . . may actually be the hallmark of male sexuality in our culture."

    For an exploration of the ways in which social structure and personality intersect from a psychoanalytic perspective, see Chodorow (1977), who argues that the root of the differences in male-female personality, and the concomitant differences in the development of psychosexual needs and responses, lie in the social structure of the family.

See also Barker-Benfield (1973) for a portrait of nineteenth-century definitions of male and female sexuality and the fear and abhorrence with which men viewed female sexuality in that era.

4. It is for this reason that studies relying on the recollection of only one spouse for their data—as most do—risk considerable distortion. Thus, for example, when Hunt (1974) reports that almost 26 percent of the married women ages twenty-five to thirty-four report having sexual intercourse between 105–156 times a year, we know only that this is the wife's perception, and we can assume that the recollection is filtered through her *feelings* about the frequency of the sexual encounter.

5. Again, Hunt's (1974) data, while not controlled for class, are suggestive. Using the 1948 Kinsey data as a comparative base, he reports that marital coitus has increased in frequency at every age and educational level. Comparing the Kinsey sample with his own at the fifteenth year of marriage, Hunt reports "a distinct increase in the number of wives who always or nearly always have orgasm. (Kinsey: 45 percent; *Playboy*: 53 percent) and a sharp decrease in the number of wives who seldom or never do (Kinsey: 28 percent; *Playboy*: 15 percent)."

6. For a rebuke of the self-styled male "experts" on women's sexuality that is both wonderfully angry and funny as it highlights the absurdity of their advice to women, see Frankfort (1973:172–180). She opens this section of her book, entitled "Carnal Ignorance," by saying:

For the longest time a woman wasn't supposed to enjoy sex. Then suddenly a woman was neurotic if she didn't achieve orgasm simultaneously with her husband. Proof of a woman's health was her ability to come at the very moment the man ejaculated, in the very place he ejaculated, and at the very rate ordained for him by his physiology. If she couldn't, she went to a male psychiatrist to find out why.

Bibliography

Barker-Benfield, Ben. "The Spermatic Economy: A Nineteenth-Century View of Sexuality." In *The American Family in Social-Historical Perspective*, edited by Michael Gordon. New York: St. Martin's Press, 1973.

Chodorow, Nancy. *The Reproduction of Mothering: Family Structure and Feminine Personality*. Berkeley: University of California Press, 1977.

Frankfort, Ellen. *Vaginal Politics*. New York: Bantam Books, 1973.

Gagnon, John H., and William Simon. *Sexual Conduct: The Social Sources of Human Sexuality*. Chicago: Aldine Publishing, 1973.

Hunt, Morton. *Sexual Behavior in the 1970's*. Chicago: Playboy Press, 1974.

Komarovsky, Mirra. *Blue-Collar Marriage*. New York: Vintage Books, 1962.

Shostak, Arthur B. "Working Class Americans at Home: Changing Expectations of Manhood." Delivered at the Conference on Problems, Programs, and

Prospects of the American Working Class in the 1970's, Rutgers University, Rutgers, New Jersey, September, 1971.

Simon, William, and John H. Gagnon. "On Psychosexual Development." In *Handbook of Socialization Theory and Research*, edited by David A. Goslin. Chicago: Rand McNally, 1969.

21

Cultural and Historical Influences on Sexuality in Hispanic/Latin Women

Oliva M. Espín

. . . Despite shared features of history and culture, attitudes towards sex-roles are extremely diverse among Hispanic women. For instance, some Latin women are willing to endorse "modern" and "liberated" sex-roles concerning education and employment, while maintaining very "traditional," "conservative" positions concerning sexual behaviors or personal relationships. Others are traditional in all respects and still others reject all traditional beliefs concerning the roles of women. Consequently, it is very difficult to discuss the sexuality or sexual behavior of Latin women without the danger of making some sweeping generalizations. The experiential and emotional distance between an immigrant worker of peasant extraction who barely knows how to write her name in Spanish and a "Latin princess" who comes to the United States to study at a private educational institution with all expenses paid by her parents is enormous. If these two women met each other, they probably would not acknowledge any commonalities between them. And yet, as their therapist, I can recognize a common thread and a historical background to their lives, a thread shared with daughters of immigrants born and raised in the streets of New York and in the rural areas of the Southwest.

What are the commonalities among Hispanic women in the United States that manifest themselves in spite of the enormous differences among them? *Historical influences* have left their mark in cultural processes and in class and race differentiation. Other commonalities have to do with the experience of separation implied in *immigration*; with the cognitive and affective effects of sharing a common *language*; and with the experience of *oppression*.

The enormous differences between the Spanish and British conquest of Latin America and North America set these two cultures apart.[1] On the one hand, the British came with their families, escaping persecution; North America became a dumping ground for religious dissidents. The Puritans and many of those who followed turned away from England with no desire to return to the homeland, seeking a place where they could remain separated and independent from all those who were different or held different beliefs. The Spaniards, on the other hand, came to America as a male army for the specific purpose of conquering new land for their king. They landed anticipating territory full of gold, silver, and abundance where land was fertile all year long. These resources, plus the centralization of power already achieved by the native Indian empires, provided an environment profoundly different from that encountered by the Pilgrims.

Most "conquistadores" were men without fortune, nobility, or other resources. The majority of them did not come with their wives or with any female relatives; marrying women of Spanish descent was practically impossible. They initially intended to return to Spain full of honors and riches in order to marry Spanish women of a higher class. Difficult communications and the hardships of an enterprise that did not produce "gold at first sight" as they had expected delayed their return to Spain indefinitely. Many of them never returned and, instead, stayed in the Americas for the rest of their lives.

Thus, the conquerors' temporary sexual use of Indian women developed into more enduring relationships. They set up homes with the native women who were originally taken only as concubines. These relationships—some temporary, some stable—created the Mestizo population of Latin America. In spite of their known cruelties, many of the Spanish conquerors were willing to legally marry Indian or black women and to recognize, support, and pass their inheritance on to their children by those marriages. A similar behavior would have been unthinkable not only to the Puritans, but to most white gentlemen in the United States to this day. It is well known that even Thomas Jefferson had children by a black woman. However, those children were never called Jefferson and that slave woman was never freed by him.

While Calvinist theology, with its emphasis on predestination, encouraged the separation of the races in North America, the Spanish Catholic clergy battled in Europe and America for the human rights of the Amerindians, following Catholic theological tenets which give the right to salvation to anyone who is baptized and fulfills appropriate duties as a Christian. Once the Indians were declared to be human by the pope, they had the right to be Catholic and, thus, children of God.[2]

The Catholic church's proclamation of the importance of virginity for all women, regardless of their race or social status, became a challenge to a social system that otherwise could have been even more oppressive to non-white women. By emphasizing that all women, regardless of race and social class, hold the duty and the right to remain virgins until marriage, and that all men were responsible to women whose honor they had "stained," the church discouraged consensual union and illegitimacy.[3] However, by upholding the standard of virginity as the proof of a woman's honorability, the church, and later the culture in general, further lowered the status of women who cannot or will not maintain virginity. This also fostered the perspective that once an unmarried woman is not a virgin, she is automatically promiscuous. These standards fell in a disproportionately harsh way on native and Mestizo women, who were less likely to be virgins because of the social and economic conditions in which they lived.

Historical circumstances combined to shape gender and race relations in Latin America in a very distinctive way. This is not to say that racial inequality or prejudice does not exist in Latin America, but that it differs from the forms found in North America. There is a fluidity in racial relationships among Latins that is difficult to understand in the United States. In Latin America, social status is affected more profoundly by factors other than race. Social class and income prevail over color.[4] Different shades of color among members of the same family are not denied. The number of political figures and upper-class Latin Americans who are "non-white" by North American standards attests to the difference in perspective. On the other hand, European ancestry and "whiteness" are highly respected. "Color" makes doors harder to open. People of color are overrepresented in the lower socioeconomic classes, and many a descendant of an interracial marriage would carefully avoid such a marriage now. The non-white woman may still be seen as not deserving the same respect as the white woman. And, if a white man fathers her children, she may not find the same protection as her white counterpart. Moreover, precisely because many of the conquerors' wives were not white, the lower status of all women was further compounded by racial factors.

Trends created centuries ago in the relationships between men and women of different races, cultures and political status persist today in Hispanic cultures. Historical influences have been modified, amplified to give a certain character and tone to the lives of Hispanic women. In addition to their shared cultural, historical and religious heritage described above, Hispanic women living in the United States today share many characteristics as a function of immigration, language, and the shared experience of oppression.

Although some Hispanic women are not immigrants, many of them come from immigrant families. A discussion of the psychological implications of *immigration* is relevant even if not applicable to all Hispanic women. Immigration or any other form of separation from cultural roots involves a process of grieving. Women seem to be affected by this process in a manner that is different from that of men. Successful adaptation after immigration involves resolution of feelings of loss, the development of decision-making skills, ego strength and the ability to tolerate ambiguities, including sex-role ambiguities. Factors pertaining to the psychological make-up of the individual woman as well as specifics of the home culture and class interplay in unique ways with the characteristics of the host culture. Newly-encountered patterns of sex-roles combine with greater access to paid employment for women and may create an imbalance in the traditional power structure of the family.

One of the most prevalent myths encountered by immigrant Hispanic women is that all American women are very free with sex. For the parents and the young women alike, "to become Americanized" is equated with becoming sexually promiscuous. Thus, in some cases, sexuality may become the focus of the parents' fears and the girl's desires during the acculturation process.

Language is another important factor in the experience of Hispanic women. To discuss the affective and cognitive implications of bilingualism and language use will take us beyond the scope of this paper. However, it is important to keep in mind that even for those Hispanic women who are fluent in English, Spanish may remain as the language of emotions because it was usually the first language heard and learned and thus it is full of deep affective meaning.[5]

The preference of one language over another, or the shift from one language to another might be an indication of more subtle processes than even the choice of words.[6] For example, in a recent study of Cuban women in Miami,[7] fluency in English appears as the single most important determinant of attitudes towards the role of women in society. Shifts between languages and the preference for one language or the other may be a means to achieve either distancing or intimacy. When the topic at hand is sexuality, the second language might be an effective tool to express what one does not dare to verbalize in the first language. Conversely, certain emotions and experiences will never be addressed appropriately unless they are discussed in the first language.[8] The emotional significance of a specific word for a particular individual generally depends on the individual personal values and his [sic] developmental history."[9]

The emotional arousal evoked by saying taboo words decreases when they are pronounced in a foreign language.[10] Presumably, erotic language is experienced differently when uttered or heard in either English or Spanish.

The condition of *oppression* under which most Hispanics live in the United States creates certain psychological effects for both men and women, although Latin women, oppressed both as women and as Hispanics, suffer from physical and psychological consequences of oppression in a profound way. The conditions of oppression originating in the economic, political and social structures of the world become psychological as the effects of these external circumstances become internalized.[11] The external oppression of Hispanic women is expressed in political, educational, economic and social discrimination. Psychologically, the oppression of Hispanic women develops through internalized attitudes that designate women as inferior to men, including Hispanic men, while designating all Hispanics as inferior to the white mainstream of North American society. Oppressive beliefs that affect all women and all Hispanics influence the lives and the sexuality of Hispanic women.

There are specific forms in which the psychology of oppression affects women from all ethnic minority groups. One involves the importance placed on physical beauty for women, and, particularly, on standards of beauty inappropriate for non-white women. Women, regardless of ethnic group, are taught to derive their primary validation from their looks and physical attractiveness. The inability of most non-white women to achieve prescribed standards of beauty may be devastating for self-esteem.

Another psychological effect of oppression for Hispanic women is to further increase their subordination to men. As a reaction towards the oppression suffered by minority men in the larger society, minority women may subordinate their needs even further to those of men. Women and children may be suitable recipients for the displaced anger of an oppressed man. Violence takes many forms: incest, rape, wife-beating. Violence against women is produced and sustained by societal messages about women. The prevalent virgin/whore dichotomy in images of women fosters and condones the violence. It is not unusual to hear supposedly "enlightened" persons defending the violent behavior of men in oppressed groups on the grounds that their only outlet is to get drunk and beat their wives. Even if the displacement can be understood in the case of each individual, to accept and justify it is to condone injustice and another form of violence against women under the guise of understanding.

In addition, women from oppressed groups may be seen as an "easy prey" for white men or as "sexier" than their white counterparts. Their sexual behavior is supposed to be freer and less restrained when, in fact, the opposite might be true. On the other hand, a young woman's sexuality might be the only asset she has in her efforts to break away from oppressive conditions.

Contemporary Sexuality and the Hispanic Woman

If the role of women is currently beset with contradictions in the mainstream of American society,[12] this is probably still more true for women in Hispanic groups. The honor of Latin families is strongly tied to the sexual purity of women. And the concept of honor and dignity is one of the essential distinctive marks of Hispanic culture. For example, classical Hispanic literature gives us a clue to the importance attributed to honor and to female sexual purity in the culture. La Celestina, the protagonist of an early Spanish medieval novel, illustrates the value attached to virginity and its preservation. Celestina was an old woman who earned her living in two ways: by putting young men in touch with young maidens so they could have the sexual contact that parents would never allow, and by "sewing up" ex-virgins, so that they would be considered virgins at marriage. Celestina thus made her living out of making and unmaking virgins. The fact that she ends by being punished with death further emphasizes the gravity of what she does. In the words of a famous Spanish playwright of the seventeenth century, "al Rey la hacienda y la vida se han de dar, mas no el honor; porque el honor es patrimonio del alma y el alma solo es de Dios."[13] This quotation translates literally, "To the king you give money and life, but not your honor, because honor is part of the soul, and your soul belongs only to God."

Different penalties and sanctions for the violation of cultural norms related to female sexuality are very much associated with social class. The upper classes or those seeking an improved social status tend to be more rigid about sexuality. This of course is related to the transmission of property. In the upper classes, a man needs to know that his children are in fact his before they inherit his property. The only guarantee of his paternity is that his wife does not have sexual contact with any other man. Virginity is tremendously important in that context. However, even when property is not an issue, the only thing left to a family may be the honor of its women and as such it may be guarded jealously by both males and females. Although Hispanics in the twentieth century may not hold the same strict values—and many of them certainly cannot afford the luxury to do so—women's sexual behavior is still the expression of the family's honor. The tradition of maintaining virginity until marriage that had been emphasized among women continues to be a cultural imperative. The Virgin Mary—who was a virgin and a mother, but never a sexual being—is presented as an important role model for all Hispanic women, although Hispanic unwed mothers, who have clearly overstepped the boundaries of culturally-prescribed virginity for women, usually are accepted by their families. Married women or those living in common-law marriages are supposed to accept a double standard for sexual behavior, by which their husbands may have affairs with other women, while they themselves are expected to remain faithful to one man all of their lives. However, it is not uncommon for a Hispanic woman to have the power to decide whether or not a man is going to live with her, and she may also choose to put him out if he drinks too much or is not a good provider.[14]

In fact, Latin women experience a unique combination of power and powerlessness which is characteristic of the culture. The idea that personal problems are best discussed with women is very much part of the Hispanic culture. Women in Hispanic neighborhoods and families tend to rely on other women for their important personal and practical needs. There is a widespread belief among Latin women of all social classes that most men are undependable and are not to be trusted. At the same time, many of these women will put up with a man's abuses because having a man around is an important source of a woman's sense of self-worth. Middle-aged and elderly Hispanic women retain important roles in their families even after their sons and daughters are married. Grandmothers are ever present and highly vocal in family affairs. Older women have much more status and power than their white American counterparts, who at this age may be suffering from depression due to what has been called the "empty-nest syndrome." Many Hispanic women are providers of mental health services (which sometimes include advice about sexual problems) in an unofficial way as "curanderas," "espiritistas," or "santeras," for those people who believe in these alternative approaches to health care.[15] Some of these women play a powerful role in their communities, thanks to their reputation for being able to heal mind and body.

However, at the same time that Latin women have the opportunity to exercise their power in the areas mentioned above, they also receive constant cultural messages that they should be submissive and subservient to males in order to be seen as "good women." To suffer and be a martyr is also a characteristic of a "good woman." This emphasis on self-renunciation, combined with the importance given to sexual purity for women, has a direct bearing on the development of sexuality in Latin women. To enjoy sexual pleasure, even in marriage, may indicate lack of virtue. To shun sexual pleasure and to regard sexual behavior exclusively as an unwelcome obligation toward her husband and a necessary evil in order to have children may be seen as a manifestation of virtue. In fact, some women even express pride at their own lack of sexual pleasure or desire. Their negative attitudes toward sex are frequently reinforced by the inconsiderate behavior and demands of men.

Body image and related issues are deeply connected with sexuality for all women. Even when body-related problems may not have direct implications for sexuality, the body remains for women the main vehicle for expressing their needs. The high incidence of somatic complaints presented by low-income Hispanic women in psychotherapy might be a consequence of the emphasis on "martyrdom" and self-sacrifice, or it might be a somatic expression of needs and anxieties. More directly related to sexuality are issues of birth control, pregnancy, abortion, menopause, hysterectomy and other gynecological problems. Many of these have traditionally been discussed among women only. To be brought to the attention of a male doctor may be enormously embarrassing and distressing for some of these women. Younger Hispanic women may find themselves challenging traditional sexual mores while struggling with their own conflicts about beauty and their own embarrassment about visiting male doctors.

One of the most common and pervasive stereotypes held about Hispanics is the image of the "macho" man—an image which generally conjures up the rough, tough, swaggering men who are abusive and oppressive towards women, who in turn are seen as being exclusively submissive and long-suffering.[16]

Some authors[17] recognize that "machismo"—which is nothing but the Hispanic version of the myth of male superiority supported by most cultures—is still in existence in the Latin culture, especially among those individuals who subscribe more strongly to traditional Hispanic values. Following this tradition, Latin females are expected to be subordinated to males and to the family. Males are expected to show their manhood by behaving in a strong fashion, by demonstrating sexual prowess and by asserting their authority over women. In many cases, these traditional values may not be enacted behaviorally, but are still supported as valued assumptions concerning male and female "good" behavior. According to Aramoni,[18] himself a Mexican psychologist, "machismo" may be a reaction of Latin males to a series of social conditions, including the effort to exercise control over their ever-present, powerfully demanding, and suffering mothers and to identify with their absent fathers. Adult males continue to respect and revere their mothers, even when they may not show much respect for their

wives or other women. As adolescents they may have protected their
mothers from fathers' abuse or indifference. As adults they accord
their mothers a respect that no other woman deserves, thus following
their fathers' steps. The mother herself teaches her sons to be dominant and independent in relations with other women. Other psychological and social factors may be influential in the development of "machismo." It is important to remember that not all Latin males exhibit
the negative behaviors implied in the "macho" stereotype, and that
even when certain individuals do, these behaviors might be a reaction
to oppressive social conditions by which Hispanic men too are victimized.

Sexually, "machismo" is expressed through an emphasis on multiple, uncommitted sexual contacts which start in adolescence. In a
study of adolescent rituals in Latin America, Espín[19] found that many
males celebrated their adolescnce by visiting prostitutes. The money
to pay for this sexual initiation was usually provided by fathers, uncles
or older brothers. Adolescent females, on the other hand, were offered
coming-out parties, the rituals of which emphasize their virginal qualities. Somehow, a man is more "macho" if he manages to have sexual
relations with a virgin; thus, fathers and brothers watch over young
women for fear that other men may make them their sexual prey.
These same men, however, will not hesitate to take advantage of the
young women in other families. Women, in turn, are seen as capable of
surrendering to men's advances, without much awareness of their own
decisions on the matter. "Good women" should always say no to a sexual advance. Those who say yes are automatically assumed to be less
virtuous by everyone, including the same man with whom they consent
to have sex.

Needless to say, sexual understanding and communication between the sexes is practically rendered impossible by these attitudes
generated by "machismo." However, not all Hispanics subscribe to
this perspective and some reject it outright. In a review of the literature on studies of decision-making patterns in Mexican and Chicano
families the authors concluded that "Hispanic males may behave differently from non-Hispanic men in their family and marital lives, but
not in the inappropriate fashion suggested by the myth with its strong
connotations of social deviance."[20] This article reviews only research
on the decision-making process in married couples and, thus, other aspects of male-female relationships in the Hispanic culture are not discussed.

In the context of culturally appropriate sex-roles, mothers train
their daughters to remain virgins at all cost, to cater to men's sexual
needs and to play "little wives" to their fathers and brothers from a
very early age. If a mother is sick or working outside the home and

there are no adult females around, the oldest daughter, no matter how young, will be in charge of caring not only for the younger siblings, but also for the father, who would continue to expect his meals to be cooked and his clothes to be washed.

Training for appropriate heterosexuality, however, is not always assimilated by all Latin women. A seldom-mentioned fact is that, as in all cultures, there are lesbians among Hispanic women. Although emotional and physical closeness among women is encouraged by the culture, overt acknowledgment of lesbianism is even more restricted than in mainstream American society. In a study about lesbians in the Puerto Rican community, Hidalgo and Hidalgo-Christensen found that "rejection of homosexuals appears to be the dominant attitude in the Puerto Rican community."[21] Although this attitude may not seem different from that of the dominant culture, there are some important differences experienced by Latin lesbian women which are directly related to Hispanic cultural patterns. Frequent contact and a strong interdependence among family members, even in adulthood, are essential features of Hispanic family life. Leading a double life becomes more of a strain in this context. "Coming out" may jeopardize not only these strong family ties, but also the possibility of serving the Hispanic community in which the talents of all members are such an important asset. Because most lesbian women are single and self-supporting, and not encumbered by the demands of husbands and children, it can be assumed that the professional experience and educational level of Hispanic lesbians will tend to be relatively high. If this is true, professional experience and education will frequently place Hispanic lesbian women in positions of leadership or advocacy in their community. Their status and prestige, and, thus, the ability to serve their community, are threatened by the possibility of being "found out."

Most "politically aware" Latins show a remarkable lack of understanding of gay-related issues. In a recent meeting of Hispanic women in a major U.S. city, one participant expressed the opinion that "lesbianism is a sickness we get from American women and American culture." This is, obviously, another version of the myth about the free sexuality of American women so prevalent among Hispanics. But it is also an expression of the common belief that homosexuality is chosen behavior, acquired through the bad influence of others, like drug addiction. Socialist attitudes in this respect are extremely traditional, as the attitudes of the Cuban revolution towards homosexuality clearly manifest. Thus, Hispanics who consider themselves radical and committed to civil rights remain extremely traditional when it comes to gay rights. These attitudes clearly add further stress to the lives of Latin women who have a homosexual orientation and who are invested in enhancing the lives of members of their communities.

They experience oppression in three ways: as women, as Hispanics and as lesbians. This last form of oppression is in fact experienced most powerfully from inside their own culture. Most Latin women who are lesbians have to remain "closeted" among their families, their colleagues and society at large. To be "out of the closet" only in an Anglo context deprives them of essential supports from their communities and families, and, in turn, increases their invisibility in the Hispanic culture, where only the openly "butch" types are recognized as lesbians. . . .

Sexual issues tend to be at the core of much family conflict concerning women and adolescent girls in immigrant families. The adoption of new ways of life or sexual behaviors, although satisfactory in many respects, may be associated with intense guilt and feelings of betrayal. In addition, because of the myths associating free sexuality with "Americanization," there is actual danger that young women may become promiscuous or self-destructive through sex. They may attribute their discomfort with their own behavior to parental influence or lack of adequate acculturation, when, in fact, they may be carrying themselves to behaviors considered "extreme" by most American women.

Each culture allows women a different range of accepted sexual behavior. This range goes from what is fully approved and expected—the ideals and values of the culture—to what is accepted or tolerated, even if it is not in conformity with the ideal. Some cultures allow a very narrow range of sexual expression to women, while others tolerate greater degrees of variation. There is a different cost in each culture for women who overstep the boundaries of allowed or tolerable sexual behavior. Knowledge about values concerning female sexuality in a given culture is not sufficient in itself to understand individual women. Each woman, in fact, positions herself at some point along the range of behaviors allowed by the culture. Each woman's choice expresses something about who she is as an individual as well as what her cultural values are. Superficial knowledge of a culture may lead [one] to accept as a cultural norm what might only be [a woman's] expression of her individuality. Conversely, a behavior that conforms to strict cultural norms or violates them at a high personal cost can be interpreted . . . as a strictly individual choice with no cultural implications. . . .

There is danger of being male-centered in the name of cultural values. Precisely because sex roles and female sexuality tend to be the last bastion of traditional cultural values while all other norms may be changing under acculturative pressures, it is possible to support these values without considering their negative effects on women. . . .

Because there is pleasure and danger in sexuality,[22] there are problems and possibilities in every aspect of sexuality. Sexual behavior may become both liberating and enslaving. Sexual choices, although deeply personal, may also be of far-reaching political consequences.

For women undergoing a process of acculturation, as many Hispanic women are, choices about sexual behavior may become important expressions of a multitude of different experiences and values. . . . Rebellion against the culture of origin or loyalty to it can, in many instances, be expressed through sexual behavior. The relative degrees of guilt or joy that may be associated with choices about sexual behavior are frequently entangled with considerations which are not fully or exclusively personal, but, rather, determined by external factors and considerations, as this paper has demonstrated.

Notes

1. For further information about this period, see C. A. Beard and M. R. Beard, *The Beards' New Basic History of the United States*, New York, Doubleday, 1968; and W. H. Prescott, *History of the Conquest of Mexico* and *History of the Conquest of Peru*, New York, Modern Library, no date (originally published in 1843 and 1847).
2. D. V. Kurtz, "The Virgin of Guadalupe and the Politics of Becoming Human," *Journal of Anthropological Research*, vol. 38, no. 2, 1982, pp. 194–210.
3. V. Martinez-Alier, *Marriage, Class and Colour in Nineteenth Century Cuba*, London, Cambridge University Press, 1974.
4. Ibid.
5. O. M. Espín, "Issues of Psychotherapy with Fluently Bilingual Clients," unpublished paper presented at the Stone Center for Developmental Studies, Wellesley College, Wellesley, Mass, 1982.
6. L. R. Marcos and L. Urcuyo, "Dynamic Psychotherapy with the Bilingual Patient," *American Journal of Psychotherapy*, vol. 33, no. 3, 1979, pp. 331–38.
7. O. M. Espín and B. Warner, "Attitudes towards the Role of Women in Cuban Women Attending a Community College," *International Journal of Social Psychiatry*, vol. 28, no. 3, 1982, pp. 233–39.
8. Espín, "Issues of Psychotherapy with Fluently Bilingual Clients," op. cit.
9. F. González-Reigosa, "The Anxiety-Arousing Effect of Taboo Words in Bilinguals," in C. D. Spielberger and R. Diaź-Guerrero (eds), *Cross-Cultural Anxiety*, Washington, DC, Hemisphere, 1976, p. 325.
10. Ibid.

11. P. Freire, *Pedagogy of the Oppressed*, New York, Salisbury, 1970.

12. J. B. Miller, *Toward a New Psychology of Women*, Boston, Beacon, 1976.

13. Calderón de la Barca, *El Alcalde de Zalamea*.

14. S. Brown, "Love Unites Them and Hunger Separates Them: Poor Women in the Dominican Republic," in Rayna Reiter (ed.), *Toward an Anthropology of Women*, New York, Monthly Review Press, 1975, p. 322.

15. O. M. Espín, "Hispanic Female Healers in Urban Centers in the United States," unpublished manuscript, 1983.

16. V. Abad, J. Ramos, and E. Boyce, "A Model for Delivery of Mental Health Services to Spanish-Speaking Minorities," *American Journal of Orthopsychiatry*, vol. 44, no. 4, 1974, pp. 584–95.

17. E. S. Le Vine and A. M. Padilla, *Crossing Cultures in Therapy: Pluralistic Counseling for the Hispanic*, Monterey, California, Brooks/Cole, 1980.

18. A. Aramoni, "Machismo," *Psychology Today*, vol. 5, no. 8, 1982, pp. 69–72.

19. O. M. Espín, "The 'Quinceañeras': A Latin American Expression of Women's Roles," unpublished paper presented at the national meeting of the Latin American Studies Association, Atlanta, 1975.

20. R. E. Cromwell and R. A. Ruiz, "The Myth of 'Macho' Dominance in Decision Making within Mexican and Chicano Families," *Hispanic Journal of Behavioral Sciences*, vol. 1, no. 4, 1979, p. 371.

21. H. Hidalgo and E. Hidalgo-Christensen, "The Puerto Rican Cultural Response to Female Homosexuality," in E. Acosta-Belén (ed.), *The Puerto Rican Woman*, New York, Praeger, 1979, p. 118.

22. Carole S. Vance, Introduction, in *Pleasure and Danger: Exploring Female Sexuality*, Boston, Routledge and Kegan Paul, 1984.

22

Styling, Profiling, and Pretending

The Games Before the Fall

Gloria I. Joseph

Afro-American culture, with all its unique features of caring, sharing, kinship networks, upward mobility aspirations, and color castes, interacts with and reacts to a racially and economically oppressive environment. This "double consciousness" (Afro-American culture and Western society), these two warring souls in every Black female and male body, become further compounded and complex as women's consciousness comes to the fore. In any discussion about Blacks we must never lose sight of these actualities; however, they must not be allowed to become excuses for any and all apolitical, irresponsible behavior on the part of Black women or men. Nor must Black women and men unwittingly enter the game of blaming the victim. What is needed is an honest assessment of the reality of the conditions that surround and exist for and between Black females and males. Knowing and facing one's reality is a necessary first step in any struggle. "Our reality, like all other realities, has positive aspects and negative aspects, and

This article was taken from the book *Common Differences: Conflicts in Black and White Feminist Perspectives*, Doubleday, 1981, by Gloria I. Joseph and Jill Lewis. The article as it appears in this book represents a much abridged and slightly revised version by author Gloria Joseph.

285

strengths and weaknesses. . . . Man [sic] is part of reality. Reality exists independent of man's will . . . those who lead the struggle must never confuse what they have in their head with reality."[1]

In this section we are concerned with the realities of the sexual relationships between Black women and Black men, with an emphasis on Black women's sexual attitudes and behaviors. In so doing, we must keep in mind that there is no monolithic group of Black women or Black men. Their conditions and situations vary according to income levels, careers, regions, age, education, and life experiences. We are interested in the underlying commonalities that exist despite social forces and circumstantial differences which have had substantial effects on the lives of Black women (and men).

The Black woman's sexuality is nothing less than her entire socialization as a Black female. The sexual socialization of the Black female is largely determined by her early childhood and adolescent upbringing, the influences of family, school, and religion intertwined with the roles played by culture and society. Of course, her socioeconomic class, religion, geographical region, and sense of self-esteem influence the child-raising practices to which she is subjected, as well as the ways in which resisting or succumbing to the cultural and societal pressures are enacted. These considerations remind us once again that Black female sexuality cannot be viewed through "monolithic lenses."

The important roles of music and dance in Black culture have always been influential in the sexual socialization of young Black females. Music—spirituals, gospel, blues, and jazz—has traditionally figured prominently in the lives of Black folks. The blues dealt with the real stuff: There's no escaping from the hard, bitter, day-to-day struggles. Female blues singers were unique in recording Black women's history and struggles via song. The legendary Bessie Smith, the Empress of the Blues, made a historical contribution to the sexual lives of Black women. Michele Russell makes this point succinctly:

> Bessie Smith redefined our time. In a deliberate inversion of the Puritanism of the Protestant ethic, she articulated, as clearly as anyone before or since, how fundamental sexuality was to survival. Where work was often the death of us, sex brought us back to life. It was better than food, and sometimes a necessary substitute.
>
> For Bessie Smith, Black women in American culture were no longer to be regarded only as sexual objects. She made us sexual subjects, the first step in taking control. She transformed our collective shame at being rape victims, treated like dogs, or worse, the meat dogs eat, by emphasizing the value of our allure. In so doing, she humanized sexuality for Black women.[2]

This attitude of Blacks toward sex has been similarly described by Bessie Head, the South African author.

People's attitude to sex was broad and generous—it was recognized as a necessary part of human life, that it ought to be available whenever possible like food and water, or else one's life would be extinguished or one would get dreadfully ill. To prevent these catastrophes from happening, men and women generally had quite a lot of sex but on a respectable and human level, with financial considerations coming in as an afterthought.[3]

As for homosexuality, especially regarding lesbians, the messages that young females receive seldom include explicit factual information. The primary message is simply to "stay away from them." The vast majority of young Black females enter adulthood with a fixed, negative idea about homosexuality. That fixed idea does not give them latitude for expressing their sexuality along any other lines than heterosexual ones. The Black woman is socialized to believe that sexual involvement occurs with man, not woman. Consequently, females with feelings of attraction for the same sex are fearful or deny their feelings, are courageous and bold, or are creative and live differently. Like most oppressed groups, they develop their own subculture.

The concept of heterosexuality (forced as it is) is readily internalized given the Black female's socialization, including the messages she receives about men and sex: men are the barometer for good times and troubled times, the other half of a partnership, the ones women can't live with and can't live without. Black heterosexual males and females must become knowledgeable about the concept of lesbianism as a political measure, as a force against sexual oppression. Present-day political lesbians are redefining women's lives in light of a raised consciousness which enables women to see their roles as women under patriarchy as oppressive and to see a need for radical change. What the Black community and, in particular, Black males are reacting to are a combination of facts, myths, and old notions coupled with a resistance to change.

The following composite discussion represents a freewheeling conversation among a group of Black women reminiscing about their experiences as young girls growing up. It dramatizes salient dimensions of their sexual socialization. The conversation is based on numerous tape-recorded sessions involving groups of women, all of whom were close friends. The following five personalities were selected: Kay, age forty-one, college graduate, master's degree, divorced, no children, social worker; Terri, age thirty, attending college part-time, married, three children, temporarily unemployed; Sue, age thirty-two, secretary, separated, two children; Edith, age twenty-eight, college graduate, teacher, single parent, one child; and Rose, age thirty-one, high school graduate, divorced, one child living with grandmother in another state, salesperson in a department store.

KAY: Terri, you said that without a father you don't know how men are supposed to treat you?

TERRI: The strange thing about it is I had a stepfather, and yet I always say, "I never had a father." You know, my real father died when I was five and everybody who knew him said he was a real nice guy. I never knew my stepfather.

KAY: Didn't you learn from your mother how a woman is supposed to be treated?

TERRI: My stepfather's role in the home was support.

SUE: But did he ever mistreat your mother?

TERRI: He kicked her ass, but when I got over the initial shock, I began to see that she needed it. I mean she really deserved it.

KAY: Really? You think some people deserve to be treated that way?

TERRI: Some people like getting their ass kicked.

SUE: That's true!

TERRI: I could say, deserving . . . liked . . . No! She *must* have liked it. She let him keep on kicking her; she never left him so she must have liked it. He'd start beating her ass and the next thing I knew, they'd be coming out of the bedroom smiling—I couldn't figure it out. [*laughter*]

SUE: Ah ha. I like that!

TERRI: When I was older I asked her why. I said, "Mommy, why did you stay with him so long?" and she said, "He was a nice man." And I said, "Ma, he kicked you down the stairs, don't you remember, and all the neighbors knew." She said, "Well, you know I did some things that hurt. There were a lot of things." And I said, "Son of a gun. Here I am screaming, 'Don't hit my mother!' and you liking it all the time!" But it's true, if you're in a home and there is no male, how do you know how he's supposed to treat you, except for what you see on TV. And if the people next door got no father—and if they do, their fathers are kicking their asses—how do you know?

KAY: Because it's just a question of plain humanity as to how people are treated.

TERRI: Honey, if everybody on the block is doing it *that's* humanity! That's your source of reference.

ROSE: Different men treat women different ways. And all women are different.

KAY: But in some ways I think they're the same.

SUE: Okay. Then tell me what is it that all women have in common.

TERRI: Pussies. They have pussies. [*laughter*]

SUE: That's it?

ROSE: They have periods and can't jump rope!

SUE: Oh, did I ever tell you about when I got my first period? I was nine years old and my grandmother scared me. Told me from now on you can't jump rope and you can't play with boys!

EDITH: [*Screaming with memory*] That's it! That's it! You couldn't jump rope and be careful with the boys—even your own brother.

SUE: Not why. They didn't tell you why. I didn't know what the hell my mother and grandma were talking about.

ROSE: It was a trip!

EDITH: I don't know if women have anything in common except they can have babies—biological features. But women have similar experiences at one point or another. They're treated different. Like I feel a part of something here. But what is it? I don't know. I guess that's what you're asking.

ROSE: Hmm. I don't know. I never gave it any thought before. [*A lull as the women reflect on what has been said.*]

SUE: I think there is an emotional understanding that women can relate to. Like I can understand Terri's experiences even though I may not agree or haven't experienced it all myself. I don't think a man could relate to that.

KAY: Maybe it's because people react to us like we're second-class citizens. I think that women play roles, especially with men, and I think that the common knowledge that there is so much role-playing going on creates a bond. It's like a common knowledge that as second-class citizens, we're not going to be considered equals to men no matter what.

EDITH: I'm gonna tell you all what I think now. I feel in fact that women are superior.

ALL: That's right! Why? In what way? I think so too.

EDITH: You know why I feel women are superior? We're emotionally stronger whereas men may be physically stronger. I mean the shit that we go through being all we have to be. You can't just be successful and a woman, you have to break the shit that men put up there for you. To be a successful woman you have to have more than a successful career. For instance, I just can't be a teacher and a woman—being a good woman means I must adequately sustain my family, be spiritual mentor for my friends, be able to deal with a man, be able to deal with other men, hold a household together, and a million other things. I dare say a man, any man, would have broken beneath the strain—any man who would have gone through what I have gone through in my life, age eighteen to twenty-eight, would have copped out. He couldn't have taken the weight, the strain, and come out smiling. They would have been a junkie—a drunkard—couldn't have took the weight! Couldn't have come out smiling.

ROSE: I think you're right.

SUE: I think men recognize that women are emotionally stronger.

KAY: They fall on that physical thing. Their strongness. They don't ever attempt to fall on their emotional or mental strongness.

EDITH: I don't even think they do that. I never had a man come to me from that point of view—where he's telling me where his strength is coming from—his physical strength, like in his arms. But because he was a *man*. Somehow he never said, "I have a dick, so I'm stronger," but you know he feels it. That's where he's coming from. They sort of think that the dick makes them superior.

TERRI: I think we're superior by virtue of having compassion and empathy.

SUE: Most men *are* physically stronger than women.

TERRI: You could karate him to death. You may not be able to fight him, but you could kick his ass.

ROSE: My virginity was broken by the super when I was five years old. I never had a father and the super was nice to me. One time he said, "Come downstairs to the basement," and he ate me for three hours. It felt pretty good. Afterward he said, "You're a very nice girl. What would you like?" I said the most money I could think of—I said seventy-five cents. Something told me not to tell my mother.

KAY: Didn't you feel ashamed?

ROSE: He didn't hurt me and I just didn't tell anyone. [*Everyone expresses understanding.*]

There is no mistaking the fact that racist, sexist, and economic deprivations have seriously influenced the socialization of the five Black women. Also apparent is the absence of constructive, accurate sex education. They had to cope with sexist attitudes and behaviors, and sexual abuses coupled with the harsh realities of growing up Black and female. The five women, who are from lower- to middle-class families with high educational aspirations, are all familiar with certain experiences common to young girls growing up in a society where sex is the dominant commodity for monetary profit, personal gains and gratifications, and human exploitation.

Their conversation revealed a recognition of female strength and solidarity based on the knowledge of a common fate which stems from sexual oppression from society and from the Black male—the former on an institutionalized basis, the latter on a personal level. Their knowledge of Black male oppression of Black females was expressed, but did not seriously hinder their sexual intimacy with Black men. The reasons for this are manifold. The word *oppression* may be somewhat inappropriate, since its popular usage implies systematic overpowering or imposition by abuse of power and authority. In the case of Black men and women if male domination occurs in sexual relations, it is not automatically transferred to other areas of social living. In addition, there are numerous Black women who neither act nor feel oppressed or overpowered in their intimate sexual relations with men. What cannot be denied is the fact that, as was pointed out by one of the women in the group, Black men in general place their number one claim to manhood in the locale of the groin palace, the home of the dick.

The emergence of an attitude toward males that is more demanding of equality in sexual and social areas is addressed more specifically in the following discussion among four Black women: Dot, age twenty-five, college graduate, social worker for the welfare department, separated; Jean, age thirty-five, two years of college, clerical worker, married; Betty, age twenty-eight, high school graduate, beautician, serial monogamy, no marriage; Sadie, age forty, dietician in a public school, twice married, now single.

DOT: I have just entered a new phase in my attitude toward sex. I was socialized to look at sex as a romantic ideal. Now that's all different.

JEAN: How's that?

DOT: The way I see sex now is—it's politics, it's cash, it's economics! I'm at the point where I see it as an exchange, but not a romantic exchange.

JEAN: I'm afraid I'm beginning to hear you.

SADIE: You mean you're going to use sex specifically as a means to obtain other things?

DOT: Well yes, and it's not my idealistic view. I wasn't raised like that, but I've become that way.

JEAN: When did you get rid of your idealistic views?

DOT: After the last three relationships. From the sexual politics that males and females play. You know, I got taken off. Trying to be nice you know, romance and all that har–di–har–di–har.

JEAN: When you say "sexual politics," just what do you mean?

DOT: Sexual politics between a man and a woman. Games. Yeah, X and Y, me and him, racking up points or trying to rack up points against one another.

BETTY: And they did you in?

DOT: Did me in! But no more. It's an exchange from now on, but on my terms!

JEAN: And what are those?

DOT: I love to have the pleasure of sex, but he's got to give me something first. I have to put it on that level because when I was giving out of my heart, I didn't get nothing in return. I was giving but I didn't get.

BETTY: I hear you. I hear you. I'm with you, sister!

DOT: Sex is pleasurable. But dig it. Just being pleasurable ain't enough. Those days are over for me. 'Cause it can be pleasurable and I still ain't got no food in the 'fridge. That does not add up. Economics, you know.

JEAN: Well, tell me this now. If you go out with a guy and he really appeals to you, wouldn't you go to bed with him because he's him? No economics attached.

DOT: Well, I don't know.

BETTY: [*laughing*] You could be persuaded.

DOT: Yeah, well, I could be persuaded. But I find it very, very difficult to get down and stay on the sexual level alone.

SADIE: It really doesn't pay to be involved with men just to be involved. The way men are, I don't trust them no more. You know. [*Others express agreement*]

DOT: And they lie about *everything*. They can't be trusted.

JEAN: You all sure are putting down the Black men when you say those things. Let's be more positive. Men are important in our lives, right?

BETTY: Oh, that's obvious.

SADIE: It's not so obvious to me anymore.

DOT: There's a lot of things that I like about them and a lot of things that I don't like about them.

BETTY: You think you can change a man?

SADIE: No, but if we change, they'll *have* to change.

BETTY: I enjoy a man's company. It's fun. I like the physical difference. I like the mental and emotional difference.

SADIE: Too often all you get is mental and emotional *stress*!

JEAN: Yeah, but we women still put up with them.

SADIE: I'm at the point now where I don't accept the man's role as the way it's been defined. You know, I don't believe in double standards where they hogwashed me all my life. Forget the double standards. Do you hear what I'm saying?

DOT: My main concern is where his head is, how he acts, you know. What are his beliefs, what kind of culture does he come from? Is it on the map? [*laughter*]

SADIE: And where you're comin' from also determines the kind of sexual activities you get involved with.

DOT: Right. If you don't have communication, somebody who may seem very nice and do all these things that you want, when it comes time for the sexual they may be very cold, or they may be very macho. You know, they may be very quiet, and you like a screamer. Personally, I prefer a small dick. You have got more chance to get clitoral stimulation with a small penis. For my build anyway.

BETTY: That's something else. Being in bed and trying to explain, "Ah . . . sweetheart, you know, that wasn't getting it. [*laughter*] Like you're trying to ram my, you know, my gizzards through my elbow. Don't do it like that. Have a little tenderness." You know a lot of men have to learn that it's not so much the heavy jamming as the communication involved.

JEAN: Establishing that communication can be a trip. Sometimes it hardly seems worth the bother.

DOT: Well, they're going to bother you anyway. And you know, we can't leave them alone. They couldn't survive and where would we be?

SADIE: In my last relationship I was making an effort to do right. I suggested that we compromise on certain things. Not always do things his way. He got an attitude. I said, "Let's deal with things like two adults. I'll lotion you down one night, you lotion me down the next night. Why I always got to be lotioning you down? Goddamnit, you know, I work too. When I want to get lotioned down, I got to go to a masseuse. I got to lotion you down, take a course on how to do it, to please you." Well, the upshot of it all was he split.

JEAN: But you know, women carry the heaviest burdens, and for years we have been putting up with an unequal exchange. And we continue to put up with them in the same old ways.

BETTY: I don't look at it so much as a burden. 'Cause I ain't going to let nothing be no burden. If you have to be a burden, go on your way! But we have to work it out together because we're in a tough situation together. It's a tough struggle for all Black people.

DOT: If it was all women, you'd have to put up with the same thing.

JEAN: No, you can't say that. It wouldn't be the same with women. There would be more sharing of loads. What do you get in exchange for the heavy load you're carrying?

DOT: I see it more as a mission than a burden.

BETTY: It's a mission and a challenge just like everything else. Black men represent our mission and our challenge. Because I think if Black men and Black women—and this is my one political reality of the day—if we don't somehow soon get together it will be catastrophic. One of the personal satisfactions in dealing with Black men is reinforcement as a person. Now I can say that I get my reinforcement as a woman by sticking by Black men.

DOT: Yeah. I used to feel strong about the continuation of our nationalism. About his Blackness.

JEAN: What do you mean *his* Blackness?

DOT: I mean the fact that Black men have been fucked over and are fucked up and we can't desert them. I wouldn't go out with a White man. I'm just going to make the Black man pay a price. No one gets a free lunch anymore.

JEAN: *You* may not go out with a White man, but they damn sure go out with White women.

BETTY: That's why I like the fact that we are maintaining the Black family. I feel very strongly about that. I'm doing my little piece by sticking with Black men.

SADIE: Maintaining the Black family?

BETTY: Black male and female relationships—yes, yes, the Black family. That's the mission. Besides you get personal gratification, you know—the fact that I made the effort within the Black family structure. You know what I'm saying? 'Cause I wouldn't want to go through that mission with another woman.

JEAN: But you already do. Mothers, sisters, aunts.

BETTY: I mean just pertaining to Black male and female relationships. Hey! My mother and father, case in point. They've been together for thirty-two years. Mom carried the heavier burden, but my father hung in there. They maintained their relationship with all their burdens.

JEAN: Okay, okay. I hear all these reasons for maintaining relationships with our Black men—on a really personal and intimate level, what do you receive from the relationship?

DOT: We receive nothing! [*laughter*] We receive nothing!

SADIE: I must say that I did get certain satisfactions from both of my marriages, but sexual intimacy wasn't the main source of my satisfaction.

BETTY: Let me say this. I like to fuck as much as anybody, and as long as Black men are around there will be fucking. They'll fuck anything! Women, other men, animals.

SADIE: I'm beginning to wonder what it really was that gave me satisfaction, pleasure, in my relationships. What was it really?

BETTY: Listen, you all. I *got* to say this—the dick is good! [*laughter*] The dick is good. And for me, I'm just the sweetest thing he done had. Shit! So I just collect a little rent and get me some threads now and then, you know, it's like that.

DOT: It *does* make you feel good.

BETTY: Oh, when you be coming ain't nothing like coming! It's the best.

DOT: I think sexual intercourse is the best relaxer around other than the sauna. 'Cause if I can't get no sex, ain't nobody giving up no money. I go to the sauna and exercise and come home and masturbate and feel real good.

JEAN: But you'd rather have the man!

DOT: If there's a choice, yes. But sometimes you don't even want the damn choice for the hassle. It ain't worth the hassle. And it's not like you can say after you've had intercourse, "Okay, get up and go home. I came already, did you come? Now you can get up and go home. I've got some work to do." You can't do that.

SADIE: My final comment is, Black women have to consider some serious changes in our relationships with black men, because we've had enough! And we know they can do better! Amen. [*group laughter and approval*]

These comments reflect Black women's experienced view of the effects of institutionalized heterosexuality on their relationships with men and an absence of a homosexual consciousness. Their remarks represent a focus on both the precarious sexual relationship between Black men and women, and the strong counterforce of uninhibited and unrestricted joy to be found in sex. The women are direct and explicit in expressing their feelings. At times they seem to vacillate; such is the actual case. There are serious problematic aspects in their relationships with men and, in trying to think through their problems and develop new strategies, there are uncertainties in their decisions, wavering and compromising behavior. The reality of Black females linking their existence to males as part of their socialization process was unmistakably reflected in their conversation. Equally represented was a showing of their independent spirit. What was also obvious was the infiltration of consumerism, with sex as the commodity.

The conversation also revealed an openness and willingness to talk about their dissatisfactions and desires regarding sexual relations. Heretofore many Black women were fearful of losing their man if they did not please him sexually, so they did not disclose dissatisfaction. Black women understand that the Black male has had severe restrictions placed on his opportunities for economic advancement. They have therefore provided ego gratification to him in the area of sexual relations. In attempting not to further damage the male ego, women have sacrificed their feelings. In the long run, this has created more problems for both partners.

In their conversation, these Black women are not only questioning their insights into their own sexuality, they are simultaneously trying to analyze and assess the realities of the conditions that have contributed to the present state of affairs between Black women and Black men.

Females have to learn at an early age (around twelve) to cope with young males who emulate older Black males in their attempts at sexual conquests. Thus, the styling, profiling, and pretending begins early on. One of the women put it this way:

> Sisters have been socialized to believe that involvement with males is a real true relationship—a sincere commitment. The brothers, on the other hand, believe that the "rap" is most important in order to get over.

"Getting over" means, initially, flattery, then the sexual conquest. Sexual politics is reduced to a game. It is a "false" relationship in the sense that the play is to *get over*, not to establish a true relationship. The games allow the woman to feel that she is not totally disrespected. She can point out to others and to herself, "See, he brings me flowers, records, and pizza"—that's the flattery. Later in the game there are groceries. If a male starts talking sex right away, with no rapping or presents, it's not considered respectable. So in most cases, games are played to keep the image of respectability (a necessity for the women) and games are played to keep women on the string (a necessity for the men). It may take three weeks, more or less, for the fuck (conquest) to be achieved—then, too often, it's good-bye. Should the games end and the woman simply say, "I'm in this for a good screw just like you, so let's stop with the games," there would be a new situation. But both the male and female roles are so ingrained that it is very, very difficult for both parties to change. (Sadie's statement during the conversation, "If we change, they'll have to change," is instructive here.)

Black women are faced with a reality today that demands changes ranging from a slight shift in posture to a complete about-face as they come to grips with their sexuality and relationships with Black men. The women's movement has provided a renewed interest and impetus for Black women to formally organize around issues of feminism and sexual equality and to informally voice their opinions and attitudes about Black female and male relationships with far less reluctance than in the past. A major reality that Black women face is the shortage of Black males. "Black women twenty-five years old and over are more than twice as likely as white women to remain never married. The situation grows far more grave among the college-educated where—within the urban population nineteen to forty-four years old—for every one hundred males there are fifty-four extra females without a mate or forced to share somebody else's.[4] Incarceration, drugs, war casualties, interracial marriages, and homosexuality increase the scarcity of available males. The problems this scarcity creates, the attitudes and opinions on sex and marriage, and the uncertainties and possible solutions are put forth in two witty, serious, insightful, and candid discussions among four Black women.

A Group Discussion: Challenges to Traditional Patriarchal Paradigms

Round I

Gathered in the home of Sandy in 1980, four women were talking about men in their lives. Ellen, age mid-thirties, two children, ages five and seven, living with husband; Sandy, age mid-forties, divorced, no children; Althea, age twenty-eight, never married, one child, age five; Margie, age thirty-one, two children, ages seven and nine, living with husband.

ELLEN: If I hit the lottery I would have another child. [*Group reacts as though statement was just casual comment, without serious intent, about winning a lottery.*]

SANDY [*responding lightly*]: Hit the lottery, have a child? What's the lottery got to do with your having a child? The lottery doesn't make babies.

ELLEN: I mean *my* child this time, not *our* child.

SANDY: You mean you'd pick out a father? Not your own husband?

ELLEN: That's right!

MARGIE: Hold on a minute. You're saying that you would pick out some dude that would suit your fancy and have this child? What kind of man would you pick? What would he look like? Muhammad Ali or a young Harry Belafonte?

ELLEN: Characteristics. Characteristics are most important. In general, good physical characteristics, teeth, eyes, etc., and intelligent. I wouldn't have to live with him.

ALTHEA: Ellen, you been holdin' out on us? Is there a new man on the scene? If so, let me know, 'cause I ain't seen nothin' worth dressing or undressing for in months. And you know, all they're saying about the new Black woman and her new consciousness, and sisters supporting and sharing with one another.

MARGIE: What "they"? Who's saying all that?

ALTHEA: Oh, you know all that shit Sandy's always talking about. Black women writing about the *new* Black women, *contemporary* Black women, *together* Black women. Feminism. We're all of that. Didn't you know? [*laughter*]

MARGIE: Yeah, I'll bet whoever or whatever Black women are writing that stuff sure ain't sharing their man.

ALTHEA: That's if they got a man. Got to have before you can share.

MARGIE: I hear a lot of feminists are lesbians. Into women.

ALTHEA: Feminism and lesbianism are not synonomous.

SANDY: You two cool out. I want to hear Ellen. I want to hear more about this "lottery child."

ELLEN: No, seriously, I believe a woman should have as many children as *she* can afford, not as many as *we* can afford. My husband is away now, taking a course for five months, and I am glad to be free. Glad that he is away. Now you know that is sad that you have to be glad that your husband is away so you can feel free and good. I think the reason that marriages are so unsatisfactory is because in our society boys are raised one way and girls another, and then they put them together at a certain age and they are supposed to get along with one another, understand one another. Boys are raised to be strong, tough, not compassionate, earn money; girls are taught to be compassionate, gentle, understanding, have feelings, empathy; and then they get married and they don't receive what they have been experiencing.

ALTHEA: But you can't have women marrying one another.

SANDY: I read that in some places in Africa they have women marrying women and the one with the power picks out a man to father their children.

SANDY: There is an increase in lesbianism, and among Blacks, too, and they're having babies too.

ELLEN: I'm not quite ready to go that way, but I can understand why a woman will live with another woman. If you are sick a woman will fix you a cup of tea and not tell you to "get up and fix yourself a cup of tea." I don't think men know anything about empathy when it comes to women. Like when I was married and we were both working, both of us would be home for lunch, and I'd be rushing around the kitchen and fixing his lunch and mine, and he'd be there sitting watching me and talking. I became pregnant soon and worked until eight months, and there I was still fixing his lunch. So I said, "Look, in five years I want to look like your wife, not your mother," so I quit working. You see, too many women are tied down to their husbands, to marriage, due to economic reasons. If I had to do it over I wouldn't. I would, say at age eighteen, select the type of job I wanted and pursue that, and once economically prepared, I would have as many children as I could afford. A woman should be allowed to have as many children as she can afford.

ALTHEA: Well, in my case, I'd still be waiting because I certainly couldn't *afford* to have any children. But once they're here, somehow you manage. And I don't get any child support from his father.

MARGIE: What you get is a lot of help from other women. Mothers, neighbors, sisters, babysitters, friends. Look at all the children Ma Gregory [*a neighborhood woman who has taken care of babies and children for generations*] took care of.

ELLEN: Now my husband is trying to be more considerate—the perfect father and husband—but I couldn't care less. I've grown indifferent.

Round II

The group has reconvened at Sandy's with wine and refreshments.

SANDY: I'm prepared for you all this time. But don't go drinking so much that you start talking a lot of foolishness, 'cause I've been thinking a lot about our last conversation and want to hear some sober thoughts.

MARGIE: [*in mocking tones*] The Black women's consciousness-raising session is now in s-e-s-s-i-o-n. [*turning to Sandy*] That's what this is, isn't it?

ALTHEA: We're just telling it like it is.

ELLEN: I was thinking the other day that my problem is deliberately wanting to live free of the bonds and binds of marriage and men, but most women have the problem of getting a man. That Black male shortage is for real!

ALTHEA: I propose that the Black female move in on the White woman's territory like she has moved in on ours.

SANDY: You advocating Black women going with White men! Miss Black Nationalist of the sixties, am I hearing correctly?!

MARGIE: White boys! You talking about going with gray boys. Out! Scratch that!

ELLEN: It is an alternative.

SANDY: Not really. If the Black men aren't there, it's taking leftovers.

ALTHEA: Listen. Things are changing. I know for sure that more and more Black women are going out with White men. They wine you and dine you in style! Some "leftovers" can be pretty good!

SANDY: Celibacy is a choice that many women follow.

ALTHEA: A choice for who? Girl, you're a trip. What kind of women follow celibacy other than nuns and even they are getting out of those habits and all. And you even got gay nuns.

ALTHEA: [*in disgusted tone*] Do y'all hear our choices? Do you hear them? Celibacy, gray boys, or White women!

ELLEN: White women?

ALTHEA: Yeah, ain't no Black women going with another woman.

SANDY: Althea, don't be ridiculous. Black lesbians exist. They're all over, everywhere.

MARGIE: Well, a choice between White men or White women is no choice at all! I'd rather share a real man with five other women than have any cracker, lowlife White boy.

ELLEN: That polygamy thing doesn't work either. I know several Black women who were into that and at first it seemed fine, but after a while, they found out that the males were still the king of the roost but this time with *several* hens under their direct command.

ALTHEA: Okay, let's add polygamy, and as far as I'm concerned, scratch that too. Let's see, now, we have celibacy, polygamy, White men, and other women.

SANDY: Now I think we should make a distinction between "other women" and lesbianism. Friendship with other women is a must, a desirable must. We offer each other support, "an ear to listen and a shoulder to cry on." And lesbianism has proven to be very satisfactory for many Black women.

MARGIE: Yeah, but on the other hand we have a lot of women fighting one another, usually over men, talking behind one another's back—catty, real bitchy. And trying to outdo one another in clothes, cooking and lies about how well their husband's treatin' them, and half of the time the ones who talk the loudest are the ones whose men beat the shit out of them.

ELLEN: How did we get that way? How come women are such contradictions? How come? Men aren't that bitchy.

MARGIE: No, because they're the reason we're bitchy. They feel all supreme because some women are fighting over them.

ELLEN: The women ought to get together and have a rebellion. Not so much because we're oppressed but because we're not being treated right. You know, those White women keep talking about being oppressed about this and oppressed about that, and how men oppress them sexually. Well, I don't feel oppressed at all when it comes to sexually dealing with men. Lots of times I could teach them a thing or two. But there is something wrong in relationships when both people can't be honest. But if you're honest you'll lose your man 'cause there'll always be several women waiting in the wings to please him no matter how much of her act is pure "D" lies.

ALTHEA: Preach, sister, preach. Get in the pulpit Sunday morning and tell it all!

SANDY: I read an article that mentioned a growing number of older women going with younger men, and the women had some positive things to say about it.

ALTHEA: Well, that won't help the numbers game, but it will provide male company. The younger men have less hang-ups, are into newer ideas. Health foods, yoga. In a way they're more interesting, less demanding.

SANDY: We have to learn, to *realize*, that singlehood is and can be a totally self-rewarding decision. We've been trained and taught to nurture, care for, everyone but ourselves. It's time for some reciprocity. And if that's not in the cards, then we must "do for self," as my mother always told me. And it's not about us ruling out men. The terms that they want to enter our lives are just not acceptable. Not in our best interests.

ALTHEA: I think we're going around in circles. Simply put, and this is my way of thinking, there aren't enough Black males and even those who are eligible need some training about dealing with women. My choices include men of other color. There are Hispanic men and even some Asians might do—especially the tall, karate types. Younger men can add a little diversion now and again. Women, well, as close as I am to some women I think that's enough. The relationship is fine without the sex, but if it should happen, that's cool. Who knows. Several years ago I wouldn't think of touching a White man, much less sleeping with one. Let the Africans keep their polygamy, and you know, even women with men need to learn to appreciate and deal with being alone, constructively. Like singlehood within marriages.

MARGIE: I feel a new challenge for Black women. I'll be able to tell my grandchildren about how the eighties was when we Black women shifted gears into different life options.

In the eighties the challenge to the Black woman is to define herself in terms of her needs, her desires, and her psychological and emotional makeup. This does not mean to negate or neglect Black men. Whether a woman defines herself as a traditional wife in a monogamous marriage, a lesbian, a celibate, a polygamous wife, or a single woman, those decisions in and of themselves tell us very little about her political aspirations or political commitments or ideology. They simply tell us who she may or may not be sleeping with. So it is incumbent upon Black women to start defining themselves in terms of a politic that is not predicated upon a sexual preference.

A woman's sexuality and sexual preference should be a complement to her well-being, not the locus of her well-being. Women always have gained strength and support from other women; this practice should be embellished and drawn upon to help women further their self-development. Women's support groups, organized and run in constructive ways, can provide an excellent source of new ideas while helping to break down old barriers and reestablish warm, rewarding female friendships.

The eighties offer the Black woman the challenge of taking a giant step into a region called "her own rights" without divorcing herself from Black culture, which embodies care, concern, and nurturance for the Black community. She must do so without negating her own sexuality, which in many instances she must redefine for herself. She must come into her own being, in relationships with and to men, but relationships that do not disallow her personal freedom, happiness, and the opportunity to pursue her aspirations.

Notes

1. Amilcar Cabral, "Guardian Voices of Revolution," *The Guardian*, January 1980, p. 17.
2. Michele Russell, "Slave Codes & Linear Notes," *The Radical Teacher*, March 1977, p. 2.
3. Bessie Head, *The Collector of Treasures* (London: Heinemann, 1977), p. 39.
4. "Where Have All the Black Males Gone?" *Black Male/Female Relationships*, Vol. 1, June–July 1979. San Francisco: Black Think Tank, Inc., p. 5.

23

The Sympathy of the Blood

Amber Hollibaugh

The bus was hot going over the Grapevine toward Bakersfield. The smell of Southern California growing valleys, of the dry land between rows of crops, and the low glaze of heat holding in the fever of the earth were drifting toward me. Images of the slightly leaning houses listing from the dust storms, the rains and the lack of money to keep them perfectly upright, and of the people who were bent over the lettuces or strawberries, reaching up for the beer hops or oranges, were rolling past my eyes like I'd never been away, like I'd never made an escape.

My mother's side of the family came to the United States after the potato famines in Ireland. Later, my grandmother was forced to uproot again, this time from the devastation of the Midwest's dust bowls. She ended up in this semi-desert town with her children and her willpower, raising her daughters alone, first as a servant and cleaning woman and then as a washwoman to the emerging upper class that was making it on the oil that had been discovered here.

Oildale, just outside Bakersfield, is a town of car mechanics, oil workers, and migrant laborers. It is made up of poor white trash like my family, or Mexicans who have settled here, many marrying Anglos.

This is Steinbeck's Hoboville, the town I was born in. I am Edna Mc-Cune's lesbian granddaughter, and I was finally going back.

I hadn't been to Oildale in 20 years, not since I had first made a break for it, running from the heat and the dead ends that seemed inevitable if I stayed there. Through 20 years I have dreamed this land, smelled it, hated it, wanted it, and been afraid to return. The running from it caused a hollowness which stretched across most of my adult life, invaded and seduced my dreams, weighed on my mind and been a part of all I feared as a radical and as a dyke.

I needed to see my grandmother before she died. She was on the critical list and I had been her favorite granddaughter. Though I had half-brothers, first, second, and third cousins, aunts and uncles, I was the only girl to survive childhood.

I broke with this side of the family when my grandmother, watching the evening news, saw me in an early anti–Vietnam war demonstration. Later that same night she received news that my cousin (I was raised with him) had been shot in Vietnam. I never went back after that. But the rift could be traced much further back to a struggle between me and my family over class and hope and the women I desired.

I am not the middle-class woman generally described in the literature used to teach women's studies classes, not like many of the new generation of lesbian-feminists. The history of my brand of lesbianism is the story of women who ran from towns like the one I fled, who joined the army, navy, or air force or who were busted when discovered with another girl and thrown into juvie hall. Or it is a quieter story of women who form a culture different from the feminist one—a life led in gay bars on Friday and Saturday nights, if you have a lover; every night, if you don't. It is about drinking too much and playing pool with style. It is an underground that runs through the phone company, the Teamsters Union, the Bank of America, and the grocery counters of this country. It is made up of women you never notice, women who pass as men and women who are femmes to butches whose bar names are Jesse and Sandy and Paul. I have lived a double life, seducing butches from the bars while working long hours writing, speaking, organizing in the feminist community. Most of the material that I write I have created so that I would see my own life on a piece of paper, see the lines in the faces of the women I grew up with and the women I have loved.

Although I had told my mother and father early on that I was a lesbian, my homosexuality and radical politics were hidden from the rest of the family. "It would hurt them," we said, masking our pain and confusion at what I was: lesbian—Marxist—organizer—feminist. My mother would return periodically to Oildale with vague stories about the city I lived in and how happy I was, but her stories were empty of any details except my general health or weight. After a few years, the family stopped pressuring her about when I was coming to annual family get-togethers, stopped asking for a phone number and address my mother could never produce.

This was the distance I had to travel to protect myself from discovery, a bitter irony of safety and sadness: I had been forced to create this wall between us in order to pursue my life and, in doing this, I had become other, unknown to them, different from anything they had thought my life would be. Yet, they continued to be the people who lived in my mind, their voices were the ones I tried to answer and to write about through all the years of separation. Their fear of my queerness came as much from my moving outside the expectations of our family as it did from sex. They generate their dignity, their lives, through the power of the family and a sympathy of the blood. It was their sense of my betrayal I most wanted to speak to.

The trailer park was very bare. It was a new one and the concrete slabs which people put their trailers on had no shrubs or trees to soften the hot, cement-grayed earth. Oildale is not very green; it takes too much water to keep lawns lush and flowers healthy.

From the moment I arrived, between visits in the morning and afternoon to the hospital, I worked with the women in my family, piling bologna and lunch meat onto trays and setting it next to loaves of bread, making potato salad, iced tea, and Kool-Aid for the kids while the men were building a wheelchair ramp at the side of the trailer. I washed grandma's glass figurines and folded her "company only" tablecloths. I went with everyone to my niece's eighth-grade graduation; I had my picture taken with the rest of the family outside the Sizzler. No one spoke of their despair at grandma's worsening condition; no one spoke of my return. We worked with the radio blaring and the kids ducking in and out of the trailer. Like always, if it wasn't said out loud, it wasn't there.

Sunday was my last day there, time to break the silence our work could not obliterate. We told stories of our childhoods together: of Jeff cutting up bumble bees on his plate during camping trips (all names have been changed); of how we had locked all the grown-ups outside one night until my father finally broke the door in, caught us, and whipped us all; of who swam further, who got caught most often, who got blamed. We remembered secrets we had sworn never to tell and instead had just forgotten as we got older.

We began to speak of getting older. All my cousins are cops or ministers or prison guards, all came back from Nam, married, and had kids. They pulled out old pictures, early baby shots, the guys around Hank's pickup truck at the rifle range, the kids at their baptisms. Wayne had finally joined AA after 20 years of being drunk—a habit he'd acquired trying to kick the drugs he'd gotten hooked on in the Me-kong delta. Artie had come back from the war and worked at the B. F. Goodrich plant, gotten sick of it, and become a county sheriff. Jeff had come back angry, tried being a cop, then settled in as a Seventh Day Adventist minister. Wayne came back in bad shape. He had trouble keeping a job and ended up a guard at the county prison.

We each dated our lives around Vietnam, they telling war stories, me trying to talk about why I'd joined the antiwar movement. Until two of the boys ripped off their shirts to expose jagged, deep pink scars and even the shrapnel still in their bodies. They asked me, yelled at me, "What do you think of these—do you think we're killers? Do you only cry for Commies when they die?" I yelled back. "Fuck you, that's what I was trying to stop. Do you think it's an accident you were drafted instead of some middle-class college kid? You had no business being there, it wasn't your fight."

I brought out the picture of my woman lover. I had told them all I was a lesbian before making this trip. Now they all stared, embarrassed, at her picture. Aunt Bev: "very handsome." Aunt Vera thought she looked "stern." None of the boys called her butch, which she is, they just thought it. "Do you think its hormonal? Were you 'one' when we were kids? Couldn't you find a guy to marry? Were you ever arrested? Does she wear men's clothes? Don't you feel you owe something to the family?"

"What did you think we were doing all those years you were gone? Did you think it was okay to just disappear and never let us know a goddamn thing? Didn't you think we would worry? What do you think we told grandmother? We thought you had joined Weathermen or something after a while, and we never heard. Did you think it was just all right to disappear from everybody? Or did you think we were too stupid to be bothered with?"

"If I had come back with my antiwar buttons on, would you have let me in the door? If I'd stood in front of the Bakersfield City Jail protesting racism, would you have busted everyone but me? If I'd ridden up on the back of my dyke lover's motorcycle, would you have asked us to stay overnight? If I had come home that way, would you have been asking when I was coming to the next big family picnic?"

We could not have talked before. We had been too arrogant, too sure we were right. But since then, we had all been pulled apart by inappropriate desires, defeat, illegal abortions, and bullets still lodged in the hip—the unexpected circumstances and forces we could not control. Finally, we could accord each other our differences.

In the last visit before I left, my grandmother didn't remember the television newscast of so long ago. She held my hand and told me stories about what kind of kid I'd been, how I'd caused her a sleepless night or two. She told me about how hard it was for her getting old.

PART IV

RELIGION

Imagine a room filled with US women. Among others, there is a high Episcopalian, a Seventh Day Adventist, a self-proclaimed witch, a member of the Armenian Orthodox church, someone who is of the African Methodist Episcopal church, an Orthodox Jew, a Hopi woman of medicine, a member of the Nation of Islam, an atheist, a Jehovah's Witness, a Buddhist, a Rastafarian, a born-again Christian, a Pentacostalist, someone of the Hari Krishna group, and on and on. This list conjures up a sweeping sense of diversity without even adding elements such as class, race, ethnicity, age, and regionality.

Certainly there would be points of shared experience among such a group of women. Yet at the base of the stark differences suggested by the labels used to describe them is the reality of religion, though we are also talking about more than religion. At issue here are ways of viewing the world, ways which are indeed connected to class, race, age, and so forth. Also at issue are efforts to explain the world, efforts which are diverse, in large measure because the "world" (that is, the totality of one's experiences) that must be explained is not the same for each of these women. Captured in these labels of religious affiliation are women's attempts to control, or at least subdue, forces in their worlds—and those forces vary.

Women, along with men and children, use magic, science, and/or religion to view, explain, and try to control their world. In doing so, there can be such variety as using historical materialism or the story of creation in Genesis to explain origins and current realities. The differences in addressing one's economic position by participating in a women's caucus of a trade union, praying to Jesus to make things better, or using a dream book to find a "magical number" that will change one's fortune can be dramatic. And of course, there are individuals who see no contradiction in seeking to change their condition by engaging in each of these activities.

This sense of the expansiveness of what is involved in "religion" is addressed in the writings and the practice of women of such diverse formations as liberation theology, feminist spirituality, and born-again Christianity. The common message in these markedly different "religions" is that women's lives cannot be divided up and placed in little boxes marked worship on the Sabbath, work on Monday, and vote on Tuesday. But the extraordinary differences and, indeed, conflicts among women of such affiliations rest in large measure in the stark ways in which their "theologies" diverge. These theologies not only explain how the world came to be, what happens to people when they die, why the rich are rich and the poor are poor, but how and why the status of women is as it is within both organized religion itself and the totality of the society at large.

For some women, women's secondary place in religion and society is all right because it is believed to be God's will. For other women, the status of women is assumed to be a reflection of *men's* misinterpretation of the will of God and is far from all right. And for still others, women's secondary status is explained not by scriptures or spiritual notions, but by the material conditions of society at a particular point in time, requiring a change of those material conditions in order to effect a complete change in that status.

As noted in the introductory essay to this book, in every one of the so-called world religions, women are rarely, if ever, the leaders, and their role in life is defined as secondary.

> The church remains as a male-dominated leadership serving a predominantly female participation. One must look at the congregation present every Sunday in our Churches. The majority are women . . . Sunday after Sunday a male-oriented version of faith is given and the role of the woman is affirmed as a passive receiver. (Dominga 1980: 173)

In the Islamic religion, unlike a number of other organized religions, there is no formal clergy and no religious hierarchy. There are, however, definitive ways in which the subservence of women is underlined, at the very same time that there are verbal praises of the importance and beauty of women. When Moslems in the United States, as all over the world, face Mecca for prayers, men stand in rows behind the prayer leader and women stand behind the men.

Statements about the secondary role of women in religion and society, however, should be placed within a time frame, for the experiences of some women were quite different at other periods of history. Judith Todd, in an article that follows, points out the egalitarian nature of traditional, that is, "pre-contact," Hopi lifeways in the non-dichotomized spheres of the sacred and the profane. This is a point that many anthropologists, notably Eleanor Leacock, make: the current subjugation of women does not prove that this has always been women's status.

To acknowledge that women in the various religious institutions in the United States are in a subservient position today is not to argue that women therefore necessarily wish to see the dissolution of these institutions. Indeed, the situation seems quite analogous to that of the contradictory role of families in the lives of many women in the United States: religion is an institution which can be simultaneously a source of exploitation and a bulwark against other exploitation. As a further complexity, it is important to note that a woman's involvement in religion, while serving as a coping mechanism, can also serve as a substitute for action. A concrete example of this is offered by Sue Taylor in her discussion of religion among older black women:

> Individual initiative may give way to dependency upon faith or prayer for solutions rather than direct confrontation with a problem. For example, one woman without heat in January due to non-payment of her fuel bill, prayed daily for a solution. An outreach worker for the area agency on aging discovered the situation and arranged for emergency fuel assistance. For the woman, the problem had been solved by prayer. She neither sought outside aid nor considered the probability of intervention by an agency. (Taylor 1982: 2–3)

I grew up in a Southern black family where the African Methodist Episcopal church we all attended was a central part of our lives in terms of the amount of time, money, and energy expended. As a teenager, and even more so as a young college student studying the anthropology of Africa and Afro-America, I was conscious of the predominance of women in the membership, the secondary role they played in the church, *and* the range of nonreligious as well as religious functions this institution served in women's lives, including my own.

There was no attempt to change the language of the scriptures, the words of hymns, or the physical images. In this black church where we sang "Jesus will wash me whiter than snow" in Sunday school, the superintendent was my great-grandfather but most of the teachers were women. We looked up at stained glass windows depicting a blond, blue-eyed image of Jesus and showing Mary as a white woman. However, as the choir my mother directed sang "Amazing Grace," Sister Minnie would begin to twitch as the spirits moved her, and she began to speak in tongues and shout and dance in expressions of "getting happy." Her religion, its imagery as Eurocentric and male as it was, also involved the retention of elements of an African religion. And importantly, it was obviously a source of tremendous relief and satisfaction to a woman who somehow had to support herself and several children on the less-than-minimum wages she received as a domestic for a Southern white lady, living in a city where even the water fountains were marked "white" and "colored."

Sister Minnie was never in the pulpit, nor did anyone who shared her gender ever hold forth as a preacher. Yet she, and other women, were always frying the chicken and preparing the potato salad that were essentials for the many church suppers. Without defending or excusing this division of labor, it is necessary to note that on those Sundays when Sister Minnie's usher board served and she brought men and women to their seats, or even more so, when, with one arm folded behind her back, she brought some of the collection plates to the minister, one saw a woman who in Mt. Olive A.M.E. church was able to play a public role of dignity and consequence denied her in much of the racist, sexist, and elitist southern United States. Outside of the church walls, like many black and Latino women, Sister Minnie was one of those known to have powers of alternative forms of healing, alternatives to the exorbitantly expensive and yet always segregated medical institutions in Jacksonville, Florida. When the social services she and her family needed were not provided by the city, state, or federal governments, it was to her sisters and brothers in the church that she turned for help. Although Sister Minnie was not among them, many in that same church joined what was then a civil rights and black power movement with a strong grounding in the religious institutions of black America.

These gender, race, and class complexities of the African Methodist Episcopal church in which I grew up in the South suggest the context within which many other poor and ethnic women struggle with the spiritual and profane sides of their lives. The double edge in Judaism is expressed this way by Cynthia Ozick:

> In the world at large I call myself, and am called, a Jew. But when, on the Sabbath, I sit among women in my traditional *shul* and the rabbi speaks the word "Jew," I can be sure that he is not referring to me. For him "Jew" means "male Jew." . . . My own synagogue is the only place in the world where I am not named Jew. (Ozick 1979: 21)

Thus for many Jewish women, while religion can be a place of refuge from a hostile and anti–Jewish world, in most of the congregations of

that same religion there is much that continues to place women outside "the Covenant."

If the place of women today in organized religion and society is not
what it should be, what is to be done to redress the situation? This is a
question to which each of the following articles speaks. Briefly noting
the nature of those responses not only introduces each of the articles,
but once again takes note of similarities and differences among US
women.

Todd argues that the distinction which many women make between political and spiritual feminism is, in the world view of the Hopi
and the Anasazi from whom they are descended, a distinction that
overlooks the interdependence and interconnectedness of all things.
Todd shows how Anasazi spiritual beliefs and Hopi opposition to strip-
mining express this world view. The fundamental notion of women's
power among these matrilineal and matrilocal people is now under
question, however, because the U.S. government imposed the rule of
Tribal Councils and maneuvered the lease of Hopi land for strip-
mining—the rape of Mother Earth. Without explicitly taking this position, the tone of Todd's article suggests that many of the contemporary
problems of the Hopi would be diminished by a "return to," or at least
a continuing adherence to, the social ideals, and religious practices
and institutions of traditional Hopi ways.

Despite a host of differences, there is a striking similarity between
the situation described by Todd and that addressed by Anne Follis in
her article, "Born Again." The book jacket describes Follis as the wife
of a minister and the mother of three children, a description that her
views inside the book would not challenge. She writes of her experience of being born again, that is, of "entering into an intimate relationship with God through Jesus Christ" (Follis 1981: 32). Although in this
article there are no explicit references to a "return to" the old-
fashioned virtues and beliefs of Christianity, such a return is clearly
what Anne Follis is suggesting.

The interesting twist to Follis's view is her feeling that to right the
wrongs of this world will require more than individual salvation
through the born-again experience. In particular, to correct the injustices suffered by women requires active political work, such as her serious involvement with championing the Equal Rights Amendment.
While disassociating herself from the hostility and antifeminism of
some fundamentalist Christians, neither does she stand with those
feminists who denounce the Bible because of what they see as its sexism, racism, and warmongering. It is between this rock and a hard
place that she seeks a solution to the condition of women: "between the
Christians who claim God is an anti-feminist and the feminists who insist Christianity is anti-woman."

Feeling estranged from the women's liberation movement because of what is perceived to be that movement's attack on traditional cultural and religious practices of white ethnic Catholic women, Barbara Mikulski presents the case for a population that she says consists of about 20 million women in the industrial cities of the United States. Mikulski describes two important aspects of these women: their democratic liberal politics and their conservative cultural lives based on ethnic traditions and religious heritage. These are not the women struggling to change the Bible to less male-centric language or the ones who want to sing folk songs in place of the traditional music of their church. Rather these are women who feel strongly that equal pay for equal work is their right. In an honest and quite moving passage, Mikulski states that these are women who want change but are intimidated and confused by threatening ideas.

In another article, Susannah Heschel also speaks of women, and men, who view feminism as a threat to their traditional religion and lifeways. Rather than seeing feminism as a threat, however, she suggests that it is the crucible for modern Judaism, for it lays bare "the failure of Jewish religious movements to cope with modernity's challenges to theology and to respond effectively to them" (Heschel 1983: xxiii). Indeed, Heschel argues, through a feminist theology of Judaism, there is the possibility of revised traditions which are more in tune with today's world of pluralism and free choice. Such a feminist theology would guarantee that when the Jewish people look to Judaism, they would see not just a reflection of the experiences of Jewish men. To go even further, such a feminist critique of and engagement with established tradition and institutions could become, it is argued, a force helping to insure an ongoing vitality in Judaism and appeal to present and future generations.

From the perspective of Carol Christ, the problems women face today in terms of that crucial part of their lives called the spiritual are even more profound then implied in Heschel's article. Noting the importance of religious symbols and rituals, Christ argues that even for women who are atheists, continuous references to "God the Father" can affect the unconscious, suggesting the anomaly of female power. What is the solution to this problem, the problem of patriarchal rule in religion as in the rest of society? Christ argues it is to replace "God the Father" with the symbol of the Goddess. Christ identifies four different "meanings" of the Goddess symbol, but notes that "at the simplest and most basic level, the symbol of Goddess is an acknowledgment of the legitimacy of female power as a beneficent and independent power" (Christ 1979: 277).

Carol Christ thus assumes that all women who are under the influence of Judeo-Christian traditions and practices are affected by the centrality of "God the Father." Here then is a commonality among a large group of U.S. women. Yet it may well be important to determine how women of the Judeo-Christian tradition are differently affected by the pervasive symbolism of God the Father as a consequence of their class, racial, ethnic, age, "denominational," and other differences.

In her article, Jacquelyn Grant discusses how and why women of color are invisible in the theology of churches in their own communities. In analyzing the situation of black women in churches Grant locates their oppression in the distinction between "prescribed support positions and policy-making leadership" (Grant 1979: 142). Grant looks to the history of the black church for illumination on the oppression of black women in the ministry, and she notes the ways in which the role and status of black women in their churches is a microcosm of their place in society as a whole. Grant argues that it is only when black women and men fully share leadership in the church *and* the community that liberation becomes possible.

Although it is not the subject of any of the articles in this section of the book, it is important to note the growing popularity of liberation theology. This movement calls for and supports a change in women's status and that of all exploited groups.

Within the so-called major religions in the Untied States, the history, place, and expected roles for women are defined, as indeed they are for men. These religions chronicle women's very existence and history as an outgrowth of man's. Women's role is that of a serving and nurturing wife and mother, and their place is specified as secondary. And yet, within each of these religions there is a strong tradition of rebellion and promise of hope to the oppressed. It is this dual message which makes religion both a participating force in women's oppression and a potential source of ideology for the transformation of that very condition.

References Cited

Christ, C. P.
1979   "Why Women Need the Goddess." In *Womanspirit Rising: A Feminist Reader in Religion*, C. P. Christ and J. Plaskow, eds., pp. 273–287. San Francisco: Harper & Row.

Dominga, M. Z.
1980   "The Role of the Hispanic Woman in the Church." *New Catholic World*, July/August, pp. 172–174.

Follis, A. B.
1981   "Born Again." In *I'm Not a Women's Libber, But. . . ."* New York: Avon.

Grant, J.
1979   "The Black Church and the Black Woman." In *All the Women Are White, All the Blacks Are Men, But Some of Us Are Brave*, G. Hull, P. Bell Scott, and B. Smith, eds, pp. 141–152. Old Westbury, N.Y.: Feminist Press.

Heschel, S., ed.
1983   *On Being a Jewish Feminist*. New York: Schocken.

Ozick, C.
1979   "Notes Towards Finding the Right Question." *Lilith*, no. 6, pp. 19–29.

Taylor, S.
1982   "Religion as a Coping Mechanism for Older Black Women." *Quarterly Contact* 5(4): 2–3.

24

Opposing the Rape
of Mother Earth

Judith Todd

Some feminists see themselves as exclusively "political feminists" or as "spiritual feminists," and many find it difficult to understand the other's point of view. The spiritualists feel that the politicalists are too narrow or insensitive to what they regard as "a more encompassing feminist consciousness," whereas the politicalists consider the spiritualists impractical and believe that they avoid "the reality of the real political issues." I think that it is extremely important for us to realize that this division between the spiritual and the political is arbitrary and unnecessarily divisive. I hope to illustrate the positive relationship between spirituality and politics by discussing the ancient Anasazi spiritual beliefs and the present day struggle of their descendants, the Hopi, to preserve their land from strip-mining.[1]

The Anasazi world view is difficult for us to talk about because our sentence structure and words, which inevitably reflect our own world view, imply distinctions that they did not make. This is a matter of metaphysics, whether we like that term or not, and it is necessary to consider yet another distinction that derives from our European western metaphysics—one that is alien to Anasazi belief. We assume a distinc-

Reprinted from *Heresies, A Feminist Publication on Art and Politics*, Issue 5, Revised, Vol. 2, No.1, 1982.

tion between "living" things, such as animals and plants, and "non-living" ones, such as rocks and water. The distinction did not exist for the early Anasazi people and still does not exist for many of their present-day descendants. For the Anasazi/Hopi, trees, insects, rocks, people, water—are all living, virtually interconnected parts of a living Whole. Earth is not just a huge chunk of inanimate matter with animate beings scurrying around on top. Mother Earth is a living being. Earth's creations cannot be reduced to inanimate atomic particles, subject only to physio-chemical laws, because no such things exist. Atoms are alive, energized by the same vitality that we experience.

Once we can view the world without separating the animate from the inanimate, we can better understand the interconnectedness of all things and the consequent possibility for what we call psychic phenomena. For the Anasazi, thought was not a mere epiphenomenon of a few pounds of cerebral cortex but was in itself a vital, viable, powerful force that could and did affect things in the world, such as the weather and other natural forces. Our own orientation confuses us when we try to understand this because as soon as we say "affect things," we assume a linear version of cause and effect. The Anasazi held a more complex concept of reality. Since they regarded all things as related to each other, cause and effect were not a simple matter of a one-two chain reaction, but rather a complex interrelationship, a network, a pattern in which they perceived cycles as well as lines, and subtle as well as gross power.

The Anasazi expressed the metaphysical truth of the interrelatedness of all things as parts in a great dynamic Whole in their ceremonial dances. These multi-sensorial, dynamic dramas were attuned to the cycles of nature and the positions of certain stars. Within the ceremony, the movements of the dancers were synchronized with each other and with repetitive, one-two drum beats, the heartbeat of Mother Earth. Each ceremony in the cycle of ceremonies was simultaneously a complete, orchestrated unit as well as an integral part of the Whole cycle. Analogously, each individual participant was an integral part of the great dynamic Whole of the dance, the cycle, and all of nature.

Anasazi architecture played an important part in the ceremonial expressions of this primary truth. . . . Some of the more extensive pueblos span about three acres. In some cases pueblos are built on top of even older ruins, which had been abandoned by earlier generations of Anasazi. The ceremonial temples, called *kivas*, were dug out of the earth, so that they are wholly or partially subterranean. The kiva is a subterranean Great Kiva and was probably used by a group of about 1000 people. Smaller kivas were also at least partially underground and usually circular. Each kiva contained a *sipapu*, a circular hole dug out of the floor. The sipapu symbolized the place of emergence from the last world.

Kivas were a part of the daily life of the Anasazi, as were their spiritual practices. They were used constantly for ceremonial preparations and rituals.[2] For the architects of these buildings, there was no distinction between the spiritual and the political, i.e., between their religious and secular lives—or for that matter between art and non-art. Religion and art were an integral part of daily life. The Anasazi's ritual ceremonies celebrated life and their daily lives celebrated the beauty of a total reality, naturally including what we call the spiritual.

The Anasazi ceremonies were held either inside the circular, partially underground kivas or in the plaza, framed by these concentric, step-like buildings. As Vincent Scully says, "Most of the dances of ritual . . . are held, now as in the recorded past, tight up against the buildings. . . . And the beat of those dances is built into the architecture, which thus dances too."[3]

The architecture's very structure expressed the metaphysical belief in the interdependence and interconnectedness of all things in a dynamic Whole. The pueblo was composed of interconnected cells, so that it was quite typical for one unit's south wall to be the next unit's north wall. The living units were all about the same size, reflecting the egalitarian social belief of the Anasazi. Each of these cellular units was owned by a woman. The Anasazi were matrilineal and matrilocal. When a daughter married, a unit was built adjacent to that of her mother and she and her husband moved in. (In case of divorce, the man moved out, leaving the woman in a relatively more secure position, since she had the house and the support of her own clan.) The layout of the Anasazi pueblo was a direct result of this matrilocal arrangement: Construction occurred only where daughters were born. A family that had many daughters could be evidenced by a cluster of pueblo units. In an area of the pueblo where only sons were born, new construction did not take place; in fact, because the clans were matrilineal, a clan that failed to have daughters became extinct.

Laura Thompson points out the value in this kind of growth pattern: "Reproduction in this organically conceived society is ideally by means of budding. As the Hopi matrilineal clan grows by adding daughter households to the mother unit, so the pueblo expands by the budding of daughter colonies from the original nucleus. Thus ideally the society is able to augment and completely reconstitute itself."[4]

This budding type of growth pattern is different from that of our architecture. For us, the basic structural unit is the building to which new rooms, patios, etc., can be added. Pueblo architecture's basic structural unit is the room itself, and growth consists of indefinite repetition of this basic unit. Although J. B. Jackson seems to consider this growth pattern inferior to our more "complex" way of building, he points out that it seems to imply "the belief in the cumulative power of infinite repetition."[5] This belief is also reflected in the Chaco Canyon masonry, which prefers small stones to large ones. Jackson says, "It is as if the builders were saying that a wall is sturdy when it is made out of a multitude of identical small fragments."[6] I think it is likely that these builders, who were members of a matrilineal, egalitarian society and who expressed their spiritual beliefs via repetitive, cyclic ceremonies did believe in the "cumulative power of infinite repetition." That idea seems difficult for Jackson to honor, but then he is a member of a patriarchal, hierarchical society whose architecture, social ideals, and religious institutions radically differ from those of Anasazi society.

Probably the most dramatic difference between Anasazi architecture and ours is the relationship of its forms to the earth. This difference is most marked in the structure of the kivas. European influenced churches are capped with phallic steeples, straining to leave the earth to reach the male God in the sky; arches cleave walls well above human height, pointing to the same exalted being. By total contrast, Anasazi architecture hugs Mother Earth, and the most sacred is the lowest and most enveloped. Kivas are dug out of the earth and are usually circular, reflecting earth's form.[7] The most sacred part of the entire pueblo, the sipapu, the place of emergence from the last world, is dug deep into the already subterranean kiva. This sacred orifice is protected by the circular kiva, whose walls may be of many thicknesses. The kiva is in turn surrounded by the pueblo, which may also have a concentric layout.

The concentric arrangement of the kivas may reflect the matrifocused spiritual beliefs of the Anasazi. The walls of some kivas are nearly two feet thick.[8] They are made up of stones, mortar, layers of plaster and (sometimes) paint. Frank C. Hibben reports that "In some kivas having many painted coats of plaster, the layers themselves made up perhaps a third of the thickness of the walls."[9] These concentric layers symbolically protect the sipapu and the people inside the kiva. For the Anasazi/Hopi, two types of labyrinth symbolize Mother Earth as she enfolds each soul, gives it birth and receives the spirit back at the end of the person's path through life.[10]

The same symbolism seems to be the underlying motive of the layout of the pueblo itself. There are two basic kinds of ground plan apparent in the pueblos throughout the Southwest that echo the two maze shapes. One is a sort of semicircular or capital letter D shape; the other is a more rectangular, roughly E shape—sometimes with the center bar missing. All of the rooms on any one level of a pueblo are connected by doorways, so that it is possible to enter a room at one end and wind one's way through the rooms to the other end. The multiple rows of rooms arranged around a central plaza create a concentric, centripetal design. That this labyrinthine structure was intended to symbolize Mother Earth is at least plausible; if it does, this is another way in which the Anasazi expressed their spiritual beliefs.

We have already discussed the intimate connection between the Anasazi's matrifocused society and the growth pattern of their architecture, and between the matrifocused spiritual beliefs and the structure of their kivas, if not the entire pueblo complex. But it is even more interesting to realize that this architecture was to a great extent built by women. Apparently the division of labor was that the men cut and laid the timber (which made the ceilings and partially framed the doors) and the women built the walls. It is not common knowledge among anthropologists that women were the major participants in building some of the most spectacular architecture in North America.[11] Not surprisingly, I came across this bit of information in male literature, which mentioned it in the process of denigrating women. The following passage, written by George Kubler, was based on the records of the seventeenth century Franciscan missionary Benavides. The passage blames certain "negative aspects" in missionary architecture on women's role in its construction, and in the process indicates that women built pueblo walls in ancient times. I quote this passage at length because its ethnocentricity and phallocentricity are so appallingly blatant as to be humorous (in an adrenalin-producing kind of way):

"The evidence of the buildings constitutes proof that two commonplace devices of European building found no use in New Mexico during the missionary era. The arch is almost nonexistent, and the dome is completely lacking, but both forms may readily be built with the local materials. Why were they excluded from the architectural repertory of the mission buildings? It is to be recalled that, to this day, the Indians themselves never use either the arch or the dome. In dealing with these negative aspects of the structure, reference must be made to the passage . . . from Benavides, pertaining to the participation of women in construction. Since Benavides, the roles have been reversed: the women now spin and weave, and the men build walls. But the women own the houses in the pueblos, and the ownership itself is perhaps a remnant from the time when building was the women's prerogative. Does this indifference to alien forms, so unlike the ready acceptance found in Mexico, stem from the women? . . . It is likely that resistance was encountered in New Mexico . . . and it seems reasonable to localize this resistance in the participation of women. The point cannot be proved by asserting that women are temperamentally more conservative, or indifferent to structural considerations: the evidence of the monuments and the known control of their construction by Indian women induce a correlation between the two, without reference to a priori considerations." Perhaps this correlation is to be expressed in terms of a traditional division of labor among men and women, the men executing the carpentry and woodwork, as indicated by Benavides, and the women opposing any increase in their own share.[12]

I certainly doubt that the absence of domes and arches is due to the women's laziness, as Kubler suggests. Nor were the women likely

to have been "indifferent to structural considerations," since prior to
the white man's encroachment they were capable of building Pueblo
Bonito, Chetro Ketl, and dozens of other multiroomed, multistoried
earthen monuments. The constructions of a mission would have been a
snap by comparison. I do, however, agree with Kubler's hint that the
women were more "conservative," for it is much that they had to con-
serve: their matrilineal, egalitarian society and their ancient earth-
reverencing spiritual beliefs. Kubler doesn't bother mentioning that
the women weren't building these missions out of devotion to the
white man's god, but because they were forced to build them. I prefer
to believe that the women's refusal to cap the buildings with domes or
the doorways with arches was a subtle way of protesting against the
white man's phallocentric religion.

Forcing the people to build missions and to attend church was
only part of the oppression the Anasazi/Hopi experienced.[13] During the
missionary era people were whipped, imprisoned and burned to death.
But in the long run, the most destructive form of oppression was a
form of indoctrination that is extremely difficult to combat. Beginning
in the late nineteenth century, Hopi children were literally stolen from
their parents and forced to go to white man's schools—far from their
homes—where they had to learn to speak in the English language and
to think in patriarchal concepts.[14] This insidious form of oppression
has had repercussions that are simultaneously political and spiritual.

Generations of indoctrination into the white man's world view
made other kinds of government influence possible. Nearly 100 years
ago, U.S. government agencies began insidious efforts aimed at gaining
control over Hopi land for mining purposes.[15] However, the traditional
Hopi way of making decisions—by clan consensus, in which every individual's view counts equally and all must reach agreement—was a constant impediment to deal-making and sellouts. So the government instituted a Hopi Tribal Council, consisting of "elected representatives."
Those sufficiently schooled in the white man's ways agreed to vote for
and support the Council. But traditional Hopi would not go along with
this manipulation of tribal government. They boycotted the elections
and refused to recognize the "elected" officials as their representatives. The traditional Hopi still do not recognize the Tribal Council, but
the U.S. government does. It was with this Tribal Council that the Department of the Interior made its contract to lease Hopi land to the
Peabody Coal Company for strip-mining. The Hopi Tribal Council
stands to gain more than $14 million over a 35-year period.[16] In Hopi-
land jobs are scarce, but they are available for those who support the
Tribal Council.

In spite of generations of attempted indoctrination, heavy economic pressures, and the demoralizing effects of watching their own
tribe members accept the white man's values, a small group of Hopi,

along with a few other Pueblo groups, remain traditional and will not consent to their land being strip-mined.[17] Their metaphysic—their spiritual beliefs, their world view—gives them this strength. They know Mother Earth is a living being and will not agree to have her raped.

This same world view, which treasures Mother Earth, allows for other phenomena that cannot be explained by our prevailing metaphysic. One such phenomenon crucially important to the traditional Hopi is prophetic visions. The Hopi have been guided by visions for countless centuries. In fact, visions guided the people to Chaco Canyon after many hundreds of years of migration throughout North and South America.[18] It is here that the Anasazi built their earthen architecture and here that their descendants still choose to live.

The white man's appearance in Pueblo country was prophesied long before he came. The prophesies predicted that if the white man came bearing the sign of the circle, he would live in beneficial harmony with the Hopi. But if he came bearing the sign of the cross, he had lost his true belief and would bring sickness and death with him. The Anasazi women understood all too well the real meaning of the cross crowning the missions that they were forced to build.

The prophetic visions revealed that this new race of people would be able to fly through the air and would speak to each other through what appeared in the visions to be "cobwebs in the sky." The visions also foretold of a road "like a ribbon" that would run through the Hopi villages. Hopi men were later forced to build such a road while working on chain gangs as punishment for resisting government attempts to educate their children.

Many of the prophesies have become realities, but there are still more that pertain to the future. A crucial prophecy, still unfolding, is that men will come to try to take what lies under Hopi land. All of Mother Earth is sacred to the Hopi. They believe that they live at the very heart of this continent, the geomagnetic center—and that tampering with Mother Earth at this sacred center will create a serious imbalance. The prophecy warns that the people should not let the men take what is under their land. For the Hopi who have been indoctrinated into the white man's world view, a view in which prophetic visions are not valued, such a warning has little meaning. Yet those who have managed to cling to their ancient world view and spiritual knowledge take the warning very seriously. These people will try to protect Mother Earth from strip-mining.

Ecology-minded feminists may oppose strip-mining and see the struggle of the Hopi with the U.S. government as a political situation. The Hopi know it is a political *and* a spiritual struggle. For them, the concepts of "political" and "spiritual" are so tightly woven that in the cloth of reality, they cannot be separated.

Both spiritual awareness and political action are urgently needed to protect the Hopi land from strip-mining and from other attempts to exploit Mother Earth. . . .

Notes

1. The name *Anasazi* is not a Pueblo Indian name. It's a Navaho word meaning *ancient ones*, although the Navaho are not descended from the Anasazi. Somewhere along the line, anthropologists started using this name for the people who inhabited the Four Corners region (where Colorado, Utah, Arizona and New Mexico meet) from about 1 A.D. through 1300. The Hopi and other Pueblo tribes are descended from the Anasazi. My discussion of Anasazi world view and social structure is based largely on what I know of the Hopi, believed by many to be the most traditional and therefore the most similar to their ancestors.

2. It is sometimes said that these kivas were men's club rooms, or that women were excluded from them. That's purely a presumptive fantasy of male anthropologists. The women took part in ceremonies both inside and outside the kivas. (Hewett, p. 68)

3. Scully, p. 61.

4. Thompson, p. 543.

5. Jackson, p. 24.

6. Ibid. p. 24. To illustrate the extent of this multiplication of pieces, it has been estimated that one of the pueblos in Chaco Canyon was constructed of 50 million pieces of stone. (Hewett, p. 299)

7. Considering all that the Anasazi knew about the nature of the Cosmos and our place in it, I'm sure they knew Mother Earth is round, but I have not yet found printed support of that claim.

8. Hibben, p. 22.

9. Ibid. p. 22.

10. Waters, p. 29. These same symbols are found all over the world. One is identical with the Labyrinth of Ariadne, as depicted on a Cretan coin.

11. None of the anthropologists I spoke with (three women and two men) knew that women built the walls of the Anasazi pueblos. Not surprisingly, the men were the most skeptical. One was overtly hostile to the very idea and the other suggested that if I wanted to study the Anasazi art from a *female* point of view, I should study the pottery—it would be "safer." Since finding the Kubler quote, I've discovered a number of other sources that corroborate the tradition of women building the pueblo walls. Some of these also state the fact in derogatory ways. Hewett (p. 75) mentions it parenthetically; Schull (p. 48) says the women built the walls, then calls the walls "man-made" just two sentences later. See also Silverberg, p. 40; Thompson and Joseph, p. 54.

12. Kubler, p. 38.

13. For various accounts, see Katchongva, Nequatewa, Silverberg, or Waters.

14. Nequatewa, p. 61 and elsewhere.

15. Budnik, p. 101. See his article for an excellent account of the nature and extent of the ecological and cultural effects of this strip-mining effort.
16. Ibid., p. 101.
17. U.S. Bureau of Competition, pp. 38–39.
18. Waters, p. 50.

References Cited

Budnik, D.
1972 "Progress Report on Ecological Rape." *Art in America* 60.

Hewett, E. L.
1936 *The Chaco Canyon and Its Monuments*. Albuquerque: University of New Mexico Press.

Hibben, F. C.
1973 *Kiva Art of the Anasazi at Pottery Mound*. Las Vegas: KC Publications.

Jackson, J. B.
1953–1954 "Pueblo Architecture and Our Own." *Landscape* 3.

Katchongva, D.
1972 *From the Beginning of Life to the Day of Purification: Teachings, History and Prophecies of the Hopi People*. As told by the late Dan Katchongva, Sun Clan. Los Angeles: Committee for Traditional Indian Land and Life.

Kubler, G.
1973 *The Religious Architecture of New Mexico in the Colonial Period and Since the American Occupation*. Albuquerque: University of New Mexico Press.

Nequatewa, E.
1967 *Truth of a Hopi: Stories Relating to the Origin, Myths and Clan Histories of the Hopi*. Flagstaff: Northland Press.

Scully, V.
1975 *Pueblo: Mountain, Village, Dance*. New York: Viking.

Silverberg, R.
1965 *The Old Ones: Indians of the American Southwest*. New York: New York Graphic Society.

Thompson, L.
1945 "Logico-Aesthetic Integration in Hopi Culture." *American Anthropologist* 47:540–553.

Thompson, L., and A. Joseph
1965 *The Hopi Way*. New York: Russell and Russell.

U.S. Federal Trade Commission, Bureau of Competition
1975 *Staff Report on Mineral Leasing on Indian Lands*. Washington, D.C.: USGPO.

Waters, F.
1963 *Book of the Hopi*. New York: Ballantine.

25

"Born Again"

Anne Bowen Follis

The phone rang just as I was sitting down to lunch. "Could you get some of your people out to talk to Senator so-and-so this week?"

It was the ERA headquarters in Springfield. It seemed that some ERA opponents had set up in the capital for legislators to visit a display, which supposedly depicted the kind of people who support the Equal Rights Amendment. To describe the display as inflammatory and pornographic would be an understatement. Using guilt-by-association smear tactics, the display lifted quotes from various feminist leaders out of context; emphasized the most radical and controversial elements of the feminist movement; and posted homosexual material, stating that these were the people who *really* support the Equal Rights Amendment.

"We thought it was so obnoxious that it would only hurt the opposition rather than help them," the caller told me, "but, would you believe, it has actually weakened a few pro legislators?"

I was annoyed and disgusted, and not in the mood to have my day ruined by the news. "Who set this thing up, anyway?" I asked.

When she told me the name, it was not familiar. "Who is she?" I asked.

"Oh, you know," the caller told me, "she's one of those *born-again* Christians."

Her voice was so sarcastic and contemptuous when she said the words "born again" that I choked on my sandwich. When I regained my composure, I said somewhat timidly, "So am I."

She was shocked into an awkward silence. Born-again Christians, I could hear her thinking, are self-righteous, overbearing people. This Anne Follis is a friend of mine. What is she saying? She can't be one of *them*.

But I am. When the country first took notice of presidential candidate Jimmy Carter, one intriguing facet of the man was the fact that he called himself a born-again Christian. Many reacted to it almost as if it was some sort of a new fad. There seemed to be a new born-again celebrity every week. Books dealing with the phenomenon began appearing even in secular bookstores and at drug counters. Whatever it was, it was marketable, and before long a certain Madison Avenue element to the born-again craze made it almost cheap. At least, it seemed that way to me.

"Born again" was more than just a slick slogan to put on a bumper sticker. For me it had been a precious, life-changing experience. And on the phone that day, as so many times since, I felt compelled to explain that, and to apologize for the excesses that are often associated with the experience.

It is possible to go to church all your life, and yet to grow up with a spiritual vacuum. Religion was secondary in my life as I went through high school and into college; what I wanted most was to find the right man, get married, and settle into a nice, comfortable, middle-class life. I wanted more than security, though. I wanted a loving relationship that would last a lifetime.

There was a certain hollowness in the friendships I acquired in those years. I couldn't quite put my finger on it, but I wanted more. Once, during a particularly lively class picnic I broke away from the festivities and went off into the woods alone. "I was looking for something," I wrote later in my diary, "but I don't know what it was, and I didn't find it." (I believe now that I was experiencing the gentle pull and tug of the Holy Spirit in my life.)

It didn't make sense, this vague yearning of mine. I had a good family, plenty of friends, and lots of things to keep me busy. But I wanted more. I convinced myself that when I finally found the right guy and fell in love, I would be happy.

The right guy took a while in coming along, and something happened in the meantime. The young woman with the big, romantic fantasies was born again.

Volumes have been written to explain just what that means, and some of them are very good. Essentially, what it comes down to is an entering into an intimate relationship with God through Jesus Christ. I had come to recognize my own failures and needs and . . . I just wanted more *substance* in my life. And I found the love and the wholeness offered in Jesus Christ to be absolutely irresistible.

I didn't go forward to an altar and have an emotional breakthrough. It happened in the quiet of my room, as I was reading the Bible (a book to which I had paid little attention, and for which I had some disdain, in spite of my religious upbringing). All my life I had felt a little like I was on a treadmill, dealing with resentment, frustration, disappointment, and trying, trying, trying to do things "right"—only to discover as I got one hole in the dike plugged up that three more had burst. But that evening I turned to the fifth chapter of Galatians and read that when we allow human nature to rule our lives the treadmills will abound, but when the Spirit controls our lives, we will have "love, joy, peace. . . . Against such things there is no law" (NIV).

I remember a surge of relief and feeling downright gleeful! The old, overworked phrase about "letting go and letting God" became a reality in my life as I got off the awful treadmill of trying to manage my own life and let the Spirit of God enter and fill the void.

There are a few problems with testimonies such as I have just shared. For one, they tend to be easily overplayed. What Christ has done in my life in the years since this experience is actually far more significant. For another, they begin to sound a little bit alike after a while, and often end with the simplistic claim that "since then everything has been perfect in my life and I haven't had any problems." That claim, I suspect, is pure fiction. At least I can't make it.

No instant, dramatic changes occurred in my life. The changing and the growth have been slow, even painful at times. There have been struggles with my own confusion, my own doubts, and the frustrations of trying to live the Christian life amid the complexities of today's world. Immediately after my decision I found myself trying to work out my beliefs and define terms, and I studied the Bible as one who had just found water after being lost in the desert. I was constantly trying to relate my faith to the present day and to my own life. How is one to be "in" the world but not "of" it? Why is there so much evil, suffering, and pain in this world? Why do I continue to sin, to fail God, to live like the "old" me?

Sometimes the pieces fit, and sometimes they didn't. Gradually, however, the feeling of urgency to find the answers lessened. When, through prayer and study and struggle some new understanding would come it was great, but as I grew in my relationship with God I learned to trust him even with that which I could not yet understand.

And I discovered joy. Rich, abundant, glowing, charged-up joy. It came unexpectedly at first: while having my coffee in the morning, or reading a book, or watching TV, or driving the car, or sitting in church. I'd think about the greatness of God's love in my life, and it would flood over me in waves. Joy, joy, joy; so much sometimes that I could hardly handle it all. Gradually the joy flowed over even into the grief, and the frustrations, and the disappointments in my life. It wasn't that God always gave me the solutions to all my problems, but that, through the problems, God's presence was there: "the everlasting arms," "the Good Shepherd," "our rock and our foundation." I found myself trusting him, and loving him, more each day. I remember telling a friend, "I thought Christ would take away from my life, but instead he's added to it."

When the feminist movement began to establish itself, I viewed it as an attack on my Christian faith and reacted with a degree of arrogance and defiance. I had the vague idea that feminism and Christianity were incompatible. As I felt myself increasingly drawn into the women's movement, a struggle began in my life. If feminism and Christianity were incompatible, which would I choose? My Christian faith was not composed merely of a set of beliefs; it was an intensely close, personal relationship with Someone I loved very much. Yet the consensus among many Christians seemed to be that feminism was essentially "un-Christian."

As I considered it, I had to agree that, yes, some *feminists* were extreme in some of their beliefs, but that feminism, or the ideal of basic equality between women and men, was entirely consistent with my Christian faith.

Sorting out the complexities of my own beliefs and feelings amid my increased involvement in a very controversial movement kept me awake many nights. What I found particularly distressing was that much of the opposition to women's rights was springing up from among the people with whom I would expect to have the closest alliance: Christians.

I have since come to realize that there was a degree of naïveté to my faith that is common to young Christians. After coming into a personal experience with Christ, we find it inconceivable to think that others who have had the same experience could be anything but loving and supportive. I was bowled over by the hostility I encountered from a number of know-it-all Christians. During my frequent trips to the capital, or at public places where I was to speak, I found myself being challenged, interrogated, and, with less frequency, accosted, shoved, and threatened. The reasoning seemed to be that God was against the Equal Rights Amendment (and women's rights). And because I was for it, I was therefore the Enemy, and fair game.

In no time the Equal Rights battle became polarized and embittered. In all fairness, I'm sure that some proponents have done their share of behaving rudely. I found it particularly upsetting, however, that the opposition, coming from the religious sector, seemed to be characterized by such anger and hatred. And, yes, I found myself often responding with anger and hatred, and I didn't like it. I felt guilty about my anger and I tried (often unsuccessfully) to overcome it. Among opponents of the ERA, however, what comes across to me is their belief that their hatred is perfectly righteous and justified.

Of course not *all* Christians joined the antiequality bandwagon; in fact, many of my richest Christian friendships developed from my ERA work. But it is a sad fact that throughout history there has been a tendency, within Christianity, to go to extremes; to take Christian liberty and turn it into license; to justify arrogance and self-righteousness against a cause which is deemed, often unjustly, as "un-Christian."

One reaction to this has been some real hostility toward the Christian faith among some feminists, as with my friend in Springfield. In another similar instance, I will never forget listening to a lecture by feminist author Marilyn French, author of *The Women's Room* (Summit Books, 1980). Her speech was earnest, compelling, and completely unselfconscious. As she spoke about the use and abuse of power, and about the vulnerability of women, I found myself moved to tears. After she spoke I was asked to say a few words, and I should have declined. I was so choked up that I fumbled all over the place like a blithering idiot.

Afterward several of us went to dinner. Marilyn French sat on the far end of the table from me (and got up only briefly to change the title on the rest-room door with a felt marker from "ladies" to "women," to our delight). After dinner I had a chance to speak with her briefly, and expressed how much her talk had meant to me.

"But," I said, "I don't agree with your denunciation of the Bible. There are people who are reassessing these narrow interpretations . . ."

I was never able to finish. I felt like I had hit a raw nerve. She took off furiously, stating that, yes the Bible has some beautiful passages, but it is an awful book, a sexist book, a racist book, a war-mongering book. Her attack was not aimed at me, and I understood that, but it left me so surprised that I was able to respond with little more than "I disagree."

I have thought about that encounter many times since. Had I had the time, and the presence of mind, I could have argued round and round with her, but I doubt if it would have accomplished a thing. Her opinions were clearly immovable, as were mine. I thought later that trying to talk me out of my faith would be like trying to persuade me that the institution of marriage is an evil to avoid. All the reason in the world wouldn't mean a thing up against the fact that I love my husband and am very happily married. Period.

It's more than security, and it's even more than faith. It's love. God isn't someone I merely intellectualize about, or, for that matter, follow and obey blindly. God is someone, as I have stated before, whom I love.

It's in the framework of that love that I've been working my way through the changes in my life these past several years. My faith and beliefs are, obviously, decidedly Christian. At the same time, I am ashamed and angered by the creeping Christian chauvinism I see in much of the Christian right-wing movement today. It is entirely possible, I believe, to hold deeply felt convictions, while respecting, and even being open to learn, from the differing views of others.

But how does one strike a chord somewhere in the middle: between strong convictions and intolerance; between the Christians who claim God is an anti-feminist and the feminists who insist Christianity is anti-woman?

I have had a few moments when I wondered if I would be able to work my way through it all and still remain true to my convictions. But as the struggle progressed I knew ... *I knew* ... that I was both a Christian and a feminist, and that the two are complementary, not contradictory. Working my way through the cobwebs and confusion became not a chore but an adventure; one that strengthened and confirmed my beliefs, all the way around.

26

The White Ethnic Catholic Woman

Barbara Mikulski

We've heard a great deal of talk about differences in the women's movement. I personally feel very much a part of a special constituency that is best represented by the phrase "European ethnic Catholic women." We are the people who represent a population of about 20 million women residing primarily in the urban areas of the North—from Boston to Baltimore, New York to Milwaukee—and other major industrial centers.

One of our problems is that many people don't understand us. We are stereotyped in the media as passive Edith Bunker types, even as reactionary. But if you know us, you will know this to be untrue. You'll find there are two themes that run through our public attitude. Number one, we are associated with the Democratic Party through the ideas of Franklin Delano Roosevelt and Jack Kennedy, and programs like Social Security. But when you look at our cultural lives, which stem from both our ethnic traditions and our religious heritage, you'll find we are somewhat conservative in our outlook. So if you know us

Excerpted from *Dialogue on Diversity: A New Agenda for American Women* edited by Barbara Peters and Victoria Samuels, 1976, Institute on Pluralism and Group Identity. Reprinted by permission of Barbara Mikulski.

as politically and economically progressive but culturally moderate, then you will understand our attitudes in relationship to the women's movement. The women in our constituency have mixed feelings about the women's movement.

Though we hate to categorize people, it seems there are two groups within the movement. There are the women's rights activists and there are the women's liberation activists. The women's rights activists have been in the forefront of those programs dealing with concrete benefits for people in terms of child care, day care, educational opportunities, senior citizens programs, Social Security reform, changing the work place, and fighting for the minimum wage to cover more people. We feel very much a part of this group.

Then there are the women's liberationists who perhaps have had the most publicity and have presented what we would regard as culturally provocative ideas. These are the people who have talked about role changes, changing life-styles and changing orientations in the family. Many of the people in our communities find these ideas very threatening and very confusing.

A History of Involvement

When we look at the question of fighting for rights, the women in our community have been involved in this struggle for a long time. We go back to the early trade union movement. We were "Rosie the Riveter." We're there now when it comes to reforming the work place. We see it in the working class communities around the country where women have organized. And it is interesting that this struggle is not necessarily for their own benefit, but is carried on in behalf of others, which has so often been the story of women. . . .

The Way We Really Are

One of the problems we face—and we find it a major problem—is the orientation of our cultural and religious backgrounds. You have to understand that those of us of European ethnic backgrounds have always felt under the gun in this country. First for our ethnicity, then for our religion, both from the outside society and even within our own society. And now the confusion over something called women's liberation. The larger culture has always baffled us because they tell us to do one thing and twenty years later they ridicule us for doing it.

When we first came to America, we helped to build the railroads, we worked on the docks and in the coal mines, and we called ourselves

Americans. But others were calling us Polack, Wop, Dago, and Honky. We were ridiculed for our funny names and our funny foods. So we became "Americans." We became superpatriots, and as we became superpatriots we found ourselves harassed in the late 1960s because we were proud to say we were Americans. We were proud to say we respected the flag and we were even proud of the fact that our men had gone to war.

While we faced this dilemma, many of us found solace and consolation in our Catholicism. We cherished our religion. There were certain nationality parishes and we had our own. In the Polish church there is a tremendous devotion to the Blessed Mother and that has always meant something to us. There's a Polish version of the Virgin Mary, which is the Madonna that guarded the capital of Poland from the time of Napoleon's invasion to the Nazi invasion. Her statue, her portrait, which is a charred face of the Madonna, has always been a symbol of freedom to the Polish people.

So as we continued to have our processions and our devotions in the 1960s, along came the liberated Jesuits. They came in with their turtlenecks and their guitars and they said: "We're going to liberate you from the oppression of the Roman Catholic Church. This is the Ecumenical Council. Throw out the statues. The Blessed Mother is out." We didn't know who was in! They didn't bring in Jane Addams or Rosie Schneiderman as a substitute. They just said: "She's out the window." And then we were told to go into folk masses.

Now, we didn't know how to sing "Go Tell It on the Mountain." In my neighborhood, children learned to play the accordion. We didn't know what the hell a guitar was. We thought it was something Elvis Presley played. At the same time as they were telling us to get with it and be part of the 1960s and the folk culture, our own folk culture was put down. We asked: "Couldn't we have a service and then afterwards have some other kind of music? Couldn't we have our traditional services?" They said no, and that was it.

It is within this context that in the past five years we began to be part of something else. It was called the women's movement. Again you have to understand how we feel. We and our mothers and grandmothers and great-grandmothers were the women of the sweatshops. The women who died in the Triangle Shirtwaist fire. And I can tell you something: when World War II was over, and *McCall's* magazine talked about family togetherness and getting out of the factory, you're damn right my aunts and other relatives wanted to get out.

They wanted to be "ladies." They didn't find it especially gratifying to work in factories or to stand there trimming tomatoes so that at seventy years old all they've got out of their work is arthritis and very little Social Security. The title "lady" meant something, and they wanted their daughters to be "ladies." That's why many of them scrubbed floors and took other menial jobs to send their children to college. So when something came along that began to threaten that dream, it became a real problem.

The Threatening Issues Cause Ambivalence

One of the things that has always held us together—whether it was the 1,000 years of oppression in Czechoslovakia, in Poland, in Latvia or Estonia—is the concept of family. No matter what king, kaiser or czar marched through your country, somehow or other that family would hold you together. The family is not only a living arrangement. It has always been a symbol of survival. When that traditional family structure is challenged by views that some of our people consider as culturally provocative, we feel threatened.

On the one hand, we want equal pay for equal work. We want the benefits that are coming into our communities. We like being out on the barricades. We like bringing about change. But when threatening ideas come along, we have a tremendous feeling of ambivalence and hurt. We feel intimidated and confused. If you see it within this context, hopefully you can understand all of these mixed feelings.

The women in our community are not hostile to the women's movement. But we're confused and we're searching. And we're looking to find ways that we can be together. Maybe one of the ways that we can begin to get together is to take a look at our cultural diversity and to respect the different feelings that we have. Respect the ambivalence, respect the reluctance, the shyness, and inhibition to participate in some areas.

One of the things we have to remember is that the women's movement is a movement, not a religion. A religion has a single dogma, a single creed. In some places it might even have a mystical language. But the women's movement is not a single truth. We are not like little boxes of crackers, uniform in size and shape. We are different. . . .

27

On Being a Jewish Feminist

Susannah Heschel

A learned, observant, and committed young woman applied in 1903 for permission to study in the rabbinical school of the Jewish Theological Seminary. Daughter of a rabbi, she had long been involved in Jewish education and was employed as an editor and translator at the Jewish Publication Society. She was clearly an applicant of considerable distinction. The faculty of this renowned center for advanced Jewish studies voted to allow her to attend all the classes, with one condition: that she not use her knowledge to seek rabbinical ordination.

Henrietta Szold attended classes, assisted Talmud professor Louis Ginzberg in editing his monumental, six-volume study of Jewish legends, translated and edited articles for other scholars in the field of Judaica, and then went on, some years later, to found Hadassah, the women's Zionist organization, the largest Jewish organization in America today.[1]

Much remains the same since Szold's lifetime . . . but a fundamental change has taken place; a modern-day Henrietta Szold would not stand alone. Increasing numbers of women are demanding entry into

Reprinted by permission of Schocken Books Inc. from *On Being a Jewish Feminist: A Reader* by Susannah Heschel copyright © 1983 by Schocken Books Inc. (excerpted).

rabbinical schools, into the quorum for communal prayer (the *minyan*), and into leadership echelons of community organizations, forming a movement of Jewish feminism that is continually gathering momentum.

The history of Jewish women is just beginning to be written,[2] but it is clear that many issues raised today under the banner of feminism represent the strivings of past generations. Legal *repons* literature from the Middle Ages, in discussing marriage and divorce, property ownership and inheritance, frequently reveals the frustration felt by many women over their restricted lives in families and communities. Occasional, minor changes were made, but the first major shift in women's status came with the ban on polygamy in medieval France and Germany—a ban recognized only by the Ashkenazic community.[3]

The advent of modern secularism and movements of religious reform did not bring many actual changes in Jewish laws pertaining to women, but did bring the possibility of escaping their control. By the nineteenth century, some women were able to elude rabbinic strictures over their lives and seek educations and professions as well as changes in the expectations of their husbands and families. In poetry, fiction, essays, and through organizations, the position of women in Judaism was challenged. Leaders of the Reform movement in Central Europe and the *Haskalah* movement [Enlightenment] in Eastern Europe rejected women's position in the synagogue and the traditional roles of women and men in the homc.[4] The movement was often felt to be for the benefit of men no less than women; Sholem Aleichem once remarked that Jews don't write novels about love because relations between Jewish men and women are so primitive. . . .

The concerns for equality within the Jewish community continued to be articulated as national organizations of Jewish women were formed in the Untied States at the turn of the century. They were also given passionate voice in the short stories and novels of women such as Anzia Yezierska and Mary Antin writing before and after World War I. The heroines of these stories usually take their shattered lives and repair them through education, careers, or financial independence, but invariably without assistance from family or community. Liberation was achieved only by breaking off and struggling alone.

The most recent wave of Jewish feminism, beginning during the 1960s, is assuming the opposite posture: not breaking away from the community, but struggling to become full members of it. Feminists are calling today for changes with *halakhah* to end discrimination in areas from divorce laws to synagogue separation; for inclusion in secular leadership; for concrete changes in the structure of the community to accommodate changing life-styles of women, from day-care centers to greater community acceptance of single mothers. At the same time, new studies concerning various aspects of women and Judaism are being published: women in the Bible, women resistance fighters during World War II; images of women in aggadic literature.[5]

Institutional changes took on rapid momentum in 1972. Sally Priesand was ordained rabbi by Hebrew Union College, the seminary of the Reform movement; Ezrat Nashim issued a "Call for Change" at the annual convention of Conservative rabbis; task forces on the status of women in the community were established by various Jewish organizations; groups of women formed throughout the country to celebrate Rosh Hodesh, the new moon, which is referred to in early Jewish sources as a woman's holiday; and feminism became a hotly debated topic in the community. . . .

Equality of women in synagogue services was a major issue from the beginning. By the mid-1970s the Orthodox community began debating the use and height of the *mehitzah*, the curtain separating women and men during prayers; the Conversative movement's Committee on Law and Standards voted to count women in the *minyan*, a decision which was ratified by many, but not all, Conservative synagogues; the Reconstructionist Fellowship granted full equality of women with men "in all matters of ritual," ordaining its first woman rabbi in 1974; and the Reform movement initated a review of sexism in its liturgy, organizations, and community life. Both Reform and Reconstructionist movements have now ordained over seventy women rabbis. The burgeoning *Havurah* movement has been strengthened by women who prefer traditional services but reject the inequality of women within Orthodoxy. Informal prayer groups of women, some including men, are beginning to flourish, as are groups for study of the traditional texts, particularly the Talmud, inaccessible to women still excluded from male-only *yeshivot*.

. . . Many women rabbis encounter prejudice, even discrimination, when they search for a job. Women who find greater equality in the synagogue often see more and more meaningful traditions eliminated. Others feel frustrated that further efforts are not being made to radically rewrite the traditional liturgy in order to rid it of sexism. . . .

Suggestions that women be ordained rabbis or simply be counted in a prayer quorum arouse protest on . . . blatantly obvious psychological—and sexual—grounds. Writing in opposition to the ordination of women as rabbis in the Conservative movement, Ruth Wisse fears that feminism will emasculate Jewish men: "Judaism's ability to create an alternative model of virility, which depended on intellectual and spiritual prowess rather than political and physical might, helped to compensate for the great social dependency of the Jews without undue sacrifice of masculine self-confidence and biological zest."[6] Her argument implies that to protect some degree of self-esteem during the long cen-

turies of persecution and ghetto life, Jewish men were justified in sub-
jugating Jewish women.

Wisse's concern for the mental health of Jewish men is echoed by
psychiatrist Mortimer Ostow and by historian Lucy Dawidowicz. Ostow, considering proposals that women receive *aliyot*, lead services,
and officiate as rabbis, warns that "there is the problem of sexual
arousal, consciously or unconsciously, by women performing [sic] on
the *bimah*. In our society it is generally true that men are far more
readily aroused by an attractive woman than women are by an attractive man. That being the case, a woman appearing as a central figure in
a religious service is likely to distract some of the male worshippers
from a reverent attitude and encourage erotic fantasies.[7] According to
Ostow, the synagogue traditionally serves as a "refuge from the struggles of the marketplace, struggles for self-worth as well as for economic survival.[8] But as women enter the marketplace alongside men, it
is imperative, Ostow insists, that the synagogue remain a stronghold of
men: "One would not wish to sponsor a program that will convert the
synagogue from a refuge to an arena where a man will feel that he
must struggle again to defend his self-esteem; this, I suspect, is the psy-
chologic truth behind the dictum: '*ishah l tikra batorah mipnei kavod
ha'tsibur*' (*Megillah* 23a): 'a woman should not read the Torah, out of
respect for the congregation.'"[9]

Dawidowicz fears the effect of women's participation on the community as well as the psyche:

> Women, when passive, can turn the synagogue into something like a pro-
> vincial Italian Catholic church. The rabbi assumes all sacerdotal func-
> tions, the women become his dutiful parishioners whose religion is part
> devotion, part ignorance, and part superstition. Religion, then, becomes a
> womanish thing. Men stay away out of contempt. But even more
> forbidding—to me at least—is the threat of female power, female usurpa-
> tion of the synagogue. Women are efficient; they can organize, raise
> funds, bring order out of chaos. They can turn the shul into a Hadassah
> chapter. Not that I disapprove of Hadassah, its activities, or its ladies. But
> I do not like the idea of their taking over the synagogue. To my mind, the
> assumption by a woman of rabbinic or priestly function in the synagogue
> undermines the very essence of Jewish tradition.[10]

By focusing on these kinds of concerns, opponents skirt the more
serious theological issues that feminism is raising—issues also missed
by some Jewish feminists who are endeavoring to answer them. Talmud professor Judith Hauptman, in her article "Rabbinic Images of
Women," sharply criticizes the position of women in classical Jewish
law and calls for the revision or elimination of those laws.[11] Yet she
raises no challenges to the halakhic system as such; on the contrary,
she calls for change according to the procedures laid down by the Tal-

mudic rabbis. Hauptman even defends the ancient rabbis, claiming they showed greater sensitivity to women's legal status than did leaders of neighboring, non-Jewish societies.

Blu Greenberg, in her recent book, *On Women and Judaism: A View from Tradition*, defines feminism as a call for the equality (though not identity) of men and women.[12] She sees feminism as an ethical movement worthy of attention by Jews who value Judaism's historic sensitivity to ethical dilemmas. Greenberg also criticizes aspects of the position of women in certain classical Jewish laws as maintained today by Orthodoxy, and calls for changing those laws. Like Hauptman, Greenberg claims it is possible to contrive to operate within the halakhic system, since she views what she dislikes in Judaism's treatment of women as the outgrowth of an earlier period and environment.

This approach may make certain Orthodox opponents more sympathetic to feminism, but it does not stem from a coherent theological position. The historical method cannot be applied only in some areas and not in others. Once we acknowledge the laws regarding women as products of a particular historical period and outlook, what is to keep us from considering other Jewish practices—such as the synagogue service—as a comparable historical outgrowth that has outlived its meaning and relevance? In fact, the entire system of *halakhah* might be similarly regarded as the religious expression of a particular community, living in Palestine and Babylonia nearly two thousand years ago. If the Talmud is the product of a particular time and particular individuals, what religious authority does it hold, and why should we return to it after discovering teachings and ruling within it that limit and oppress us? . . .

. . . Both the most traditional Jew and the most radical feminist would agree that thorough and rigid sex-role differentiation is deeply imbedded in Judaism. Judith Plaskow, writing in this volume, puts the matter bluntly: "Our legal disabilities are a symptom of a pattern of projection that lies deep in Jewish thinking, one that must be addressed and rooted out at its core." She concludes that women cannot be fully part of Judaism without a complete transformation of the bases of Jewish life. The Jewish feminist writers represented in this volume have moved beyond criticizing specific traditions and institutions to recognize the marginality of Jewish women extending beyond the synagogue, Orthodoxy, tradition, and *halakhah*. The problem, as today's writers see it, runs throughout the course of Jewish history, penetrating the basic theological suppositions of Judaism: its imagery of women and men, its liturgy, its conceptions of the Jewish people and community, its understanding of God as Father and King. Woman as

Other is expressed, for instance, by Judaism's "purity" laws, in which women convey impurity not to themselves or to other women, but only to the men with whom they come into contact. Similarly, women enter into discussions in Judaism's law codes only as they affect men's lives; there exists no Talmudic tractate discussing the experiences of women's lives, how they are to be guided halakhically and interpreted religiously. In another example, women are placed behind a curtain in some synagogues, or denied *aliyot* and positions of leadership, not for any reasons concerning them, but because their visible presence might affect the concentration of men at prayer.

These issues, all concerning the authority and relevance of key aspects of Judaism, lie at the root of the feminist challenge. Here the question arises: if feminists do indeed bring about all the changes their critique implies, what will remain as recognizably Judaism? What criteria, what grounds of authority, will be used to retain some aspects of Judaism while rejecting or radically modifying others?

The implications of the feminist inquiry clearly involve more than the repair of particular laws or traditions, as suggested by Wohlgelernter and Poupko, or by Greenberg and Hauptman. The very bases of Judaism are being challenged—from *halakhah* to the prayer book to the very ways we conceive of God. The challenge emerging today demands a Copernican revolution: a new theology of Judaism, requiring new understandings of God, revelation, *halakhah*, and the Jewish people in order to support and encourage change....

Questions arose with the beginnings of modern Judaism, over two hundred years ago, regarding the place of *halakhah* in an age of individualism and decline in regard for rabbinic authority; the implications of history to an oral and written tradition held as timeless and immutable; the real nature of God in an era when our images and language are understood to be human projections. Feminism's challenge to *halakhah*, for example, is at bottom an extension of these earlier challenges to theology. If we view a tradition as having developed in a far different period and setting than ours, and as proclaiming values inimicable to ours, what authority can it claim over us? On the other hand, if we become the authority over the tradition, what relevance does it retain as God's commandment?

While theoretical questions still await resolution, the practical implications of modernity already display their impact. Before the modern era, when Jewish law and tradition encompassed all of life, even the most threatening of issues were taken on by the leadership, often with dramatic concessions resulting. Yet since the advent of modernity Jewish law has become increasingly rigid, ignoring the exigencies of life as it ceases to govern that life. One example is the dilemma of the *agunah*, the woman whose husband has deserted her without granting her a divorce—a problem more pressing when modern times bring increased mobility, freedom from rabbinic power, and the option of civil marriage. Yet despite the worsening situation, no solution has gained acceptance. A living legal system never has the luxury to ignore a serious conflict; it must respond in one way or another. Only when a legal system dies can problems be ignored or passed over.

The issue is not that feminism poses insoluble problems to Jewish law, but that Judaism has long ago died in the way it had existed for nearly two thousand years. The crisis has not been brought on by feminism, but feminism clearly discloses the morbid condition of Judaism that has continued, untreated, throughout the modern period.

Thus, from Judaism's perspective, the conflict emerges not so much from the particular agenda of feminism, but from the weakness of Jewish theological responses to modernity, which are thrown into relief by the challenge of feminism. In reality, a large part of the opposition to feminism arises from displaced concern over the impact of secularism. Attacks on feminist demands for changes in *halakhah* simply reveal the absence of a coherent position regarding the authority of Jewish law in an age of relativism. Claims that feminism violates Jewish principles and values reveal general confusion over what constitutes Judaism in today's context of pluralism and free choice.

Feminists, often unaware of the magnitude of the problem, have attempted to seek accommodation within one of the religious denominations of American Judaism—Orthodoxy, Conservatism, Reform, or Reconstructionism. In raising issues ranging from rabbinical ordination to divorce proceedings feminists have achieved greater or lesser degrees of success. Indeed, during the past decade, these denominations seem to have been occupied more with questions raised by the women's movement than with any other single issue.

Yet feminists may be misdirecting their efforts by attempting to remain within the frameworks of the denominations, whose confrontations with feminism raise the question whether these branches of Judaism have succeeded in their ostensible goal of meeting modernity's challenges. Modernity strikes not so much at the specifics of traditional theology, but at the general concept of theological absolutism. Yet these Jewish denominations have responded to modernity by substituting new dogmas for the older traditional ones. For Orthodoxy, the absolute core is *halakhah*, while Reform lays claim to a spirit or idea, and Conservatism and Reconstructionism adhere to an historical consciousness or civilization of the Jewish people.

Yet none of these approaches provides clear, normative criteria for implementing the changes called for by feminism. In fact, the

changes made by these denominations in response to particular feminist demands were made not by applying the central principles of each
movement. Whatever progress made during the past decade by feminists was not because of, but in spite of, the core ideas of each of the
movements. . . .

All the denominations are struggling to meet the challenges of the
modern world and to determine just what constitutes Judaism. They
fear that the changes feminists call for will be the final blow of modernity, shattering whatever links to tradition and history the denominations preserve to guarantee a Jewish future.

But this book argues the contrary. It is not feminism which poses
the threat to Judaism, but the denominations' own inability to come to
terms with the challenges posed by modernity; the threat lies in their
own inability to develop constructive theological positions which can
respond to modernity's challenges—including feminism. It is the weaknesses inherent in modern Jewish theology, and not feminism, that are
bringing about the impasse of today.

Also clear is that feminists cannot turn to one or more of the denominations in hope of developing a positive, constructive reconciliation with Judaism. Not only are such efforts naively optimistic about
the ability of the movements to cope with the changes demanded, but
they also function discretely, lacking their own coherent theological
positions.

Until now, feminists have concentrated on individual, isolated issues within Judaism, such as changing divorce laws or attaining leadership positions within Federation. Gradually a fuller picture is
emerging that shows the connections among these various issues. . . .
Older, biblical, rabbinic, and medieval images continue to thrive even
in secularized contexts. These images reveal not who women really
are, but how women are made to appear and function from a male-
dominated perspective. When opponents describe the sexual danger of
ordaining women as rabbis, for example, they cannot point to statistics
of women assaulting men in the synagogue. Rather, they unconsciously draw on ancient Jewish legends such as those describing the
mysterious, threatening power of Lilith, the mythical female demon. In
their struggle with contemporary discrimination, feminists are actually wrestling with these unspoken, hidden images which often keep the
community from making changes even when no rules forbid them. . . .

Clearly, there is a need for theological reinterpretations to transform women in Judaism from object to subject. For only theology can
offer the solution to the present problem, determining the role of rabbinic tradition in contemporary Judaism and its application to the
lives we lead. Theology must apply feminism's concern for women's

dignity and humanity in examining the meaning of religious symbols, traditions, and beliefs, and strive to give answers to humankind's ultimate questions.

Religious beliefs and observances have life cycles of their own. They may take different shapes, flourish, or wane. Some die because of their incredibility or irrelevance; others receive new life through reinterpretation. This process proves the vitality of a religious tradition, not its instability or impending demise. Theology establishes a relationship to Judaism as a whole, guiding this process of growth not simply by changing one or another particular points of *halakhah*, but by creating a framework for understanding larger questions of revelation, tradition, authority, and change. A feminist theology of Judaism must resonate with women's experience, must ground women's lives in a Jewish dimension. The outcome may be new or revised traditions, observances, and prayers. But above all, in the future when a woman looks to Judaism, she should not see only a reflection of the experiences of Jewish men.

In helping to create a new theology, women will become receivers and transmitters of Judaism, not onlookers. That shift can be illustrated through a parable by Franz Kafka, "Before the Law."[13] In Kafka's parable, a man from the country arrives at a door, seeking entry into the law, but the doorkeeper tells him that entry is impossible; a guard sits before each of many doors, and each guard is larger and fiercer than the one before. The man from the country sits down before the open door and remains there for years, until his death, begging and bribing the doorkeeper for permission to enter. Finally, as the man faces death, he asks why no one else has ever sought admission during the many years. The doorkeeper informs him that this door was intended solely for him—and then shuts it.

Although the doorkeeper forbids entry into the law to the man from the country, in reality he cannot prevent it. The man from the country fails to gain entry when he passively assumes that authorities are obstacles to the law, instead of taking the initiative and walking through the door himself. His error becomes twofold: first, he believes he can achieve his aim only through the guard and only if he begs and bribes him correctly, and, second, he blames his failure to gain entry on the doorkeeper, whose refusal to give help is seen as unfeeling and evil.

Many women in recent years have come seeking entry into Judaism. Some give up and eventually leave. Others plead and argue for admission, and are offered counterarguments, warnings, barriers, and a few ameliorating changes.

By assuming a posture like that of the man from the country, women continue their relation to Judaism as outsider or Other—even if they walk past the guards and through the doors. A profound error underlies this approach. Kafka's parable applies well to the situation of modern Judaism, which has built the doors of denominations, guarded by rabbis, institutions, and ideologies. But Judaism is not an edifice lying behind doors and guards and we should not have to go through a denomination to reach it. Rather, our relations should be with the diversity and totality of Jewish tradition, unmediated by one of its modern forms. There are no doors, there are no guards. Through theological exploration Judaism can belong to all who desire it.

Notes

1. Several biographies of Henrietta Szold have been published; not one explores her decision to attend the seminary or her academic interests. See Elma Ehrlich Levinger, *Fighting Angel: The Story of Henrietta Szold* (New York: Behrman House, 1946); Rose Zeitlin, *Henrietta Szold* (New York: Dial Press, 1952); Alexandra Lee Levin, *The Szolds of Lombard Street* (Philadelphia: Jewish Publication Society, 1960); Irving Fineman, *Woman of Valor: The Story of Henrietta Szold* (New York: Simon and Schuster, 1961); Joan Dash, *Summoned to Jerusalem: The Life of Henrietta Szold* (New York: Harper and Row, 1979).

2. Sondra Henry and Emily Taitz, *Written Out of History* (New York: Bloch Publishing Co., 1978) is a good general introduction, although it is based on secondary sources and so contains some inaccuracies.

3. The ban on polygamy is generally attributed to Rabbi Gershom ben Judah of Mainz, Germany (c. 960–1028). But Ze'ev Falk, in his study *Jewish Matrimonial Law in the Middle Ages* (London: Oxford University Press, 1966), pp. 14 and 18, argues that "Gershom did not himself proclaim the ban. . . . An examination of sources dating from the eleventh and twelfth centuries thus apprises us that monogamy found its way into French/German Jewry by slow degrees, and not as a result of a single legislative act."

4. Changes in the Jewish family in nineteenth-century Germany are discussed by Julius Carlebach, "Family Structure and the Position of Jewish Women," in *Revolution and Evolution: 1848 in German-Jewish History*, ed. Werner Mosse, Arnold Pauker, and Reinhard Rurup (Tubingen: J. C. B. Mohr, 1981). For discussion of the Jewish family in America during the late nineteenth and early twentieth centuries, see Charlotte Baum, Paula Hyman, and Sonya Michel, *The Jewish Woman in America* (New York: Dial Press, 1976).

5. Aviva Cantor, ed., *On the Jewish Woman: A Comparative and Annotated Listing of Works Published 1900–1979* (Fresh Meadows, N.Y.: Biblio Press, 1979); Ora Hamelsdorf and Sandra Adelsberg, *Jewish Woman and Jewish Law: Bibliography* (Fresh Meadows, N.Y.: Biblio Press, 1980).

6. Ruth Wisse, "Women as Conservative Rabbis?" *Commentary*, vol. 68, no. 4 (October 1979), pp. 63–64.

7. Mortimer Ostow, "Women and Change in Jewish Law," *Conservative Judaism*, vol. 29, no. 1 (Fall 1974), p. 6.

8. Ostow, p. 11.

9. Ostow, p. 11.

10. Lucy Dawidowicz, *The Jewish Presence: Essays in Identity and History* (New York: Holt, Rinehart, and Winston, 1977), pp. 52–53.

11. Judith Hauptman, "Images of Women in the Talmud," in *Religion and Sexism*, ed. Rosemary Ruether (New York: Simon and Schuster, 1974), pp. 184–212.

12. Blu Greenberg, *Women and Judaism: A View from Tradition* (Philadelphia: Jewish Publication Society, 1982).

13. Franz Kafka, "Before the Law," *Parables and Paradoxes*, trans. Willa and Edwin Muir (New York: Schocken Books, 1946), pp. 61–80.

28

Why Women Need the Goddess

Phenomenological, Psychological, and Political Reflections

Carol P. Christ

At the close of Ntosake Shange's stupendously successful Broadway play *For Colored Girls Who Have Considered Suicide When the Rainbow Is Enuf*, a tall beautiful black woman rises from despair to cry out, "I found God in myself and I loved her fiercely."[1] Her discovery is echoed by women around the country who meet spontaneously in small groups on full moons, solstices, and equinoxes to celebrate the Goddess as symbol of life and death powers and waxing and waning energies in the universe and in themselves.[2]

> It is the night of the full moon. Nine women stand in a circle, on a rocky hill above the city. The western sky is rosy with the setting sun; in the east the moon's face begins to peer above the horizon. . . . The woman pours out a cup of wine onto the earth, refills it and raises it high. "Hail, Tana, Mother of mothers!" she cries. "Awaken from your long sleep, and return to your children again."[3]

What are the political and psychological effects of this fierce new love of the divine in themselves for women whose spiritual experience has

"Why Women Need the Goddess" from *Womanspirit Rising: A Feminist Reader in Religion* by Carol P. Christ and Judith Plaskow. Copyright © 1979 by Carol P. Christ and Judith Plaskow. Reprinted by permission of Harper & Row, Publishers, Inc.

been focused by the male God of Judaism and Christianity? Is the spiritual dimension of feminism a passing diversion, an escape from difficult but necessary political work? Or does the emergence of the symbol of Goddess among women have significant political and psychological ramifications for the feminist movement?

To answer this question, we must first understand the importance of religious symbols and rituals in human life and consider the effect of male symbolism of God on women. According to anthropologist Clifford Geertz, religious symbols shape a cultural ethos, defining the deepest values of a society and the persons in it. "Religion," Geertz writes, "is a system of symbols which act to produce powerful, pervasive, and long-lasting moods and motivations"[4] in the people of a given culture. A "mood" for Geertz is a psychological attitude such as awe, trust, and respect, while a "motivation" is the *social* and *political* trajectory created by a mood that transforms mythos into ethos, symbol system into social and political reality. Symbols have both psychological and political effects, because they create the inner conditions (deep-seated attitudes and feelings) that lead people to feel comfortable with or to accept social and political arrangements that correspond to the symbol system.

Because religion has such a compelling hold on the deep psyches of so many people, feminists cannot afford to leave it in the hands of the fathers. Even people who no longer "believe in God" or participate in the institutional structure of patriarchal religion still may not be free of the power of the symbolism of God the Father. A symbol's effect does not depend on rational assent, for a symbol also functions on levels of the psyche other than the rational. Religion fulfills deep psychic needs by providing symbols and rituals that enable people to cope with limit situations[5] in human life (death, evil, suffering) and to pass through life's important transitions (birth, sexuality, death). Even people who consider themselves completely secularized will often find themselves sitting in a church or synagogue when a friend or relative gets married, or when a parent or friend has died. The symbols associated with these important rituals cannot fail to affect the deep or unconscious structures of the mind of even a person who has rejected these symbolisms on a conscious level—especially if the person is under stress. The reason for the continuing effect of religious symbols is that the mind abhors a vacuum. Symbol systems cannot simply be rejected, they must be replaced. Where there is not any replacement, the mind will revert to familiar structures at times of crisis, bafflement, or defeat.

Religions centered on the worship of a male God create "moods" and "motivations" that keep women in a state of psychological dependence on men and male authority, while at the same time legitimating the *political* and *social* authority of fathers and sons in the institutions of society.

Religious symbol systems focused around exclusively male images of divinity create the impression that female power can never be fully legitimate or wholly beneficent. This message need never be explicitly stated (as, for example, it is in the story of Eve) for its effect to be felt. A woman completely ignorant of the myths of female evil in biblical religion nonetheless acknowledges the anomaly of female power when she prays exclusively to a male God. She may see herself as like God (created in the image of God) only by denying her own sexual identity and affirming God's transcendence of sexual identity. But she can never have the experience that is freely available to every man and boy in her culture, of having her full sexual identity affirmed as being in the image and likeness of God. In Geertz' terms, her "mood" is one of trust in male power as salvific and distrust of female power in herself and other women as inferior or dangerous. Such a powerful, pervasive, and long-lasting "mood" cannot fail to become a "motivation" that translates into social and political reality.

In *Beyond God the Father*, feminist theologian Mary Daly detailed the psychological and political ramifications of father religion for women. "If God in 'his' heaven is a father ruling his people," she wrote, "then it is the 'nature' of things and according to divine plan and the order of the universe that society be male dominated. Within this context, a *mystification of roles* takes place. The husband dominating his wife represents God 'himself.' The images and values of a given society have been projected into the realm of dogmas and 'Articles of Faith,' and these in turn justify the social structures which have given rise to them and which sustain their plausibility."[6]

Philosopher Simone de Beauvoir was well aware of the function of patriarchal religion as legitimater of male power. As she wrote, "Man enjoys the great advantage of having a god endorse the code he writes; and since man exercises a sovereign authority over women it is especially fortunate that this authority has been vested in him by the Supreme Being. For the Jews, Mohammedans, and Christians, among others, man is Master by divine right; the fear of God will therefore repress any impulse to revolt in the downtrodden female."[7]

This brief discussion of the psychological and political effects of God religion puts us in an excellent position to begin to understand the significance of the symbol of Goddess for women. In discussing the meaning of the Goddess, my method will first be phenomenological. I will isolate a meaning of the symbol of the Goddess as it has emerged in the lives of contemporary women. I will then discuss its psychological and political significance by contrasting the "moods" and "motivations" engendered by Goddess symbols with those engendered by

Christian symbolism. I will also correlate Goddess symbolism with themes that have emerged in the women's movement, in order to show how Goddess symbolism undergirds and legitimates the concerns of the women's movement, much as God symbolism in Christianity undergirded the interests of men in patriarchy. I will discuss four aspects of Goddess symbolism here: the Goddess as affirmation of female power, the female body, the female will, and women's bonds and heritage. There are, of course, many other meanings of the Goddess that I will not discuss here.

The sources for the symbol of the Goddess in contemporary spirituality are traditions of Goddess worship and modern women's experience. The ancient Mediterranean, pre-Christian European, native American, Mesoamerican, Hindu, African, and other traditions are rich sources for Goddess symbolism. But these traditions are filtered through modern women's experiences. Traditions of Goddesses', subordination to Gods, for example, are ignored. Ancient traditions are tapped selectively and eclectically, but they are not considered authoritative for modern consciousness. The Goddess symbol has emerged spontaneously in the dreams, fantasies, and thoughts of many women around the country in the past several years. Kirsten Grimstad and Susan Rennie reported that they were surprised to discover widespread interest in spirituality, including the Goddess, among feminists around the country in the summer of 1974.[8] *WomanSpirit* magazine, which published its first issue in 1974 and has contributors from across the United States, has expressed the grass roots nature of the women's spirituality movement. In 1976, a journal, *Lady Unique*, devoted to the Goddess emerged. In 1975, the first women's spirituality conference was held in Boston and attended by 1,800 women. In 1978, a University of Santa Cruz course on the Goddess drew over 500 people. Sources for this essay are these manifestations of the Goddess in modern women's experiences as reported in *WomanSpirit, Lady Unique*, and elsewhere, and as expressed in conversations I have had with women who have been thinking about the Goddess and women's spirituality.

The simplest and most basic meaning of the symbol of Goddess is the acknowledgement of the legitimacy of female power as a beneficent and independent power. A woman who echoes Ntosake Shange's dramatic statement, "I found God in myself and I loved her fiercely," is saying "Female power is strong and creative." She is saying that the divine principle, the saving and sustaining power, is in herself, that she will no longer look to men or male figures as saviors. The strength and independence of female power can be intuited by contemplating ancient and modern images of the Goddess. This meaning of the symbol of Goddess is simple and obvious, and yet it is difficult for many to comprehend. It stands in sharp contrast to the paradigms of female de-

pendence on males that have been predominant in Western religion
and culture. The internationally acclaimed novelist Monique Wittig
captured the novelty and flavor of the affirmation of female power
when she wrote, in her mythic work *Les Guérillères,*

> There was a time when you were not a slave, remember that. You walked
> alone, full of laughter, you bathed bare-bellied. You say you have lost all
> recollection of it, remember . . . you say there are not words to describe it,
> you say it does not exist. But remember. Make an effort to remember. Or,
> failing that, invent.[9]

While Wittig does not speak directly of the Goddess here, she captures
the "mood" of joyous celebration of female freedom and independence
that is created in women who define their identities through the symbol of Goddess. Artist Mary Beth Edelson expressed the political "motivations" inspired by the Goddess when she wrote,

> The ascending archetypal symbols of the feminine unfold today in the
> psyche of modern Every woman. They encompass the multiple forms of
> the Great Goddess. Reaching across the centuries we take the hands of
> our Ancient Sisters. The Great Goddess alive and well is rising to an-
> nounce to the patriarchs that their 5,000 years are up—Hallelujah! Here
> we come.[10]

The affirmation of female power contained in the Goddess symbol has
both psychological and political consequences. Psychologically, it
means the defeat of the view engendered by patriarchy that women's
power is inferior and dangerous. This new "mood" of affirmation of female power also leads to new "motivations"; it supports and undergirds women's trust in their own power and the power of other
women in family and society.

If the simplest meaning of the Goddess symbol is an affirmation of
the legitimacy and beneficence of female power, then a question immediately arises, "Is the Goddess simply female power writ large, and
if so, why bother with the symbol of Goddess at all? Or does the symbol
refer to a Goddess 'out there' who is not reducible to a human potential?" The many women who have rediscovered the power of Goddess
would give three answers to this question: (1) The Goddess is divine female, a personification who can be invoked in prayer and ritual; (2) the
Goddess is symbol of the life, death, and rebirth energy in nature and
culture, in personal and communal life and (3) the Goddess is symbol
of the affirmation of the legitimacy and beauty of female power (made
possible by the new becoming of women in the women's liberation
movement). If one were to ask these women which answer is the "correct" one, different responses would be given. Some would assert that
the Goddess definitely is *not* "out there," that the symbol of a divinity
"out there" is part of the legacy of patriarchal oppression, which

brings with it the authoritarianism, hierarchicalism, and dogmatic ri-
gidity associated with biblical monotheistic religions. They might assert that the Goddess symbol reflects the sacred power within women
and nature, suggesting the connectedness between women's cycles of
menstruation, birth, and menopause and the life and death cycles of
the universe. Others seem quite comfortable with the notion of Goddess as a divine female protector and creator and would find their experience of Goddess limited by the assertion that she is not *also* out
there as well as within themselves and in all natural processes. When
asked what the symbol of Goddess means, feminist priestess Starhawk
replied, "It all depends on how I feel. When I feel weak, she is someone
who can help and protect me. When I feel strong, she is the symbol of
my own power. At other times I feel her as the natural energy in my
body and the world."[11] How are we to evaluate such a statement? Theologians might call these the words of a sloppy thinker. But my deepest
intuition tells me they contain a wisdom that Western theological
thought has lost.

To theologians, these differing views of the "meaning" of the symbol of Goddess might seem to threaten a reply of the trinitarian controversies. Is there, perhaps, a way of doing theology which would not
lead immediately into dogmatic controversy, which would not require
theologians to say definitively that one understanding is true and the
others are false? Could people's relation to a common symbol be made
primary and varying interpretations be acknowledged? The diversity
of explications of the meaning of the Goddess symbol suggests that
symbols have a richer significance than any explications of their meaning can express, a point literary critics have long insisted on. This phenomenological fact suggests that theologians may need to give more
than lip service to a theory of symbol in which the symbol is viewed as
the primary fact and the meanings are viewed as secondary. It also
suggests that a *thea*logy[12] of the Goddess would be very different from
the *theo*logy we have known in the West. But to spell out this notion of
the primacy of *symbol* in thealogy in contrast to the primacy of the *explanation* in theology would be the topic of another paper. Let me simply state that women, who have been deprived of a female religious
symbol system for centuries, are therefore in an excellent position to
recognize the power and primacy of symbols. I believe women must develop a theory of symbol and thealogy congruent with their experience
at the same time as they "remember and invent" new symbol systems.

A second important implication of the Goddess symbol for women
is the affirmation of the female body and the life cycle expressed in it.
Because of women's unique position as menstruants, birthgivers, and
those who have traditionally cared for the young and the dying, wom-
en's connection to the body, nature, and this world has been obvious.
Women were denigrated because they seemed more carnal, fleshy, and

earthy than the culture-creating males.[13] The misogynist anti*body* tradition in Western though is symbolized in the myth of Eve who is traditionally viewed as a sexual temptress, the epitome of women's carnal nature. This tradition reaches its nadir in the *Malleus Maleficarum (The Hammer of Evil-Doing Women)*, which states, "All witchcraft stems from carnal lust, which in women is insatiable."[14] The Virgin Mary, the positive female image in Christianity, does not contradict Christian denigration of the female body and its powers. The Virgin Mary is revered because she, in her perpetual virginity, transcends the carnal sexuality attributed to most women.

The denigration of the female body is expressed in cultural and religious taboos surrounding menstruation, childbirth, and menopause in women. While menstruation taboos may have originated in a perception of the awesome powers of the female body,[15] they degenerated into a simple perception that there is something "wrong" with female bodily functions. Menstruating women were forbidden to enter the sanctuary in ancient Hebrew and premodern Christian communities. Although only Orthodox Jews still enforce religious taboos against menstruant women, few women in our culture grow up affirming their menstruation as a connection to sacred power. Most women learn that menstruation is a curse and grow up believing that the bloody facts of menstruation are best hidden away. Feminists challenge this attitude to the female body. Judy Chicago's art piece "Menstruation Bathroom" broke these menstrual taboos. In a sterile white bathroom, she exhibited boxes of Tampax and Kotex on an open shelf, and the wastepaper basket was overflowing with bloody tampons and sanitary napkins.[16] Many women who viewed the piece felt relieved to have their "dirty secret" out in the open.

The denigration of the female body and its powers is further expressed in Western culture's attitudes toward childbirth.[17] Religious iconography does not celebrate the birthgiver, and there is no theology or ritual that enables a woman to celebrate the process of birth as a spiritual experience. Indeed, Jewish and Christian traditions also had blood taboos concerning the woman who had recently given birth. While these religious taboos are rarely enforced today (again, only by Orthodox Jews), they have secular equivalents. Giving birth is treated as a disease requiring hospitalization, and the woman is viewed as a passive object, anesthetized to ensure her acquiescence to the will of the doctor. The women's liberation movement has challenged these cultural attitudes, and many feminists have joined with advocates of natural childbirth and home birth in emphasizing the need for women to control and take pride in their bodies, including the birth process.

Western culture also give little dignity to the postmenopausal or aging woman. It is no secret that our culture is based on a denial of aging and death, and that women suffer more severely from this denial than men. Women are placed on a pedestal and considered powerful when they are young and beautiful, but they are said to lose this power as they age. As feminists have pointed out, the "power" of the young woman is illusory, since beauty standards are defined by men, and since few women are considered (or consider themselves) beautiful for more than a few years of their lives. Some men are viewed as wise and authoritative in age, but old women are pitied and shunned. Religious iconography supports this cultural attitude towards aging women. The purity and virginity of Mary and the female saints is often expressed in the iconographic convention of perpetual youth. Moreover, religious mythology associates aging women with evil in the symbol of the wicked old witch. Feminists have challenged cultural myths of aging women and have urged women to reject patriarchal beauty standards and to celebrate the distinctive beauty of women of all ages.

The symbol of Goddess aids the process of naming and reclaiming the female body and its cycles and processes. In the ancient world and among modern women, the Goddess symbol represents the birth, death, and rebirth processes of the natural and human worlds. The female body is viewed as the direct incarnation of waxing and waning, life and death, cycles in the universe. This is sometimes expressed through the symbolic connection between the twenty-eight-day cycles of menstruation and the twenty-eight-day cycles of the moon. Moreover, the Goddess is celebrated in the triple aspect of youth, maturity, and age, or maiden, mother, and crone. The potentiality of the young girl is celebrated in the nymph or maiden aspect of the Goddess. The Goddess as mother is sometimes depicted giving birth, and giving birth is viewed as a symbol for all the creative, life-giving powers of the universe.[18] The life-giving powers of the Goddess in her creative aspect are not limited to physical birth, for the Goddess is also seen as the creator of all the arts of civilization, including healing, writing, and the giving of just law. Women in the middle of life who are not physical mothers may give birth to poems, songs, and books, or nurture other women, men, and children. They too are incarnations of the Goddess in her creative, life-giving aspect. At the end of life, women incarnate the crone aspect of the Goddess. The wise old woman, the woman who knows from experience what life is about, the woman whose closeness to her own death gives her a distance and perspective on the problems of life, is celebrated as the third aspect of the Goddess. Thus, women learn to value youth, creativity, and wisdom in themselves and other women.

The possibilities of reclaiming the female body and its cycles have been expressed in a number of Goddess-centered rituals. Hallie Mountainwing and Barby My Own created a summer solstice ritual to celebrate menstruation and birth. The women simulated a birth canal and birthed each other into their circle. They raised power by placing their hands on each other's bellies and chanting together. Finally they marked each other's faces with rich, dark menstrual blood saying, "This is the blood that promises renewal. This is the blood that promises sustenance. This is the blood that promises life."[19] From hidden dirty secret to symbol of the life power of the Goddess, women's blood has come full circle. Other women have created rituals that celebrate the crone aspect of the Goddess. Z. Budapest believes that the crone aspect of the Goddess is predominant in the fall, especially at Halloween, an ancient holiday. On this day, the wisdom of the old woman is celebrated, and it is also recognized that the old must die so that the new can be born.[19a]

The "mood" created by the symbol of the Goddess in triple aspect is one of positive, joyful affirmation of the female body and its cycles and acceptance of aging and death as well as life. The "motivations" are to overcome menstrual taboos, to return the birth process to the hands of women, and to change cultural attitudes about age and death. Changing cultural attitudes toward the female body could go a long way toward overcoming the spirit-flesh, mind-body dualisms of Western culture, since, as Ruether has pointed out, the denigration of the female body is at the heart of these dualisms. The Goddess as symbol of the revaluation of the body and nature thus also undergirds the human potential and ecology movements. The "mood" is one of affirmation, awe, and respect for the body and nature, and the "motivation" is to respect the teachings of the body and the rights of all living beings.

A third important implication of the Goddess symbol for women is the positive valuation of will in a Goddess-centered ritual, especially in Goddess-centered ritual magic and spellcasting in womanspirit and feminist witchcraft circles. The basic notion behind ritual magic and spellcasting is energy as power. Here the Goddess is a center or focus of power and energy; she is the personification of the energy that flows between beings in the natural and human worlds. In Goddess circles, energy is raised by chanting or dancing. According to Starhawk, "Witches conceive of psychic energy as having form and substance that can be perceived and directed by those with a trained awareness. The power generated within the circle is built into a cone form, and at its peak is released—to the Goddess, to reenergize the members of the coven, or to do a specific work such as healing."[20] In ritual magic, the energy raised is directed by willpower. Women who celebrate in Goddess circles believe they can achieve their wills in the world.

The emphasis on the will is important for women, because women traditionally have been taught to devalue their wills, to believe that they cannot achieve their will through their own power, and even to suspect that the assertion of will is evil. Faith Wildung's poem "Waiting," from which I will quote only a short segment, sums up women's sense that their lives are defined not by their own will, but by waiting for others to take the initiative.

> *Waiting for my breasts to develop*
> *Waiting to wear a bra*
> *Waiting to menstruate*
>
> . . .
> *Waiting for life to begin, Waiting—*
> *Waiting to be somebody*
>
> . . .
> *Waiting to get married*
> *Waiting for my wedding day*
> *Waiting for my wedding night*
>
> . . .
> *Waiting for the end of day*
> *Waiting for sleep. Waiting . . .*[21]

Patriarchal religion has enforced the view that female initiative and will are evil through the juxtaposition of Eve and Mary. Eve caused the fall by asserting her will against the command of God, while Mary began the new age with her response to God's initiative, "Let it be done to me according to thy word" (Luke 1:38). Even for men, patriarchal religion values the passive will subordinate to divine initiative. The classical doctrines of sin and grace view sin as the prideful assertion of will and grace as the obedient subordination of the human will to the divine initiative or order. While this view of will might be questioned from a human perspective, Valerie Saiving has argued that it has particularly deleterious consequences for women in Western culture. According to Saiving, Western culture encourages males in the assertion of will, and thus it may make some sense to view the male form of sin as an excess of will. But since culture discourages females in the assertion of will, the traditional doctrines of sin and grace encourage women to remain in their form of sin, which is self-negation or insufficient assertion of will.[22] One possible reason the will is denigrated in a patriarchal religious framework is that both human and divine will are often pictured as arbitrary, self-initiated, and exercised without regard for other wills.

In a Goddess-centered context, in contrast, the will is valued. *A woman is encouraged to know her will, to believe that her will is valid, and to believe that her will can be achieved in the world*, three powers traditionally denied to her in patriarchy. In a Goddess-centered framework, a woman's will is not subordinated to the Lord God as king and ruler, nor to men as his representatives. Thus a woman is not reduced to waiting and acquiescing in the wills of others as she is in patriarchy. But neither does she adopt the egocentric form of will that pursues self-interest without regard for the interests of others.

The Goddess-centered context provides a different understanding of the will than that available in the traditional patriarchal religious framework. In the Goddess framework, will can be achieved only when it is exercised in harmony with the energies and wills of other beings. Wise women, for example, raise a cone of healing energy at the full moon or solstice when the lunar or solar energies are at their high points with respect to the earth. This discipline encourages them to recognize that not all times are propitious for the achieving of every will. Similarly, they know that spring is a time for new beginnings in work and love, summer a time for producing external manifestations of inner potentialities, and fall or winter times for stripping down to the inner core and extending roots. Such awareness of waxing and waning processes in the universe discourages arbitrary ego-centered assertion of will, while at the same time encouraging the assertion of individual will in cooperation with natural energies and the energies created by the wills of others. Wise women also have a tradition that whatever is sent out will be returned and this reminds them to assert their wills in cooperative and healing rather than egocentric and destructive ways. This view of will allows women to begin to recognize, claim, and assert their wills without adopting the worst characteristics of the patriarchal understanding and use of will. In the Goddess-centered framework, the "mood" is one of positive affirmation of personal will in the context of the energies of other wills or beings. The "motivation" is for women to know and assert their wills in cooperation with other wills and energies. This of course does not mean that women always assert their wills in positive and life-affirming ways. Women's capacity for evil is, of course, as great as men's. My purpose is simply to contrast the differing attitudes toward the exercise of will *per se*, and the female will in particular, in Goddess-centered religion and in the Christian God-centered religion.

The fourth and final aspect of Goddess symbolism that I will discuss here is the significance of the Goddess for a revaluation of woman's bonds and heritage. As Virginia Woolf has said, "Chloe liked Olivia," a statement about a woman's relation to another woman, is a sentence that rarely occurs in fiction. Men have written the stories, and they have written about women almost exclusively in their relations to men.[23] The celebrations of women's bonds to each other, as mothers and daughters, as colleagues and coworkers, as sisters, friends, and lovers, is beginning to occur in the new literature and culture created by women in the women's movement. While I believe that the revaluing of each of these bonds is important, I will focus on the mother-daughter bond, in part because I believe it may be the key to the others.

Adrienne Rich has pointed out that the mother-daughter bond, perhaps the most important of woman's bonds, "resonant with charges ... the flow of energy between two biologically alike bodies, one of which has lain in amniotic bliss inside the other, one of which has labored to give birth to the other,"[24] is rarely celebrated in partriarchal religion and culture. Christianity celebrates the father's relation to the son and the mother's relation to the son, but the story of mother and daughter is missing. So, too, in patriarchal literature and psychology the mothers and the daughters rarely exist. Volumes have been written about the oedipal complex, but little has been written about the girl's relation to her mother. Moreover, as de Beauvoir has noted, the mother-daughter relation is distorted in patriarchy because the mother must give her daughter over to men in a male-defined culture in which women are viewed as inferior. The mother must socialize her daughter to become subordinate to men, and if her daughter challenges patriarchal norms, the mother is likely to defend the patriarchal structures against her own daughter.[25]

These patterns are changing in the new culture created by women in which the bonds of women to women are beginning to be celebrated. Holly Near has written several songs that celebrate women's bonds and women's heritage. In one of her finest songs she writes of an "old-time woman" who is "waiting to die." A young woman feels for the life that has passed the old woman by and begins to cry, but the old woman looks her in the eye and says, "If I had not suffered, you wouldn't be wearing those jeans/Being an old-time woman ain't as bad as it seems."[26] This song, which Near has said was inspired by her grandmother, expresses and celebrates a bond and a heritage passed down from one woman to another. In another of Near's songs, she sings of a "hiking-boot mother who's seeing the world/For the first time with her own little girl." In this song, the mother tells the drifter who has been traveling with her to pack up and travel alone if he thinks "traveling three is a drag" because "I've got a little one who loves me as much as you need me/And darling, that's loving enough."[27] This song is significant because the mother places her relationship to her daughter above her relationship to a man, something women rarely do in patriarchy.[28]

Almost the only story of mothers and daughters that has been transmitted in Western culture is the myth of Demeter and Persephone that was the basis of religious rites celebrated by women only, the Thesmophoria, and later formed the basis of the Eleusian mysteries, which were open to all who spoke Greek. In this story, the daughter, Persephone, is raped away from her mother, Demeter, by the God of the underworld. Unwilling to accept this state of affairs, Demeter rages and withholds fertility from the earth until her daughter is returned to her. What is important for women in this story is that a mother fights for her daughter and for her relation to her daughter. This is completely different from the mother's relation to her daughter in patriarchy. The "mood" created by the story of Demeter and Persephone is one of celebration of the mother-daughter bond, and the "motivation" is for mothers and daughters to affirm the heritage passed on from mother to daughter and to reject the patriarchal pattern where the primary loyalties of mother and daughter must be to men.

The symbol of Goddess has much to offer women who are struggling to be rid of the "powerful, pervasive, and long-lasting moods and motivations" of devaluation of female power, denigration of the female body, distrust of female will, and denial of the women's bonds and heritage that have been engendered by patriarchal religion. As women struggle to create a new culture in which women's power, bodies, will, and bonds are celebrated, it seems natural that the Goddess would reemerge as symbol of the newfound beauty, strength, and power of women.

Notes

1. From the original cast album, Buddah Records, 1976.
2. See Susan Rennie and Kristen Grimstad, "Spiritual Explorations Cross-Country," *Quest*, 1975, *I* (4), 1975, 49–51; and *WomanSpirit* magazine.
3. See Starhawk, "Witchcraft and Women's Culture," in Carol P. Christ and Judith Plaskow, eds., *WomanSpirit Rising: A Feminist Reader in Religion* (San Francisco: Harper & Row, 1979).
4. "Religion as a Cultural System," in William L. Lessa and Evon V. Vogt, eds., *Reader in Comparative Religion*, 2nd ed. (New York: Harper & Row, 1972), p. 206.
5. Geertz, p. 210.
6. Boston: Beacon Press, 1974, p. 13, italics added.
7. *The Second Sex*, trans. H. M. Parshleys (New York: Alfred A. Knopf, 1953).
8. See Grimstad and Rennie.
9. *Les Guérillères*, trans. David LeVay (New York: Avon Books, 1971), p. 89. Also quoted in Morgan MacFarland, "Witchcraft: The Art of Remembering," *Quest*, 1975, *I* (4), 41.
10. "Speaking for Myself," *Lady Unique*, 1976, *I*, 56.
11. Personal communication.
12. A term coined by Naomi Goldenberg to refer to reflection on the meaning of the symbol of Goddess.

13. This theory of the origins of the Western dualism is stated by Rosemary Ruether in *New Woman: New Earth* (New York: Seabury Press, 1975), and elsewhere.

14. Heinrich Kramer and Jacob Sprenger (New York: Dover, 1971), p. 47.

15. See Rita M. Gross, "Menstruation and Childbirth as Ritual and Religious Experience in the Religion of the Australian Aborigines," in *The Journal of the American Academy of Religion*, 1977, *45* (4), Supplement 1147–1181.

16. *Through the Flower* (New York: Doubleday & Company, 1975), plate 4, pp. 106–107.

17. See Adrienne Rich, *Of Woman Born* (New York: Bantam Books, 1977), chaps. 6 and 7.

18. See James Mellaart, *Earliest Civilizations of the Near East* (New York: McGraw-Hill, 1965), p. 92.

19. Barby My Own, "Ursa Maior: Menstrual Moon Celebration" in Anne Kent Rush, ed. *Moon, Moon* (Berkeley, Calif., and New York: Moon Books and Random House, 1976), pp. 374–387.

19a. In Georia Kaufman's videotape, "Women, Ritual, and Religion," 1977.

20. Starhawk, op. cit.

21. In Judy Chicago, pp. 213–217.

22. "The Human Situation: A Feminine View," in *Journal of Religion*, 1960, *40*, 100–112, and reprinted in Christ and Plaskow, ed., op. cit.

23. *A Room of One's Own* (New York: Harcourt Brace Jovanovich, 1928), p. 86.

24. Rich, p. 226.

25. De Beauvoir, pp. 448–449.

26. "Old Time Woman," lyrics by Jeffrey Langley and Holly Near, from *Holly Near: A Live Album*, Redwood Records, 1974.

27. "Started Out Fine," by Holly Near from *Holly Near: A Live Album*.

28. Rich, p. 223.

29

Black Women and the Church

Jacquelyn Grant

It is often said that women are the "backbone" of the church. On the surface, this may appear to be a compliment, considering the function of the backbone in the human anatomy. Theresa Hoover prefers to use the word "glue" to describe the function of women in the Black church. In any case, the telling portion of the word "backbone" is "back." It has become apparent to me that most of the ministers who use this term are referring to location rather than function. What they really mean is that women are in the "background" and should be kept there: they are merely support workers. This is borne out by my observation that in many churches women are consistently given responsibilities in the kitchen, while men are elected or appointed to the important boards and leadership positions. While decisions and policies may be discussed in the kitchen, they are certainly not made there.

A study I conducted recently in one conference of the African Methodist Episcopal Church indicated that women are accorded

Chapter 14 in *All the Women Are White, All the Blacks Are Men, But Some of Us Are Brave: Black Women's Studies* edited by Gloria T. Hull, Patricia Bell Scott, and Barbara Smith. Reprinted by permission of Orbis Books and the author.

greater participation on the decision-making boards of smaller rather
than larger churches.[1] This political maneuver helps to keep women
"in their place" in the denomination as well as in the local congregations. The conspiracy to keep women relegated to the background is
also aided by the continuous psychological and political strategizing
that keeps women from realizing their own potential power in the
church. Not only are they rewarded for performance in "backbone" or
supportive positions, but they are penalized for trying to move from
the backbone to the head position—the leadership of the church. It is
by considering the distinction between prescribed support positions
and policymaking leadership positions that the oppression of Black
women in the Black church can be seen most clearly.

For the most part, men have monopolized the ministry as a profession. The ministry of women as fully ordained clergypersons has always been controversial. The Black church fathers were unable to see
the injustices of their own practices, even when they paralleled the injustices of the white church against which they rebelled.

In the early nineteenth century, Rev. Richard Allen perceived that
it was unjust for Blacks, whether free or slaves, to be relegated to the
balcony and restricted to a special time to pray and kneel at the com-
munion table. Yet because of his acceptance of the patriarchal system,
Allen was unable to see the injustice in relegating women to one area of
the church—the pews—by withholding ordination from women as he
did in the case of Mrs. Jarena Lee.[2] Lee recorded Allen's response when
she informed him of her call to "go preach the Gospel":

> He replied by asking in what sphere I wished to move? I said, among the
> Methodists. He then replied, that a Mrs. Cook, a methodist lady, had also
> some time before requested the same privilege; who, it was believed, had
> done much good in the way of *exhortation*, and *holding prayer meetings*:
> and who had been permitted to do so by the *verbal license* of the preacher
> in charge at the time. But as to women preaching, he said that our Disci-
> pline knew nothing at all about it—that *it did not call* for women
> preachers.[3]

Because of this response, Jarena Lee's preaching ministry was delayed
for eight years. She was not unaware of the sexist injustice in Allen's
response:

> Oh how careful ought we be, lest through our by-laws of church govern-
> ment and discipline, we bring into disrepute even the word of life. For as
> unseemly as it may appear nowadays for a woman to preach, it should be
> remembered that nothing is impossible with God. And why should it be
> thought impossible, heterodox, or improper for a woman to preach, see-
> ing the Savior died for the woman as well as the man?[4]

Another "colored minister of the gospel," "Elizabeth," was greatly troubled over her call to preach, or, more accurately, over the response of men to her call to preach. She said:

> I often felt that I was unfit to assemble with the congregation with whom I had gathered. . . . I felt that I was despised on account of this gracious calling, and was looked upon as a speckled bird by the ministers to whom I looked for instruction . . . some [of the ministers] would cry out, "You are an enthusiast," and others said, "The Discipline did not allow of any such division of the work."[5]

When questioned some time later about her authority to preach against slavery and about her ordination status, she responded that she preached "not by the commission of men's hands: if the Lord had ordained me, I needed nothing better."[6] With this commitment to God rather than to a male-dominated church structure, she led a fruitful ministry.

Mrs. Amanda Berry Smith, like Mrs. Jarena Lee, had to conduct her ministry outside the structure of the A.M.E. Church. Smith described herself as a "plain Christian woman" with "no money" and "no prominence."[7] But she was intrigued with the idea of attending the General Conference of 1872 in Nashville, Tennessee. Her inquiry into the cost of going to Nashville brought the following comments from some of the A.M.E. brethren:

> "I tell you, Sister, it will cost money to go down there; and if you ain't got plenty of it, it's no use to go"; . . . another said: "What does she want to go for?" "Woman preacher; they want to be ordained," was the reply. "I mean to fight that thing," said the other. "Yes, indeed, so will I," said another.[8]

The oppression of women in the ministry took many forms. In addition to their not being granted ordination, the authenticity of "the call" of women was frequently put to the test. Lee, Elizabeth, and Smith spoke of the many souls they had brought to Christ through their preaching and singing in local Black congregations, as well as in white and mixed congregations. It was not until Rev. Allen, now Bishop Richard Allen, heard Jarena Lee preach that he was convinced that she was of the Spirit. He still refused, however, to ordain her. The "brethren," including some bishops of the 1872 General Conference of the A.M.E. Church, were convinced that Amanda Berry Smith was blessed with the spirit of God after hearing her sing at a session held at Fisk University. Smith tells us that "the Spirit of the Lord seemed to fall on all the people. The preachers got happy. . . ." This experience brought invitations for her to preach at several churches, but it did not bring an appointment as pastor to a local congregation, nor the right of ordination. She summed up the experience in this way: "After that many of my brethren believed in me, especially as the question of ordination of women never was mooted in the Conference."[9]

Several Black denominations have since begun to ordain women.[10] But this matter of women preachers having the extra burden of proving their call to an extent not required of men still prevails in the Black church today. A study in which I participated at Union Theological Seminary in New York City bears this out. Interviews with Black ministers of different denominations revealed that their prejudices against women, and especially women in the ministry, resulted in unfair expectations and unjust treatment of women ministers whom they encountered.[11]

It is the unfair expectations placed upon women and blatant discrimination that keep them "in the pew" and "out of the pulpit"— sometimes to ridiculous extremes. At the 1971 Annual Convocation of the National Committee of Black Churchmen,[12] held at the Liberty Baptist Church in Chicago, I was slightly amused when, as I approached the pulpit to place my cassette tape recorder near the speaker, Walter Fauntroy, as several brothers had already done, I was stopped by a man who informed me that I could not enter the pulpit area. When I asked why not, he directed me to the pastor, who told me that women were not permitted in the pulpit, but that he would have a man place the recorder there for me. Although I could not believe the explanation was a serious one, I agreed to have a man place it on the pulpit for me and returned to my seat in the sanctuary for the continuation of the convocation. The seriousness of the pastor's statement became clear to me later at that meeting when Mary Jane Patterson, a Presbyterian Church executive, was refused the right to speak from the pulpit.[13]

As far as the issue of women is concerned, it is obvious that the Black church described by C. Eric Lincoln has not fared much better than the Negro church of E. Franklin Frazier.[14] The failure of the Black church and Black theology to proclaim explicitly the liberation of Black women indicates that they cannot claim to be agents of divine liberation. If the theology, like the church, has no word for Black women, its conception of liberation is inauthentic.

The Black Experience and the Black Woman

For the most part, Black churchmen have not dealt with the oppression of Black women in either the Black church or the Black community. Frederick Douglass was one notable exception in the nineteenth century. His active advocacy of women's rights was a demonstration against the contradiction between preaching "justice for all" and practicing the continued oppression of women. "He, therefore, dared not claim a right [for himself] which he would not concede to women."[15] These words describe the convictions of a man who was active both in the church and in the larger Black community. This is significant because there is usually a direct relationship between what goes on in the Black church and in the Black secular community.

The status of Black women in the community parallels that of Black women in the church. Black theology considers the Black experience to be the context out of which its questions about God and human existence are formulated. This is assumed to be the context in which God's revelation is received and interpreted. Only from the perspective of the poor and the oppressed can an adequate theology be created. Arising out of the Black Power Movement of the 1960s, Black theology purports to take seriously the experience of the larger community's struggle for liberation. But if this is indeed the case, Black theology must function in the secular community in the same way it should function in the church community. It must serve as a "self-test" to see whether the rhetoric or proclamation of the Black community's struggle for liberation is consistent with its practices.

How does the "self-test" principle operate among the poor and the oppressed? Certainly Black theology has spoken to some of the forms of oppression which exist within the community of the oppressed. Many of the injustices it has attacked are the same as those which gave rise to the prophets of the Old Testament. But the fact that Black theology does not include sexism specifically as one of those injustices is all too evident. It suggests that the theologians do not understand sexism to be one of the oppressive realities of the Black community. Silence on this specific issue can only mean conformity to the status quo. The most prominent Black theologian, James Cone, has recently broken this silence:

> The Black church, like all other churches, is a male-dominated church. The difficulty that Black male ministers have in supporting the equality of women in the church and society stems partly from the lack of a clear liberation-criterion rooted in the gospel and in the present struggles of oppressed peoples. . . . It is truly amazing that many Black male ministers, young and old, can hear the message of liberation in the gospel when related to racism but remain deaf to a similar message in the context of sexism. . . .[16]

It is difficult to understand how Black men manage to exclude the liberation of Black women from their interpretation of the liberating gospel. Any correct analysis of the poor and oppressed would reveal some interesting and inescapable facts about the situation of women within oppressed groups. Without succumbing to the long and fruitless debate of "who is more oppressed than whom," I want to make some pointed suggestions to Black male theologians.

It would not be very difficult to argue that since Black women are the poorest of the poor, the most oppressed of the oppressed, their experience provides a most fruitful context for doing Black theology. The research of Jacquelyne Jackson attests to the extreme deprivation of Black women. Jackson supports her claim with statistical data showing that "in comparison with Black males and white males and females, Black women yet constitute the most disadvantaged group in the United States, as evidenced especially by their largely unenviable educational, occupational, employment, and income levels, and availability of marital partners."[17] In other words, in spite of the "quite insignificant" educational advantage that Black women have over Black men, they have "had the greatest access to the worst jobs at the lowest earnings."[18] It is important to emphasize this fact in order to elevate to its rightful level of concern the condition of Black women, not only in the world at large, but in the Black community and the Black church. It is my contention that if Black theology speaks of the Black community as if the special problems of Black women do not exist, it is no different from the white theology it claims to reject precisely because of its inability to take account of the existence of Black people.

It is instructive to note that the experience of Black women working in the Black Power Movement further accentuated the problem of the oppression of women in the Black community. Because of their invisibility among the leadership of the movement, they, like women of the church, provided "support": they filled the streets when the numbers were needed for demonstrations; they stuffed envelopes in the offices and performed other menial tasks. Kathleen Cleaver, in a *Black Scholar* interview, revealed some of the problems in the movement which caused her to become involved in women's liberation issues. While underscoring the crucial role played by women as Black Power activists, Kathleen Cleaver, nonetheless, acknowledged the presence of sex discrimination:

> I viewed myself as assisting everything that was done. . . . The form of assistance that women give in political movements to men is just as crucial as the leadership that men give to those movements. And this is something that is never recognized and never dealt with. *Because women are always relegated to assistance*, and this is where I became interested in the liberation of women. Conflicts, constant conflicts came up, conflicts that would rise as a result of the fact that I was married to a member of the Central Committee and I was also an officer in the Party. Things that I would have suggested myself would be implemented. But if I suggested them the suggestion might be rejected. If they were suggested by a man the suggestion would be implemented.
>
> It seemed throughout the history of my working with the Party, I always had to struggle with this. The suggestion itself was never viewed ob-

jectively. *The fact that the suggestion came from a woman gave it some lesser value.* And it seemed that it had something to do with the egos of the men involved. I know that the first demonstration that we had at the courthouse for Huey Newton, which I was very instrumental in organizing, the first time we went out on the soundtrucks, I was on the soundtrucks; the first leaflet we put out, I wrote; the first demonstration, I made up the pamphlets. And the members of that demonstration for the most part were women. I've noticed that throughout my dealings in the Black movement in the United States, that *the most anxious, the most eager, the most active, the most quick to understand the problem and quick to move are women.*[19]

Cleaver exposed the fact that even when women had leadership roles, sexism lurked in the wings. As Executive Secretary of the Student Non-violent Coordinating Committee (SNCC), Ruby Doris Robinson was described as the "heartbeat of SNCC." Yet there were "the constant conflicts, the constant struggles that she was subjected to because she was a woman."[20]

Notwithstanding all the evidence to the contrary, some may want to argue that the central problem of Black women is related to their race and not their sex. Such an argument then presumes that the problem cannot be resolved apart from the Black struggle, I contend that as long as the Black struggle refuses to recognize and deal with its sexism, the idea that women will receive justice from that struggle alone will never work. It will not work because Black women will no longer allow Black men to ignore their unique problems and needs in the name of some distorted view of the "liberation of the total community." Consider the words of President Sekou Toure on the role of African women in the revolution: "If African women cannot possibly conduct their struggle in isolation from the struggle that our people wage for African liberation, African freedom, conversely, is not effective unless it brings about the liberation of African women."[21] Black men who have an investment in the patriarchal structure of White America and who intend to do Christian theology have yet to realize that if Jesus is liberator of the oppressed, all of the oppressed must be liberated. Perhaps the proponents of the argument that the cause of Black women must be subsumed under a larger cause should look to South African theologians Sabelo Ntwasa and Basil Moore. They affirm that "Black theology, as it struggles to formulate a theology of liberation relevant to South Africa, cannot afford to perpetuate any form of domination, not even male domination. If its liberation is not human enough to include the liberation of women, it will not be liberation."[22]

A Challenge to Black Theology

My central argument is this: Black theology cannot continue to treat Black women as if they were invisible creatures who are on the outside looking into the Black experience, the Black church, and the Black theological enterprise. It will have to deal with women as integral parts of the whole community. Black theology, therefore, must speak to the bishops who hide behind the statement, "Women don't want women pastors." It must speak to the pastors who say, "My church isn't ready for women preachers yet." It must teach the seminarians who feel that "Women have no place in seminary." It must address the women in the church and in the community who are content and complacent with their oppression. It must challenge the educators who would reeducate the people on every issue except the dignity and equality of women.

Black women represent more than 50 percent of the Black community and more than 70 percent of the Black church. How, then, can an authentic theology of liberation arise out of these communities without specifically addressing the liberation of women? Does the fact that certain questions are raised by Black women make them any less Black concerns? If, as I contend, the liberation of Black men and women is inseparable, then a radical split cannot be made between racism and sexism. Black women are oppressed by racism *and* sexism. It is therefore necessary that Black men and women be actively involved in combatting both evils.

Only as Black women in greater numbers make their way from the background to the forefront will the true strength of the Black community be fully realized. There is already a heritage of strong Black women and men upon which a stronger nation can be built. There is a tradition which declares that God is at work in the experience of the Black woman. This tradition, in the context of the total Black experience, can provide data for the development of a holistic Black theology. Such a theology will repudiate the God of classical theology who is presented as an absolute Patriarch, a deserting father who created Black men and women and then "walked out" in the face of responsibility. Such a theology will look at the meaning of the total Jesus Christ Event; it will consider how God through Jesus Christ is related not only to oppressed men, but to women as well. Such a theology will "allow" God through the Holy Spirit to work through persons without regard to race, sex, or class. This theology will exercise its prophetic function and serve as a "self-test" in a church characterized by the sins of racism, sexism, and other forms of oppression.

Until Black women theologians are fully participating in the theological enterprise, it is important to make Black male theologians and Black leaders aware of the fact that Black women are needed not only as Christian educators, but as theologians and church leaders. It is only when Black women and men share jointly the leadership in theology and in the church and community that the Black nation will become strong and liberated. Only then will there be the possibility that Black theology can become a theology of divine liberation.

One final word for those who argue that the issues of racism and sexism are too complicated and should not be confused. I agree that the issues should not be "confused." But the elimination of both racism and sexism is so crucial for the liberation of Black persons that we cannot shrink from facing them together. Sojourner Truth told us why in 1867, when she spoke out on the issue of suffrage, and what she said at that time is still relevant to us as we deal with the liberation of Black women today:

> I feel that if I had to answer for the deeds done in my body just as much as a man, I have a right to have just as much as a man. There is a great stir about colored men getting their rights, but not a word about the colored women; and if colored men get their rights, and not colored women theirs, you see the colored men will be masters over the women, and it will be just as bad as it was before. So I am for keeping the thing going while things are stirring: because if we wait til it is still, it will take a great while to get it going again. . . . [23]

Black women have to keep the issue of sexism "going" in the Black community, in the Black church, and in Black theology until it has been eliminated. To do otherwise means that they will be pushed aside until eternity. Therefore, with Sojourner Truth, I am arguing for "keeping the thing going while things are stirring. . . ."

Notes

1. Study of the Philadelphia Conference of the African Methodist Episcopal Church. May 1976. (The study also included sporadic samplings of churches in other conferences in the First Episcopal District.) For example, a church of 1660 members (500 men and 1160 women) had a trustee board of 8 men and 1 woman and a steward board of 13 men and 6 women. A church of 100 members (35 men and 65 women) had a trustee board of 5 men and 4 women and a steward board of 5 men and 4 women.

2. Jarena Lee, *The Life and Religious Experience of Jarena Lee: A Colored Lady Giving an Account of Her Call to Preach the Gospel* (Philadelphia, 1836), printed in Dorothy Porter, ed., *Early Negro Writing, 1760–1837* (Boston: Beacon Press, 1971), 494–514.

3. Ibid., p. 503 (italics mine). Carol George, in *Segregated Sabbaths* (New York: Oxford Univ. Pres, 1973), presents a very positive picture of the relationship between Jarena Lee and Bishop Richard Allen. She feels that by the time Lee approached Allen, he had "modified his views on woman's rights" (129). She contends that since Allen was free from the Methodist Church he was able to "determine his own policy" with respect to women under the auspices of the A.M.E. Church. It should be noted that Bishop Al-

len accepted Rev. Lee as a woman preacher and not as an ordained preacher with full rights and privileges thereof. Even Carol George admitted that Lee traveled with Bishop Allen only "as an unofficial member of their delegation to conference sessions in New York and Baltimore"—"to attend," not to participate in them. I agree that this does represent progress in Bishop Allen's view from the time of Lee's first approach; on the second approach, he was at least encouraging. Then, he began "to promote her interests" (129)—but he did not ordain her.

4. Ibid.
5. "Elizabeth: A Colored Minister of the Gospel," reprinted in Bert James Loewenberg and Ruth Bogin, eds., *Black Women in Nineteenth-Century American Life* (University Park, Pa.: The Pennsylvania State Univ. Press, 1976), 132. The denomination of Elizabeth is not known to this writer. Her parents were Methodists, but she was separated from her parents at the age of eleven. However, the master from whom she gained her freedom was Presbyterian. Her autobiography was published by the Philadelphia Quakers.
6. Ibid p. 133.
7. Amanda Berry Smith, *An Autobiography: The Story of the Lord's Dealing with Mrs. Amanda Berry Smith, the Colored Evangelist* (Chicago, 1893), reprinted in Loewenberg and Bogin, *op. cit.*, p. 157.
8. Ibid.
9. Ibid., p. 159.
10. The African Methodist Episcopal Church started ordaining women in 1948, according to the Rev. William P. Foley of Bridgestreet A.M.E. Church in Brooklyn, New York. The first ordained woman was Martha J. Keys.

   The African Methodist Episcopal Zion Church ordained women as early as 1884, when Mrs. Julia A. Foote was ordained Deacon in the New York Annual Conference. In 1894, Mrs. Mary J. Small was ordained Deacon, and in 1898, she was ordained Elder. See David Henry Bradley, Sr., *A History of the A.M.E. Zion Church*, Vol. II:1872–1968 (Nashville: The Parthenon Press, 1970), pp. 384 and 393.

   The Christian Methodist Episcopal Church enacted legislation to ordain women in the 1970 General Conference. Since then approximately 75 women have been ordained. See the Rev. N. Charles Thomas, General Secretary of the C.M.E. Church and Director of the Department of Ministry, Memphis, Tennessee.

   Many Baptist churches still do not ordain women. Some churches in the Pentecostal tradition do not ordain women. However, in some other Pentecostal churches, women are founders, pastors, elders, and bishops.

   In the case of the A.M.E. Zion Church where women were ordained as early as 1884, the important question would be: What happened to the women who were ordained? In addition, all of these churches (except for those which do give leadership to women) should answer the following questions: Have women been assigned to pastor "class A" churches? Have women been appointed as presiding elders? (There is currently one woman presiding elder in the A.M.E. Church.) Have women been elected to serve as bishops of any of these churches? Have women served as presidents of Conventions?

11. Yolande Herron, Jacquelyn Grant, Gwendolyn Johnson, and Samuel Roberts, "Black Women and the Field Education Experience at Union Theological Seminary: Problems and Prospects" (New York: Union Theological Seminary, May 1978).
12. This organization continues to call itself the National Committee of Black Churchmen despite the protests of women members.
13. NCBC has since decided to examine the policies of its host institutions (churches) to avoid the recurrence of such incidents.
14. E. Franklin Frazier, *The Negro Church in America;* C. Eric Lincoln, *The Black Church Since Frazier* (New York: Schocken Books, 1974), passim.
15. Philip S. Foner, ed., *Frederick Douglass on Women's Rights* (Westport, Conn.: Greenwood Press), p. 51.
16. James Cone, "Black Ecumenism and the Liberation Struggle," delivered at Yale University, February 16–17, 1978, and Quinn Chapel A.M.E. Church, May 22, 1978. In two other recent papers Cone has voiced concern on women's issues, relating them to the larger question of liberation. These papers are: "New Roles in the Ministry: A Theological Appraisal" and "Black Theology and the Black Church: Where Do We Go from Here?"
17. Jacquelyne Jackson, "But Where Are the Men?" *The Black Scholar, op. cit.,* p. 30.
18. Ibid., p. 32.
19. Kathleen Cleaver interviewed by Sister Julia Herve. Ibid., pp. 55–56.
20. Ibid., p. 55.
21. Sekou Toure, "The Role of Women in the Revolution," *The Black Scholar* 6: 6 (March 1975): 32.
22. Sabelo Ntwasa and Basil Moore, "The Concept of God in Black Theology," in *The Challenge of Black Theology in South Africa*, ed. Basil Moore (Atlanta, Ga.: John Knox Press, 1974), pp. 25–26.
23. Sojourner Truth, "Keeping the Things Going Whilst Things Are Stirring," reprinted in Miriam Schneir, ed., *Feminism: The Essential Historical Writings* (New York: Random House, 1972), pp. 129–30.

PART V

POLITICS

I‌T is the women's movement that has most systematically and effectively raised issues of gender inequality. One can question which issues are raised and which women are affected by them; one can criticize the tactics and strategies used in raising certain issues; and one
can even doubt the ultimate effectiveness of something called a wom-
en's movement—but one cannot ignore the women's movement as a
kind of politic in contemporary U.S. life. The articles in this chapter
make that clear, for in each, no matter from what perspective it is written, "the women's movement" becomes a force to be dealt with—
defended, attacked, explained, but definitely not ignored.

There is a question, however, that is far more profound than
whether or not one can ignore the women's movement. The question is:
has the women's movement made a difference in the lives of a few,
some, many, or all US women? In short, is there less sexism in the lives
of US women? Or, if one prefers different words, is there less oppression of women, less gender inequality? In the most conservative terms,
the response must be that the women's movement—the twentieth-
century organizational form in which feminism is expressed—has concrete accomplishments to which it can point. All over the United
States, there is an awareness of something called "women's issues" or

371

a "woman's agenda," and terms such as "sexism" and "patriarchy" have moved into the general lexicon of the U.S. public. Although for some, these concepts and words elicit a negative response, there is more discussion about them today than there was twenty years ago. Challenges to the use of gender-biased language are certainly the result of the women's movement. Saying "chairperson" rather than "chairman" does not fundamentally change the condition of women. However, to the extent that language reflects thought patterns, attitudes, and even future possibilities, more is involved than a mere name change. Today, women are in certain positions where there were no females ten, fifteen, or twenty years ago. There are presently more women in college; more women are elected to public office; there is more sensitivity to gender bias in scholarship and more scholarship about women. All of this, in large measure, is tied to the women's movement. Issues such as violence against women and reproductive rights are open to more public discussion. Charges of sexual discrimination in employment are rarely laughed at and not so immediately dismissed.

On the broad level on which these accomplishments have been spelled out, they are irrefutable. However, once one asks a series of other questions, the assessment takes on a different tone. Who are the women who have benefited from these changes? What have been the changes for the masses of US women in such basic areas of life as employment, decent and affordable day care, and the burden of the double shift? Or one might ask, who are the leaders of the women's movement, and who are the majority of the participants? The response remains: middle- to upper-middle-class white women.

The gains that can be attributed to the women's movement, and specifically to affirmative action legislation, have often served to further divide white women from women of color. Among women of color, there is the perception, and often accompanying evidence, that when an "affirmative action slot" can be filled by a white woman or a woman or man of color, it is the white woman who is chosen again and again. Affirmative action legislation was won in large part as a result of the organized and protracted struggle of people of color. Ironically, white women felt the immediate benefits of those efforts sooner than did those who did so much of the fighting.

The racial and class composition of the women's movement today represents a continuation of patterns set in the 1860s. The origins of the current women's movement date back to the suffrage movement of the late nineteenth and early twentieth centuries. After the victory of gaining the right for women to vote—a victory which also caused a deep split between white women suffragists and many black men and women who saw their rights as a people given a secondary status— there was a forty-year lull in mass political activity.

The reemergence of the women's movement occurred following the 1959 publication of Betty Friedan's *The Feminine Mystique*, a book which put before the public the case of the white, well-educated, middle-class suburban woman. When Friedan helped to found the National Organization of Women (NOW) in 1966, the "older branch" of the movement was clearly established.

There were, as Jo Freeman puts it, two branches of the movement, drawn from two different age sets, involving women's different styles and orientations (Freeman 1984: 544). But they were predominantly white women. In the 1960s, the younger branch of the women's movement consisted of those who saw themselves as purposefully less structured and more radical than the founders of the movement, who were represented in NOW, the National Women's Political Caucus, and close to 100 different other organizations and caucuses of professional women. The younger branch created a technique which was clearly a variation on a form that was a part of the black power movement: the rap group. One function of the rap group, as Freeman notes, was to bring women together so that they might compare common concerns. A second was a mechanism for social change known as "consciousness-raising": a public sharing of experiences which led women to see that their individual concerns and problems were in fact based in social causes and subject to political solutions (Freeman 1984: 545–546).

Consciousness-raising and rap groups continue to function. However, in the 1980s there is yet another process which is intimately associated with the women's movement: networking. Although this process of sharing information and skills, being supportive, and getting things done among a group of women is working in grass roots and community formations, as well as in the highest circles of power in which women travel, the term has the ring of establishment tactics—so that "networks or even old girls' networks raise the echo of old boys' clubs in our brains" (Steinem 1983: 196). Steinem challenges this association, but the challenge is not convincing when she gives concrete examples such as the following:

> Networks may conjure up the status quo. That is, until you put *women's* in front of it. And until you realize that it's used generically to include everything from specialized national coalitions like the National Women's Health Network or the Feminist Computer Technology Project to such local luncheons and information exchanges as the Women's Forum in New York or the Philadelphia Forum for Executive Women. (Steinem 1983: 198)

Once again, on a certain level, this is an important statement of change and to some extent empowerment. But it is also important to ask: who are the women with access to the most information which they can then share? Who are the women with the education and contacts to pick up the most helpful skills? Who are the women in the New York Women's Forum?

The campaign of Geraldine Ferraro as vice presidential candidate for the Democratic party was truly an historic event and one very definitely tied to the modern women's movement. Yet the fact that a black woman, Shirley Chisholm, was a candidate for president of the United States in 1972 and another black woman, Angela Davis, has been a vice presidential candidate several times on the Communist party ticket is seldom mentioned.

In the following article by Ferraro, the connection between her candidacy and the women's movement is explicitly stated:

[The Ferraro candidacy] was the result of hard work by many individuals. First, the ground was laid by thousands of feminists who launched the modern Women's Movement in the 1970's. (Ferraro 1985: 1)

However, in a crucial statement, Ferraro implies that such a movement of women was necessary, but not sufficient, for putting a woman on the ticket of one of the two major parties. For what was decisive, she argues, was the presidential nominee of the Democratic party. In her words, "Luckily enough, the nominee turned out to be someone who was a committed feminist" (Ferraro 1985: 2). The point here is not to debate the assessment of Walter Mondale as a feminist, but rather to underscore the idea that working within the political system, the electoral politics with which the center of the women's movement is associated, is not and cannot be a separatist movement. Such work depends on the support of men, individuals whom radical/separatist feminists would define as outside of their movement, indeed as the enemy; individuals whose intimate involvement in corporate and governmental structures make them the permanent adversaries of socialist feminists.

The Reagan/Bush victory raises serious questions for that part of the women's movement committed to electoral politics as the major avenue for social change. Reagan/Bush won a majority among white women who voted while Mondale/Ferraro won 90 percent of the Afro-American vote (male and female). While debates continue as to exactly what this means, it is certainly clear that voting patterns by white women are not based exclusively on gender.

Additionally, there is an assumption that women administer and govern differently from men: women, it is argued, consult and network more, are less hierarchical, are more concerned about the "bread and butter issues" which affect our lives. That may be true in some cases, but the tenure of Jean Kirkpatrick in the Untied Nations, Sandra Day O'Connor on the Supreme Court, Anne Gorsuch at the Environmental Protection Agency, and Linda Chavez on the U.S. Commission on Civil Rights challenge that assumption.

The articles in this chapter represent some of the many variations on women's movement politics symbolized by the candidacy of Representative Ferraro and alternatives posed to it. The article by Barbara Deckard gives a detailed account of the political organizing of certain sectors of the women's movement in response to violence against women: rape, wife beating, and pornography. This kind of organizing is expressive of certain basic tenets and characteristics of the women's movement. First, it addresses problems to which all women are potentially subjected: rape, sexual abuse, and misogyny are not restricted to a certain class, race, age group, or sexual preference. Yet neither are they experienced equally by all groups of women. Physical violence does occur in lesbian relationships, but all indications are that the incidence is far less than in heterosexual relationships. Rape is a fear of all women and a reality for many, but the actual incidence of rape is far greater for poor women and women of color. Unfortunately, Deckard's account does not reflect these differences among women. What the article does do, however, is offer concrete examples of the kind of political organizing that one sector of the women's movement has pursued. Such organizing has significant potential power if it is based on a sound analysis of the roots of violence against women in our society *and* if it incorporates all women's experiences into the active efforts to stop such forms of violence.

The most frequently voiced criticism of the women's movement is that it does not incorporate the concerns, particular circumstances, and experiences of all groups of women. In response to that narrowness in definition and activity, some women have sought radically different groups and organizations. Others have raised their criticisms and called for reforms within the women's movement, using some of the same strategies for which it is most known, but incorporating a wider spectrum of women. We see this later approach in the article by Yvonne Duffy: a call is made for inclusion of more disabled women within the women's movement. Several women Duffy worked with "felt alienated from the women's movement. Having suffered more serious discrimination as a result of being differently abled than being women, they thought that most feminists neither understood nor even acknowledged this problem" (Duffy 1981: 167). This was often the case at the center of the women's movement in its early stages, and Duffy addresses ways in which disabled women themselves can undergo a change in consciousness that will improve their situation ("How do we further handicap each other in our mutual struggle for full acceptance?" [Duffy 1981: 166]) But her discussion does seem oblivious to the experiences of differently abled women of color. There is not a single mention of what may be the particular problems of women of color with disabilities. She notes that disabled women often do not feel that they are discriminated against as women because others never get beyond their disability. What might be the case of, for example, an Asian American woman who is disabled? Will her "race" serve as the first line of discrimination, then her disability and then her gender?

The women's movement has also been charged with insensitivity to the special needs and concerns of older women. There is no such specific criticism in the conversations and reminiscences of two elders, as they are shared with us in the article by Rosette Capotorto and Kathleen D'Arcy. And yet what these women speak of is a penetrating criticism of how our society responds to women who are old and who are physically incapacitated. Redressing that situation must be on the agenda of a movement which aligns itself with the interests of women.

In the brief scenes from the lives of these two women, we encounter vivid examples of the complex dynamics of commonalities and differences among US women. The two women are of different racial and class backgrounds, but similar tragedies lead to their residency in a geriatric institution. Within that institution, they each experience the indignities of being treated like children, and of worrying more about the quality of how they are living than the details of when and how they will be dying. Through even these brief glimpses, we sense that class and race continue to make a difference in the lives of these women.

Paula Gunn Allen, describing the situation of Native American women, presents a different set of realities. For Native women, the issue is very simply that of biological and cultural survival as distinct peoples. What is very important to understand about the severity of their situation is that extreme assaults on their communities from the outside produce assaults on them from within their communities. The high incidence of sexual assaults on Indian women by Indian men reflects a definitive decline in women's status since European contact. The response of some of the women to the assaults they suffer from all directions is to "just give up." Yet in a moving statement of the truism in human history, "Where there is oppression, there is also resistance," Allen reminds us that even after almost 500 centuries of brutality many Indian women continue to honor their traditions in music, in poetry, and in art.

The women's movement, operating within the boundaries of traditional political activity, had as its first serious challenge a split between lesbian and nonlesbian women. It was after Ti-Grace Brown's 1969 accusation of homophobia in NOW that the first overt expressions of a lesbian political presence appeared within feminism. (See Snitow *et al.* 1983: 29–34 for a summary of this political presence and the effects on the women's movement.) However, from the very beginning of that lesbian politic, those who waged it were most often mirror images of their nonlesbian sisters in terms of class and color. Thus, women of color who were also lesbians moved increasingly into their own organizations. The article by Barbara Smith follows an open and insightful conversation among four black lesbian feminists concerning their political organizing efforts. These women address a number of issues seldom discussed in the women's movement: issues revolving around being a leader; class and homophobia; internal color distinctions among black and other women of color. The crucial contribution this article makes is the detailed description and discussion of the range of ways in which these women act as political beings: sometimes in all lesbian formations; sometimes in groups where their blackness is emphasized; sometimes in coalitions on gay/lesbian issues; sometimes in coalitions on issues such as nuclear disarmament.

The idea that issues such as nuclear disarmament are of concern to women, including women in the United States, was at the heart of the U.N. End of the Decade Conference on Women, held in Nairobi, Kenya, in July of 1985. For some U.S. feminists, this is not a new issue. In a 1983 speech in which Adrienne Rich talked about some of her experiences in Nicaragua, there is a clear statement on what constitutes "women's issues."

> [In Nicaragua] I found myself having to think about "women's issues" not just as reproductive issues or the problems of rape, woman-battering, child abuse, but as literacy, infant mortality, the fundamental issue of having something to eat. (1983: 4)

The final article is written by Sasha Hohri, a Japanese American who works for a women's foundation and defines herself in very straightforward terms as a revolutionary. Avoiding what is often posed as a choice between viewing class *or* race/ethnicity *or* gender as the primary determinant of her oppression, Hohri makes key connections when she says:

> I see socialist revolution as the basis for the elimination of women's oppression in this country and see the future of Asian women as most closely connected to the future and struggles of our people as a whole because of racism and national oppression. . . . But Asian women are not only oppressed by this American government and society which is based only on what is profitable, Asian women are also oppressed inside our communities by the force of Asian feudal tradition. This tradition continues to define us as so-and-so's daughter, mother or wife. (Hohri 1983: 42, 44)

The various political positions presented in this chapter are not easily reconciled. If others, such as radical separatist feminism were added, the chance of agreement on fundamental issues would be even slimmer. Yet there may be one point on which there is now sufficient agreement for discussion, although not for resolution. It is the same

point on which this volume has been shaped: there are commonalities
which we women share, and there are diversities among us. To ignore
the commonalities is to participate in the kind of divisiveness which is
not in the interest of women, of men, of our society. But to ignore our
differences is to participate in practices of racism, classism, heterosex-
ism, ageism, handicapism, and regional, religious, and ethnic chauvin-
sim. The mere recognition of our differences does not guarantee that
we can respect them, build on them, and most importantly unite for
needed social change. However, not to recognize them is to delay inter-
minably the processes of our liberation.

References

Duffy, Y.
1981   . . . *All Things Are Possible*. Ann Arbor, Mich.: A. J. Garvin and Associ-
       ates.

Ferraro, G.
1985   "The 1984 Campaign and the Women's Movement: Where Do We Go
       From Here?" Speech delivered to the Organization of California
       Elected Women, Sacramento, Calif., February 27, 1985.

Freeman, J., ed.
1984   *Women: A Feminist Perspective*. 3rd ed. Palo Alto, Calif.: Mayfield.

Hohri, S.
1983   "Are You a Liberated Woman?" *East Wind: Politics and Culture of
       Asians in the U.S.* 2, no. 1: 42–45. San Francisco, Calif.: Getting Together
       Publications.

Rich, A.
1983   "Women in Struggle." Unpublished speech.

Snitow, A., C. Stansell, and S. Thompson, eds.
1983   *Powers of Desire: The Politics of Sexuality*. New York: Monthly Review
       Press.

Steinem, G.
1983   "Networking." in *Outrageous Acts and Everyday Rebellions*, pp. 197–
       205. New York: Holt, Rinehart and Winston.

30

The 1984 Campaign and the Women's Movement
Where Do We Go from Here?

Geraldine Ferraro

One of the best things this organization does is to give elected women a chance to get together and share their experience. . . .

Now that the campaign has been over for several months, it is possible to have some perspective on what we went through. And today I would like to share with you my thoughts about what that long campaign meant for the women's movement—and where we go from here.

On the night of November sixth, I conceded the election to Mr. Reagan and Mr. Bush, but on another level I do not believe that Walter Mondale and I lost in 1984. For our ticket was truly a breakthrough. We opened a door that will never again be closed, and that is something that both women and Democrats can be proud of for years to come.

That breakthrough was the result of hard work by many individuals. First, the ground was laid by thousands of feminists who launched the modern women's movement in the 1970s. Soon groups like this one were talking about the importance of electing women to public office. And then in the beginning of 1984, some people even be-

From a speech delivered to the Organization of California Elected Women, Sacramento, Calif., February 27, 1985. Reprinted by permission of Geraldine Ferraro.

gan talking about putting a woman on the national ticket. But all along, ultimately we always knew that the decision lay in the hands of whoever was going to be the Democratic nominee in 1984.

Luckily enough, the nominee turned out to be someone who was a committed feminist. Walter Mondale has been a defender of equal opportunity all his life. He has fought for civil rights, fair housing, and medical care for the elderly. He has joined every fight for social justice for more than twenty years. He was always one to take a chance for something he believed in, and in 1984 he took yet another chance— probably the most daring in his career—when he chose me to be his running mate.

Instantly, that decision touched a nerve in our country. I, for one, received mail—tens of thousands of letters—almost overnight, from people congratulating me and wishing me well. One theme common to many of the letters was the feeling of surprise people felt: they had not expected to be so moved by the nomination of a female vice presidential candidate. But, much to their surprise, millions of Americans were.

One woman wrote me a letter on the night I was nominated. She was a young mother of twins, and she wrote the following: "I ran into the bedroom to see if the twins were still awake so I could tell them. They are four years old and took the news casually, since they don't know yet that this is an historic first. It means more to me than I can ever express that the childhood lessons they learn will include your name."

During my acceptance speech at the Democratic National Convention, I was surprised to see usually hard-bitten reporters with tears in their eyes.

People who previously had not been involved in campaigns were suddenly drawn into politics for the first time in 1984. Susy Willson organized a fundraiser in San Jose in which a group of waitresses, who had never before contributed to a political campaign, gave sixty-five dollars. They couldn't really afford that money, but they were determined to contribute anyhow because they had found in our ticket new hope for all American women.

One day, I was telling a story in St. Paul about a woman who had come up to me and said, "I'm eighty years old, and I never thought I'd live to see this." When I finished the speech and was leaving, an elderly woman who was leaning on a walker by the door of the hotel motioned to me, and said, "You know that story about the eighty-year-old woman? Well, I'm ninety-one, and I never thought I'd live to see this day."

Now, I knew that all these people, and many more, were not moved just by Geraldine Ferraro but by the breakthrough we had made with a woman on the ticket. A lot of women could have done what I did. But I was lucky. I had the chance to stand in for millions of women. And together, I think we did a very good job.

Above all, people were proud that their country had finally taken down this enormous barrier and declared the equality of all Americans. And not just equality: we were declaring that the tyranny of expectations is over. Women can be whatever we want to be.

We can walk in space and help our children take their first steps. We can be corporate executives and also wives and mothers. We can be doctors and also bake cookies with our six-year-old future scientists.

Or we can choose none of these things. We don't have to be superwomen. For the first fourteen years of my married life, I worked at home as a mother and wife. That was a fine profession. Then I decided to work outside the home, and that was also the right decision for me. Not every women would agree with the decisions I have made. But the point is, they were my decisions, I made them for myself, and women should take pride in whatever they decide to do.

And whatever we choose to do, we want to be judged by the quality of our products. We aren't women doing men's jobs. We're women doing work.

This is a new age for American women. It's easy to forget that only twenty years ago in the United States, equal pay for equal work was not even the law of the land. Only twelve years ago, there was no law guaranteeing women's right to compete in school athletics. Only ten years ago, a woman was not entitled to credit in her own name. And only one year ago, the pension rights of many women were routinely violated, until the Congress enacted a law I wrote and President Reagan signed it—without, I should add, inviting me to the signing ceremony. I wonder why he did that?

We're making great progress on the question of equal rights. But there's much more to be done. Above all, I see two areas where we need to concentrate in the next few years.

First, we need to step up our participation in politics. Remember that Eleanor Roosevelt was thirty-six before she cast her first vote. What a waste. She should never have been barred from choosing public officials. She should have been one.

Today, there are thousands of talented women who should be in politics but are not. And it's our job to bring them in, especially younger women. Groups like this one have been vital in that effort. The 1984 campaign itself awakened some women to the possibilities of politics. I was very pleased to read that a survey by the National Women's Political Caucus found that 27 percent of the interviewed people are now more likely to vote for a woman candidate than before the election of 1984. And 64 percent said that having a woman on the ticket made no difference at all to them. That second figure may be the more important one, for it shows that at last we're removing gender as an issue in elections.

During the campaign, someone told me that she was riding on an airplane and overheard the woman behind her say, "I'm not very political, you know. I don't vote the party. I vote the woman."

We're making headway. We have two very good governors—Madeleine Kunin and Martha Layne Collins. But, after all, there are fifty states, aren't there? In 1986, we want to see more women in politics, more women voting, and more women elected to office than ever before. That's the best thing we can do for women. And it will be good for men, too.

Second, we must continue to press the right for pay equity. When I was in the House, I cochaired hearings in which we learned that tree trimmers in Denver were paid more than emergency room nurses, and dog pound attendants were paid more than child care workers. Now, I'm not running down any worker, but the fact is, women are paid less because they are women. And that is wrong.

We should pay people for their time, their skills, their experience, and the worth of their labor—and not according to whether or not they happen to be female or male, black or white or Hispanic.

I think most men agree. I'm not speaking just to women today. You don't have to be a woman to be offended by discrimination. Most men are too. You don't have to be poor to hate poverty. You don't have to be black, Hispanic, or Asian to loathe bigotry. Every American should, and most Americans do.

Every father is diminished when his daughter is denied a fair chance. Every son is a victim when his mother is denied fair pay. But when we lower barriers, open doors, and free women to reach wherever their dreams will take them—our talents are multiplied, and our country is stronger.

That is why I have always said that the cause of women is really the cause of our country. And it is one we can wage not just in public, not just every two or four years, but in our own private lives, every day.

When we move ahead in our careers, we must have the courage to speak up for those left behind. When we are struggling to reach the top, we must have the commitment to help others starting at the bottom. Especially now, when some people are saying that a conservative mood has overtaken our society, I urge you to stoke that courage and keep that commitment. I know you will. . . .

31

Violence Against Women

Barbara Sinclair Deckard

In the early 1970s, rape became a major feminist issue. The increase in rape and growing feminist consciousness led to a questioning of society's views on rape and a new, specifically feminist analysis.

The common view holds that rape is committed by a few sick men driven by insatiable sexual urges. Not infrequently, it is assumed that the crime is usually committed by black men on white women. But society's view toward the victim is at best ambivalent. It is frequently assumed that she asked for it, that nice women don't get raped. Even if the victim can show that the attack was completely unprovoked, she is stigmatized. Somehow, it is felt, she is to blame for having been raped. These attitudes are lodged deep in the consciousness of most men and women. All consciousness-raising groups include sex and female sexuality as a major topic of discussion. Such discussions frequently begin with the participants' sexual hangups and progress to an analysis of the socialization process that produced them. Early consciousness-

From Chapter 13 (pp. 431–442), "Current Issues of the Women's Movement: Women Against Violence," in *The Women's Movement: Political, Socioeconomic and Psychological Issues* by Barbara Deckard. Copyright © 1983 by Harper & Row, Publishers, Inc. Reprinted by permission of Harper & Row, Publishers, Inc.

raising groups often did not carry the analysis much further, but as the movement's awareness increased, women came to see the relationship between sex and dominance in our society. Men often see sex as something men do *to* women, an act that certifies the male's superordinate position. The connection between sex and violence is not restricted to hardcore pornography; words like *fuck* and *screw* signify both sexual intercourse and doing someone in. Women came to see that frequently their sexual relationships had had masochistic-sadistic overtones, at least on the psychological level. They learned to acknowledge that, whatever their rhetoric, many men still regarded sexual relationships as conquests.

When the topic of rape came up, most women would say: Yes it's a problem, but it's never happened to me. As the discussion progressed, however, women would frequently realize that their denial was not completely accurate. Almost all had been sexually harassed by men. Being shouted at and followed on the street, being pressured into bed through the use of psychological warfare (the threat of being labeled a "cock teaser, frigid bitch") were common experiences. Even the use of threats and physical force by "dates" was not unusual. Such experiences left women feeling not just sexually used but psychically put down. The essence of such situations was not sex but domination. Sexual harassment was men's way of asserting their supremacy, of warning women to stay in their place.

From an understanding of the sex-dominance relationship, a new analysis of rape emerged. Rape, women discovered, is a political act, not a sexual one. It is a political act of terror against an oppressed group. According to one of the first feminist analyses of rape, by Pamela Kearon and Barbara Mehrhof, "rape teaches . . . the objective, innate and unchanging subordination of women relative to men."[1]

Kearon and Mehrhof's 1971 analysis has become a feminist classic. They say:

> [In our sexist society the] sexual act [is] a renewal of the feeling of power and prestige for the male, of impotence and submission for the female. Rape adds the quality of terror. . . ."[2]

Society's real attitude toward rape is shown by its treatment of the victim. Frequently the accused rapist is treated better than the victim. Police often refuse to believe rape took place unless the victim can show severe injuries. They ask demanding questions, such as "Did you enjoy it? Did you come?" The victim is repeatedly forced to describe the rape in excruciating detail to various male police officers. Her past sex life is scrutinized. A woman who once says yes to a man who is not her husband is assumed to have lost her right to say no to any male. Eva Norman, a founder of the Los Angeles Commission on Rape, says:

"The crime of rape has no parallel. It is the *only* crime in which the victim is treated like a criminal by the police, the hospitals, the courts."[3]

Not infrequently, the police will make only a nominal effort to catch the rapist. "If he is white, and middle class, forget it. They figure that the chances of getting a conviction in court wouldn't be that good."[4] If a woman has let a man into her apartment and he has raped her, she might as well forget it too. Both the police and juries take that as consent. If the accused rapist is black or lower class and the woman is white, the police are more likely to pursue the matter.

In 1972, 46,497 forcible rapes were reported. Criminologists estimate that only 1 out of 10 rapes are reported.[5] Given the police harassment of the victim, the low reporting rate is hardly surprising. But even if a woman is willing endure the experience of going to the police, the chances of conviction are very slim. In 1972, 3,562 rapes were reported in Chicago; 833 arrests were made, 23 defendants pleaded guilty; and 8 were found guilty and sentenced after a trial. Thus fewer than 1 percent of the rapes resulted in jail sentences.

The situation is not new, nor was it a well-guarded secret. But it required a strong feminist movement and a new analysis of rape to make women see that collective action was necessary. The first political action was a Rape Speak Out organized by the New York Radical Feminists in 1970.

The first rape crisis center seems to have been the one in Washington, D.C. Formed in the summer of 1972, it at first concentrated on counseling and giving emotional support to rape victims. Since then it has gone more heavily into helping women deal with hospitals and the police. Members accompany the woman to the hospital and to the police. They make sure the medical examination form is filled out properly. This is necessary for conviction, but according to one of the members, "the intern, either out of ignorance or not wanting to testify, fudges the report" unless watched.[6]

The presence of rape crisis center members not only provides emotional support to the victim but results in better treatment by the police and the hospital. The police take the case more seriously and moderate their behavior. The Washington center's existence has even had an effect on the treatment of victims who come in independently. A member explained: "When we first started, we wouldn't say that we were members of the Rape Crisis Center—we would simply say that we were friends of the victim. So, now, whenever a woman comes in with a friend, they assume that she is from the Crisis Center, even if she's really not, and they behave very nicely."[7] Members accompany the women to court and can refer her to a free lawyer. They are also involved in the D.C. Task Force on Rape, which is working for changes in police, hospital, and court procedures.

Such services, while essential, will not directly prevent rape. Thus the center has also set up self-defense classes to aid women in protecting themselves. Karate, judo, and street-fighting techniques are taught. Asked how effective the classes were, a member replied

> No matter how much karate or self-defense you know, it's not worth shit if you don't have the mind set to use it. What we try to do is politicize the women. Middle-class women, especially, are very afraid of being aggressive. We try to break that down and make women realize that if someone is fucking her over, she has the right to hit him back—just enough so that she can get out of the situation and run.[8]

Rape crisis centers have sprung up by the dozen. As Mary Ann Langen of NOW said in 1977, "In 1972 there were three rape crisis centers in this country. Today there are over 150."[9] Frequently centers are started by former rape victims. Many are modeled on the D.C. center; its booklet, "How to Start a Rape Crisis Center," is often used as a guide. Every center has a crisis line that women who need help can call. Most try to staff the line 24 hours a day, but because this is often difficult, compromises are frequently made. Center members check out hospitals to determine which offer the best and most sympathetic care. They compile lists of gynecologists, VD clinics, and Planned Parenthood chapters where further medical help can be obtained. A list of sympathetic, nonsexist psychiatrists and psychologists is also necessary.

Some women may need professional help, but many find that talking to previous victims working at the center is even more useful. Because society tends to blame the victim for the rape, women often need to be reassured that they are still worthwhile people, that in fact they are not responsible. The Washington, D.C., center sets up meetings at which rape victims and their families can discuss their reactions and learn from each other to overcome their shame and fear. Rape crisis centers frequently get calls from women who were raped years before. Often it is the first time the woman has told anyone about the experience. Center members will accompany a victim to the police if she decides to report the crime. But the decision is left up to the woman. Most women agree in principle that all rapes should be reported and prosecuted, but the emotional ordeal involved is such that few women feel they should persuade someone who is reluctant to go to the police.

Some centers have managed to establish reasonable relationships with police and prosecutors' offices. In a number of areas, rape crisis personnel are even involved with police training. Janet Taggart of Seattle's Rape Reduction Project says, "We do a part of each new patrol person's training. It is very extensive and it's generally been successful."[10] Even if these officials cannot be made more sympathetic by reasoned discussion, the presence of an active center often has a salutary effect. If they know that any misbehavior will be publicized, they tend to be more careful.

A center organized on different lines began operation in May 1973 in Philadelphia. Women Organized Against Rape (WOAR) has its headquarters in Philadelphia General Hospital, where rape victims are examined. When a rape victim enters the hospital, the WOAR room is notified and a member on duty is immediately available for help. Because of its location, WOAR sees all rape victims who report the crime. A member explained why they worked so hard to get their location inside the hospital: "It was obvious to us that hotlines and crisis centers which work outside the system would reach mostly middle-class and movement women. We felt we had to be available to poor and Third World women who are particularly vulnerable to rape, and who are the most abused by medical and legal agents of the patriarchy.[11]

Getting into the establishment took a 3-year campaign. In August 1970, women began to collect the names of people interested in starting a rape crisis center. In November, WOAR was formed by 150 women. WOAR talked to various prominent Philadelphia women—a district attorney, a judge, members of the city council, and several black leaders. WOAR's documentation of the abusive treatment of rape victims persuaded these women to serve on the WOAR board of directors and to use their influence to get the group into the hospital. Opposition collapsed under this kind of pressure, and during its first 3 months, WOAR counseled over 300 rape victims. Of these, 90 percent were black and 60 percent were girls under 16.[12] This approach has begun to spread; in several other cities, centers are now located in hospitals.

Action against rape has taken a variety of other forms. Most centers do some community education such as giving talks at schools and to local organizations. Self-defense for women has become more prevalent. Classes, how-to booklets, and even schools are proliferating.

Efforts to educate those who deal with rape victims is continuing. In 1981, the Los Angeles Commission on Assaults Against Women undertook a survey of the needs and problems of rape victims in Los Angeles County. The worst problems, the survey found, were medical.[13] According to the survey, the county's emergency rooms were frequently unhelpful and insensitive. "We found out minors were being turned away if they didn't have parental consent. This is illegal. Women who did not report the rape to the police were being turned away from treatment. By and large, rape victims were seen as low priority," the commission's executive director reported.[14] Evidence was often improperly collected and preserved, making prosecution difficult or impossible. Rape victims were forced to wait in public waiting rooms, and police officers were often present during the medical examination. To change this deplorable situation, the commission, along with the National Council of Jewish Women and the Los Angeles Police Department, has launched an educational program for hospital emergency room personnel. By late 1981, almost half of the hospitals in the county have signed up for the program. Similar educational efforts undoubtedly are needed across the country.

But, the progress that has been made is now threatened. In the late 1970s and early 1980s, cuts in government spending for social services severely affected rape crisis centers. Although most were established by volunteers on shoestring budgets, the costs of maintaining a center are high. Many eventually obtained some government funding and, when such money became scarce, were forced to cease operation. In mid-1981, before the full effects of the Reagan budget cuts were felt, about a quarter of the approximately 600 centers that had been established during the 1970s had closed.[15] Some centers have managed to tap private funding sources effectively. For example, the Santa Monica Rape Treatment Center, a model hospital-based, comprehensive-treatment center, has developed a reliable support base among the affluent Los Angeles liberal community.[16] For most centers, however, relying upon purely private funding will mean at best a hand-to-mouth existence. Furthermore, if more cuts in government social spending are made, the competition for private funds will become even more fierce.

Not all the news is bad. The campaigns to change rape laws and judicial proceedings launched in the 1970s have shown important results. Most states have made some reforms in their rape laws, with the most frequent change being a restriction on the admission of evidence about the victim's previous sexual history. But although progress has been made, recent rape cases show that the old misogynist assumptions are far from dead. In Madison, Wisconsin, a teenage boy convicted of raping a 16-year-old girl was "sentenced" to a year of supervision by his parents. In explaining his leniency, the judge called the rape "a normal reaction . . . to sexual permissiveness and provocative clothing."[17] Feminist groups and other outraged citizens organized a recall petition drive in which they obtained almost twice the required number of signatures. The judge was removed from the bench in September 1977 in the first judicial recall election in Wisconsin history. He lost to a feminist candidate. Another Wisconsin judge, hearing a case in which a 24-year-old man sexually assaulted a 5-year-old girl, blamed the attack on the girl. Incredibly, he called the 5-year-old "an unusually sexually permissive young lady" and "the aggressor" in the assault.[18] A recall campaign is now underway.

More important than these judges' attitudes is the response they have provoked. Attitudes about rape do seem to be changing. The feminist position has received considerable favorable coverage in the press.

Because of its large audience, the "All in the Family" episode in which Edith Bunker is raped may have contributed significantly to a change in public perceptions of rape. People who work with rape victims also report a change. "The women I get today feel better about themselves as women," said Paula Klein of the National Coalition Against Sexual Assault. "They are less willing to hold themselves responsible for what happened."[19]

A major change in attitudes was a prerequisite to raising the problem of marital rape. Even now it is difficult to get many legislators to treat it as a serious issue. "If you can't rape your wife, who can you rape?" a California state senator said to a group of feminist lobbyists.[20] The campaign on marital rape is still in its infancy. Marital rape is considered a crime in only a few states. The National Center on Women and Family Law has conducted a study of the marital rape exemption in the states' criminal laws and provides information to feminists who want to launch reform campaigns.[21] This is an area in which a great deal of public education is needed. A campaign to change the law, even if it is not initially successful, is an excellent way of focusing public attention on the problem.

The feminist movement has also forced people to look at other aspects of reality that many would rather pretend did not exist. One of these seldom-discussed subjects is wife-beating. Contrary to myth, this is not a rare occurrence, nor is it restricted to the "lower classes." During 1973, approximately 14,000 wife-abuse complaints reached the New York State Family Courts.[22] And cases that make it to court are only the tip of the iceberg. Virtually all police personnel agree that wife-beating is the most underreported of all crimes; it has been estimated that a million women a year are subjected to domestic violence.[23]

Guilt and fear frequently prevent battered women from reporting the crime. As with rape, prevalent attitudes in our society are such that women who have been beaten often believe that somehow it's their fault. Many feel a public admission would expose them as failures at the role of wife. Economically dependent upon their husbands, lacking any place to go, battered wives fear that calling the police will only increase their husbands' wrath.

If a battered wife does call the police, her complaint is often not taken seriously. The husband will be arrested only at last resort and only if he has inflicted considerable injury. Police do not like getting involved in domestic conflicts, and unfortunately, too many seem to believe that there's nothing wrong about a husband slapping his wife around a little. Yet according to a Kansas City study, 96 percent of that city's family homicides had been preceded by at least one "domestic disturbance" call.[24]

The magnitude of the problem first became apparent in London. A

Women's Aid center, opened in 1971 to provide advice and support to women, found battered women coming in seeking shelter. The refuge that was established provided shelter to almost 5000 women and children in its first 3 years.[25] There are now about 50 such shelters in England. The first center in the United States had a similar history. Women Advocates of St. Paul, Minnesota, started in 1972 as a phone service for answering women's legal questions.[26] Staffers were soon deluged by women seeking emergency housing, which was not available. A fund-raising campaign resulted in enough money to open a shelter in 1974. Rape hot-lines also frequently received calls from battered women desperate for someplace to go.

Although a number of privately funded shelters for battered women have been opened around the country, the need much exceeds the supply. Lengthy waiting lists are intolerable when delay may mean serious injury or death. Because of the high cost of operating shelters, government funding has often been sought. A group in Orange County, California, obtained federal grant money to open a shelter. The NOW Wife Assault Task Force in Ann Arbor, Michigan, which provides emergency housing as well as other services, paid one full-time staff member out of Federal Government Comprehensive Employment and Training Act (CETA) funds.[27] A Brooklyn program operated jointly by the YWCA and the National Congress of Neighborhood Women received a $200,000 grant from New York State as start-up money.[28] The California legislature provided money for a pilot program to establish a limited number of shelters there.

By 1978, there were about 300 shelters, and the National Coalition Against Domestic Violence had been formed. Trying to develop reliable funding sources has been a top priority. Several states have been induced to increase their marriage license fees and earmark the money raised for spouse-abuse prevention programs. Florida took the lead in 1978. Since then Montana, California, Michigan, Kansas, North Dakota, and Ohio have followed. Indiana has imposed an antiabuse fee on divorce filings. This source of funds has been of immense help to those shelters that receive it because it is not dependent upon the vagaries of politics or the whims of private donors. The fees are not sufficient, however, to support the total budget of most shelters. Mercy House, one of four shelters in Montana, is probably typical. About $18,000 of its $60,000 budget comes from fees; the rest must be raised from foundations, churches, the United Way, and individual donations.

The National Coalition Against Domestic Violence, supported by other feminist groups, mounted a campaign to establish a federal program. In 1979 the House and in 1980 the Senate passed a domestic violence bill authorizing $65 million over 3 years, mostly for emergency shelters. The House passed the bill easily, but in the Senate, the vote was 46–41. Incredibly, conservative Christian groups targeted the bill for defeat and, led by the Moral Majority, subjected Senators to intense pressure. These groups opposed the bill because in the words of Senator Gordon Humphry, the federal government had "no business" intruding in family disputes. In the end, the Moral Majority defeated the broad coalition of women's, civil rights, and social service organizations who supported the bill. Although the conference report was easily approved in the House, opponents of the legislation threatened a fillibuster in the Senate and, because it was so late in the session, killed the bill.

The defeat of the bill proved to be a tragedy because the little federal money shelters had been getting from other government programs fell victim to Reagan's 1981 budget cuts. Shelters may still get some money from federal block grants to the states, but competition for these funds will be fierce. Unfortunately, retrogression is a real possibility in many areas. Many women will be forced to endure abuse because they have nowhere to go.

While essential, sufficient emergency housing is by no means a solution to the problem. Social service agencies and the police must be made more sensitive to domestic violence. A good deal of feminist effort is going into getting the police to enforce the law. In New York, a class-action suit on behalf of battered wives was filed in 1976. The suit charged that the police "deny the existence, prevalence, and seriousness of violence against married women or treat it as a private privilege of marital discipline."[29] The police frequently refused to respond to requests for assistance from battered wives and were extremely reluctant to arrest the husband.[30] In June 1978, the New York City Police Department entered into a consent judgment with the plaintiffs. In the agreement, the police bound themselves to guaranteeing battered women the same police protection and assistance afforded other crime victims. What this obligation entails is spelled out in considerable detail.[31] That this settlement represents an important victory indicates how little protection battered women formerly received from the police. A massive monitoring campaign to make sure the police live up to the agreement is underway. Encouragingly, the settlement appears to be having an impact beyond New York. Feminists, using it as a model, have pressured police departments in a number of cities to change their procedures.[32] The National Center on Women and Family Law has prepared a comprehensive training module to aid advocates for battered women.[33]

The roots of the physical abuse of women lie in our society's beliefs about appropriate sex roles and the institutional arrangements that result from these beliefs. Men are expected to be aggressive and physically assertive, to be head of the household. Women are expected to be dependent and passive. Within the traditional family structure, women are economically dependent upon their husbands and thus basically powerless. Under these circumstances, it is not altogether surprising that men take out their frustrations by beating their wives—often the only person over whom they have power. A real solution thus requires basic changes in attitudes and power relationships.

Some of the uglier symptoms of the underlying attitude toward women in our society are the prevalence of violence against women in films and the bizarre record jackets put out by a number of reputable firms and popular rock groups. On the record jackets, women have been shown badly beaten and seemingly enjoying it. Women Against Violence Against Women was formed to combat such outrages. The group forced a billboard advertising one such record to be removed and organized a boycott of the companies involved. After a 2½-year struggle, Warner Communications, Inc., one of the worst offenders, agreed to renounce such promotional tactics. "The WCI record group opposes the depiction of violence, against men or women, on album covers and in related promotional material," the company's president said in a joint statement issued by WCI and WAVAW in Los Angeles and New York.[34] Although this was a major breakthrough, it was only one battle in a much bigger war.

Recently, some feminists have extended the attack to include pornography. The image of women in pornography is extremely negative and demeaning. In it, women are depicted as objects, not as feeling individuals. Violence against women is a major theme in pornography, and women are frequently shown as enjoying it. Although all feminists oppose pornography's depiction of women, there is some argument about what should be done. Some advocate censorship; others are concerned that this would violate the right to freedom of speech. Large reputable record and film companies can be subjected to the pressure of public opinion as was done with WCI. This tactic is, unfortunately, much less likely to be successful with the small and more marginal companies that produce pornography and that do not have reputations to lose. The best answer in the long run is to destroy the market for pornography through education. In the short run, there may not be an answer short of breaching the First Amendment.

Notes

1. Pamela Kearon and Barbara Mehrhof, "Rape: An Act of Terror," *Notes from the Third Year*, 1972, p. 80.
2. Ibid.
3. Quoted in Kirsten Grimstad and Susan Rennie, *The New Woman's Survival Catalog*, 1973, p. 155.

4. Quoted in ibid, p. 145.

5. Ibid, p. 150.

6. Quoted in ibid., p. 145.

7. Ibid.

8. Quoted in ibid., p. 146.

9. Quoted in *In These Times*, March 9–15, 1977.

10. Quoted in ibid.

11. Quoted in Grimstad and Rennie, *Catalog*, op. cit., p. 147.

12. Ibid.

13. *Los Angeles Times*, December 13, 1981.

14. Ibid.

15. *New York Times*, August 31, 1981.

16. *Los Angeles Times*, October 18, 1981.

17. *Los Angeles Times*, June 3, 1977.

18. *National NOW Times*, January/February 1982, p. 6.

19. *New York Times*, August 31, 1981.

20. *Express*, May 16, 1980.

21. *Women's Rights Law Reporter* 6 (spring 1980), 159.

22. Judith Gingold, "One of These Days—Pow Right in the Kisser," *Ms.*, August 1976, p. 52.

23. *In These Times*, May 18–24, 1977.

24. Gingold, op. cit., p. 54.

25. Kirsten Grimstad and Susan Rennie, *The New Woman's Survival Sourcebook*, 1975, p. 214.

26. *Do It Now*, June 1976.

27. Ibid.

28. *In These Times*, May 18–24, 1977.

29. *Ms.*, April 1977, p. 19.

30. Laurie Woods, "Litigation on Behalf of Battered Women," *Women's Rights Law Reporter* 5 (fall 1978), 7–34.

31. Ibid., 28–31.

32. Ibid., p. 31, n. 156.

33. *Women's Rights Law Reporter* 6 (spring 1980), 159.

34. *Los Angeles Times*, November 9, 1979.

32

. . . All Things Are Possible

Yvonne Duffy

. . . As Differently Abled women in the latter part of the twentieth century, what can we do to support one another as we strive for self-actualization? How do we handicap ourselves and each other? What is our role in the women's movement? How do we fit into society as a whole?

I recently received in the mail a paper entitled "Disabled Women: Sexism Without the Pedestal" (Fine and Asch, 1981) in which the term "rolelessness" is used to describe the status of Differently Abled women in society. Whereas Differently Abled men have the choice of identifying either with their disability or with their maleness—a more positive image—according to the authors, women have no real option, since both identities are seen as equally powerless. To what extent is this true?

Because of her specific physical condition (systemic lupus), Dahtee sometimes must use a wheelchair and at other times can walk unassisted; from this unique vantage point, she has been able to study how the same persons' attitudes toward her changed according to whether she was Differently Abled or able-bodied:

> Before I was disabled, I was always very popular . . . very strong personality, infectious laugh, good listener as well as a good talker, and I knew how people responded to me then. . . . And then, when I was disabled, I went through these amazing realizations of how people treat disabled people. . . . I was always so used to people being respectful of my intelligence and my knowledge, and suddenly, I had people leaning down and slowly articulating into my face, "Are you all right, dear?" type of things. . . . I was not allowed to be respected. . . . I did not feel that anybody could see any of the beauty in me.

With nothing else changed but her legs' physical ability to carry her around, Dahtee's status vacillated between that of a pretty, well-educated, young woman and a mentally impaired illiterate. She was fortunate in possessing a strong sense of self. For those of us whose egos may not have been so fully developed when we became Differently Abled or who have faced this kind of oppression since early childhood, finding suitable roles is bound to be more difficult, however. For example, Connie L. stated,

> I have no role in society and feel really rotten about it . . . this is perhaps the hardest and most devastating question . . . because it has forced me to confront myself and how I have allowed myself to diminish to a point where I hardly feel I exist anymore.

Anet emphasized that we must make an effort toward self-determination:

> One thing that is disturbing to me is how easy it is for people with disabilities to give up their right to make their own decisions and to control their own lives. Somehow, we are convinced very early in our disability, whether the disability occurs to us as a child or in mid-adulthood, . . . that we are totally dependent, helpless, and this is just not true. . . .
>
> Eight years of isolation in San Francisco taught me how easy it is to get into an attitude of helplessness, of just deciding that there is no cure for the situation of isolation. It takes a lot more aggressiveness and assertiveness than we really want to have, to get out and be a member of society, to find answers for our needs. They just don't exist at home. . . . If I want to take a class in art, I should be able to do that and not just say, "Well, it's too much of a hassle to cope with transportation getting there. . . ." We just have to fight the ease with which we can slip into an apathetic state, so it entails changes in behavior patterns that many times create problems.

There is an interesting parallel here in the dependent wife who relies on her husband to make all her decisions, to supply her with opinions on all major issues, and, in fact, to define her world for her. Sanctioned by a large segment of society, this cocoon type of existence becomes more and more comfortable as one relinquishes her mind and heart to the control of another, and this can be a very difficult mold from which to break away.

Taking responsibility for one's own life is risky; one may make poor decisions and have to live with them without shifting blame to anyone else; one may be faced with tremendous challenges, physically, mentally, and spiritually.

What are the rewards? To determine one's own existence can be exciting. The book from which this article is taken could never have been written, for example, if twelve years ago, I had not relinquished my easy, dependent existence with an aunt and uncle to try living independently in Ann Arbor. It has not been easy, and I still don't feel quite as self-determining as Colleen Moore, a California paraplegic, who said, "I know I can create the events of my life as I wish." But I continue to grow more self-reliant even as my physical abilities weaken, because independence is a state of mind, not a state of body, and even my worst days, are better than those comfortable eons I passed doing nothing more strenuous than crocheting and watching T.V.

Do we take a back seat to Differently Abled men? Thinking back over the years to the numerous committees, boards, task forces, etc., on which I have served with other Differently Abled persons, the most vocal, the most assertive, the most adamant about the need for change, I recall, have been women. This trend appears to be continuing in the younger generation; one of my helpers, who served at a camp for Differently Abled children last summer, observed that the female children were usually the most assertive.

Women have emerged as early leaders in the struggle for equality waged by other minorities. Harriet Tubman and other black women who risked their lives daily so that others could take the Underground Railroad to freedom come first to mind. Perhaps those who suffer double oppression are first to recognize the necessity of liberation and, being already at the bottom of the totem pole, have the least to risk by speaking against the system.

As many of us become leaders and spokeswomen in our movement for equal rights, what can we do to support each other as we all seek the roles, traditional or non-traditional, best suited to us? Anet and Lola expressed their thoughts on this subject:

> There really needs to be more thought put into how disabled people can become independent. And there has to be more discussion of philosophy of independence that is not connected at all with the number of things a person has to be dependent upon. That is, independence really starts within you. . . .
> I've known many attendant/disabled person relationships that I would call very unsatisfactory because the disabled person doesn't think

of the attendant as an employee but . . . as a caretaker or parent figure, getting back to the opposition between philosophies of self-reliance and caretaking. These are two philosophies that are directed at the disabled, and I don't think [she] is getting enough of the self-reliance philosophy. . . .

We need to counsel newly disabled and children who are disabled on self-reliance and decision-making in evaluating where we are in life and what our status is in connection with the rest of society and learning how to improve it.

[Lola] would like to see more handicapped people in the various media, more active, less stereotyped portrayal . . . not just as main characters but also . . . supporting roles, bit parts—how about a handicapped secretary or neighbor, a handicapped woman sitting in a bar or restaurant that the main character walks into.

Also, it has occured to me that I've never seen a handicapped person on a game show. Do they think we don't like money? . . . I've never seen anyone handicapped doing a commercial. We buy all that stuff too.

Certainly, economic pressure is a valid tool, used with varying success by other minorities. Two things are important to remember when boycotting products and services to protest discrimination. First, sufficient numbers of persons must participate in order to make a financial impact; so it is a good idea to enlist the support of relatives, friends, and classmates, etc. Second, the proprietors should be informed of the reasons you and others are boycotting them as well as the changes you expect them to make.

How do we further handicap each other in our mutual struggle for full acceptance? Although stereotyping, a natural strategy we all use to put some order into a chaotic world, does not have to be prejudicial, it all too often locks us into others' expectations of us. It is essential that we examine our own attitudes regarding persons with other specific physical conditions to be sure that we are not hindering them from attaining their full potential.

Dahtee related her growth in self-awareness upon suddenly becoming Differently Abled:

I remember being just amazed when I realized my own stereotypes and my own prejudices against disabled people. That was the greatest learning experience for me when . . . I realized that . . . here I was sitting in a wheelchair with my own personal problems, and I knew nothing about the deaf world, I knew nothing about the blind world—cerebral palsy scared me to death—wouldn't allow myself to give them the intelligence that I so wanted people to give me.

She went on to explain how her world expanded as she overcame her bigotry:

I've gotten very involved with sign language, in going for my certification as an interpreter because one of the men that I met and became sweet-

hearts with was a deaf man . . . so I began using sign on a daily level for
communication . . . because I was seeing him all the time, and I began to
really respect this beautiful language system, with the beautiful, honest
concepts and grammar—everything about it.

Patting ourselves on the back because we are farther along the
road to independence than others with similar physical conditions is a
form of snobbery we can all do without, for, certainly, in diminishing
the accomplishments of others, we diminish ourselves. Expressing
how she felt about this tendency was Rebecca Burns:

> I bitterly hate the feeling of stigma I have among other handicapped peo-
> ple because I live with my mother. I feel that they think I'm backward, and
> I hate the feeling of having less confidence in some ways than some of my
> peers.

Several respondents felt alienated from the women's movement. Having suffered more serious discrimination as a result of being Differently Abled than being women, they thought that most feminists neither understood nor even acknowledged this problem. Mary James
said,

> Disabled women are the symbol of the most major form of "oppressed
> people" in this country, but I don't feel the women's movement is doing
> any recognizing of this. I am definitely a feminist but have no allegiance
> with women's groups. Their . . . problems seem so trivial as compared to
> those of the disabled women.

Michelle felt "left out. . . . I am a feminist—radical probably—but I
seem that as a separate part of my life from disability . . . there is no
arm of the movement concerned about disabled women." Deena remarked, "We do fit in but only on the outside like some sort of mas-
cot."

Personally, I feel that there is little genuine concern displayed for
Differently Abled women except by some lesbians in the women's
movement. Besides being more conscious of the sexual myths and taboos that can hurt us all, lesbians often seem more politically aware of
other minority movements than other feminists. The Michigan Wom-
en's Music Festival stands as an illustration of how we can be accom-
modated at meetings and gatherings with minimal financial expense
when planners are sensitive to our needs and creative about meeting
them.

The following women discussed the discrimination we face and
how they felt the women's movement was benefiting us:

Connie L. described the evolution of her thinking about our relationship to the women's movement:

> At first, though I've always considered myself a supporter of the feminist
> movement, I felt rather isolated from it. I could understand their outrage

at being judged wholly or primarily on the basis of their sex, but my problem was having people recognize that I had a sex.

As time went on though, I felt disabled women fit well into the women's movement. The need to fit into a particular mold in order to be considered a "real woman" was lessened by the movement . . . a sensitizing of men, a reevaluation of what they considered important in a woman and a relationship, couldn't help but make life better for disabled women. And, of course, the more wide open the choice of life styles, the better it is for us highly "irregular" types; so I think disabled women could not only benefit from the changes but have a lot to offer in helping to bring them about.

Jenny Jones, a paraplegic since birth, spoke.

We, in a way, have a double problem. Once you buck the disability, then you're next bucking the fact that you're a woman. I don't think I've had the discrimination because I'm a woman because they never saw beyond the disability, which may also be the factor in the fact that they don't know you.

Added Martha Merriweather,

We have to fight architectural barriers, attitudinal barriers, employment barriers . . . in addition to all that, we're also women. I think this takes a great deal of endurance, stamina, determination, but I intend to pursue it to the best of my abilities. I have wondered when I receive my degree in journalism, where I will go from there. Will I be accepted even though I am handicapped? I would hope that my personality is strong enough, that my skills are sharp enough, . . . that I am going to get the job that I want when the times comes.

Carol Sea, a social worker, thought the women's movement had been especially beneficial to us by helping others

realize that individuals should do the jobs that they are best at doing rather than doing jobs that they think they are supposed to do. In other words, because of the shift in the emphasis of women being homemakers, . . . in my relationship with my partner, I can go out and earn money at an intellectual job . . . and my partner could stay home and do the manual stuff.

Mae Evans summarized,

Before I was disabled, I had a comfortable identity as a wife, mother, and community leader. . . . I thought "women's rights'" were for others who had not lucked into a good life situation. After paraplegia, things were different. I lost my comfortable identity because I could no longer function in that role. I had to find some other way to operate, but there was no other way because I was no longer able to do the things that a female person "does" to be worthwhile. When I went into therapy for post-paraplegia depression, I became angry that the depression was not caused by the leg loss; it was caused by my original low self-esteem which pre-

vented me from accepting leg loss. I discovered that I had been a victim of
cultural attitudes on women and didn't even know it.

Disabled women can learn from the women's movement how they
have been held back by things other than their own disabilities. We may
not be able to improve our personal physical situation, but we can change
how we and others feel about our being women.

Reciprocal relationships in which we are able to give as well as receive are generally more satisfying, and this is no less so in our liaison
with the women's movement. Pooh Grayson noted,

Disabled women are good problems-solvers, good managers, and have
endless determination, or they don't survive. Those of us who have made a
life of our own would be a great asset to the women's movement.

Mae Evans went a step further:

Able-bodied women can learn from the disabled, who have had to learn
this before they can truly cope, that the physical body is not as important
as the person who lives inside; that one is first, a person and second, a female; that sex is less important than sexuality, and individuality is more
important than these two; and that every woman who is honestly involved
in her own personal growth is making a contribution to the women's
movement whether she is aware of it or not.

What were the major concerns of the Differently Abled women in
this study? Certainly, the desires they expressed, financial and emotional security, sexual happiness, barrier-free access to the community, and legal rights, are no different than those of most able-bodied
women. Overwhelming all other concerns, however, even when they
appeared to be talking about something else, has been the need to be
fully accepted as women rather than as asexual objects of pity. Sally
Smith related:

I am new in the community . . ., and I'm also newly married. One of my
bigger concerns is that I be accepted as one of the housewives . . . rather
than a poor disabled female . . . I do not want this type of concern/
sympathy, and I find it very difficult to become one of the girls. In fact, it
has been impossible so far. . . . I would like to be more a person—me, Sally
Smith, the person—rather than me, that poor girl in the wheelchair.

Woodie stressed:

First and foremost, I want people to know that I'm a person regardless of
whether I have a disability. I have wants and needs and fears; I'm happy
and I'm sad just like anybody else. I'm not immune to feelings and because I do have feelings I am a person. . . .

Secondly, I'm a woman. I do consider myself liberated—if not physically liberated, legally liberated, . . . spiritually liberated. Being a woman
is very important to me. . . .

Last but by no means least, I am a disabled woman. That also brings with it a few added concerns, but my disability is *not* the biggest most important thing in my life. I do not want people to judge me simply because I am disabled.

Woodie would probably agree with Martha Merriweather, who said,

> I love people who accept me for what I am—people who forget the fact that I'm in a wheelchair and will bring a chair to the table at dinner for me and then apologize and say, "Oh gee, I forgot." I find that extremely complimentary.

Indeed it is. My ideal person will do whatever is necessary to help me function independently, then, will forget about my specific physical condition and treat me as me—lover, friend, writer, or whatever I am in relation to that person.

When *we* can forget about being Differently Abled, I am convinced that it helps others to do so. Forgetting about it does not mean being passive or giving up the fight for accessible buildings and transportation, equal opportunities for employment, and legal rights. On the contrary, we must become even more assertive about obtaining these; having them will render us more independent and, thus, make it easier to concentrate on others rather than on ourselves and our limitations. Being more creative in finding new methods of doing things may help us forget about it for longer periods of time. Becoming better organized in daily activities may mean less time with an attendant; everyone needs some time alone every day to think and dream.

Most of all, forgetting the specific physical condition does not mean ignoring or failing to accept its existence. The period of solitude each day is particularly essential in truly coming to grips with it, for in really accepting the limitations, whatever they may be, while still striving to realize one's full endowment lies the key to full personhood.

Becoming a full person and not just *"a poor girl"* is not easy; it takes a lot of effort, but then most worthwhile achievements do. In closing, Elizabeth Mark and Deena gave us a glimpse of the rewards. Elizabeth Mark says,

> I love so much. There is not much I hate. Maybe other women who are disabled will realize, as I did, that there is love in our world—you just have to push yourself to your potential.

Deena contributed:

> I don't have any more hates since I just made the miraculous discovery that I accept myself as what I am, and I am loved more for the right reasons because of this discovery.

33

Broken Hips

Rosette Capotorto and Kathleen Walsh D'Arcy

The personal narratives that follow are taken from a collection of elder women's life stories. These women generously share their past and their present in the belief that the record of their lives will be useful to younger generations of women. Their histories are ethnically and economically diverse. They were homemakers, professors, laborers, dancers, cooks, writers, and factory workers. They are mothers, daughters, single, and widowed, but all have gender, age, and community membership in common. They live together in an institution, more specifically, in a "skilled nursing facility."

These storytellers live in an "SNF" nursing home because they have, or once had, an acute illness or disability that requires twenty-four-hour medical care. To the nonmedical observer, their residence looks like any other hospital, with busy corridors, harsh lighting, nurses' stations, and small, sparsely furnished rooms. Rigidly scheduled meals arrive on steel trolleys; drink is served in Styrofoam and food eaten with plastic utensils. But this is not a hospital, and these women are not patients who check in for a week or two. They are called "residents" in a geriatric facility which is their *only* home.

The tales of the events that led each woman to the door of the institution are uncanny in their similarity. Only dates and details change in the relentless scenario: Catastrophe (a fall, a traffic accident, a stroke) strikes an independent, elder women in her home or on the street. She is taken by ambulance to a hospital for treatment or surgery. Social workers and/or family decide she cannot return to her autonomous life-style. An ambulette transports her to a nursing home, an intermediate solution that often proves to be final.

The participants in this women's history project are alert, articulate, and politically savvy. They are a minority group in an establishment that houses large numbers of mentally impaired and "regressed" elders. Many bright and lucid women had already found each other in dining rooms and day rooms, but they were delighted to join a larger network of women for oral history collection. They saw the project as a connection to women outside, an opportunity to speak out and be heard. Their fascinating stories are filled with warnings and advice for all women.

These women are formidable critics of a system that evaluates their daily performance without ever asking for their expert appraisal of the geriatric industry. "They treat us like children" is the most common complaint, as they struggle to preserve their dignity and individuality in a system that labels them "inmates" instead of the health care consumers they are.

Anne Russell's and Gladys Carter's stories illustrate the collective experience of their sisters in American nursing homes. Their very different paths crossed only because each of them "fell" in the inexorable chain of events that brought them to the nursing home. With strong voices, they describe their home and critique the institution from within.

In 1898, Anne Russell was born into an old Massachusetts family whose white Protestant roots in America were two centuries old. She was a child of privilege, an only daughter in a large and loving family. After her mother's death and her high school graduation, she assumed the family caretaker role while her brothers went on to college and careers. Many generations of Russells called her "Sister." She says, "I was called Sister, and it was a man's world. For responsibility they came to Sister. I took things in my stride. There was no anger or resentment. I guess responsibility followed me because at this age, I've actually outlived every member." Besides her sense of family responsibility, she continued to have a great awareness of the world outside.

When Anne slipped in her bathroom and broke her hip, she was able to recuperate from the surgery at home, in her own apartment. Friends and neighbors looked in on her, and with the aid of a visiting nurse, she fully recovered. It was the second fall and hip fracture that changed everything. Surgical complications left her paralyzed, and she couldn't go home. Eighty years of independence, financial security, and caring for others did not prepare her for the shock of being confined to an institution for life.

> So here I am, but I'm very thankful and philosophical. If I hadn't come here I wouldn't have met you people. [She laughs.] It's remarkable. I'm in this room most of the time—and the people I've met!

When she entered the nursing home, Anne brought her political activism with her. Xeroxed copies of newspaper articles relating to nursing home investigation and legislation are stacked on her bedside table for easy distribution. Although she rarely leaves her room or her bed, a steady stream of visitors, including off-duty staff members, act as her information network. She records and reports daily news items, such as deaths, staff changes, and other incidents of vital importance to her community:

> The greatest problem facing this whole country today—it's not war—is that the government is running out of money for Medicare and Medicaid. Isn't that terrific? So how about a nursing home? I came to this one because I wanted to have my own physician who was a personal friend. A lot of nursing homes don't want your personal physician. You ought to see what they have here, and what they send in to her [points to roommate's bed]. That's why I'm here. And until last Friday, he came the first of every month, all these years I've been here, and he finally announced—eighty-one years old—that he was retiring, and he's recommended someone else. So I shall miss him terribly, because I can tell *you* what goes on here!
>
> They came to me and they wanted to stick a needle in me. I said, "What is this?" Mrs. G. said, "Everybody has to take the flu shot." Now I know from past experience that you can be worse with the flu shot than if you caught the real flu germ. They gave it to her [points to roommate] and they were very remiss. They're supposed to take a temperature every day. She was just about burning up, when the person in charge came. She wears the old-fashioned flannel nightgown in the wintertime. Very pretty. Mrs. G. said, "No wonder you're warm, you're wearing a hot nightgown," and here she was burning to the sky. Well, that had gone on dangerously far, so on the next shift we have this nice Betty. So finally, when she was just about ready to pass out, Betty came in to take up the supper trays and she said, "That's no hot nightgown, that's heat pouring out of her. I bet if I got a thermometer her temperature is up in the sky. If I can't get it down before I go off duty, I'm calling the hospital and we'll take her over." When she came in at eleven o'clock she said, "It's down to a hundred,

thank God," and she told the person coming on to watch her carefully. This has gone on since November. December, January, February, March—it's the first time, yesterday, she felt normal.

Dedicated and compassionate staff members are always greeted with Anne's praises when they enter her room. She stores their names, and even their birthdays, in her incredible memory bank. She also stores away the details of unpleasant exchanges between patients and staff, and relates these stories with a calm but chilling voice:

> I can even remember the exact date, Monday the 7th. The person in charge, very temperamental, high strung, loving to take it out on others because she was a nobody, she took me in to give me a shower, and getting me back into the chair she got my foot caught. "Sit down!" I said, "I can't," so she banged me and said, "Sit down!" she kept banging me until I screamed, and she looked, and this foot [points to foot] was just swollen way out, black and blue. The only thing that saved her was a little thin skin so that the blood couldn't get out. I've never heard the word; it's called "hemo"—that's for blood—"toma." All the blood vessels burst. Well, she was afraid I would tell. You know, they're supposed to be occupied at all times. The minute she'd see someone come in she'd rush to the sink to make believe she was washing her hands, thinking I would be a tattletale. Wherever I went, she was in, so she'd be sure I wouldn't tell.

Gladys Carter is an eighty-year-old black woman who was born in New York City and graduated from high school in 1922. Her plans for a secretarial career ended abruptly during a job search:

> I'd go to apply for a job and as soon as they'd see who I was they made excuses. I got the message. My color. Never mind my knowledge. Behind the doors they would never know, but if I came out and they'd see my face, forget it . . .

Gladys returned to school for another diploma, this time in cooking and food management, so she could "get jobs and make money because that's the main idea." She worked as a live-in cook until an accident, a broken hip, brought her to the institution.

> You see, age is what got me in here. Otherwise, I would never be in here. I'm eighty years old and I've been on my own for a long time and I've got to do this because I have nobody to depend on, no family. Now you see, when I came here—I fell in the street. My legs buckled under me and they put me in the hospital. Naturally when they put me in the hospital my friends didn't keep my place. That's why I haven't got no place now. It's pitiful. Since I've been here there's people crying and carrying on. People don't come to see them. I'm not worried. I haven't got anybody to come to see me, so it don't matter. If friends don't come, it's perfectly all right. If they don't want to remember me for what I was, forget it. I can forget it too. [She laughs.]

Gladys lives, literally, in the lobby of the nursing home, and only sleeps in her semiprivate room. This is her unique coping strategy, her way of bridging the gap between "outside" and "inside." Each day, she sets up her chair by the front door and observes the comings and go-ings of residents, relatives, and staff. Gladys speaks with a gatekeep-er's view of the institution:

> When I get up in the morning the first thing I hear is "Nurse, nurse, nurse." I get mad at the nurses because they take their time, and there's a lot of temperamental old people, grouchy, and a lot of them mean too. And hollering at them; I don't like that. That's why I don't like to stay up there. I'll snap like a—I don't like it. I don't think you should be abused like that.
>
> And you know, a lot of them got big families and they're crying and they won't be bothered with them, and they don't come to see them at all. Oh, good Lord, I'll tell you the truth, I'm thankful that all mine are gone. I won't have to worry about it 'cause I don't think I could take it, what I see going on around here; old people crying and carrying on. They don't come. I say, "Don't worry, they'll come. They'll come." I keep trying to cheer them up like that. But it's heart rendering to think that you did all you could, brought them in the world, and then they leave you in this place. I came into this place because I had no place else to go.
>
> I heard a woman, I heard her begging down in the lobby. They brought her down in a wheelchair, begging to go home. He gave her some kind of excuse. That poor old soul. I realize he couldn't do nothing. She's in a wheelchair, plus the fact they don't want to have the trouble to take care of her. If not, they got to hire somebody to take care of her and fix meals for her. That's the way it goes.
>
> I look at them when I sit down in the lobby. They bring the old lady downstairs in the wheelchair. One little boy—I thought it was a shame. They had to almost spank him to make him kiss Grandma. Poor old soul was sitting in the chair, you know. She don't look too beautiful but she still was his grandmother, you know. He was more or less afraid of her. Oh my Lord. "Go, go, go, get over there and kiss Grandma." My Lord, and the poor little thing didn't want to do it.
>
> It's pitiful, really. One woman, she made me so mad when she asked me, "Gladys, who's going to bury you when you die?" I said "Jesus Christ." "Uh-oh," the girl said, "don't bother with her!" I said "I'm not worrying about dying. I'm worrying about living." And you see those cockroaches, how they fight for their life? That's me.

34

Angry Women Are Building
Issues and Struggles Facing
Native American Women

Paula Gunn Allen

The central issue that confronts American Indian women throughout the hemisphere is literally *survival*, both on a cultural and biological level.

In the United States the population of American Indians according to the last census is just over 1,000,000. Some researchers put our pre-contact population at upwards of 45 million, while others put it around 20 million. The US government used the imaginary figure of 450,000 for almost 200 years. If as some researchers insist, around 25% of Indian women and 10% of Indian men in the United States have been sterilized without informed consent; if our average life expectancy is, as the best informed research presently says, 45 years; if our infant mortality rate continues at well above national standards; if our average unemployment for all segments of our population is between 60% and 90%; if the US government continues in its policy of termination, relocation, removal and assimilation along with the destruction of wilderness, reservation land and its resources, and severe curtail-

Adapted from *The Sacred Hoop* by Paula Gunn Allen. Copyright © 1986 by Paula Gunn Allen. Reprinted by permission of Beacon Press.

ment of hunting, fishing, timber harvesting and water-use rights, then the tribes are still facing extinction.

For women, the current struggle for physical and cultural survival means fighting alcoholism and drug abuse (our own and that of our husbands, lovers, parents and/or children); poverty; affluence (a destroyer of people who are not traditionally socialized to deal with large sums of money); rape, incest, battering by Indian men; assaults on fertility and other health areas by the Indian Health Service and the Public Health Service; high infant mortality rate due to substandard medical care, substandard health and nutritional information; poor educational opportunities or education that takes us away from our traditions, language and communities; suicide, homicide or similar forms of self-hatred; lack of economic opportunities; substandard housing; sometimes violent and always virulent racist attitudes and behaviors directed against us as Indians by an "entertainment" and "educational" system that wants only one thing from Indians: disappearance. They coerce our silence, our invisibility and our collective death.

A headline in the *Navajo Times* in the fall of 1979 said that rape was the number one crime on the Navajo Reservation. In a report published in Listening Post, A Periodical of the Mental Health Programs of Indian Health Services (VI: 2 April, 1982), Phyllis Old Cross Dog has reported that incest and rape are common among Indian women seeking services and that they are increasing. "It is believed that at least 80% of the Native Women seen at the regional psychiatric service center (5 site area) have experienced some sort of sexual assault," she says. Among the forms of abuse being suffered by Native Women, Old Cross Dog cites a recent phenomenon, something called "training." This form of gang rape is "a punitive act of a group of males who band together and get even or take revenge on a selected woman." Certainly these and other cases of violence against women indicate that the status of women within the tribes has suffered a serious decline since contact, and the decline has gained speed in recent years. The amount of violence against women, as well as the incidence of violence, abuse and neglect by women of their children, have both increased; and both were virtually unheard of among most tribes 50 years ago—contrary to popular white American opinion.

In the face of these multiple threats on our sanity, survival, and sense of self, many of us just give up. Many are alcoholics, many are addicts; many abandon the children, the old ones; many commit suicide; many become violent, go insane; many go "white" and are never seen or heard from again. But enough hold on to their traditions and their ways so that even after almost 500 brutal years, we endure; and even write songs and poems, make paintings and drawings that say, "We walk in beauty. Let us continue."

Media images, literary images and artistic images, particularly those embedded in popular culture, must be changed before the Indian women will see much relief from the violence that destroys so many lives. Colonizer revisions of our lives, values and histories have devastated us at the most critical level of all—that of our own minds, our own sense of who we are, to the extent that American Indian men have been deluded into acting out the widespread belief that they are blood-thirsty, heartless savages who treat women with cruelty. Native Women struggle against government and corporations, as well as against all individuals or interest groups who will stop at nothing in their dedication to obliterating American Indian peoples. They alter our life support base, steal our tribal lands, colonize our cultures and cultural expressions and revise our very identities. We must work to maintain tribal status; we must make certain that the tribes continue to be legally recognized entities, sovereign nations within the larger United States, and we must wage this struggle in a multitude of ways— political, educational, literary, artistic, individual and communal. We are doing all we can; as mothers and grandmothers; as family members and tribal members; as professionals, workers, artists, shamans, leaders, chiefs, speakers, writers and organizers; we daily demonstrate that we have no intention of disappearing, of being silent, or of going quietly along with our extinction.

35

Black Lesbian/Feminist Organizing

A Conversation

Barbara Smith

Tania Abdulahad, Gwendolyn Rogers, Jameelah Waheed, and I met on June 13, 1982 to discuss our experiences as activists and organizers. All of us had attended the second National Third World Lesbian and Gay Conference in Chicago in November of 1981 and it was there that I began to think about the possibility of our doing an article about our political work.

Prior to our conversation, I sent everyone an outline of the questions I hoped we would cover and we relied on these questions during our talk. We talked for almost three hours and the conversation here is of course a condensation, although virtually all of the topics we discussed are included.

Tania Abdulahad is a member and past president of Sapphire Sapphos, a Black Lesbian organization in Washington, D.C.

Gwendolyn Rogers is National Coordinator of the Lesbian and Gay Focus of the People's Anti-War Mobilization and a national organizer for the All People's Congress.

Excerpted from "Black Lesbian/Feminist Organizing: A Conversation" in *Home Girls: Black Feminist Anthology*. Reprinted by permission of Barbara Smith and Kitchen Table Press.

*Jameelah Waheed is the Coordinator of the Political Action Com-
mittee of Salsa Soul Sisters Third World Womyn Inc., an eight-year-old
Third World Lesbian organization based in New York City.*

BARBARA: How did each of you get involved in doing political organizing?*

GWENDOLYN: I started doing political organizing in a serious way when I came
out into the Lesbian community. After taking a very long time to come out, I
got very, very involved with Lesbian feminist politics and embraced that
whole-heartedly. I worked in that context for a while, but after a period of time
I felt that there were certain contradictions that working in the Lesbian feminist community alone did not answer.

About a year and a half ago, I attended a coalition meeting which had been
called to launch a new anti-war movement. A number of Lesbians, including
several Black Lesbians, and gay people were there. Many of us found the prospect of working within a progressive coalition as "out" Lesbians and gays,
thrilling. I got very drawn into that initiative, and started reevaluating very seriously how and where I wanted to focus my major energies in terms of political activity.

JAMEELAH: The reason I began political organizing with Salsa Soul Sisters was
the need to preserve my woman-identified woman freedom. Many Third World
Lesbian sisters were being deported back to Africa, the Caribbean, and other
places because they were living openly in the Lesbian community. The problems of mere survival for myself and my sisters caused me to take all the
knowledge and energy I have and put it toward trying to work collectively with
others in ending our oppressions. Organizing in this manner takes grassroots
people and progressive individuals to bring about a change in the attitudes of
government officials and community people.

This process is not an easy task. I have spent the past two years doing consciousness raising within the organization and the Lesbian community as a
whole. The main challenge of organizing for me has been working with Third
World gay male groups and Black male heterosexual community organizations to make them aware of Third World Lesbians and how their sexist attitudes perpetuate our oppression. I mean, as long as males view our liberation
as the least important to their liberation, then none of us will ever be liberated.

BAR: What about you, Tania?

TANIA: My actually getting involved in Lesbian feminist politics was for the
most part through organizing cultural events. We did coffee houses and
brought in people like Meg Christian and Holly Near. One of the things that I
found real different about being in the women's community was that there
weren't a whole lot of Black Lesbian feminists that I saw. Pittsburgh had a real
small women's community and it also had a mostly white women's community, so almost everybody that I knew and did work with were white women.
But I always had it in the back of my mind that obviously there were Black Les-

---

*Although Jameelah joined us after the conversation was underway, she responded in
writing to the first question.

bians; they just weren't in Pittsburgh. Or I would only see them if I went out to a bar, or a party, or something like that. But I never saw them at any political events. And I thought that was rather strange because I knew that Black women were certainly involved in women's issues. But in terms of the Lesbian issues and just being an "out" Lesbian feminist, it was real hard to find out where people were coming from. . . .

BAR: What kinds of organizing are you involved with now and how is it relevant to Third World women?

GWEN: At this point, I am working primarily on the grassroots resistance movement that targets Reagan's program, and on building a new anti-war movement unlike the old peace movement which excluded so many oppressed people. We're trying to involve many more communities and to work closely with the poor people's movement. I've been working nationally on the struggles of Black women under apartheid. I'm also working on campaigns which specifically affect the women's community, and the Lesbian and gay community: the so-called "Family Protection Act," repressive legislation in general, reproductive freedom, and so forth. I think it's very important to organize among Black Lesbians, Lesbians in general, and gay males. I also think it's very important to bring the issue of Lesbian and gay oppression to the overall movement and for Black and other Third World people to have that as something they must grapple with and identify with consciously in a political context.

TAN: Up until last weekend I was the president of Sapphire Sapphos, a Black lesbian organization in D.C. Until Sapphire Sapphos got started there was no Black Lesbian feminist organization out there for Black Lesbians to plug into, so it's served a definite need. The work I've done for the most part has been pretty much keeping the organization together. . . .

I've spent the last two years in Sapphire Sapphos trying to develop some politics for a lot of the sisters in the organization, trying to make sure that the organization begins to see itself outside of just meeting every other Sunday and as part of the broader gay community.

I've also been working recently with some other Black women's groups that have sprung up. A lot of these women have come from nationalist movements and still have nationalist sentiments, but they understand that they have to talk about some of the things that they've experienced specifically as Black women. That's been useful for me too.

BAR: What I'm doing now, mostly, is writing and also working on Kitchen Table: Women of Color Press, which is the first press that has the commitment of publishing the work of women of color both in the U.S. and internationally. That's very exciting to me, because I see it as an expansion of my politics from Black women's organizing to Third World women's organizing, which is a direction that we're probably all moving in. The other thing that I wanted to mention was my involvement in the Combahee River Collective, which was a group of Black feminists, primarily Lesbians, that began in Boston in 1974. Many people are familiar with the Collective by now. That was just such a dynamic chapter in my life. One of the things that's most important about it, is that it shows you *can* do Black women's organizing. You can raise those "funky" issues that nobody wants to talk about and live to tell about it. Later I want to talk about the organizing we did around the murders of Black women in Boston in 1979, because I think that work illustrates what's possible as far as coalitions are concerned. You can raise the hardest issues and have grassroots Black women relate to them.

I wanted to talk more about the difficulties of organizing Black women. What have you found to be problems?

TAN: An ongoing problem of Black women's organizing, particularly as it relates to the work I've done in Sapphire Sapphos, has been what kinds of commitments will people make to challenging themselves to be political. . . .

Another thing that's really hard to do in terms of organizing Black Lesbian feminists is getting people to do coalition work. Many Black Lesbians still identify the feminist movement with white women and they have real problems with white women. All of it I'm sure has its historical roots, but I think that we're at a different stage now. We are talking about history moving on. We have a bigger world and broader questions that we have to relate to and we can't operate in these old narrow vacuums. I think that white women can be challenged on their racism; they can be challenged on their ignorance and their backwardness. But if we don't, if we only leave it to three or four of us to do that all the time, we are constantly over-utilizing those same women. And also we are burning them out. Burn-out is a real syndrome.

The other thing that I find really difficult in organizing is making it possible for Black women who are Lesbian and Black women who are straight to work together. That's because a lot of Black Lesbians are still at a point where they don't want the Black community to know that they're Lesbians. But I see that as real contradictory, because I hear some of the same Black Lesbians talking about their identification with the Black community. Well how can you unquestioningly identify with the Black community when they are really not supportive of who you are as a person or of your right to live in a society where you're not just tolerated, but accepted?

I've found that in dealing with the Black community, confining yourself to labels doesn't help. If you say first I am Black, and second I am a woman, third I am a Lesbian, fourth I am a feminist, fifth I am a worker, and so on, then, of course, every single time that you think about what you are going to do and how you're going to relate to something, it is always along those lines and in that order. Those are difficult decisions to make, because you are *all* of those things at once and they're all important to you. . . .

GWEN: I can identify and relate to the difficulties you described in working in the Black Lesbian community. But I find it's very different when you're organizing Black Lesbians who have not been touched by a community movement.

I hesitate to say it's easier, but in a certain sense it is, when you're working with and organizing the sisters on the street, or when you're doing outreach to the working Lesbian who really has not been enmeshed in or demoralized by the various movement controversies or intimidated by the pejorative use of labels.

Working within a multi-issue, multi-national context, the difficulties are somewhat different. I see two main difficulties. One entails the whole question of channeling our rage—maintaining the focus of who is being targeted. Who is the real enemy, who are we organizing against, and what are we organizing for? In other words, how to maintain a class perspective which helps us see how all oppression flows from an exploitive system. Again, this is more of a problem when we look at issues as being isolated. . . .

JAM: I was listening to what both of you were saying. What is the reason for distrust? We have to look at that. Why do sisters distrust other sisters who say they are networking, building coalitions, whatever? I can speak about my organization. The reason why I think they distrust other women, who come from the outside, who are Third World Lesbians or Black Lesbians, is because they're not dealing with our issues, that is, basic survival. Survival is the basic thing that we're constantly dealing with and our survival entails all issues.

Housing is one of the main things that we can all relate to. Another thing we all can relate to is what type of health care we get as Black women. Education and jobs are issues we can relate to, because they are constant struggles. We have sisters in the community who are constantly calling each other, saying "Hey, I'm getting ready to be put out of my house" or "I'm getting ready to lose my children." "I can't find proper health care." It's constant so we are working together to build solutions.

You raised dealing with the Black community. One of our long range goals is to work with the Black community. We have to because that's where we live. We've got to have them deal with the issue of homophobia and not lose our focus of who we are. The strategy by which the Political Action Committee proposes to do this is to get involved in their organizations as out Black Lesbians and to work with them on issues that we all rally behind. Two of the issues that we rally behind, at this point, are the issue of South Africa and the issue of racism. Our participation lets them see that we are an autonomous body, but we do work and support the movement. . . .

TAN: I don't disagree with what you're saying, Jameelah. But the context I am talking from is probably a very unique situation from the situation in New York. I don't have any problems with that, but D.C. is definitely different. The Black Lesbians that I'm talking about are Lesbians who work for the federal government.

JAN: They're elitist.

TAN: No, no, no. I'm talking about people who feel that there is a lot more at stake for them to be out politically because of what they have been socialized to believe in. I waver sometimes myself on the question of what makes people elitist. Black people, in the sense that I use the term, are not elitist. And these Black women I'm talking about may be backward, extremely so, but they're definitely not elitist because they don't have those kinds of power positions. What they do have are jobs that are substantial enough to give them a certain mobility that they are not real sure they want to lose. And what I see happening particularly in Sapphire Sapphos, is those women come and project for the organization what the direction is going to be.

JAM: They come and project this?

TAN: Yes, in terms of their influence. They come with skills which we need. We have accountants. We have lawyers. We have people in medical school. We don't tell these women that there's no place for you in our organization, but we know that those women have a certain perspective about what the organization should be, that it should operate like the National Council of Negro Women (Laughter) only it should be for Black Lesbians. What we say is that there is room for you in this organization, but there is also room for sisters who are on welfare. There is also room for sisters who have childcare needs. There are sisters who are students who have some needs. And there are sisters who come from the women's movement, who are strong feminists, and who want to be identified as that. . . . I don't have any problems with sisters who make $30,000 a year, especially if they're contributing to keep the organization that I believe in together. But, if that $30,000 a year perspective is going to be the sole basis on which things are decided in terms of politics, I have problems with that.

BAR: I just want to jump in here to say that it seems like what we're talking about is difference and how we deal with it among ourselves.

GWEN: Yes.

BAR. We're talking about political differences, class differences, and differences in values. But sometimes what gets defined as a class difference is not about actual income levels, it's about values and what you're aspiring to. And that's very complex for us. But in Sapphire Sapphos or in Salsa Soul, some of this stuff has obviously been dealt with head on. So clearly it's possible, it can be done.

GWEN: We have talked a little bit about something that Jameelah raised that I want to get back to and that is the whole issue of where distrust comes from in terms of organizing with Black women. . . . Often the distrust comes from forces outside of us. That's something we don't always acknowledge. We need to ask ourselves why it is if we're talking with a group of welfare mothers they're less likely to ask, "Why is *she* here?" You don't find that attitude as prevalent as when you're approaching a group of Black Lesbians that has been defined as being *in* the movement or in a community. And we need to look at why that is. I think primarily it has to do with the nature of our oppression. A group of Black Lesbians are a very powerful force. And anybody who opposes us who has any sense would say: that's a potentially powerful force, and we need to make sure it doesn't really coalesce and come together in the way it needs to. That's why it is so important not to feed divisiveness in any way. . . .

JAM: You know, when I think about the history of Black Lesbian organizations, so many times sisters have come from outside and outside means sisters who do not deal with the community itself as a whole, who are not there.

GWEN: What community?

JAM: The Black Lesbian community. These sisters, when they finally do come, have used a highly sophisticated way of dividing and conquering the community or the organization. So many times, there is distrust because there has to be a level of safeguarding one's self or safeguarding your organization. So what it boils down to is not letting yourself be led into a direction that gets you away from your basic issues. And that's something that we have to constantly remind ourselves of. It's not that we don't want other sisters to come into the community with new ideas. I mean, there's constant sharing and exchanging of new ideas and perspectives. That's what keeps an organization growing and thriving. Yes, there's going to be conflict. There has to be conflict. That's the only way that we learn from each other. If an organization's running smooth with no problems then we all are basically saying the same thing. Rhetoric. That's what you get. No one's growing. And we're not challenging anything. But it keeps going back to this: the sisters who bring things into the community also have to be a part of the community. And that sometimes means crying with people over common issues. And that means sometimes getting your behind kicked out there. Sisters have shared a lot in these communities. And that's why when someone comes with something new, and you don't know what they have been through, you don't necessarily trust them. . . .

We get sisters who, if all of a sudden, they get some type of notarization from the white community, then they consider themselves our leaders. It appears they think they can answer all of the problems of Black feminist Lesbians. There's no way in hell that you can do that. None of us can really say what all the problems are, because we don't know. We can take a consensus of what our groups or a majority of Lesbians are saying is the problem and deal from there. But we cannot speak for them. . . .

BAR: My question is, is it possible to be in an organization, to be a part of the community and demonstrate leadership abilities? In other words, Gwendolyn is talking about doing national organizing which means on some level she's getting national recognition. I've gotten to travel all over the country and speak and that's a kind of organizing as well. How do the parts mold together? How do they join together? . . .

TAN: I wanted to say something concerning leadership and how it's developed or not developed. I understand where Gwendolyn is coming from as well as Jameelah. I came to some conclusions about this as a result of experiences I had in another kind of group. I was in an organization for a number of years that was a left group. For a long time there were a lot of things that the group did that I definitely was opposed to. But as a member of a group you have a certain unity about being in the group, so you hash the differences out internally. As a result of that experience, I found that when I left that group I became real hard in terms of being leery of the left, because I had been burned. I'm not saying that what happened to me has been to the detriment of how I think about all left groups. It just means I am in a much better political situation now to understand and to analyze what the questions are. . . .

BAR: I want to switch the discussion at this point and talk about the values and virtues of being out as Lesbians in relation to whatever politics we're doing.

TAN: I guess the value for me in being out is it gives me the opportunity to at least know how to answer questions from the opposition. . . .

My being out is also an opportunity to convince other people to do it. To inspire people and let them know that there are positive Lesbian role models. Being out has also helped me be able to cross lines, like in my building you don't get nobody to talk more about tenants' rights than me. I make sure that I'm right on the case when them tenants' meetings is happening. And I talk to the resident manager and I talk to the people in my building and I tell them about things that are going on in the community. I use the bulletin boards to advertise about community events, so people usually know that whenever they see something posted in my building, it's me that put it up there. I think that as long as you give people the opportunity to see you functioning on many different levels, then what they obviously have to recognize is that you are about more than your quote/unquote "sexual preference." You begin to challenge other people to deal with you seriously.

GWEN: I just thought of yesterday's disarmament demonstration. A group of us including several Black Lesbians were marching with other progressive groups and Third World groups and carrying the Lesbian and Gay Focus (of P.A.M.) banner. We were in a section of the march which primarily focused attention on the threat of nuclear war in South Africa, Lebanon and the war in the Middle East. One Palestinian woman was quite struck by our banner, she kept peeking at it and peeking at it. She approached us and we started rapping. Our being there, visibly there, raised her consciousness, and gave her an opportunity to ask some questions. She was wondering why we, as Black Lesbians, were in that section of the march. She was curious about the whole business of how we defined our issues.

BAR: I really love what you're saying because my experience has been that the more down-to-earth people are and the more pressed they are in their actual day-to-day situations, the more open they probably are to us as Lesbians. 'Cause, you see, they don't have time for bullshit. They know that the fact that we are woman-identified and are sexual with each other in the great scheme of things doesn't undermine their ultimate freedom. What we've noticed is that it's the well-educated Black middle-class intellectuals in this country who are the ones who are going nuts over this. It's the *Black Scholar* magazine variety that are getting on our cases, people who have the leisure to think that we are messing with their program. Conscious people who are truly in life and death struggles know that we're on their side. . . .

BAR: I want to discuss coalitions with other women of color who are not Afro-American. I feel like we're at a breakthrough point as far as making those links is concerned and I wanted to know what each of you have thought about this recently.

JAM: I can admit that it's a challenge. We at Salsa have been trying to deal with that challenge. One of the things that I'm finding with the Asian sisters, with the Hispanic sisters, and I'm being very frank about this, is it seems that some have problems relating to Black Lesbians. We have found a lot of them in this area feel more comfortable working with white Lesbians, or with other groups and not working with us. I feel this is a form of racism that is perpetuated by the white male dominant society. Unfortunately these attitudes filter into Third World communities, and cause separatism to continue. A lot of them basically say, we'd rather work together or work with the white community. When they do come around, they say, "You're not organized." And I say, how aren't we organized? We've been existing for eight years and we're not organized? Then they say, "You're not political enough." Well we have a sub-committee that's a political committee, that deals with the political issues. If you feel there's more that you can bring in to help the organization grow, because this is our base, this is your organization also, then bring it in. It doesn't appear as though they want to give it. And we've made the space. We don't care what the sister is. If she's Asian, if she's Cuban, if she's Chicana, if she's Hispanic, whatever she is. If she's a Native American, Indian, Black, Cuban, because we do have a mixture there. But we have a tendency with sisters who are not "Afro-American" quote/unquote, to get the sisters from those populations who are a darker color. They are from the same places, but some of them are of darker complexion. So people automatically assume they're all Afro-American. And they're not. But the sisters who are a lighter complexion, they have a tendency to be with the white, privileged community.

BAR: So you're talking about internal racism?

JAM: Yes.

BAR: This is a question that you can respond to or not. How do you imagine it feels to come into an all-Black women's group when you're one of something else? 'Cause I think that it feels a lot like how we feel when we go into an all-white group and we're the only one. You're dealing with cultural isolation. I think that's hard.

GWEN: This may be a little presumptuous of me to answer, but I'd like to comment. I'm living with a Native sister—she's Eastern Cherokee, and very strongly Third World identified, *and* very fair-skinned. We've been in situations where I as a dark-skinned Third World person feel pressured to say, "But her father is Black and Indian." It's very painful to her to be confronted with the assumptions people make because she is light. She's constantly dealing with invisibility and isolation. On the one hand whites almost always assume she's white—which drives her up a wall. In situations with darker Third World people her presence and identity might be questioned. I've had to deal with my response to her reactions to the isolation. It's really made me look at the issue of being a Third World person in a much more political way. Someone once said to me: "Well if she isn't Black and she ain't colored, then there's no way. She doesn't feel the oppression the same way." Well in a way that may be true but it's pretty clear that that attitude obliterates history. It obliterates the history of what it means to be colored in terms of her people. It obliterates the history of the genocide and oppression of Native people which continues today. It also obliterates the history of the relationship between Black and Native peoples. Thinking about working with other Third World people and the kinds of alliances we have to make in the Native community, the Puerto Rican community, in the various Third World communities, it's crucial for us as

Black Lesbians to understand the commonality of our struggle and the struggles of other Third World women.

Some people have expressed the notion that among Third World people, we as Blacks are more privileged and consequently have the power to be racist. I think the history of our oppression is such that we may not always interpret the dynamics between us and other Third World people correctly, and sometimes when we echo the kinds of racist shit which stems from a class system, we aren't sure if we've being racist—prejudiced or whatever. Seeing as how racism by definition has as its basis the concept of white superiority, I don't think it's correct to describe the insensitivities we may exhibit toward each other as racist. Racism is not a personal affliction. It's a system of attitudes and behaviors. It's institutionalized and is a means to justify exploitation. We as Black people do not have at our disposal the means to enforce a system of superiority and exploitation. But if we as Black Lesbians are talking about being woman-identified, that by necessity must also mean Third-World-woman-identified. . . .

JAM: Well, that goes to another problem. A lot of people in an organization are not quote/unquote "political" and they cannot be a lot of places all the time. You have to accept this. We cannot just go and deal with everyone's struggle.

GWEN: But they're not everyone else's struggles. That's part of the problem, how we define our struggle also defines how we relate to our other Third World sisters. . . .

TAN: I find in D.C. that there obviously has not been a lot of consciousness raising among Black women around the need for people to identify with other Third World women. I know that that's particularly true in Sapphire Sapphos. I agree that sometimes it is very easy for us to assume people are operating out of a racist context, because racism is the first thing we've always addressed when somebody has really bad attitudes about us. It is scary when Black people get called on being racist, but I certainly see a lot of times Black people follow society's negative trends too. Those are the kinds of things I think we have to take some responsibility for. For example, in an article that another Black woman and I did for *Off Our Backs* about the Third World Lesbian and Gay Conference last November, we didn't mention that there was participation by Native American women. *Off Our Backs* got a letter from Beth Brant, who had attended the conference, that I obviously had to decide whether I was going to respond to or not. Of course I felt really terrible about it. But I felt not saying anything was probably worse than my feeling terrible. So I had to think of something to say and in putting together a letter, it at least maybe opened a door that, had someone not responded, might have been shut forever.

36

Are You a Liberated Woman?
Feminism, Revolution and Asian American Women

Sasha Hohri

[This article is] about Asian women and feminism, but probably not what you expect. My job is with a feminist foundation—the Ms. Foundation for Women. In my job capacity, I read and evaluate proposals from women's groups and women's projects nationally. I also participate in discussion, with other staff and Board members, on the parameters and definition of feminism. Much of what I say in those discussions is contained in my article below. But I must say that my views as expressed are my own, and that I know there are those within the feminist community who would not agree and some who would agree, with all or parts of it.

I think this is because I see socialist revolution as the basis for the elimination of women's oppression in this country and see the future of Asian women as most closely connected to the future and struggles of our people as a whole because of racism and national oppression.

For Asian women, this is a confusing period of time—personally and politically—as the pull between Asian tradition and America becomes sharper, and as the U.S. drifts rightward becoming more conservative and racist. What I try to do below is to lay out some problems fac-

*ing Asian women, and some alternatives or paths to take to resolve
those problems.*

Let me begin by saying that I "came of age" in the late 60's and early
70's and that much of my consciousness was shaped by participation in
the massive social movements taking place in this country at that time.
I grew up in the Midwest—Chicago to be exact. I got active in high
school around the anti-Vietnam war movement, and student and civil
rights issues.

It's important to remember if you're over 30, or understand, if
you're under 30, that 10–15 years ago there was no Asian American
studies, no *Roots, Counterpoint*, etc. Growing up, Asian American literature was *5 Chinese Brothers*. Asian American theater was "Flower
Drum Song." As far as the educational system was concerned, Asian
Americans and Asian people, much less Asian women, did not exist.

The anti-war movement sparked our national consciousness by
giving us both victims and heroes to identify with. Of course, I was initially outraged by the injustice, racism, and inhumanity of the war—
the napalm, the anti-personnel bombs—and then began to understand
that those "helpless victims" were actually winning the war—and that
I wanted them to because we all had the same enemy—U.S. imperialism. I saw Asian women fighting wars for the liberation of their
people—carrying equal, if not more responsibility—in positions of
leadership. So for me, consciousness of being Asian arose simultaneously with developing an understanding of being a woman.

A decade has elapsed from those times until now. Gains have been
made, won through hard struggle and sacrifice. But Asian working
women still face triple oppression as women, as Asian women and as
Asian women workers—oppression by sex, race and class.

Examples highlighting the accomplishments of Asian women "success stories" who may have gone through some struggles in the past
but now have their lives together, figured out, no rough edges or hard
times, no anger or struggle, make us wonder why our lives are still so
hard and why the majority of us still work in some sweatshop, behind a
typewriter or doing some other job mainly relying on our hands. They
make us wonder what's wrong with us?

I think as our collective sojourn/history becomes longer in America, some Asian sisters manage to make it through various strata of society to become lawyers, doctors, scholars, television newscasters, or
some other type of professional. But I think the true measure of our
progress has to be seen in relationship to what the majority of us do,
and to the obstacles that our most oppressed Asian sisters face. When
looked at in this light, things have not changed all that much. As the

rightward trend of American society continues, what little gains we have made are being threatened. Except for a few tokens, we are again being relegated to invisibility or worse yet to the revival of degrading, sexist stereotypes along the lines of "Dragon Ladies" or "Susie Wongs."

So what do the majority of us do? The overwhelming majority of Asian women work in clerical, service and light industry. We work in hospitals, downtown offices, hotels, kitchens, and sweatshops in some of America's biggest cities. The economic exploitation and inequalities that Asian women suffer allow the capitalist class to make extra money off of our labor and keep us "in our place." By and large, the labor of women—including tens of thousands of Asian women—is essential to the functioning of society. It is the woman worker who sews your clothes, types the letters, and takes care of the children. It's a trip to think about where the rich and powerful would be without the unpaid and underpaid labor of women. They couldn't live. Ronald Reagan wouldn't have clean socks.

The capitalist class needs to justify our special oppression, so they develop racist and sexist ideology. Perhaps the cruelest blow of this ideology is that it tries to get us to think that there's no problem at all or that we're the ones who have messed up . . . we can't do anything about it because we're too passive and marginal . . . or we're too ugly, not socially skilled enough to make it. So the problem must be with us. It's not that the system is messed up and has to be changed. That's where we get to seeing ourselves as the oppressor sees us, believing the lies, limiting ourselves. Systematic national oppression slams doors in our faces, limits our options and opportunities for growth. Racist ideology tries to get people in society to see us in a certain way but also tries to get us to see ourselves that way too. This facilitates our oppression by getting us to think that we are incapable, unattractive, not worth it, and tries to get us to close the doors on ourselves.

Racism and national oppression tries to twist our values, and denies us our heritage of struggle, perseverance and resistance. It is painful to me to realize how difficult and long it took to learn to value and appreciate the strengths and bamboo resistance of my mother and grandmothers against all that would uproot and obliterate us. Because of my political involvement, I have been able to understand their lives in a broader social context. For Nisei and Issei women to continue to struggle to keep the family together through the incarceration of the camps and beyond is quite something. For me it is hard to imagine going ahead, as my mother did, after a war when she was put in a prison camp as the enemy, to a strange city to find a place to live for her parents and three younger sisters. It is just as difficult to put myself in the shoes of my grandmother watching these tall white men take away her husband, my grandfather, on Pearl Harbor day. Being able to continue to live, persevere through these awful conditions are not characteristics that are valued, understood or promoted in capitalist society.

But Asian women are not only oppressed by this American government and society which is based only on what is profitable, Asian women are also oppressed inside our communities by the force of Asian feudal tradition. This tradition continues to define us as so-and-so's daughter, mother, or wife. Such feudal ideas serve to keep us quiet and think "family first." Endless layers and rituals of obligation try to smother us, make us lose ourselves or we must be "bad" mothers, "bad" daughters and "bad" wives. Is there a balance?

From all sides, we are challenged to define and redefine our lives, history and role. For Asian women there is beginning to be a heritage we can learn from, a heritage we are beginning to understand, speak of and be proud of. We have only begun to understand the sufferings of our older generations of Issei and Nisei women as we have begun to appreciate their incredible strength and courage in their collective testimony at the Commission hearings on the concentration camps. Their candor, honesty and anger laid bare the outrageous injustices of the camps, breaking 40 years of silence. This new appreciation, definition and heritage can be seen as many of those "decade ago women"—like Miya wrote about—have matured, had families, worked and continued to be active in the political movement around issues close to the heart and future of our people.

For many of us, this has meant going *against* tradition and role models, and creating new ones in their place, by speaking out and being politically active in the Asian American movement. This has been the case in my own life.

I am a Sansei, one of those "decade ago women," still a revolutionary and now a single parent of two daughters. I have been all the "bads" by divorcing the father of my daughters—who is not really a monster—but whom I no longer loved, having been married at 19, by speaking my mind, and by becoming a revolutionary (at best, society says these things should be left to men). Having broken so many rules—I didn't finish college either—perhaps the easiest thing to do would have been to turn my back on the community, tradition, and family who had raised me. Kind of say "goodbye to all that mess. I must get on with my own life and you people don't understand or appreciate me anyway." And there are some things about being Japanese that I absolutely can't stand sometimes like the indirectness, silent suffering, guilt tripping, and deferential treatment of men and status—all remnants of feudal culture.

But I realized that I could separate the positive and negative parts of growing up Japanese in America. I could reject the suffocating feudal remnants and capitalist stereotypes, and still retain the best in what my grandmother and mother have stood for as Japanese women. I could see myself as part of the collective struggle of my people in relation to society as a whole. I think this is because no matter how much I may struggle with those questions/oppressions internal to the community, changing those things in and of themselves will not qualitatively change our lives if we are still oppressed by those "outside" things. So I choose to stay in the community and deal with those feudal and backward ideas that exist in the context of taking up issues that affect our people as a whole. I see the struggle for the emancipation of women in this context. We must fight to be free and to fight to be free, Asian women must fight against feudal sexist tradition and attitudes that prevent us from fully participating in the struggles which will determine our future.

Because of being a revolutionary, I can better understand my relationship to the world—what brought me here and made me what I am, and how those social forces affect me, my children, family and people in general. So that when I look at my own life and the lives of my Asian sisters, and of my mother and grandmother, I see that consciously, women have always had to put family first, self second, which is a legacy from feudalism. Further, I see that feudal, oppressive family relations are one thing—family/future in the context of racist America and struggling for a new society is another. Family at the expense of woman's active participation in political struggle is one thing. Family as part of deepening that understanding and commitment, and building a better future is another. I love my children very much. I see my role as trying to give them the tools to understand the world and the confidence, hope and determination to fight for what's best for all people.

For Asian women and working class people in general, conditions are worsening—economically and politically. It's a challenging period to grow up in or to raise kids by ourselves. Tradition tells us to fulfill familial expectations—get married, have children, preferably sons. Society tells us to be passive and sexy. Some "liberated women" tell us to reject all that and fulfill our own potential to its fullest. In the ultimate sense, we want this for all people. But it is not possible for Asian women in this society to fulfill their human potential.

It is not possible for us to live in this society free from exploitation and oppression. It is impossible for my children to grow up without having felt and experienced racism and sexism. I recall a discussion a few years back around "are you a liberated woman?" Now what the hell does this mean and further, what does it imply? If we don't think we're liberated, are we politically unhip or out of it? Is liberation a state of mind? Is oppression a state of mind? Maybe for some professional Asian women it is, but for the majority of Asian women, it is a tangible and real thing that we live with every day of our lives. In that sense, I am not liberated. I am oppressed. These kinds of questions anger me because their impact is to confuse the issues and play around with words and ideas that have meaning to people's lives.

I am a revolutionary. I am very serious about ending the oppression of women. I continue to deepen my understanding of the extent that sexism and racism keep us from thinking of ourselves as capable of changing society. I also understand the extent that middle class ideology—me first, second, and third: up by the bootstraps—can make some women think they can do it on their own. And some of these women do make it on their own. They achieve some professional recognition and marry white men. This is fine for them, but let's not fool ourselves that this is the path to end the oppression of Asian women.

Because of the confused and mixed messages (feudalism and sexist and racist ideas) promoted in society, sometimes Asian sisters close the doors on ourselves. Some sisters choose to opt out—the most oppressed and lost, through drug addiction and suicide. It is easy to succumb, and in a lot of ways, much harder to fight. Capitalism and feudalism breathe these messages to us in subtle and not so subtle ways. How do we see ourselves if we are invisible, if our most courageous acts are unrecognized? How do we understand our role and place in society if we are not "success stories"?

For me, the strength to fight comes from understanding our situation, and taking a path which sees political struggle as an integral and fundamental part of my life. It comes from seeing myself continuing in the best tradition of my people and of the working class—scrappy fighters, survivors, makers of history. And the women are the glue. It comes from appreciating the struggles of mothers, grandmothers, sisters and comrades across nationality lines. It comes from my participation in the movement to end the oppression of Asian peoples and the working class, and seeing that the movement will develop and grow through twists and turns.

Suggested Readings

A. Lynn Bolles

This list of suggested readings augments the bibliographies already cited in this volume. Its content draws from a substantial body of work on U.S. women from the social sciences, history, and literature.

Commonalities and Differences

Blicksilver, Edith, ed. *The Ethnic American Woman: Problems, Protests, Lifestyle*. Dubuque, Iowa: Kendall/Hunt, 1978. 381 pp.

This edited volume of poetry, essays, and exerpts from novels and novellas by ethnic U.S. women brings to light the literary contributions made by those writers outside the "great literary tradition"—particularly women of color. The book is organized to express common problems faced by all women, e.g., life, love, death, and family, in a way that the cultural differences are also recognized. Some authors included in the volume are Maxine Hong Kingston, Alice Walker, Mahalia Jackson, Grace Paley, Adrienne Rich, Buffy Sainte-Marie, and Mary McCarthy.

Seller, Maxine. *Immigrant Women*. Philadelphia: Temple University Press, 1981. 341 pp.

This book is a collection of narratives and essays of women of different nationalities who immigrated to the United States during the eighteenth to the twentieth centuries. Their individual stories reflect the range of emotions and concrete realities that immigration is all about. Coming to the United States by force, by choice, fulfilling filial and wifely obligations, or championing her own cause, the woman found the new land frontier or city to which she emigrated to be everything or nothing that she had expected during the long overseas passage. Sellers' introduction discusses the differences between the male and female immigrant experiences. What has been written about immigration has been primarily from the perspective of men, therefore *Immigrant Women* is corrective women's studies scholarship at its best.

Woloch, Nancy. *Women and the American Experience.* New York: Alfred Knopf, 1984. 567 pp.

In her preface, Woloch states that women's history is something like a stroll though a mine field. The more research that is uncovered, the more "depth"–defying knowledge is demanded. Relying on women's own voices to reconstruct the past, this historical work discusses the development of female associations, the significance of women's institutions, and women's individual and collective strategies. The book is divided into four large segments—a standard periodization of American history. In each chapter, the case of an "exceptional" "white" woman is examined, followed by a general history of topics closely associated with the era discussed in the chapter. For example, in the 1860–1920 period, Jane Addams is the exceptional woman highlighted, and issues and events discussed include shrinking families, college women, professional women, club women and crusaders, educated homemakers, and women's organizations. Care is taken to address women and their stories in terms of class and race, but a drawback is that none of the exceptional women in Woloch's book are women of color.

Work

Jensen, Joan M. *With These Hands: Women Working on the Land.* Old Westbury, N.Y.: Feminist Press, 1981. 295 pp.

With These Hands is a historical overview of U.S. women who have worked as farmers, ranchers, sodbusters, traditional agriculturalists, slaves, and sharecroppers. Jensen provides the introductory analysis to the secondary essays, letters, exerpts from other works, and a photo essay. The book is divided into sections: Native American, black American, Chicana, and white ethnic women's experiences on the land are explored at length. One discussion concerns the relationship between native American women and Mormon women during the early days of the religious groups' settlements in Utah. This book is part of the Feminist Press series on Women and Work.

Kessler-Harris, Alice. *Out to Work.* New York: Oxford University Press, 1982. 400 pp.

In the book's preface, the author states that "the diversity of women's experience as wage workers is complex" and that she "was able to suggest only some of the outlines." Gender, race, ethnicity, and class constitute the moving forces in this women's history.

Out to Work begins with the colonial period, then moves to early industrialization. The ideological barriers in place about women's roles in society are analyzed in terms of the new order imposed by a rapidly industrializing economy. The section ends with the standardization of the sexual division of labor in the work force. Consumerism of the 1920s, new ideas about women's wage labor in the 1930s and 1940s, which were expanded in the 1950s, are explored in depth. The discord between ideology and reality explodes with the women's movement and results in the contemporary debate over the proper role of women.

Out to Work provides a readable historical overview of women, work, and the social rules and laws that govern them both.

May, Martha. "The Historical Problem of the Family Wage." *Feminist Studies* (1981) 8(2): 373–398.

The idea of a family wage is the backbone of industrial capitalism. May documents Henry Ford's tactic of using the family wage as a means of manipulating the work force in his automobile factories in the early 1900s. Ford's strategy had such an impact on the automobile industry that it has been applied across the board to industries worldwide. The consequences the family wage has had on women, men, and children are both economically and ideologically based.

This is an exciting article, offering a concise, documented examination of an issue that plagues arguments concerning women's and children's roles in industrial capitalism.

Sasson-Koob, Saskia. "The New Labor Demand in Global Cities." In *Cities in Transformation*, Michael P. Smith, ed., pp. 139–171. Beverly Hills, Calif.: Sage Publications, 1984.

This is a major theoretical study on the restructuring of the U.S. economy. It focuses on two geographical locations, Los Angeles and New York City, and the transformation of the work process. Although it does not focus on women per se, it is women whose labor has been affected by the major growth in the "new industries."

High-income professional and technical jobs, associated with the growth of computer services have expanded. Simultaneously, there has been an upgrading of a variety of jobs which used to be considered middle-income jobs. Unionized shops have been transformed into sweatshops, and much industrial work is now done at home. Clearly, all of this job restructuring has affected women, work, and families.

Also included in this article is a discussion on the impact on and utilization of immigrant labor in the work force, particularly unskilled laborers.

This article provides excellent data for discussions concerning relations among women across class, ethnic, and racial lines.

Zimmerman, Jan. *The Technological Woman.* New York: Praeger, 1983. 296 pp.

Unlike what the title might imply, *The Technological Woman* is not a volume of articles by and for women scientists or "lady" engineers. It is about understanding the role of technological innovations in every aspects of women's lives: work, family, sexuality, politics, etc. There are thirty-one articles divided into four parts in this fascinating book. Part one includes articles on "sexism in tech talk," and black women inventors. In part two, ladies "home technology" is the topic. Part three deals with work and contains an article with the lively title, "Bambi Meets Godzilla: Life in the Corporate Jungle." Part four focuses on the politics of the future, again offering a variety of articles which discusses issues of surrogate motherhood, females futures, women's science fiction, and organizing women in the office.

In a 1985 review of Zimmerman's book in *Signs* (10,4:804–5), Carolyn Lee Arnold notes that this volume fills in theoretical and factual gaps and examines issues from several class and race perspectives, unlike other books on the same subject. Also, Zimmerman makes amends for not including a full discussion on the interplay between technology and capitalism, and for not describing the needs and struggles of lesbian and older women.

Despite these exclusions, *The Technological Woman* is an exhilarating book to read which again calls for women to challenge technology and to understand how it is a force which separates women ideologically and economically from men.

Families

Day, Kay Young. "Kinship in a Changing Economy: A View from the Sea Islands." In *Holding on to the Land and the Lord*, R. Hall and C. Stack, eds., pp. 11–23. Athens, Ga.: University of Georgia Press, 1982.

The Sea Island community of Mt. Pleasant on the coast of South Carolina has a unique history of a black, landowning peasantry. Over the years, however, family incomes which once came from traditional farming, fishing, marketing, and wage labor on plantations now derive from industrial wage labor in the city of Charleston. Day examines how kin and community organization sustained Mt. Pleasant blacks in their transition from an agrarian to industrial society.

Securing a livelihood is a family affair, and women's paid and unpaid labor is an integral part of the process. Certain rights and obligations are shared by "close family," while others may be recruited into this domestic network. Reciprocity and mutual responsibility have bound members of families together. The solidarity of kin and community is still a primary support for the blacks of Mt. Pleasant in their interactions with the law, medical, and welfare institutions, and employers.

Day provides a semirural example of the importance of kin networks. As she quotes a Mt. Pleasant adage, "My family is me. Anything you do to them, you do to me."

Johnson-Reagon, Bernice. "My Black Mothers and Sisters or on Beginning a Cultural Autobiography." *Feminist Studies* (1981) 8(1): 81–96.
Marshall, Paule. "The Making of a Writer: From the Poets in the Kitchen." In *Reena*, pp. 1–12. Old Westbury, N.Y.: Feminist Press, 1983.
Walker, Alice. "In Search of Our Mothers' Gardens." *Ms.*, May 1974, pp. 64–70.

Each author of these three articles pays homage to and offers words of appreciation for the mothers, sisters, wives, grandmothers, "aunties," and female role models whose language, support, and very beings influenced them as black women, and as writers. The amazing thing about the three articles is the simple, but majestic language spoken by the female sources of inspiration in the kitchen, on the back porch, and in the garden. The strength of these foremothers and the way their spirituality comes through in the writings of Johnson-Reagon, Marshall, and Walker is most special. When Bernice Johnson-Reagon portrays "Miss Nana's relationship with God," you can hear her sing. When Paule Marshall recalls the expression "Soully-gal, talk you talk," you can feel the rhythm, and when Alice Walker describes "the sunflowers, petunias, roses, dahlias, forsythia, spirea, delphiniums, verbena" of her mother's garden, you can see it.

None of this black beauty is free from struggle, but because of these women's cultural resistance to sexism, racism, poverty, broken dreams, and so forth, when read one after another, the collective force of these foremothers is contagious.

Joyce, Rosemary. "The Life of Sarah Penfield, Rural Ohio Grandmother: Tradition Maintained, Tradition Threatened." In *The World of Women*, E. Bourguignon, ed., South Hadley, Mass.: Bergin Publishers, 1980. pp. 271–303.

This is a life history of a woman of Appalachian Ohio. Through Sarah Penfield's voice, the changes the region has undergone just in the twentieth century become direct and vivid. Inherent in social change is conflict. Here Sarah's life story offers a look at the traditional folkways of her parents. How Sarah passes on those cultural ways of seeing and dealing with the world illustrates how social change can be painful.

The author inserts Sarah's narrative whenever possible, lending this article "ethnographic life." Can her conflicts, attitudes, ambivalences, be seen as idiosyncratic, representative, or what? The author calls for more research of this type not only on the women of Appalachia, but on women in general whose voices must be heard.

Thorne, Barrie, with Marilyn Yalom, eds. *Rethinking the Family*. New York: Longman. 1982. 246 pp.

This edited collection discusses feminist thought on the family as a political, economic, historical, religious, and ideological construct. The authors

come from a variety of disciplines, each challenging the mainstream opinion
on the family or providing insightful contemporary analysis on aspects of the
institution. Five themes provide the structure of the book. They include challenging prevalent assumptions, using gender analysis as a basis for family theory; understanding families as a set of individuals who experience family in
different ways; regarding the families not in isolation but as parts of a wider
political, social, and economic framework. These themes are repeated in different ways in the eleven essays.

Sexuality and Reproduction

Boston Women's Health Book Collective. *The New Our Bodies, Our-
    selves.* New York: Simon and Schuster, 1984. 647 pp.

The Boston Women's Health Book Collective met once a week for twelve
years. In that time, three editions of *Our Bodies* have appeared. Not only has
the collective survived, but the issues concerning women's health and hygiene,
nutrition, disease, and mental health problems have survived too. Also during
that time, the medical system has become a business and is closely tied to
other businesses in this "profit-oriented economy." The collective restates its
original goals for this volume, now, as ever, essential for women's well-being.
Those goals include providing women with access to information; the opportunity to hear different voices and experiences; tools so women can take greater
charge of their own health care; support for those working for change within
and outside the existing health care system; and a more just society in which
good health is a right, not a luxury.

This volume should be made available to every U.S. woman.

Ehrenreich, Barbara, and Deidre English. *For Her Own Good.* New
    York: Anchor Press/Doubleday, 1979. 369 pp.

The subtitle to this volume is most telling—"One Hundred and Fifty
Years of the Experts' Advice to Women." As nonprofessional health and science historians, the authors document how women's health and medical care
has been taken out of the hands of women healers and midwives, and put into
the hands of male experts. With the professionalization—or male intensifica-
tion—of health care delivery, women became objects, and their bodies became
unknown to them as individuals.

In the chapters under the heading "The Rise of the Experts," every story
one needs to know about the genesis of the "aura of the white lab coat" is
present. The classic chapters on "Microbes and the Manufacture of Housework," and "Witches, Healers, and Gentleman Doctors" are included. The second section, the "Fall of the Experts" is not as strong because it leans heavily
on popular feminist literature of the 1970s as universal fact rather than temporal, class-biased information.

Nicola-McLaughlin, Andrée. "White Power, Black Despair—Vanessa
    Williams in Babylon." *Black Scholar* (1985) 16(2): 32–39.

This article delves into the underlying issues of sexism and racism which led to the Miss America controversy over Vanessa Williams, the first black woman crowned. Not too far beneath the heavily sexist/racist acts of the Miss America Pageant officials lies the political reality. Vanessa Williams was not so much the issue, rather the "tide of new conservatism embracing the nation aimed at keeping oppressed groups locked out and powerless in American society." Nicola-McLaughlin discusses the history of the pageant itself, the institutionalization of capitalizing on women's sexuality, the details of Vanessa's downfall, and finally she examines the U.S. society's perverse morality.

Not only does this article put the Vanessa Williams case in a theoretical perspective, but it shows how black women are still exploited, regardless of material gain.

Weibel, Kathryn. *Mirror Mirror.* New York: Anchor Press, 1977. 256 pp.

This volume documents the images of women reflected in popular culture. One of the first contemporary works on the subject, *Mirror Mirror* focuses on the images of women in fiction, television, movies, women's magazines, and magazine advertising. Popular culture makes common the images necessary for the society to function as it deems fit. To diffuse a strong image, women struggling for heady concerns like comparable worth are still referred to as a bunch of "bra burners." It is necessary to understand the operations of this system in order not to be made a victim of it.

Some of the statements made in the book are now history. But as background information, the book provides useful data.

Religion

Christ, Carol P., and Judith Plaskow, eds. *Womanspirit Rising.* New York: Harper & Row, 1979. 287 pp.

Christ and Plaskow's edited volume is an important addition to the study of women and religion from the Judeo-Christian perspective and the alternatives which arise from those traditions. Included in the volume are some essential articles on feminist religious theory. For example, Mary Daly's "After the Death of God the Father," Judith Plaskow's "The Coming of Lilith," and Carol Christ's "Only Women Need the Goddess," are all a part of this book.

It is imperative to remember that this collection does not go outside one religious tradition, and its interpretation of that tradition is primarily white and middle-class.

Falk, Nancy A., And Rita M. Gross, eds. *Unspoken Worlds.* New York: Harper and Row, 1980. 292 pp.

The subtitle of this edited volume is all-telling—"Women's Religious Lives in Non-Western Cultures." How Falk and Gross structure *Unspoken Worlds* portrays how religion is a social organization which permeates cultures and societies. Religion is not a separate entity that functions sporadically or periodically. Sections include: ritualized rebellion, rituals for housewives and mothers, women in male-dominated systems, women and men as equals, male domination, and women's power. The first section features the work of two extraordinary women—an East African diviner and a Hindu woman guru who renounce all worldly life. Of course, many of those "non-Western" religions are found in the United States. Therefore, those religions influence U.S. women's roles in their racial or ethnic communities. Kern's article on black Carib women, Friedl's work on Islam, Falk's study of Buddhism, and Shimony's piece on the Iroquois represent some of the more obvious U.S. links with "non-Western" religions.

McCarthy, Mary. *Memories of a Catholic Girlhood*. New York: Harcourt Brace Jovanovich, 1957. 243 pp.

This collection of autobiographical essays and articles reveals the early life of novelist/critic Mary McCarthy and the influence her religious socialization had on her as a literary person and as a U.S. woman. McCarthy begins by recalling her idyllic home life which is tragically changed when both her parents die suddenly in an influenza epidemic. The events which follow include being forced into Catholicism, being victimized by child abuse, schooling in a prestigious convent, and entering the Episcopal seminary where she begins her transition from girlhood to womanhood.

McCarthy is honest in this account, but her admitted tendency to fictionalize leaves the reader to guess whether or not some chapters were real or invented. It makes for good reading.

Ruether, Rosemary, and Eleanor McLaughlin, eds. *Women of Spirit*. New York: Simon and Schuster, 1979. 400 pp.

Female leadership in the Jewish and Christian traditions is the topic of this edited book. It is important reading because it focuses on the way women have assumed leadership in two male-dominated religions. How women have derived authority at different historical moments is imperative for a corrective history of religion and the study on sociocultural continuity and change.

Unlike a number of volumes of feminist perspectives on the history of women in the Jewish and Christian traditions, black women are included in an article on women in the holiness movement of the nineteenth century. Articles on women Quakers, and sectarian Christians (Shakers, Mormons, Christian Scientists, Pentecostals, etc.) provide a wider scope of U.S. religion than the Christ and Plaskow book.

Politics

Eisenstein, Zillah R., ed. *Capitalist Patriarchy and the Case for Socialist Feminism*. New York: Monthly Review Press, 1979. 394 pp.

Zillah Eisenstein has assembled a series of some of the well-known articles on feminist political theory from a socialist perspective. The goal of the book is to try to develop a different understanding of the relationship between patriarchy and capitalism. One premise is that theory must grow out of reality as well as offer a vision for the future.

Sections of the book focus on theory, motherhood, reproduction and male supremacy, historical analysis, patriarchy in revolutionary societies, and socialist feminism in the United States. The volume serves as a useful one-stop reference for materials written from a socialist feminist perspective.

Evans, Sara. *Personal Politics.* New York: Vintage Books, 1980. 275 pp.

Evan's historical analysis links three influential political movements of the 1960s in the United States together—the Civil Rights, the New Left, and the women's movement. The purpose is to see how the women's movement benefited from or was influenced by the course of events in the other two popular fronts.

Clearly written from a white middle-class perspective, Evans's work does have an important message to convey to its readers. Like it or not, white women were active participants in the Civil Rights movement and the New Left. The inherent sexism in those two movements served as an impetus for certain directives in the women's movement. What it does not address is the inherent classism and racism of the women's movement, which demands as close a documentation and analysis as the influences of other popular movements of the time. There are important data in this book that make it worthwhile.

Sargent, Lydia, ed. *Women and Revolution.* Boston: South End Press, 1981. 373 pp.

This anthology was inspired by the controversy over Hartmann's lead essay "The Unhappy Marriage of Marxism and Feminism Towards a More Progressive Union." As the title suggests, Hartmann considers how the political left has delegated women's emancipation to a second-class status. What follows are articles which further illuminate areas in which Marxism overshadows feminism and criticize the connection between patriarchy and capitalism. The underlying theme is to define a means toward proletarian and women's emancipation.

Index

Note: *n* refers to both a parenthetical citation following a quotation and a source appearing in a list of references, as opposed to a discussion in the text.

Horner, Matina, 133
House of Representatives, U.S., 382, 390, 391
Housewife, 81, 83, 88, 123
  fatigue of, 128
  suburban, 8, 111, 121, 136
  syndrome, 122
  and tranquilizers, 128
Housewifery, 7, 85
Housework, 84, 126, 127, 128; *see also* Work, household
  pay for, 160
  unpaid, 6, 31
Howe, Julia Ward, 245
Hubbard, Ruth, 236, 237n
Human life amendment, 232
Hune, Shirley, 2, 3, 29n
Hunt, Morton, 257, 269n, 270n
Hurst, Lynda, 137
Husband-seeking, *Look* magazine article on, 125
Hyde Amendment, 232, 242, 252
Hyman, H., 195, 197n
Hyman, Paula, 201

IBM Corp., 158
"If One Generation Can Ever Tell Another" (Friedan), 129n
"I Love Lucy," 138
Immigration, 3, 275
  of domestic workers, 47–70
  immigrants in "pink-collar" jobs, 48, 49, 53, 65
  permanent resident status, 48
  quotas, 53, 95
  reasons for migration, 67n
  sponsorship, 35, 48, 50, 51
Immigration and Naturalization Service (INS), 50
Incest among Native Americans, 408
Indian Health Service, 250, 408
Inequality
  gender, 5
  sexual, 5
Infanticide, 241
Information industry, 32
Institute for the Study of Educational Policy on Blacks and Higher

Education (1980), 190, 196n
Interdepartmental Committee on Puerto Rico, 251
Internal racism, 418
Interracial marriage, 274
Islam, 307
  religion, 308
  and women, 141

Jackson, J. B., 317, 318, 322n
Jackson, Jacquelyn, 364, 369n
Jacoby, Susan, 26
Japanese Americans, 377
  in America, 423
  in prison camps during World War II, 422, 423
  women, 424
Jardim, A., 36, 38n
Jefferson, Thomas, 273
Jesus Christ, 326, 327, 366, 406
Jews
  cousins club, 203
  extended family 202, 203
  families and holidays, 203, 204
  family kinship networks, 203
  family life, 199
  feminism, 335, 336
  feminists, 200, 337
    writers, 338
  laws pertaining to women, 335
  legends, 334
  nuclear family, 199
  Orthodox women, 204
  traditional, 337, 338
  values, 202
Jewish Conservative movement, 336
Jewish Publication Society, 334
Jewish Reform movement, 335, 336, 340
Jewish Theological Seminary, 334
Jewish women
  and divorce rate in Jewish families, 335, 340
  and family, 114
  Mama, 204, 205
  and marriage, 335
  mother/daughter relationship, 204–207

Third World women's organizing, 412, 413
Thompson, Laura, 317, 322n
Thompson, S., 32, 38n
Tixier y Vigil, Yvonne, 110
Todd, Judith, 309, 311
Torah, the, 337
Touré, Sekou, 365, 369n
Trade-union movement, 331
"Trapped Housewife, The" (CBS television program), 123
Triangle Shirtwaist fire, 332
Trudeau, Margaret, 159, 170n
Truth, Sojourner, 367, 369n
Tubman, Harriet, 396

Underground Railroad, 396
Unemployment, 9
of black men, 9, 116
Unions, 33, 74, 76, 77, 99
United Nations End of the Decade Conference on Women, 377
United States
immigration policies, 97
imperialism, 421
United States Practical Receipt Book, 242
United Steel Workers, 74
Uri, Connie, 250

Valerio, Anita, 16, 17n, 30n
Vance, C. S., 230, 237n
Vatican, the, and women, 141
Vietnam war, 41, 303, 305
Violence, 276; *see also* Sex and violence
in the family, 133
and pornography, 392
against women, 276, 277, 372
Virgin Mary, 278, 332, 351, 352, 354
Virginity
and black women, 290
and Hispanic women, 278, 280

Wages
discrimination in, 9
for migrant domestic workers, 67n
Wall Street Journal 1980 study on

black managers, 190–191
Warner Communications, 392
Waxman, Chaim I., 199, 214n
Weber, Max, 166
Welfare, 36, 39–42, 101–106, 145
and child-raising, 39–42
mothers on, 415
white females on, 101–106
Wells, Ida B., 27
West Indian women in domestic work, 46–70
Western culture, 351, 353, 354, 356
Western religion, 349
Whyte, William, 159, 160, 164, 169, 170n
Wildung, Faith, 353–354
Wisse, Ruth, 336, 337, 343n
Witchcraft, 351
Wittig, Monique, 349, 357n
Wives; *see also* Corporate wives
dependent, 395
as housewives, 381
as unpaid workers, 112
Wives of Management, The (Whyte), 160, 164, 169, 170n
Wolfe, Ann, 13, 13n, 30n, 200
Woman Rebel journal, 246
WomanSpirit magazine, 348
Women
biological features, 289
as business executives, 81, 133
and careers, 119
of color, 313
and religion, 313
in word processing, 32
and the double shift, 372
economic survival, 133
earnings compared with men, 131
elected officials, 24, 379
emancipation, 121
employment, 372
in factory work, 32
in Judaism, 335
in leadership and power, 23
in paid labor force, 31
political equality, 243
power, 348, 349
in public office, 372